Understand and Enjoy Modern Art

Understand and Enjoy Modern Art

GEORGE A. FLANAGAN

Revised Edition

Thomas Y. Crowell Company, New York, Established 1834

To Marge

Originally published under the title of
How to Understand Modern Art

Contents

Color Plates

1   It Won't Go Away

Thousands of interested and intelligent people have been puzzled by modern art. They know that modern art is the generally accepted art of our time, yet when they look at modern pictures and sculptures, they find them either partially or totally incomprehensible. And they suspect that modern art *does* have a meaning. They wish they knew what it was.

Innumerable people must have said to themselves, "If only somebody would tell me—in a few well-chosen words—what modern art is all about!" Subconsciously, one hopes that some day a wizard *will* come along with the magic sentence that will immediately and completely unlock the mystery.

But that never happens. Actually, it can't happen—because there is no *trick* in modern art to be revealed; no *secret* to be unlocked by a magic phrase.

Modern art can be explained, but unfortunately—because it is so big and broad and far-reaching in its many implications—*it cannot be explained in just a few words*. In fact, if one *does* attempt to condense the meaning of modern art into a few words or sentences, he finds himself forced to speak in such broad generalities that the explanation becomes just as abstract and baffling as the modern pictures themselves.

To really explain modern art, it is necessary to go back to its origins and follow the development of its basic ideas, step by step. When the ideas are understood, their end-results in practice—the pictures—become readily comprehensible. Now all this may seem a bit formidable, possibly a little more than one bargained for. But, in return for a longer and more detailed explanation, the reader can be promised this—the telling should at least be interesting. For the story of modern art is a lively one. In its dynamic and occasionally explosive history there is, as the familiar saying goes, never a dull moment.

And another promise can be made. In tracking down the reasons-for-being of modern art, one will come upon a better understanding of *all* art. Interesting new light will be shed on the art of the past, as well as the present.

Modern art displays an undeniable vitality. From time to time, over the years, it keeps popping into the public consciousness. It just won't go away.

This is in spite of the fact that modern art has been criticized with the utmost bitterness—many, many times. It has been subjected, throughout its history, to a veritable mountain of ridicule. It has often been denounced as a fraud (which is nonsense, because modern art is *not* a fraud in any sense. The only thing fraudulent is the cry of "fraud" itself). Yet, like "Old Man River," modern art just keeps rolling along. As one critic puts it, every year larger and larger armies of people swing over from old ways of thinking about art to an enthusiastic acceptance of modernism.

With but a few die-hard exceptions, authoritative art criticism has long since accepted the modern way of painting as a legitimate form of art. Today, modern pictures are to be found in all the important museums of the world (the Metropolitan Museum of Art purchased its first Cézanne in 1913). In New York's gallery area, north from 57th Street, it is now the exceptional art dealer who does *not* show modern pictures. Some of the earlier modern artists have already become enthroned as "old masters."

It would appear that modern art is here to stay. It has been growing by leaps and bounds for seventy-five years.

Why do not more people appreciate modern art?

Many of them want to, very much, but find themselves confronted by a number of difficulties. Some of these are:

1. Modern art is very different from the art to which they have become accustomed. It is not possible for the average person to just look at a modern picture for the first time and immediately comprehend what it is all about.

2. In fact, to the average person, trained to think about pictures in the prevailing academic, realistic way, modern paintings often appear ugly, badly drawn, deformed, or just completely incomprehensible. Misunderstanding the artist's purpose, the observer is likely to become confused and discouraged. It may take some time for him to see the *other*, different kind of beauty which is the whole point of modern art.

3. Modern art has never been adequately explained to the *general public*. A great many books have been written about modern art, never-

theless, it does not seem as if the gap between the average man's conception of art and a true understanding of modern art has as yet been successfully bridged.

4. The normal education of the average American does not provide him with adequate means for evaluating a modern picture when he sees it. In comparison with such subjects as mathematics or science or English literature, very little art is taught in the schools, and that little art teaching has generally been ultraconservative in its viewpoint (for which lack the schools need not be censured. Art is difficult to "teach." It is something of a wildflower, does not cultivate well in the formal rows of the classroom).

5. Consequently, lacking any other approach, many people attempt to judge modern pictures by *literary* standards (with which they are more familiar)—*which does not work at all.* Modern art is an inherently *anti-literary* kind of art.

6. Modern art is too *big* to explain in a few words, or a few paragraphs, or a few pages. Developing and growing for three-quarters of a century, it now embraces many ideas and many widely differing kinds of work. Each of these different approaches requires its own explanation.

7. Finally, all the art ideas, all the many subtle influences on the average person's thought along artistic lines, are those that belong to the academic-realistic period of art of the last century, whereas the modern artists have moved on to a new period of art. Whether we realize it or not, most of us are so thoroughly immersed in the academic atmosphere that we find it difficult to think—or rather, *see*—any other way than the academic way. Unintentionally, perhaps, but almost instinctively, the average person tends to resist a kind of art that brusquely violates the most cherished academic rules, the only rules he knows.

To appreciate modernism, we must disentangle ourselves from ingrained academic ways of thinking and approach the new kind of art, which has an entirely different set of standards, with as unprejudiced a spirit as possible. We must, in fact, be willing to pioneer just a bit ourselves, and not permit conservatism to build a wall around our minds.

The *edge* of the Grand Canyon of the Colorado rises in a lip a few feet above the surrounding country. Hence, it is possible to stand a few feet away from the Grand Canyon, down in a little depression, and not see the canyon at all, no matter how hard we look.

But if we move our position only 25 feet or so and climb the little hill, the whole tremendous panorama of the canyon, one of the most breathtaking sights on earth, is suddenly revealed at our feet.

Understanding modern art is something like that. If we linger at our old point of view—that is, attempt to judge modern pictures by academic standards—we will never "see" modern art, no matter how hard we look.

But if we are willing to make a little excursion—move on to a new point of view about art in general—we can find modern art happily revealed to us. And, as in the case of the Grand Canyon, it is an exciting experience.

There are times in the history of art when men seem to *see* entirely differently from the men of other times. For example, it would appear as if the painters of the Renaissance saw everything in a relatively flat light and spread out before them from left to right on a wide, but shallow, stage. They saw every contour clearly and distinctly. The baroque artists of a century later, however, saw everything in a dim and capricious light, with objects illuminated mysteriously from the side and seen as if looking down a long, narrow hall. To baroque eyes, fascinated with the dance of lights and shadow, contours often faded away entirely.

Again, how different is the *feeling* of Greek sculpture and Renaissance sculpture, frequently so similar in subject matter. There are the same warriors, the same nudes, the same equestrian pieces. But how *calm* and smooth-flowing is the touch of the Greek, how nervous and restless the quivering line of a Donatello or a Michelangelo!

Finally, how many startlingly different versions are there of the face of Christ, from the time of the early Christians to the present!

The artists of the sixteenth century seemed to see things pretty much in one general way. The artists of the seventeenth century also saw things with a collective vision, but one that was entirely different from that of the previous century. These times, in art history, when men appear to see alike are sometimes called "periods," although it is not always easy to say where or when a period begins or ends. Nor can we say that one period is better than another, for there is no pattern of *progress* in art as there is in practical science. The present period of art is not superior to the period of classical Greece, or of the amazing stone age cave men of Altamira.

Each period, then, has its own kind of greatness, which is *different* from that of other periods. And each period, each aesthetic vision-world, makes its own rules as to what *is* art, and what isn't, and these rules may conflict sharply with the rules of other periods. The artists, critics, and public of one time tend to believe that their art is the true art, the art that always has been. They find difficulty in appreciating another art period, the rules of which seem to conflict with their own.

This difficulty prevails today. Although many of the artists have gone on to a new period in art—the *modern*—much of the general public still lives in what might be called the *academic-realistic* period. In a broad sense, the *academic-realistic* period comprises the traditional, conservative art of the last hundred years.

The name "academic" derives from the French Royal Academy of Fine Arts, established on an official basis in 1664 by Louis XIV. Today, "academic" means "official," "established," "traditional." It has also acquired an additional meaning of "hackneyed" or "imitative." This latter, somewhat derogatory meaning does not apply *always*, of course. But it is, it must be admitted, fairly descriptive of a great deal of late nineteenth century traditional art.

The word "realism," or "realistic," also has a rather special sense when it is applied to this period. It represents a very wholehearted, thoroughgoing kind of realism—a whole philosophy of painting—somewhat similar, in fact, to the *realism* of recent literature. It is in this *emphasis* on realism as a primary objective that nineteenth century academic-realistic art differs from earlier post-Renaissance art. Earlier painting—since the Renaissance —often achieves a high degree of realism, but the realism is merely incidental, subservient to other artistic objectives.

Hence, the name *academic-realistic*. The officially favored art of the late nineteenth century—which is essentially the same allegedly "traditional" art admired by the general public today—is both *academic* and *realistic*. The specialized nature of this art becomes even more apparent when we glance at the main historical trends of French * art in the nineteenth century.

The nineteenth century opened on the "Classical Revival" style of David and Ingres. Officially dictated, this art was cold, and stilted, bound by innumerable rules of correct "classicism." It produced "noble" pictures of Greeks and Romans—frozen tableaux that were later to be referred to, by irreverent art students, as "machines."

Then, in the 1820's, this anachronistic, backward-looking art was displaced by the stormy Romanticism of Géricault and Delacroix. Figures in violent action; twisting, writhing compositions; "broken" color; exotic subjects—men on rearing horses, Algerian chieftains, crusaders—suddenly became the vogue. It was revolution—but, alas, only an abortive one. Romanticism lacked staying power; it was, after all, only "escape" art, doomed by its own sense of futility. It could not withstand the dominant nineteenth century march toward realism.

But before realism finally triumphed, there was an intervening, transitional period. Sentimentalism, and a switch to outdoor subjects, were the keynotes of this era, which was best represented by the dreamy, hazy landscapes of Corot and the sentimentalized peasants of Millet.

By the time the century was half over, true realism had arrived, ushered in by the rough Courbet, "who didn't paint angels because he never saw one." Courbet, followed later by Manet and Degas, established untrammeled *realism* as the basic theme of mid-nineteenth century art. These bold individuals tossed "noble" subjects out the window and painted common everyday scenes and people just as they saw them.

Somewhat paradoxically, Courbet, Manet, and Degas are today recognized as great artists—not because of their realism, but rather in spite of it—because, regardless of their intent, they did not entirely lose the

---

* French, because France was the undisputed center of Western art during the greater part of the nineteenth century. With the passing, early in the century, of Goya in Spain and of Constable, Blake, and Turner in England, artistic "competition" from other countries ceased.

CLASSICISM. David: *Death of Socrates*. A cold, formal type of art. Frozen tableaux.

METROPOLITAN MUSEUM OF ART

METROPOLITAN MUSEUM OF ART

SENTIMENTALISM. Corot: *The Ferry man*. A sentimental interlude of dreamy, softly painted landscapes. Primarily a depiction of happy out door life.

emotional personal touch, or that individuality and freshness of style that remains perpetually interesting. Their work is not photographic. Nevertheless, through their masterly draughtsmanship and their rejection of any "idealizing" of subject matter, they tended to lead less-gifted artists nearer to photographic representation.

As each of the new trends in nineteenth century art made its appearance, it incurred the violent opposition of the protagonists of the preceding trend. Then, both trends gradually merged. The total effect of this merging was greatly to strengthen traditionalism, even though some of the traditional precepts had to be changed from time to time. The traditionalists were soon able to control the official *salons*, or exhibitions, and also to influence critics and public in their favor. It became ever more difficult for radical artists to get a showing, and each successive school faced an increasingly stiffer fight to attain recognition.

As the second half of the century wore on, all the aforementioned trends—Classicism, Romanticism, Sentimentalism, and Realism—had

6

ROMANTICISM. Delacroix: *The Abduction of Rebecca*. Characterized by figures in violent action, twisting compositions, exotic subjects; brooding, stormy moods.

METROPOLITAN MUSEUM OF ART

REALISM. Courbet: *Young Ladies of the Village*. The dominant academic trend of the latter half of the 19th century. An earthy, everyday-subject type of art.

METROPOLITAN MUSEUM OF ART

largely been absorbed, or were being absorbed, into the prevailing traditionalism. The result was the *academic-realistic* art that became firmly entrenched in the 1880's and 1890's, and which has not entirely vanished today.

From the Classicists, academic-realistic art inherited a tendency to censor and dictate, to insist on moral and uplifting, if not "noble," subject matter. From the Romantics, it accepted historical and exotic subjects and, perhaps, a somewhat looser style of painting than the earlier Classicists would have permitted. The Sentimentalists were absorbed with ease. Realistic subject matter proved more difficult to digest, but realism in execution was not only accepted but was carried forward almost to the point of colored photography. Among the more typical academic-realistic artists of the last century were such men as Meissonier, Bouguereau, Cabanel, Couture, and Breton.

Academic-realistic art continued into the twentieth century, though with constantly diminishing prestige. It is the kind of art best understood

7

and preferred by a large part of the general public today. Needless to say, this public's ideas about art in general, its artistic judgments, are precisely those of the academic-realistic period, and it tends to believe that the rules of academic-realistic art are the laws of all art for all time (which, of course, they are not).

For purposes of orientation, it might be helpful to point out some of the notable characteristics of academic-realistic art. These characteristics are:

1. It is a very realistic art.
2. Unlike earlier periods of art which were often restricted in their choice of subjects, it now embraces an unlimited variety of subject matter.
3. As befits an art that has centuries of art knowledge behind it, it places great emphasis on technical skill and dexterity, *on technique in general*.
4. It delights in story-telling. It is illustrative, journalistic, literary, with a strong leaning toward sentiment.

The important point is that every academic picture is a picture *of* something.

It is a picture of a person, of a house, of a landscape, of a still life, of a scene, of a bowl of flowers, or of anything else.

TYPICAL ACADEMIC-REALISTIC PICTURES

Cot: *The Storm*. Bouguereau: *The Two Sisters*. Merle: *Falling Leaves*.

It is an *image* or a *representation*—on canvas or paper—of a real object. The image on the paper is not the selfsame thing as the object itself, but it looks like the object. It looks *real*. And we like it to look real. And so does the painter of the picture (regardless of how much he may like to dabble in technique or other artistic hokus-pokus). If the picture does not look real, we all find fault with it—immediately.

This insistence on realism, so characteristic of the academic-realistic period, does occur at other times in history. But also, *there are many periods of art which do not share this academic desire for realism.* The Egyptian, Early Greek, Etruscan, Byzantine, Saracen, Celtic-Medieval, Early Renaissance, and all primitive arts are relatively *non*-realistic in their point of view. In these non-realistic eras a picture did *not* necessarily have to be a picture *of* something. It could, for example, be an abstract *symbol* referring to some religious *idea* or *emotion.* And as such it must be accorded as much right to be considered *art* as a realistic picture of a bowl of flowers.

Modern art is a non-realistic type of art. Its rejection of realism is its most fundamental point of difference from academic-realistic art.

So steeped is the general public in academic-realistic conceptions of art, that not a few people today believe that the more realistic a picture is, the better it is. They notice that some pictures are more accurate in their realism than others, and so, apparently, they assume that some artists are *unable* to paint as literally as others. The greatest artists, they likewise

METROPOLITAN MUSEUM OF ART

METROPOLITAN MUSEUM OF ART

appear to believe, are those whose paintings achieve the greatest realism.

Now this is not true at all. The paintings of Michelangelo, Leonardo da Vinci, Raphael, Titian—yes, even Rembrandt—have been surpassed in sheer photographic accuracy by many artists whose work never got into a museum at all.

Realism—even "craftsmanship"—on its own, has nothing to do with greatness in art. A great picture *can* be characterized by realism, but *it is not the realism* that makes the picture great. In fact, *excessive*, photographic realism, by its overexacting demands on the artist, can well prevent a picture from being great.

Another characteristic of the academic-realistic art world is its deep respect for literary, story-telling qualities in a picture.

All pictures, even the fairly abstract ones, tell or suggest a story to some extent. But some pictures tell a great deal more story, put more emphasis on the story *idea*, than do others. Generally speaking, in one kind of picture, the story is the most important consideration; in other kinds, the story is only secondary; it is the *manner of painting* that comes first.

The once very popular "September Morn" is an example of a story-telling picture; so are the many pictures of doctors attending sick children, the Maxfield Parrish illustrations of Grecian myths, the Norman Rockwell magazine covers, and so on. Although such pictures are often also painted with great technical skill, their primary interest lies in the story they tell. The story—*not* the manner of the painting of the picture—supplies the real drama, the interest, the attraction.

Generally, such story-telling pictures are very realistic, because a realistic depiction heightens the dramatic literary effect. And conversely, many realistic painters try to weave story-telling subjects into their pictures to make the pictures more interesting. In academic-realistic art, the liaison between realism and story-telling is very close.

In the *modern* period of art there is a sharp reaction against story-telling in pictures. From its beginnings about 1870 up to 1920, modern art moves farther and farther away from story-telling (as it also moves away from realism) until finally, in extreme Cubist and "non-objective" abstractions, there is practically no story-telling content at all. From 1920 on, however, with the arrival of *Dadaism* and *Surrealism*, story-telling elements began to creep back into modern pictures.

Modern art's claim is that it is the picture itself that must be interesting—not the story that the picture tells.

There is a fatal flaw in an art that depends too much on its story-telling interest—a flaw that leads to lack of permanence. Such art doesn't wear well over a long period of time.

For example, a picture with a clever story-telling idea might catch one's eye immediately and cause one to purchase and hang the picture on a wall where he can see it often. Hanging on the wall, however, day after day, week after week, month after month, the clever idea loses its charm. In fact, the more clever the idea the more tiresome it is likely to become—like a novelty phonograph record that is played over and over again.

10 Possibly this is unfair. Possibly the example is too extreme. Very well,

let the story-telling picture be a bit simpler and more profound, not merely superficially clever. Perhaps the picture reproduces some happy scene that has often thrilled us in real life. Suppose, for instance, it is a pleasant, sunlit bay in New England.

Nearby is a group of clean white houses with people moving about near them. At the water's edge, the docks are weatherworn and full of interesting color. White and red sails sway and dip as they slide across the intensely blue surface of the bay. Dancing wave-tops flash in the sunlight. Gulls fly about;. and overhead, soft little clouds drift lazily by.

It is a lovely picture, and the artist has caught it perfectly. Hang it on your wall and love it.

But then what happens? At the real life scene, things would change. The sunlight would vary, the shadows would lengthen, the colors would change with the light. The waves would look different when the wind veered. Birds and people would change in position. Even the sky and water and ground would appear different. Naturally, such a constantly varying *real life* scene could well continue to be interesting.

But with the picture, this would not happen. Once the painter stopped painting, not a single blade of grass, not a single wavelet, would move forever after. Gulls would remain transfixed, in mid-air. Every motion— sails, waves, people—would be eternally frozen. Nor would light and color change in the slightest degree—except, perhaps, to get brown and dirty with age. The picture, alas, would be born dead.

Of course, this would not become immediately apparent to the owner of the picture, because it might take some time for him to become familiar with its many details. (He may *never* look at the picture enough to get really acquainted with it.) But sooner or later, if he looks at the picture long enough, he must subconsciously realize that he is looking at the same unmoving, unchanging scene.

And eventually (it may take a long time and he may not realize, himself, what is happening), this unchanging scene may bore him to the extent that his eyes no longer see the picture on his wall. The picture is then *really* dead—forever.

"But," you exclaim, "this can happen to *any* picture!"

And the reply comes—"It can happen to any picture whose main interest lies in the real-life scene it reproduces, in the story it tells, in the memories it evokes. But there is another, different kind of picture that does not wear out so easily—a picture whose appeal is not to the *memory*, but to the *eye*. It is the picture whose structure, whose design, is such that it interests the eye in itself, and need not depend on outside memories and nostalgias."

The *modern* artist attempts to create this latter, visually interesting type of picture. In so doing, he is akin to the old masters, who did not neglect design or the other purely artistic qualities of their pictures. (How dull is so much of their *subject matter* to us today, and how interesting their manner of painting!)

Although the general public still lives in the *academic-realistic* period of art, the more daring artists have long since moved on into a new period

REALISTIC PERIODS IN ART HISTORY

Late Greek

Roman

Late Renaissance *(Maroni)*

NON-REALISTIC PERIODS IN ART HISTORY

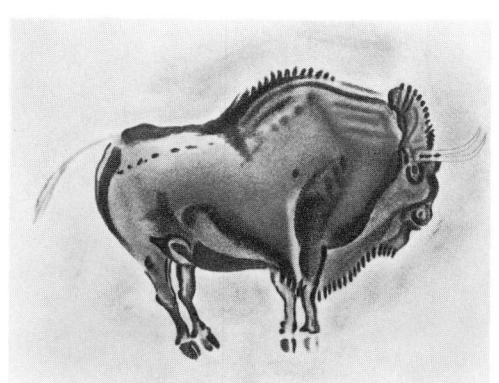

Prehistoric *(Altamira caves)*

Egyptian (1225-1215 B.C.)

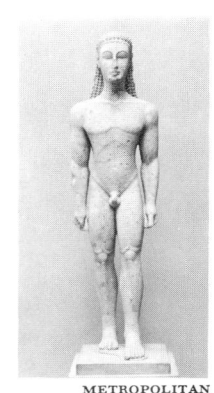

Early Greek (700 B.C.)

Renaissance Florentine

Renaissance French

Academic *(Fagnani)*

In non-realistic periods, *design* is more important than realistic representation. It is a curious fact that the realistic periods are quite often eras of wealth, power, and materialism, whereas in non-realistic periods spiritual and moral values often tend to reassert themselves.

Etruscan (500 B.C.)

Byzantine

Saracen

African

American Indian

Modern *(Picasso)*

—the *modern*. This is as it should be. The artists are always ahead of their public when artistic styles change. But what made the artists do this? Why did they not stay where they were?

Answer, part one. The artists were not satisfied with realistic pictures. They were tired of looking at realistic pictures—tired of painting realistic pictures. They knew that realistic painting had been around for a long, long time—and strongly sensed that it was time for a change. (And art *must* change, must grow and develop, or it dies.)

If this may seem a bit strange to some of us who enjoy seeing realistic pictures, let us remember that we look at only a *few* pictures, and for a short time. The artist not only makes a lot of pictures, but he looks at many more. He lives, sleeps, and eats with art, day in and day out. It is his *business* to guide the public in matters of art.

Answer, part two. The artists' dissatisfaction with the realistic pictures of their time was also caused by the fact that they thought something was *missing*. The great paintings of the past, the old masters, seemed to them to have contained something that the more recent academic pictures lacked.

The history of modern art is the story of the search for that *essence* of art that seemed to be lost or on the point of getting lost in realistic academic pictures. Behind the movement toward abstraction was a continuing attempt to get at the *real spirit and meaning of art and to distill it into a picture*.

14

OLIVER B. JENNINGS COLLECTION

3   Comes a Revolution!

When the modern movement was born, back in the 1870's, and during the early years of its growth in the '80's and '90's, art's long march toward realism was reaching a climax. It had at last become possible to paint a picture as perfect in its realism—as photographically accurate—as any human being could reasonably hope to paint on a flat surface. Perfection, or at least very near perfection, had been reached.

In evidence of this, one has only to look at the work of William Michael Harnett (1848-1892), an ex-engraver who painted oils of astonishing realism. When Harnett paints a picture of a violin hanging on the wall, it takes very little imagination to believe that you are looking at a real violin, not merely the painted image of one. The hot, live sparks he depicts spilling out of a smoker's pipe seem to glow with such a genuine fire that one feels inclined to dash forward and brush away the dangerous embers.

Harnett was a clever illusionist and delighted in exhibiting his skill in producing startlingly realistic effects. He painted with a cunning and patient craftsmanship. Today, if nothing else, his work stands out as a milestone of art's progress in one direction—it demonstrates, superbly, that art's goal of consummate realism had been achieved at last.

15

Yet, Harnett's work is only a single instance among many. The latter half of the nineteenth century, and the beginning of the twentieth, witnessed the painting of thousands of infallibly accurate, photographically realistic pictures. Realism—sometimes delicately infused with sentiment, sometimes cleverly linked with an intriguing story-telling idea—but always realism—was the order of the day.

Needless to say, this type of painting became enormously popular with the general public. No one had the slightest difficulty understanding such a picture. No one needed to know anything about "art." Just make a picture realistic enough, and the average man could like it or leave it alone.

Not long before an event had occurred of tremendous significance in the history of art—the discovery of photography. Presto! The new invention did—*perfectly*—in a fraction of a second and at a cost of a few cents, what an artist could only approximate after hours and days of diligent labor! Of course, a nineteenth century photograph and an artist's painting were not *exactly* the same thing. But as photography improved technically, embraced color as well as black-and-white, and as artists painted more and more literally, the gap narrowed.

The impact of photography on art was felt quickly. To the realist who wished to paint nature exactly as he saw it, here was a scientific device more reliable than his own eyes (or so it seemed), ready at hand to correct and instruct. The photograph confirmed him in his realism—helped to drive out everything *but* realism from his pictures.

On the other hand, the very perfection of photography encouraged those other artists who did *not* want to be too realistic—who sought *other* values in painting: inspiration, individuality, creativeness—to move still farther away from realism, to react violently against it. *They* saw in photography a heaven-sent blessing that at last would relieve art of its ancient practical chores—would relieve it of the burden of providing propaganda for church and state, of recording scenes and events, of picturing and perpetuating the faces of people who considered themselves important. Now art could be itself—paint and draw for its own pleasure—please itself alone.

Thus photography served as a powerful impelling agent to widen the breach between those nineteenth century artists who wanted to paint realistically and those who wanted to break away from realism. It did much to hasten the approaching revolution in art.

Modern art did not "just happen." No sustained style of art ever "just happens"—it grows naturally out of the cultural background of its time.

This does not mean that art must precisely mirror or symbolize the trends of its time. It need not even be sympathetic to the outstanding ideas of its day; it can react violently in revolt against them. But, sympathetic or antagonistic, art has always been influenced in *some* way by the cultural atmosphere in which it was produced.

Modern art came into being in the third quarter of the nineteenth century. Its origin, its development, its continuation far into the twentieth century, are all closely intertwined with the cultural history of that period.

The nineteenth century was marked by tremendous changes in the social, economic and political structure of the entire western world. In this period, ancient agriculture-based ways of living were replaced by a new industrial civilization; feudalism was abolished; the modern national state was founded. The early years of the century were rocked by almost continuous revolution. The later years, though more tranquil politically, witnessed profound social and economic changes. The early years liberated the individual, freed him from the oppressive authority of absolute monarch and landed church. The later years found the individual beginning a new struggle against the economic domination of the great bourgeoisie (that is, "big business," the capitalists).

It was the original bourgeois class—merchants, bankers, investors of money—who reaped the fruits of the Industrial Revolution and gained control of the great machines that not only produced wealth with fantastic rapidity, but also brought their owners social influence and political power. To the great bourgeoisie went the prestige that belonged formerly to the autocratic monarchs, and earlier, to the feudal nobility. By 1870 the bourgeois triumph was complete.

Needless to say, bourgeois taste and ideals—middle class, materialistic, conservative—quickly dominated the arts. Science, useful to the machine age, was eagerly promoted. Painting and literature simultaneously discarded the romantic "nonsense" of the earlier era and turned to strict realism.

The "correct" art of the bourgeois civilization was represented by the official annual exhibition—the Salon—at Paris, and by the offerings of the fashionable galleries of Europe and America. Here bourgeois wealth "acquired" its contemporary pictures (when it was not too busy collecting old masters from poverty-shaken former owners). Here academicism flourished and produced a stream of pictures that were slick, clever, sentimental, and above all, realistic.

Modern art, in its first stage, was a violent reaction, both against the materialistic spirit of the times and against the near-photographic realism of bourgeois art. Revolt against the greedy, self-satisfied nineteenth century civilization re-echoes in the writings (as well as the pictures) of the pioneers of modern art. Wrote Vincent van Gogh: *

> Therefore because I see so many weak ones trodden down, I greatly doubt the sincerity of much that is called progress and civilization. I do believe in civilization, even in this time, but only the kind that is founded on real humanity. That which costs human life I think cruel, and I do not respect it.

There were many reasons why the artists should find themselves out of sympathy with "the businessman's civilization." First, of course, the keenly observant and aesthetically sensitive artists were quick to resent the drab ugliness and the squalor of the factory towns.

Second—as those whose inner creative life cannot exist without freedom of the spirit—the artists found themselves often in bitter conflict with

---

* Editor, J. Van Gogh-Bonger, *The Letters of Vincent van Gogh to His Brother*. It is interesting to note that Van Gogh liked to refer to himself as "a laborer."

the revived "puritanism," the smug respectability, the veiled hypocrisy, and the sheer dullness of middle-class living. (Behind the bourgeois love of respectability was the desire to create a social atmosphere favorable to that wealth-accumulating class, to discourage violence and uncertainty, and hence, to protect precious property rights.) "Bohemianism" was one form of the artists' revolt against bourgeois respectability.

Another grievance—perhaps the most pressing of all—was the economic dislocation of the artists themselves. Before the French Revolution, the artist-craftsman, protected by his guild, worked for king, noble, and church. The arrangement was not always perfect but, generally speaking, the artist fitted into a functional economic niche. The revolutions ended all that, however, by abolishing both aristocracy and guilds, which left the artist one of two choices—either to paint for art's sake and starve, or to peddle his pictures as best he could to the wealthy bourgeoisie, a class that understood neither him nor his works.

Furthermore, the artistic standards of the bourgeoisie were very low— far inferior to the sophisticated tastes of the old aristocracy. Lacking any real knowledge of art, the nouveau riche banker or manufacturer preferred the safely conservative, the obvious, the outwardly slick and showy. Some artists pandered to this taste, but a great many others could not help but rebel against it, even though their rebellion cost them lives of poverty and discontent.

Feeding the spirit of revolt among the artists were the revolutionary traditions handed down from the Romantic era of Delacroix and Géricault. Although Romanticism itself had largely collapsed, many of its precepts lived on in the hearts of the younger artists—the emphasis on emotionalism, the demand for the freedom of the individual, the readiness to revolt and seek something different.* The early modernists revered the memory of Delacroix and looked up to him as a sort of idol and shining example. They considered themselves his heirs in spirit.

But in spirit only. Delacroix and his Romanticism had little else in common with modernism. The modern movement is *not* a continuation of Romanticism. The Romantic uprising was only a phantom revolution, an evasion—at least as far as art was concerned. The Romantic artist beat against the walls of his naturalistic prison, carried on furiously, but remained imprisoned, frustrated. The modern revolution, on the other hand, was a triumphantly successful one. *Its* artists demolished the ancient prison and started to build new structures in its stead. They were more successful because their revolt was more determined and complete, because it reached below surface appearances and based its attack on fundamentals.

While the first modern artists rebelled against the materialism, the smug respectability, and the dullness of bourgeois living, modern art did not remain aloof from other aspects of the times. For example, it was immensely impressed by *science* and the spirit of scientific research. This becomes particularly apparent as modern art develops in the twentieth century. *Cubism* is primarily a *research* into the fundamental first principles of art—a probing analysis that might well have been inspired by

18   * All of which was a natural inheritance from the French Revolution itself.

the efforts of twentieth century scientists to unlock the secrets of molecule and atom.

It is interesting to note that modern artists, by and large, *did not draw pictures of machines* as such (although many design motifs were borrowed from machinery forms). It was the *thinking* behind the making of the machines that seemed more interesting to the artists—the experimentation, the invention, the breaking-down and rebuilding. In spirit, Picasso and Einstein are not so many light-years apart as might be supposed.

Were the originators of modern art—Cézanne, Van Gogh, Gauguin, and others—willful trouble-makers, upstart disturbers of the peace? What about some of their contemporaries—Charles Darwin, Karl Marx, Nietzsche, Baudelaire, Bismarck, Richard Wagner, Hertz, Koch, and a host of others?

Impressed by the new triumphs of science, some of the more imaginative artists of the 60's and 70's also began to *experiment*—starting with a more intensive study of outdoor sunlight, the most recent natural phenomenon to be included in the domain of pictorial art. The immediate result of the experimenting with sunlight was the development of a revolutionary new way of painting called *Impressionism*. Impressionism mightily shocked the art critics of its time. It also left its mark on all subsequent art. Its importance as a revolutionary movement, however, has somewhat faded over the years. It flared up, burned brightly, then subsided. Today, the Impressionists sleep peacefully—and expensively—with the Old Masters. But while its own flame of violence was a fleeting one, Impressionism acted as the kindling that started a far greater conflagration—the *modern movement* that has been sweeping the world of art for seventy-five years.

Simultaneously with this experimenting with sunlight, some of the same restless artists, in their discontent with the pat realism of the times, had begun to restudy the old masters analytically—at first, the works of Rubens, Tintoretto, and Poussin, and later the Michelangelos, the Leonardos, and the Rembrandts. This was only natural, as most of the young artists had been largely if not entirely "self-taught" (nothing unusual in art history. Many a great master has been primarily self-taught) and had learned the "theory" of their art by copying the old masters in the museums. The birthplace of modern art was the Louvre.

The artist-experimenters constantly searched for something more fundamental in art than just the slavish copying of nature. Their reason for turning to the Louvre was the strong feeling that photographically realistic art seemed to lack something that the works of the old masters possessed, and that this missing something was important. In the great paintings of the past there seemed to be a noticeably greater vitality, a greater strength and power, a lasting interestingness that did not fade away.

19   Furthermore, some of these adventurous nineteenth century artists

(Cézanne in particular) not only noted the greater vitality of the old masters, but also came to some definite conclusions as to what *elements* in the old pictures produced this vitality. Having isolated these elements, just as a chemist isolates the vitamins in food, the artist-experimenters tried to inject them into their own work. This is the motivation of the painting of Cézanne—this is *why* he painted the way he did (and not because he had defective vision, or because he couldn't draw, as some of his academic critics claimed). And this is the primary motive that guided the followers of Cézanne, the modern artists of the world.

What were the elements the early modernists saw in the works of the old masters that were being lost in realistic art? Risking the dangers of over-simplification, we may say that they saw two things. First they noticed an underlying *structure, of design*, that was deeply woven into the painting of the picture. Second, they saw a remarkable *personal expressiveness* that lifted these paintings far above ordinary pictures.

Design structure and expressiveness are marks of the mind and hand of the artist, not of the subject matter. Hence, as pictures grew more realistic, the former structure and expressiveness were lost, because the form and color of the subject matter necessarily dictated how the artist should paint.

Here was a parting of the ways. Either one could paint realistically, guided by the "nature" before him, or he could paint expressively, on a strong structural framework, guided by his own spirit and feeling. It seemed *impossible to follow both paths to a conclusion at the same time.* Thus the early moderns chose to develop structure (design) and expressiveness (personality) at the expense of realism—thereby starting modern art on its way.

The two cornerstones of modern art are (1) emphasis on *structure*, or *design*, and (2) a continuing attempt to achieve great personal *expressiveness*. Let us examine each in turn.

4   The Structure of a Picture

On pages 22 and 23 you will find a picture and a diagram. The picture is the "Daniel" of Michelangelo, a small section of his tremendous fresco painting on the Sistine Chapel ceiling at Rome. This Sistine painting is a recognized world masterpiece, one of the greatest of all time.

Look at the picture of Daniel for at least two full minutes, timing yourself with a watch. View the picture as a whole, then study its details. Now set the book up on a chair and step back about five or six feet. Look at the picture from this distance for at least a minute more.

Then pick up the book and turn the picture *upside down*. Look at the upside down picture for at least two minutes—by the watch. Next, study the diagram for a minute or two. Turn it upside down, too.

Now just a minute, please. If you haven't followed the instructions and studied the pictures for the required length of time, please go back and do so before reading on. This Michelangelo reproduction, with its diagram, contains an important clue to the meaning of modern art. Shouldn't it be well worth spending a total of six minutes trying to *see* it?

Very well, what is the purpose of all this looking, turning upside down, and so forth?

What is hoped is that the reader will see that there is something else about this picture than merely a representation of a figure.

It is hoped that he will forget about the figures, Daniel and the Cherubs, for a moment, and instead become aware of the strong *design structure* that is woven into the picture. This structure—of lines, of areas of dark and light, of well-placed masses—seems to *organize* the painting.

Indeed, this picture appears to be fitted firmly together, *built* with a sort of architecture of its own. The strong major lines and edges are like girders in this architecture. The whole picture is firm and stable within its borders.

Also, this painting includes within itself a certain *motion* of its own. One's eye is led from point to point—sweeps around curves. There seems to be a *circular* movement around the picture. This is part of the picture's structure, part of its design.

When one turns the picture upside down, or looks at it from a distance, it is usually much easier to see the internal design structure, because then one's eye becomes much less preoccupied with the subject matter of the painting. The diagram, too, is intended to act as a guide in seeing this structure. Look at the diagram, then look back at the picture itself.

In the sketching of the diagram it quickly became apparent that almost any diagram would be painfully inadequate, because the design structure created by Michelangelo extends *completely through the picture*. To indicate it fully with all of its subtleties, one would have to reproduce the painting itself. The diagram had to content itself with the segregating of some of the *main* lines and areas only.

It will be seen that this diagram, or the picture itself when looked at upside down, forms, more or less, an *abstract design*. This design serves as the structure, the "skeleton," of the picture. And one will note, if he concentrates on it to see it clearly, that the design is an aesthetically pleasing and interesting entity in itself. It makes *another* picture—an *abstract* picture—quite apart from the original subject.

Or, to put it another way—while Michelangelo gives us an adequately convincing representation of the prophet Daniel (and some cherubs), he also succeeds in making the lines and areas of his picture fall into a beautiful design. The design strengthens and enlivens the original picture. In fact, it does more; it contributes, more than anything else, to making the picture immortal. This quality of *design* characterizes all the really

21

Michelangelo: *Daniel, Sistine Chapel Ceiling.* Both representational drawing and powerful *design* are combined in this world-famous masterpiece.

Michelangelo *(Diagram)*. In this diagram, the picture reproduced on the opposite page has been simplified to suggest the underlying de-sign pattern more clearly.

great masterpieces of art. It is one of the reasons, perhaps the foremost reason, why they *are* masterpieces.

But what has this to do with modern art? A great deal, because, in a later chapter, we shall analyze a picture by the modern artist Cézanne and show that it, too, has the same type of design structure as the Michelangelo painting. Nor will the similarity be an accident. It was deliberately sought after by Cézanne—and by all the moderns who followed him.

This basic structural design is what Cézanne saw when, dissatisfied with the academic art of his time, he studied the great masterpieces in the Louvre. It is a key to modern art—a key to all great art.

If you *don't* see this design picture, look at the diagram and picture some more. Try not to see the human figure—try to see the lines and shapes, and the way they fit together. If you can see the powerful design of Michelangelo now, it will not be too difficult to see the same kind of design (or structure) later—in a Cézanne, a Braque, or a Picasso.

5   That Word "Design"

It is hoped that the reader doesn't think of the word "design" as something *dull*, or remote, or unimportant. It is really a very exciting word, when one appreciates it fully, as the moderns do. Unfortunately, however, we have been living in the art world of the academics for a long time—

A. ORIGINAL SCENE. The natural scene used by the artist as a subject for his picture seldom composes itself perfectly. Everything is haphazard; the location is full of pictorially undesirable objects.

B. COMPOSITION. The academic artist composes his picture by *rearranging* the objects before him and by eliminating undesirable material (such as telephone poles, and so on). But his painting still remains a *realistic* picture.

C. DESIGN. The *modern* artist, not concerned with maintaining realistic appearances, uses the natural scene as raw material to construct into a *design*. He *distorts* or changes natural shapes at will to develop the design.

D. DESIGN ALWAYS INVOLVES SOME DISTORTION. The degree of distortion may be very slight, as in certain old master paintings, or it may be very great, as in extreme *abstractions*. But *some* distortion is involved, or there is no *design*.

A.

obeying the aesthetic laws of the academics, seeing everything through the enveloping atmosphere of academic thought. Therefore, because academic art makes little use of genuine design, it would not be surprising if one *did* think of design as being dull or remote.

And for a logical reason. Academic art wanted to be realistic and it wanted to "tell a story." Design, too much design, interferes both with realistic representation and with the story-telling function. (If an artist wants to depict a story-telling emotion, such as an expression of joy or agony, on a face, he can do it much more convincingly with a realistic rendering than with an abstract design.)

Not finding it useful, academic art relegated design to the background. Academic pictures contain a minimum of design—only that small amount that does not seriously interfere with the realism or story-telling qualities of the pictures. Indeed, we are likely to think of design—in this academic world—as having only a utilitarian purpose. A design is something that decorates a curtain or a rug; something that has engineering connotations, such as the design of a new car; or something traditional, such as the fancy cornices or the Greek columns on the county courthouse.

Because so many of these things are done in hackneyed manner, and because we see their like a hundred times a day, they become so familiar that we scarcely notice them at all. Our conception of design becomes debased.

Furthermore, the passing academic era in art—the art of the last hundred years—has offered us surprisingly little in the way of good *original* design, in any field. This period that exalted realism in painting is the same one that gave us Victorian architecture—the aimless, imitative "battle of the styles." It gave us gingerbread decoration. It filled our homes with the strange gimcracks of the Victorian and post-Victorian periods. The fresh air of modernism was needed finally to sweep this accumulated junk out of our houses and off the walls of our buildings.

B.

C.

D.

In contrast, during the great art periods of the past, a feeling for original design has been very much in evidence, not only in the fine arts, but in the humblest utilitarian crafts as well. Greek sculpture was full of design, and so were Greek temples, vases, weapons, and furniture. And as Greek art declined, emphasis on design faded in fine and applied arts alike. And, interestingly, the representation of figures became much more *realistic!*

Weakness, dullness, and imitativeness in design is an indication of lack of creative inspiration, and all the arts are likely to show it at the same time.

In speaking of pictures, it is interesting to note that the modern artist nearly always uses the word "design," while the academic artist generally prefers to use the word "composition."

Although the two words overlap somewhat in meaning, an important distinction between them has grown up. Today, the academic artist's *"composition"* does not mean quite the same thing as the modern artist's *"design."*

By "composition," the academic man meant the *arrangement* of the parts of his picture in a pleasing or interesting way, but not in any way that destroys the essential realism of his painting.

He painted a picture of a barn, a road, a tree. When he *composed* his picture, he *arranged* barn, road, and tree "to best advantage" (often following a simple design-motif like an S-shape, or an oval). But the barn was still a realistic barn, the tree a realistic tree. Some details might have been omitted, or some added, but all remained realistic; there was no distortion.

The modern artist, on the other hand, means much more than this when he uses the word "design." The modern concept is as follows:

1. Design is bigger than composition, *includes* composition. The modern is not restricted by any self-imposed obligation to be always realistic.
2. Design, as envisaged by modern artists, *necessarily* implies *some* distortion of natural forms.
3. Design is creative. It is a *making something* out of nature, not merely a copying of nature.
4. The "touch" of design permeates every part of a picture, every detail. It involves far more than just an arrangement of the larger elements.
5. In a modern picture it is the *design* that is more important, not the realistic subject matter.
6. The element of design varies in quality and interest, of course. It may be dull or hackneyed, or it may be exciting, original, highly creative (depending upon the abilities and inspiration of the artist).

Academic art, with its strong literary bias and its constant desire for realism, had imprisoned design and reduced it to the impotent form of "composition." Modern art sets design free—restores it to the high level it formerly held in the great historical periods of art.

In this explanation of modern art it will be necessary to use the word "design" many times. For after all, modern art *is* design—design *and* expressiveness. Consequently, in using the word, we will not be thinking in terms of the emasculated academic conception of design, but rather of the larger, more important, more glorious concept—*design* as understood by the moderns—and by the ancients.

When we say that design involves *some* distortion of natural forms, it does not mean that the distortion need be great. It may only be a slight alteration of nature. On the other hand, the distortion may be considerable—in which case the picture tends to become *abstract*.

But there *is* some distortion—some change—always, because design is not a copy of nature; it is man's *comment* on nature. It is (first) his analysis of nature and then (second) his re-creation of nature to suit his own aesthetic sense. Designing is an imaginative, creative process—a process which can be applied to the painting of a picture as readily as to the formulation of a bookplate, a trade-mark, or a totem pole.

It is the *distortion* that makes pictorial design possible—that permits the artist to build the structure of his painting strong and solid. It permits the structural pattern (or design) to amalgamate with every part of the picture, not just with the major units, as in academic composition.

There are some who may throw up their hands in horror at the mention of the word "distortion." The idea of artists distorting nature! Yet artists do it every day—and not only modern artists.

What about those comic-strip cartoons everyone enjoys so much? Aren't they distorted, to an extreme degree? The conventionalized flowers on draperies—they are distortions of nature, too. Yet, because we've all become accustomed to seeing these things, none of them are shocking to anyone.

What is more significant is the fact that the works of the great masters, such as Michelangelo, are also to some extent distorted—and distorted for purposes of design, too.

No human body could fit into the gigantic and exaggerated proportions of most of Michelangelo's figures; nor would any natural draperies likely fall into the folds imposed by this and other old masters solely for uses of design. And it has been said that some of Michelangelo's muscles (how the Renaissance painters *loved* muscles!) are not to be found in any medical anatomy book.

Partly because of the skill of these artists in creating illusions of reality, and partly because of our long (and somewhat uncritical) familiarity with their works, we fail to notice these distortions. But if one could carefully compare the works of every great master with comparable photographs, he would soon find not only *some* deviation from 100 per cent realism in every one, but an amazing amount in many of them.

Yes, there is plenty of distortion in art throughout the ages, sometimes a great deal of it at a time. But why worry about it? Distortion bothers people only when they have decided to *insist* that all art must be photographically realistic, and nothing else.

As the moderns see it, design is something that permeates every part of a picture. It is not only the skeleton of the picture, but the flesh, the bloodstream, the arteries, veins, capillaries, and skin as well.

TRUE DESIGN PERMEATES EVERY PART OF A PICTURE.

Consequently, small sections of a designed picture readily form designs themselves.

The extension of design into all parts of a truly designed picture can be indicated by a simple experiment. In a piece of cardboard or heavy paper, cut a small hole about an inch square. Move this opening over the Michelangelo picture. Note how even the small details of the painting, as revealed in the opening, seem to fall into design shapes of their own.

Design sometimes may be dull or cold—but it need not be. Those designs made by the simplification (that is, the mere conventionalizing or the formalizing) of natural objects, such as flowers, are the most elementary examples of design—the common garden variety. It is the kind of design most frequently applied to utilitarian objects, and, of course, can easily be uninspired and hackneyed.

But design in art can also rise far above this. Great design can have a lore, a language of its own—a language that is not unintelligible to persons with a keen aesthetic sense.

The sensitive eye can find interest in the delicate tensions and balances of the parts of a good design. One can be intrigued by the complexity of the design's organization, or can find pleasure in the movement of its swirling curves, its dynamic thrusts, or the interplay of its contrasting lines and colors.

One won't find too many of these things in the patterns of a basement store couch cover, but he will find them on the title page of the Book of Kells or the Lindisfarne Gospels, in the Gothic tracery of a fine church window or fan-vaulted ceiling, or in the exquisite form of a Taj Mahal. Or, in great paintings.

6   Expressiveness

The first of the two cornerstones of modern art, we have noted, was emphasis on structure—*design*. The second cornerstone is an ever-continuing attempt to achieve great *expressiveness*.

Expressiveness in art is an elusive quality, difficult to define or delimit, difficult even to describe in anything like specific terms. It is an emotional quality, subtle, and sometimes deceptive. But it undoubtedly exists in great pictures. It manifests itself in many different ways.

Of course the term "expressiveness" is a rather broad one and has many shades of meaning. But applied to *art* it has a rather special meaning. For example, in the field of literature, a novelist's writing may be said to display expressiveness if it delineates his characters clearly and sharply, so that they are quickly understood by the reader. This is expressiveness in the literary sense. *It is not the kind of expressiveness we are now talking about in connection with art.*

No, art's expressiveness transcends, goes beyond this literary, descriptive (and a bit pedestrian) kind of expressiveness. Art's version of the word

Michelangelo: *Pietà*. The personal *expressiveness* given to his work by a great Renaissance master is displayed in this beautiful statue.

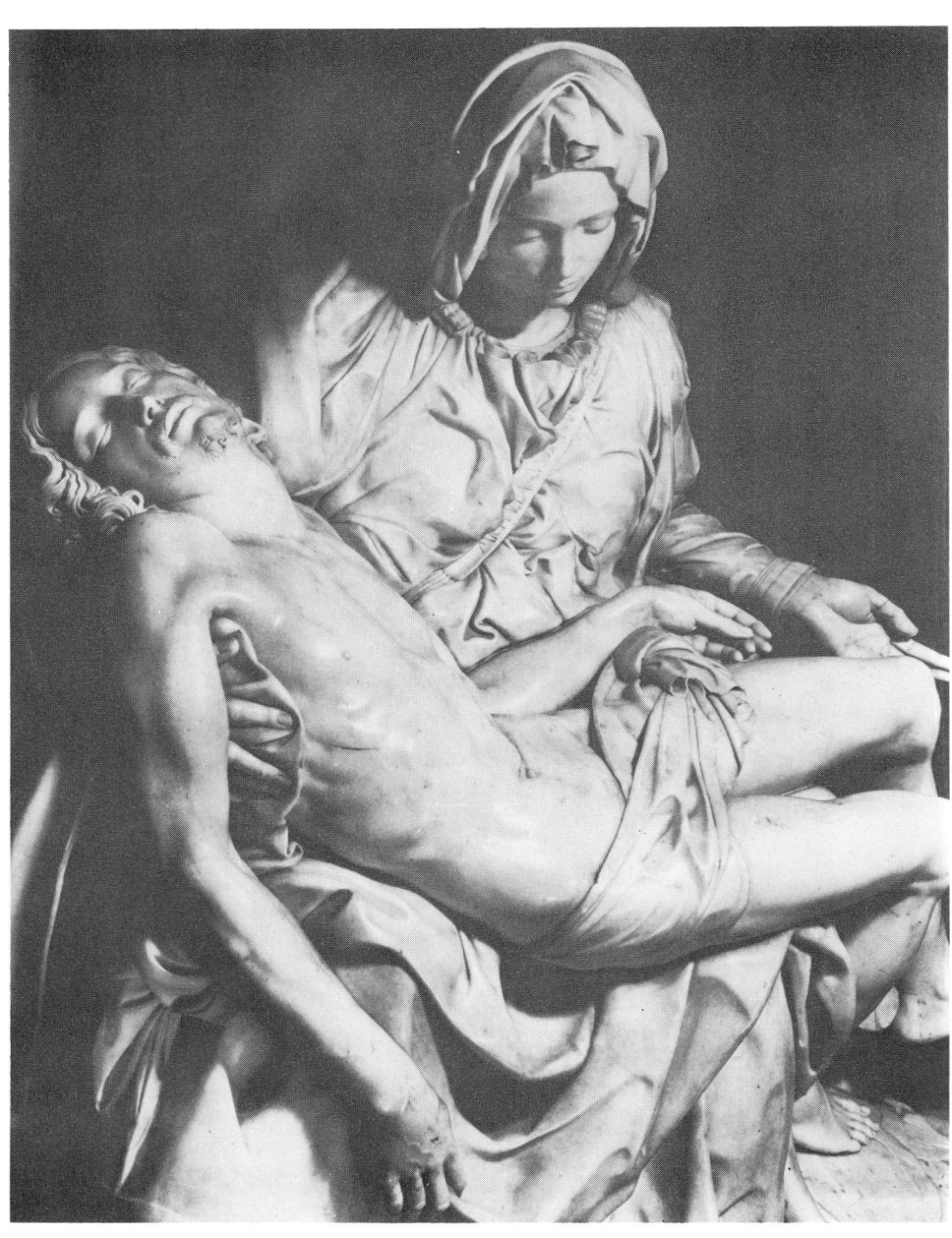

is much more nearly identical with *music's* concept of expressiveness. It is that *extra* something that Fritz Kreisler might add to the playing of a simple melody—a something that the village fiddler, for example, would lack. Art's expressiveness does not describe, portray, or analyze—it sings, it dances, it excites! It appeals to the aesthetic sense. It reaches for the soul, not the intellect.

There is a reproduction of Michelangelo's sculptured *"Pietà"* at the beginning of this chapter. The quality of expressiveness is abundantly evident in this beautiful work.

Here expressiveness takes the form of a great tenderness that touches every line, every form, every movement of the statue. The limpness of the hands, the squeezing of the flesh, the hang of the heads, the contour and direction of every fold in the draperies—all bespeak an intense and sensitive over-all *feeling* that comes right from the heart of the artist—a feeling so strong that it melts hard unyielding marble into music. A tragic but beautiful poetry flows through the entire statue.

This poetry, this tenderness, this expressiveness derives *from the artist himself*. It was not there in any models, to be copied. Michelangelo made it. Michelangelo's great feeling and emotion made it.

This is expressiveness.

It is interesting to note the close analogy between this expressiveness and the *design* we discussed in Chapter 5. True design, it was pointed out, entered into every part of a picture or sculpture—and true expressiveness does the same thing.

This quality of expressiveness is constantly displayed in the paintings of Rembrandt. The author once asked an artist friend what it was about Rembrandt's work that made him great. The artist answered immediately, "Rembrandt's *majestic drawing!*"

That phrase seems to be most revealing. Not so much the word "drawing" (anyone can see that Rembrandt's drawing is consummately accurate), but the word *"majestic."*

The *majestic* quality that imbues his every brush stroke is what sets Rembrandt's work apart from that of other men. It is particularly apparent in his glorious portraits. It is the heart-painting, the unwritten signature of the master—Rembrandt Harmensz van Rijn.

Well-meant, but silly statements have been made about this master's painting. It has been stated, somewhere, that Rembrandt was such a super-draughtsman that he could depict not only the faces of his models, but also the workings of their minds, their inner psychologies. Nonsense!

Were Rembrandt such a draughtsman—or indeed, that type of artist—all we would think of when we viewed his pictures would be the characters of the people who posed for them. Saskia, Titus, Hendrickje Stoffels, Rembrandt's father, and all the rest would immediately monopolize our attention and the artist would be entirely forgotten.

Actually, of course, nothing of the sort happens. When we go to a museum and *look at the pictures*, we are scarcely conscious of the subjects at all. Because all the paintings seem to be insistently repeating one word. They shout it, again and again: "REMBRANDT! REMBRANDT! REMBRANDT!"

Rembrandt: *Man With a Magnifying Glass.* The ma
jestic quality of Rembrandt's paintings derives from
himself, not from his models. His painting is an ex
ample of *expressiveness*, the inspired *personal* touch o
a great artist.

El Greco: *The Repentant Peter.* In El Greco, persona
expressiveness reaches its greatest heights. *Expressive*
ness is the reflection of the artist's emotional *feeling*

In New York's Metropolitan Museum are a number of Rembrandt paintings. One who has visited this section of the museum a few times need not bother to read the little labels on the pictures to tell which are the Rembrandts. With very little practice one can spot them instantly —*from twenty feet away.*

How beautiful are the faces portrayed by this master! How mysterious, how haunting, how grand!

Do not be deceived. One would have to seek far over the world to find as many hauntingly beautiful *real* people as are to be found on Rembrandt's canvases. And surely, there were not that many in Rembrandt's little circle in his own time.

No, the beauty and the glory of these faces did *not* come from the models, they came from the artist, from Rembrandt alone. This is expressiveness—the emotional, deeply felt expression of the painter himself, *not* of his subject matter. He created—he did not copy.

Furthermore, he did something else. When he changed the shape of a nose—though ever so slightly—when he deepened the color of a pair of eyes or transformed the line of an eyebrow into a line of poetry, he was taking liberties with nature. He was, though in infinitesmal degree, *distorting* nature (which, however, should disturb only those who, in art, insist on nature above man—fact above spirit).

Expressiveness differs in character in the work of each individual artist. In the Michelangelo and Rembrandt examples just cited, its nature was relatively subtle and delicate, and it disturbed the general realism of those works only very slightly.

But in the mighty canvases of El Greco, expressiveness becomes bold and forthright. It dominates the picture forcefully, and it does not hesitate to twist and distort form violently to suit its purposes.

In Michelangelo's *Pietà*, the expressiveness was characterized by exquisitely sensitive line, by tenderness of feeling and poetry of design. In Rembrandt's portraits, it was a haunting mysteriousness, a majesty of spirit, an amazing, form-understanding draughtsmanship. El Greco's expressiveness, however, consists of sheer *power* and *intensity*. It sweeps the picture with the force of a hurricane.

Bodies are elongated, the head and shoulders of a man loom up like a mountain peak, arms resemble tree trunks, rocks writhe and twist, and light comes from cold blue-green flashes of lightning.

El Greco's pictures are so powerful that the paintings of most of the greatest artists in the world seem to pale and weaken when placed near his. El Greco's art is the very soul of expressiveness. Here are some of the most intensely emotional pictures ever created. Here the feeling of the artist is supreme and subject matter is merely incidental.

The close kinship between *expressiveness* and *design* has already been suggested. True design permeates every part of a picture, and so does expressiveness. True design implies at least *some* distortion of nature (if only a tiny amount), and so does expressiveness. Both design and expressiveness derive from the artist, rather than from the subject painted.

In such a picture as El Greco's *The Repentant Peter*, for example, the factors that make for expressiveness and the design-structure of the picture seem to overlap and melt into each other. Indeed, some artists consider

33

expressiveness and design to be one and the same thing. Whether or not this is always true, the ever-present and intimate relationship between these two picture qualities cannot be denied.

It may have suggested itself by this time that expressiveness might well be the *essence* of all real art. (The pioneer modern artists thought it was —when it was firmly linked with design). It embraces all the factors that give life and vitality to a picture. Emotion, interest, sensitivity, majesty, poetic design, individuality, personality, mystery, movement, understanding and sympathy, intensity, power, grandeur, drama, richness, all are wrapped up in or closely linked with the term *expressiveness*.

Regardless of the form it takes, or of its specific application, expressiveness must always be remembered as an *expression of the artist himself*. It is that part of a painting that comes from within, not from without.

The first modern artists sought to apply the old master principles of design and personal expressiveness to their own painting, which happened to be the most advanced art of the time, airy, sunlight-loving Impressionism. All of these founders of modern art—Cézanne, Van Gogh, Seurat, Gauguin, and Renoir—thought of themselves originally as Impressionists, *were* Impressionists, at least for a time.

To *their* Impressionism, however, they added the stout backbone of strongly emphasized design and the life-giving touch of expressiveness. The impact of a powerful urge for design—with its natural tendency to distort form—on the weaker fabric of Impressionism (which even itself broke up the contours of form) had the effect of turning the stream of art in an entirely new direction—away from realism and toward increasing abstraction. This was the beginning of modern art.

Modern art did not happen in a day. It developed slowly, gradually, logically, over a long period of years. The story begins officially about 1870, when certain French artists began experimenting with the thought of depicting sunlight in painting.

This was named by the critics, in derision, "Impressionism."

7   Impressionism

Many people try to guess at the meaning of Impressionist art from the *name* "Impressionism." This is a mistake. If one guesses this way, he is almost certain to be misled.

For example, there is one thing that Impressionism does *not* mean. It does *not* mean that an artist sits down and paints his *impression* of some object. After all, there is nothing unique in that. As Edward Alden Jewell has pointed out, *every* work of art ever created "is one artist's impression of the object or mental image depicted."

Not a few of the name labels attached to trends in modern art tend to be notoriously undescriptive, and "Impressionism" is no exception. Just as Cubism has nothing to do with cubes, Impressionism is very little concerned with *impressions,* as such.

To clear up all misunderstanding, it is important, before proceeding further, to note exactly how Impressionism *did* get its name. Turn back to Paris, capital of the world of art, in the years immediately following the Franco-Prussian war.

At that time, there was only one generally accepted way for an artist to get his pictures before the public—he must exhibit at the official annual "Salon," sponsored by the French government. Paintings to be exhibited had to pass a jury. This jury, however, was composed of painters staunchly devoted to tradition, and any painting that varied too much from the accepted style was promptly rejected.

As a result, to have their pictures seen at all, the more revolutionary painters of the day found themselves obliged to organize an exhibition of their own. This they did, in the spring of 1874, enrolling as many artists as possible to help defray expenses. The name assumed by the group was the *Société anonyme des artistes peintres, sculpteurs, et graveurs du 15 avril au 15 mai 1874.* There were about thirty exhibitors in all.

Not all the artists painted the same way or belonged to the same schools of thought about painting, but every one was an independent of one kind or other. Each wanted to paint his own way, and not the way dictated by the conservative Salon jury.

The exhibition opened April 15, 1874, at the studio of the photographer Nadar, 54 Boulevard des Capucines. (This Nadar, incidentally, must have been a remarkable man. He has been described as not only an accomplished photographer, but a wit, a caricaturist, an art lover, a scholar, and an aeronaut as well.) At the time, these artists—for the most part, young men in their thirties—were quite obscure. Today their names are not so obscure. Included in the group were Auguste Renoir, Edgar Degas, Claude Monet, Paul Cézanne, Camille Pissarro, Alfred Sisley, and Berthe Morisot.

The exhibition attracted a surprising amount of attention in the press, but it was anything but a favorable type of attention. Critics and public alike were outraged.

It so happened that, by the merest chance, Claude Monet had given one of his pictures the title, *"Impression, soleil levant."* ("Impression, sunrise.") This was a hazy dawn scene of fishing boats, very reminiscent of the English Turner. It was not a particularly startling picture by present-day standards, certainly nothing one would expect to start a furore of any kind.

Nevertheless, the title of the picture immediately caught the eye of a hostile critic, Louis Leroy of the Paris *Charivari,* and he made it the theme of an abusive review which he entitled: *"L'Exposition des Impressionistes."*

"Impressionists, forsooth!" wrote the indignant Leroy, "These wild men, these stubborn savages, disdained—was it laziness or impotence?—

to finish their pictures. They were content to dab on a few 'impressions.' What humbugs. Impressionists!" *

Thus the name "Impressionism" was given to the world by the Impressionists' worst enemy.

It is interesting to observe that what Leroy meant by "Impressionist" was "fragmentary," "incomplete." Of course Impressionist pictures are *not* incomplete fragments. They are completely and carefully painted—almost to a fault. But they *seemed* incomplete to an age that wanted its realistic, story-telling pictures painted smoothly and in great detail, that is, photographically.

The artists did not like the name "Impressionism." It did not accurately describe what they were trying to do. (Some of the artists in the exhibiting group were not of the Impressionist school at all.) But the public had seized on the name, talked about it, made it a popular catchword.

There was nothing for the artists to do but to term themselves "Impressionists," too, regardless of whether or not it correctly described what they were trying to do.

Very well, what *is* Impressionism? It is a way of painting—a point of view about painting—put into practice by certain painters, of whom Claude Monet is generally admitted to be the most typical and perfect example. The resultant paintings have distinctive characteristics which, today, immediately identify them as *Impressionist* paintings.

Impressionism has four outstanding characteristics:

1. First and foremost, it attempts to depict light—*sunlight*. It sees all objects in terms of light.

2. It is *primarily* concerned with landscape painting, and most particularly, landscapes painted in the open air, on the spot—*not* in the studio.

3. Its technique, in comparison with other art of its time, was daring, extreme, revolutionary. It did everything possible to turn color and pigment into a representation of light.

4. Its intent is entirely realistic. It is *not* inspirational especially, *not* imaginative or sentimental, *not* symbolic. It is not so much concerned with what the artist *feels* about his subject—most definitely not with what he *remembers* about it—but only with what he *sees* at a given moment.

Atmosphere, as well as light, interested the Impressionists, because light is conveyed to the eye through the medium of atmosphere.

Camille Mauclair, a biographer of Monet, explains: "All things that exist are enveloped and colored by the solar atmosphere. It follows that a picture is not the representation of a set of objects, but rather of the atmosphere in which these objects are immersed."

Nothing has a fixed color, there is no absolute "local" tone—colors change because of the effect of the surrounding atmosphere. But it is *light*, shining through atmosphere, that we see.

* Edward Alden Jewell and Aimee Crane, *French Impressionists*.

Wilhelm Uhde * writes that Impressionism "aimed at reproducing objects not in their material aspect but in the colored analysis created by sun, light and air."

Furthermore, the Impressionist painters attempted to depict the sparkle, the vibration, the shimmer of sunlight through the use of many little dabs of pigment of different colors—"broken" or "divided" color.

Sometimes grass in the sunshine is seen as a glistening, bright yellow-green. To render such grass, an Impressionist would intermingle little dabs of pure yellow side by side with dabs of green. Close by, the scene would be obscured by all the little spots and streaks of pigment, but if one stepped back and viewed the picture from a distance, the green and yellow dabs would blend and give a convincing effect of the glistening, yellow-green grass.

Of course, the grass might be represented by a flat area of yellow-green paint, but such a representation would lack the shimmering effect of *sunlight,* which was precisely what the Impressionists wanted to capture.

Some critics have averred that the purpose of this "broken color" painting was to increase the *intensity* of the *color.* For example, it has been said that spots of pure yellow and pure blue, mingled and seen from a distance, would produce a brighter green than could be obtained by merely mixing pigments. This may be true enough, but the original Impressionist painters seldom if ever actually produced green this way. They could get their green, amply bright enough, straight from the tube.

No, it was not brilliance of color that was desired, but rather the vibration, the shimmer of sunlight and sunlit atmosphere. As a matter of fact, brilliant sunlight tends to kill color rather than intensify it, and there was no need for these artists to seek mere brilliancy of color. They did, however, brighten their palettes by omitting the dull earth colors.

The Impressionists were the first artists in history to paint their landscapes on the spot, entirely and completely in the open air. Landscapes had been painted before—some artists even made use of outdoor *sketches* —but the pictures were finished in the studio, and the touch of the studio is upon them.

The Impressionists, on the other hand, worked face to face with nature, deliberately, almost fanatically, day in and day out, year after year. They very soon discovered many facts about nature that the studio artists never dreamed existed. Particularly about the true colors of outdoor objects, and about shadows.

It is curious to note that for hundreds of years, from the Renaissance on, artists had painted the foliage of trees brown. Furthermore, the color of trees was accepted by artists, critics, and public as brown—apparently because trees had always been painted brown.

When, in the early years of the nineteenth century, the English artist John Constable insisted that foliage was really green, an angry public refused to believe him—and it was necessary for him to place an old violin on the grass, to prove to one critic that grass and violin were not of the same color.

* William Uhde, *The Impressionists.*

Though influenced by him at first, the Impressionists went far beyond Constable, and discovered more about the colors of natural objects. They observed that while, in general, foliage is green—green is the "local color" —it is not always *seen* as green. In certain conditions of light and atmosphere, at certain distances, foliage might appear actually blue, or white, or almost black. (Mountains may be covered with green trees, but seen from a great distance, a mountain range generally looks purplish-blue, not green.)

The discerning eyes of the Impressionists discovered something else. They noted that shadows were not mere "darkness," to be painted in gray or black, but were actually full of light and color. Some of this color was reflected from nearby objects. Some came from a natural optical effect— the reaction (in the eye of the beholder) of a bright color on the other colors surrounding it.

For example, as has been demonstrated many times, when a bright yellow is placed next to a neutral gray, the gray appears to take on a slightly violet cast. A bright red makes neutral gray seem slightly greenish. In each case the gray takes on a bit of the contrasting *complement* of the bright color. (Violet is the color complement of yellow; green is the complement of red.)

Outdoors, in the brilliant illumination of sunlight, this effect of "simultaneous contrast," as it is scientifically called, may be considerably intensi-

Monet: *Haystacks*. Claude Monet painted the same haystacks dozens of times—at every hour of the day and under every condition of *light*. It was the *sunlight* that interested him, rather than the haystacks.

fied. Hence, the shadow of a bright yellow stone often appears violet. The Impressionists noted this recurring phenomenon and painted it into their pictures.

Today, nearly all shadows are painted full of color, along the lines established by the Impressionists, and no one thinks anything of it. But in the solemn 1870's, colored shadows seemed utterly "crazy," both to the studio-bound conservative artists and to the public.

Considered in terms of subject matter, Impressionist pictures may be compared to "snapshots," instantaneous views of living nature. This is in contrast to the staged, story-telling *tableaux* (such as scenes of ancient Greece and Rome) so often presented in the traditional French art of the mid-nineteenth century.

Almost of necessity, because of the constantly changing aspects of sunlight and clouds, Impressionist painting presented a given scene at a given moment. Monet could only paint his famous haystack for a short time before the light changed. Therefore, to continue his picture he had to come back the next day to work again in approximately the same light.

Although the Impressionists were forever attempting to capture the fugitive light and atmospheric effects of the moment, it must not be thought that their work was hurried or careless, or fragmentary or sketchy. They worked hard and long on their pictures, analyzed the scenes before them with utmost care, and painted with great completeness.

The instantaneous "snapshot" visualization was not entirely original with the Impressionists, but was derived from the somewhat earlier "Realists," Courbet and Manet. From the Realists, too, the Impressionists inherited the practice of painting commonplace everyday scenes—*not* the imagined scenes of history or story.

Impressionism fits logically into the slowly unfolding history of art. Up to the time the Impressionists went into the open air and painted sunlight, artists had painted just about everything *but* outdoor sunlight.

Impressionist methods—the use of "broken" color, the painting in dabs of pigment, even the point of view, or the type of "vision," that sees only atmosphere and vibration of light rather than line and form—had their prototypes in the work of earlier artists.

For example, the baroque art of the seventeenth century is closely akin to Impressionism in spirit. It, too, debased classic *line*, made its forms indefinite, sought after the shimmer and movement of light (*studio* light, however, *not* outdoor sunlight). In this sense, one can follow the lead of the famous critic Woelfflin and consider Impressionism an extreme form of baroque.

Painting at the beginning of the nineteenth century, the Englishman John Constable also foreshadowed Impressionism in many ways. The earlier paintings of the Impressionist artists are strikingly similar, in general appearance, to the works of Constable.

The line of succession then passes through the French Romantic, Delacroix, who preceded Impressionism in making use of a form of broken color. The young Impressionist painters regarded Delacroix as an idol to be revered and studied his style.

But a more timely influence—an influence openly admitted by the Impressionists themselves *—was that of the great English master, J. M. W. Turner. During the Franco-Prussian war of 1870, Monet and Pissarro visited London, where they saw and were deeply impressed by Turner's work. Undoubtedly, the impact of Turner's own daring and dramatic handling of light did much to give Impressionism its final, mature form.

Two perplexing names in the history of Impressionism are those of Edgar Degas and Edouard Manet (not to be confused with Claude Monet). Manet, for instance, has been called both the leader of the Impressionists and the originator of the movement. Yet when we look at the bulk of Manet's paintings, we see little if any resemblance to the familiar Impressionist style.

As a matter of fact, judging solely from the viewpoint of artistic style, Manet was not an Impressionist at all. Manet, painter of the *Olympia* and the *Dejeuner sur l'herbe*, was a "Realist," as also was Degas. Both of these men were stout realistic draughtsmen. Their love of *drawing* was much too great to permit them to go very far toward accepting the formlessness of true Impressionism. It is significant that Manet, in spite of his close personal ties with the Impressionist painters, refused to join them in their

* Though with some qualifications. Turner was not responsible for Impressionism; it had largely taken form when Monet and Pissarro went to London. But the English master's work was the culminating influence that confirmed the Impressionists in their ideas and clearly inspired them to work in a bolder and more colorful style.

group exhibitions, and that Degas, although he exhibited with them, constantly objected to the use of the name "Impressionist" in connection with the exhibitions. It is true that in their *later* work, both Manet and Degas were to some extent influenced by Impressionist ideas, particularly in coloring, but this late influence was never important enough to overturn their essential realism.

There are two points of view about the meaning of the word "Impressionism." One—the viewpoint followed here—sees it as a *style*, an *artistic approach*. The other—advanced by the English critic, R. H. Wilenski, and some others—sees it as the work of a *group of painters*, who worked closely together for a number of years. The point of difference in the two viewpoints lies in the obvious fact that *all* of the painters in the group did not paint in the same style.

If we accept the "group" point of view, it is easy to see how Manet could be called the leader of the Impressionists. The *group* began to form in the early 1860's, nearly ten years before the Impressionist *style* was developed. Actually, however, the landscapes produced by these artists in this early period (the decade 1860-1870) bear little resemblance to what the world today thinks of as *Impressionism*. The art of this period is much better described as a form of realism, painted with considerable "looseness" or "sketchiness" of technique. Naturally, the master, Manet, dominated this period—it was his style—and the others, very young men and barely more than students at the time, followed his lead.

But the art of this period should not be termed *Impressionism*, because true Impressionism had not yet been born. The typical characteristics of mature Impressionism—the rainbow palette, the broken color, the studied analysis of sunlight—did not appear until near the end of the decade, and were developed *independently of Manet*. Indeed, the whole trend of fully developing Impressionism, after 1870, was *away from* the leadership of Manet.

Nevertheless, Manet might well be termed the "godfather" of Impressionism, if not its "father." As a fighter against the dictation of the traditionalists, as an already "notorious" rebel in his own right, Manet served as an inspiration to these younger artists. In the years before the War of 1870 (and before their own Impressionism was fully developed) he presided over their meetings at the famous Café Guerbois. He later invented devious ways to assist financially his near-namesake Monet, when that artist found himself sorely beset by poverty.

But Manet never exhibited with the Impressionists. Nor could the influence of his color and technique on them have been as great as some critics claim, because, as a matter of fact, the color (and technique) of the *mature* Monet and Pissarro is even more different from Manet's than Manet's was from the traditionalists.

For a long time, the Impressionist painters had a hard time making a living. They painted and exhibited for nearly twenty years before their pictures began to sell at all. One difficult winter Monet and Renoir subsisted on potatoes they had grown themselves.

A potent cause of this lack of economic success was the bitter barrage
of ridicule leveled at the Impressionists by the critics and the press. Typical

of this criticism was the comment by Albert Wolff of the *Figaro* on the occasion of an early exhibition: *

> The Rue Peletier is unfortunate. Following upon the burning of the Opera-House, a new disaster has fallen upon the quarter. There has just been opened at M. Durand-Ruel's an exhibition of what is said to be painting.
>
> The innocent passer-by enters, and a cruel spectacle meets his terrified gaze. Here five or six lunatics, of whom one is a woman, have chosen to exhibit their works. There are people who burst out in laughter in front of these objects. Personally I am saddened by them.
>
> These so-called artists style themselves Intransigeants, Impressionists. They take paint, brushes, and canvas; they throw a few colors on to the canvas at random, and then they sign the lot. In the same way the inmates of a madhouse pick up the stones on the road and believe they have found diamonds.

Nevertheless, in spite of many such criticisms, in spite of the people who had to be prevented from thrusting umbrellas through their canvases, in spite of the gallery visitors who burst out laughing even before entering the doors of an Impressionist exhibition, in spite of the cruelly funny music-hall jokes, the Impressionists painted on.

Finally, near the end of the century there was a turnabout. A few courageous collectors and dealers had continued to purchase these unpopular pictures—until others began first to wonder why and then to purchase. Suddenly a demand was created and prices of the pictures skyrocketed, bringing a belated measure of prosperity to those of the artists who were still alive.

Today, the works of Monet, Pissarro, and Sisley are reverently displayed in the conservative museums as old masters. The long controversy—art's "Battle of Impressionism"—is not only over but well-nigh forgotten. Indeed, just past the midpoint of the twentieth century, the nineteenth-century Impressionist paintings had begun to lead all others in gallery popularity.

It has been pointed out that, in order to produce an effect like the sparkle of sunlight, the hazy shimmer of atmosphere, the Impressionists applied their paint in little dabs of color. One inevitable result of this practice was that lines became blurred, form obscured. The pictures assumed a sort of "soft-focus" effect, which, however, grew somewhat clearer as the observer moved back away from the canvas.

With the debasement of line, those parts of the pictorial structure that depended on line were undermined. The familiar *linear* perspective (the railroad tracks that seem to meet at a horizon or "vanishing point") was greatly weakened. Consequently, the true Impressionists emphasized the non-linear, *aerial* perspective (the blurring or fading away of distant objects) to obtain the illusion of distance.

* Theodore Duret, *Renoir*.

Use of the little strokes of color had another significant effect. By blurring line, they made accurate drawing impossible, and insidiously encouraged the possibility of distortion—a distortion that might naturally be influenced by the artist's sense of design. Hence, intentionally or not, Impressionism contributed to the development of true modern art.

Indeed, the *brush strokes* of the first *moderns* plainly reveal this Impressionist heritage. The "bricks" in Cézanne's pictorial "architecture" are his small, rectangular, chisel-like brush strokes—brush strokes obviously derived from Impressionist technique (though applied with a decidedly *non*-Impressionist purpose).

With another early modern, Seurat, the rough Impressionist dabs became precise little dots of pure color, carefully laid in side by side— *pointillism*. On the other hand, Vincent van Gogh's dabs, under the stress of impatient emotion, lengthened out into long streaks of pigment. Again, Renoir subordinated his Impressionist color spotting sufficiently to allow him to represent the human form solidly and roundly, yet retained enough of the "broken" technique to keep his paintings loose and fluid.

All of these men—the moderns—broke away from the literal-minded, essentially realistic representation of sunlight sought by the true Impressionists, Monet, Pissarro, and Sisley. The moderns borrowed from Impressionism but did not let Impressionist theory block their path to a new art. And conversely, that part of Impressionism that lent itself to *realistic* uses (which is a great deal of it) has long since been absorbed into present-day realistic *academic* art.

Along with Impressionism, there appeared for the first time an entirely new influence on the world of art. An important new influence destined to grow—the influence of *modern science*.

Monet's patient rendering of the same haystack, again and again, each time under a different condition of light and season (a friendly farmer left the stack for him, untouched in the fields) bears a striking similarity in spirit to the equally patient experimentation of the scientist in his laboratory.

A new concept in art—the idea of a picture as an *experiment*, as a *finding* of something hitherto unknown—is foreshadowed in these light-pictures of Monet. As modern art develops, this idea of experimentalism develops with it.

Again, many of the color theories of the Impressionists are paralleled or preceded by the discoveries of scientists in the field of optics. A notable instance is that of the French physicist Chevreul, whose findings were published in his now-famous book, *"De la loi du contraste simultane des couleurs"* (1839). Scientific treatises of this nature directly influenced the late-Impressionist school of the *pointillists*, and quite possibly influenced the earlier Impressionists as well.

Artists are not scientists. The application to art of what the average artist conceives to be science may be something to make Isaac Newton turn in his grave. Nevertheless, the fact that, in however garbled form, the world of science at last impinged on the world of art was a highly significant milestone in art history.

43   It meant that the Greeks and the Romans, the saints and the doges,

the shepherds and the nymphs had had their day, and that in art, as in everything else, the twentieth century could no longer be concealed behind an antique statue.

Like a Wagnerian leitmotif, the science-inspired spirit of experimentalism recurs again and again in modern art. It reaches a grand climax in the series of bold experiments ushered in by Cubism.

8   Old Masters and a New Art

Turn back to the Michelangelo picture and diagram at the beginning of Chapter 4. Compare these with the two Cézanne pictures—and diagrams—at the beginning of this chapter. The three paintings are quite different in subject matter—one is a figure, one a still life, and the third a landscape—but it should be apparent, after a little looking, that all three have the same thing in common. *All three are strongly organized by a definite design-structure.* (The kind of design structure suggested by the diagrams, and described in Chapter 4.) They are not drawn haphazardly; every line, every brush stroke is guided by the inner urge of the artists to *design* as well as to draw.

In each case, the design is subtly woven into every detail of the painting. In each case, the underlying design pattern controls lines and forms, dominates the pictures, and does not permit itself to be destroyed by any desire for too complete realism.

Emphasis on design is the link between modern art and the great art of the past. The rediscovery of design in painting is the starting point of modernism. If one can sense the common quality of design in both these Michelangelo and Cézanne examples, he will have begun to understand modern art.

There is one interesting difference between Michelangelo's design and that of Cézanne. In the Michelangelo reproduction and diagram, note the swirling motion of the main lines, the powerful circular action around the picture, the dynamic thrust of the figure's arm and shoulder.

In contrast, there is no such sweeping action in the Cézanne paintings. What movement there is exists in the interaction of the various details of the pictures. The pictures, as a whole, are much quieter than the turbulent Michelangelo.

Movement in Michelangelo's design is a whirlwind; in Cézanne's it is the rippling of waves on the surface of an ocean.

The reason for this is that Michelangelo and Cézanne are typical examples of two fundamentally different breeds of artists. Michelangelo belonged to that restless class of painters who delight in violence, movement, action. Cézanne, on the other hand, belonged in the more peaceful category of those who work *first* for order, balance, taste, "rightness" in every detail—the "classics." *

The inner spirit that guided Cézanne's brush was akin to that of those men who built the Parthenon (and also to their descendants who, later, built the Hagia Sophia at Byzantium). Unity, perfection, completeness—the ideals of the Greeks—apply easily to the *design* of Cézanne.

Cézanne, however, did not remain all at peace with his inner self. Curiously, the artists whose work he most admired were those of the "violent" group—Tintoretto, Rubens, Delacroix. He tried consciously to imitate them, but his deeper emotion, his inner nature, guided his brush in the other direction. Studying at the museums, he copies a Rubens—faithfully enough as to drawing—but the very way his pencil renders on the paper contradicts and defeats all of the spirit of Rubens. The Rubens sketch comes out—a Cézanne.

This contradiction, this conflict within himself (one of several conflicts), had the effect of enriching Cézanne's art and of making it more interesting to look at. Some evidence of this struggle, perhaps, may be reflected in the designs of the two pictures reproduced at the beginning of this chapter.

Cézanne's masterpiece *Pines and Rocks* (see page 46) is an over-all *pattern*, reminding one, in a way, of a rich Oriental rug. Some parts of the design—the solid rock forms at the base, the rigid vertical lines of the tree trunks, the rectangular brush strokes—argue for stability. Yet, at the same time, the twisty, curving branches and the many frivolous, restless little areas of color conspire to upset this stability. The picture remains at rest, yet is full of interior movement. In it, the stout classic framework uneasily suppresses the revolt of the baroque details.

And the very struggle—as struggle always seems to do in art—gives the painting a lasting interest, a continuing fascination it would not have if it were wholly static, or wholly active.

The same occurs in the *Still Life* (page 47). Within the strong major forms, anchored by straight horizontals and verticals to the frame of the picture, are busy little details, active curves, contrasting edges. Design like this cannot be dull—it increases in interest the more we look at it.

Both Cézanne and Michelangelo were *transition* artists. Each stands near the midpoint of a great change in the history of art. Behind Michelangelo was a long Byzantine-Medieval tradition, spiritual in inspiration and strong in design; ahead of him was the new naturalism of the fully developed Renaissance. Conversely, Cézanne stands halfway between the established realism of the nineteenth century and the new, abstract modernism of the early twentieth century.

Each artist strives mightily to attain a new art, without quite shaking off the influence of the old. Michelangelo's work is still strongly designed;

* "Classic" is a word with many meanings. Here we are comparing the inner *spirit* of Cézanne's art with the *spirit* of ancient classic art. (Michelangelo's work also can be termed "classical," but in an entirely different sense, not relevant to this discussion.)

Cézanne: *Pines and Rocks*. This richly *designed* picture suggests a patterned curtain or an oriental rug, as well as a picture of trees and rocks.

Simplified here is the underlying *design* that flows through Cézanne's picture. Each part relates harmoniously to the next part, forming an even *pattern* from frame to frame.

Cézanne: *Still Life*. This "Still Life" is *designed* rather than copied from nature. The distorted sides of the decanter were deliberately made that way to satisfy the aesthetic requirements of the design.

Intended to "bring out" the *design*, this diagram shows the interplay of curving and contrasting lines—the segments that seem to fit together like a perfect jig-saw puzzle—the vertical and horizontal lines that anchor the curving shapes firmly to the sides of the picture.

Cézanne wanders a short way from realism. Nevertheless, each artist applies his greatest effort, his utmost knowledge and subtlety, to the developing of the art to come.

Hence, Michelangelo's greatest enthusiasm is for the realistic effects of drawing and modeling he has discovered. The appearance of three-dimensional reality is what he strives for.

To Cézanne, moving in the opposite direction, it is just the other way around. It is realism that is now "old hat," the urge for design that is new and exciting. Cézanne's attitude toward realistic drawing is irreverent, careless, perfunctory, whereas his treatment of design, on the other hand, is carefully thought out, developed as fully as possible, and presented in great subtlety.

In this treatment of design lies at least part of the "explanation" of Cézanne's art—of *why* his drawing seems crude and sketchy from a purely realistic viewpoint; of *why* it is worthwhile to "live" with a Cézanne picture for a while, in order gradually to discover the inner design that so many people now find so exciting and so lastingly interesting.

To most people, untrained in looking at pictures critically, the design in Cézanne's painting cannot be seen at a glance, as can, for example, the flowered pattern on a tablecloth or a chair cover.

Cézanne's design is not that obvious. It takes time and looking to see it, because it is artfully concealed in the rough brush strokes, in the *apparently* "sketchy" and unpolished manner of his painting. (Actually, of course, every single stroke was carefully premeditated.)

And it is this very fact—that Cézanne's design is *not* too obvious, that it is subtle and not immediately apparent—that does much to make his pictures continually satisfying to the onlooker. The more one looks at a Cézanne painting the more he sees.

Accustomed to formal academic designs, or to commercialized versions of modern design, we may be tempted to think that all design must have hard edges, or must always be perfectly balanced and symmetrical, and therefore, after a little viewing, just a trifle dull and boring. This is not true.

A design can easily be a picture in itself. It can have pictorial qualities, and the artist can make free use of pictorial devices. If he chooses, he may, like Cézanne, resort to "suggestion" rather than attempt to tell all in a "complete statement."

In referring to *drawing*, artists sometimes use the terms "loose" or "free" to mean drawing that is quick, spirited, careless of detail and exact contour, but which, nevertheless, retains the general *effect* of the object portrayed. The opposite of "free"—or "loose"—drawing is "tight" drawing —accurate, photographic, painstaking, detailed. This same concept of "tight" and "loose" can also be applied to *design* as well as drawing. A design may be "tight"—formal, carefully rendered, completely stated—or it may be "loose" and "free."

Use of a roughly or incompletely stated type of design is an important factor in the development of modern art. It occurs again and again. It has a special value, a special usefulness, in that it permits the artist to amalgamate the somewhat abstract quality of *design* with the more personal quality of *expressiveness.*

9   Cézanne

The little events of Cézanne's life had almost no bearing on his art. He lived only for his painting, and that was his real life. Perhaps that is all that should be said. Nevertheless, to avoid misunderstanding, a few "guide-post" facts are needed.

Paul Cézanne was born January 19, 1839, at Aix, in Provence. He was given a somewhat better than average education—was graduated from the Collège Bourbon, even studied law for a while, until his stubborn determination to become a painter ended all possibility of the legal career his father had planned for him.

His schoolmate, and the inseparable friend of his youth, was the novelist-to-be, Émile Zola. Zola encouraged him in his artistic leanings, but he never learned to appreciate Cézanne's art, which may have been one reason for the cooling of their friendship in later life.

In 1861, at the age of 22, Cézanne went to Paris to study art. Like not a few other famous artists, he was almost entirely self-taught. In the mornings he sketched at the Atelier Suisse, which provided models but no formal instruction. In the afternoons, he copied at the Louvre or painted in his studio.

He early became acquainted with the young rebels who were to found the Impressionist school of art—Camille Pissarro, Claude Monet, Auguste Renoir, and Alfred Sisley. These men remained his good friends throughout his life. Cézanne exhibited with the Impressionists in their first exhibition in 1874, and again at the third exhibition in 1877. The storm of criticism and ridicule that greeted these showings seemed to single him out as the worst offender, not merely as a bad artist, but as something malevolent, a monster, a vicious enemy of society. This apparently was too much for the timid, conservative Cézanne. He did not again exhibit publicly in France for eighteen years.

Then, in 1895, the art dealer Ambroise Vollard came across some Cézanne canvases in the art-material shop of the "Père" Tanguy. Enormously impressed, Vollard gathered together other canvases, and put on the famous first one-man show of Cézanne. This show, that brought that nearly forgotten artist back into public view, ranks with the Salon des Refusés exhibition of 1863 and the first Impressionist exhibition of 1874 as one of the most influential art exhibitions in the nineteenth century.

As a result of this exhibition and the attendant publicity, Cézanne's position in the public esteem began slowly (ever so slowly at first) to rise. More important at the moment, however, was the much greater influence exerted on the younger painters of the day, the men who were to carry on the torch he had lighted. The outcast Cézanne, the "hermit of Aix," was finally to be recognized as a great master—to be hailed (in the words of

Clive Bell) as "the Christopher Columbus of a new continent" in art. But Cézanne himself was not to see that day.

In the fall of 1906 he had written to Émile Bernard, ". . . But I am old and ill, and I have sworn to myself to die painting, rather than to go under in the debasing paralysis which threatens old men . . ." *

Barely a month later, Cézanne kept his promise. Attempting to paint outdoors in stormy weather, his diabetes-weakened body collapsed, and a few days later, on October 22, 1906, at the age of 67, he died.

A biographical fact of real importance is that Cézanne's father was a wealthy banker and could afford the allowance of $720 a year that his artist son, the woman Hortense Fiquet who became Paul's wife, and their child, Paul, Jr., lived on. It was a difficult arrangement, but the meager allowance permitted Cézanne to continue painting, which was fortunate, because his pictures were practically unsalable during his lifetime, and he had no talent other than that of artist.

After his father's death in 1886, Cézanne received a little more money, and when his mother died in 1897, he inherited a third of an estate of 1,200,000 francs. The inheritance, however, made little difference in his manner of living. He continued to live frugally and spent all his days painting.

Cézanne's temperament—like his art and his education—was Latin and Mediterranean, through and through. Quick-tempered, yet trouble-avoiding; shrewd and suspicious, yet often foolishly generous; clear-eyed and unsentimental, yet capable of great aesthetic emotion—he was a perfect reflection of his Italian-Provençal blood and of the Mediterranean environment in which he grew up.

To this should be added mention of his somewhat more individual stubborness. Said Zola, "To convince Cézanne of anything is like trying to persuade the towers of Notre Dame to dance a quadrille." It turned out to be a valuable quality, however. It saw Cézanne through a life of disappointments that would have crushed a less obstinate spirit.

Cézanne lived two lives. The second was his inner life—his artistic life. It was filled with a never-ending struggle to "realize," as he put it. This artistic history divides naturally into two periods, (1) an early period of limited accomplishment, and (2) a more mature and successful later period. What is striking is the vast difference between the types of art produced in each period.

The early period was a period of fumbling and groping, caused largely by Cézanne's trying to produce a kind of art that was totally alien to his nature. A classic in spite of himself, he tried desperately to imitate such anticlassic artists as Delacroix, Rubens, and Tintoretto, and he failed utterly. His attempts at baroque compositions merely look amateurish. Nor was there any use of his trying to work from pure imagination—to construct literary and mythological scenes, à la Poussin, from an "inner vision"—because he was completely lacking in that type of imagination. Yet all these things he tried to do for more than ten years.

The paintings of this period were somber, contrasty, heavy-handed,

50   * *Paul Cézanne Letters*—Edited by John Rewald.

sometimes almost grotesque. Paint was lathered on in thick layers with a palette knife. Backgrounds were often very dark. Occasionally, there was an indication of great strength, of the master-to-be, of a growing sense of picture organization, but these flashes were exceptional. For a long time Cézanne seemed to be getting nowhere because he was turned in the wrong direction.

Then, about the year 1873, Cézanne came strongly under the influence of Camille Pissarro and of the Impressionist doctrine. That was the turning point, and the beginning of the second period. Under the gentle, but mature and deeply convinced guidance of Pissarro, the younger artist quickly found himself. The somber coloring and heavy layers of paint fell away and were replaced by the sunny, airy vision of Impressionism. And also, brought face to face with nature for the first time, Cézanne at last found something he could really get hold of. The baroque contortions and the feeble dabbles in mythology were cast aside for something to him much more promising.

This introduction to Impressionism acted as a trigger release for the true Cézanne. Impressionism, however, was not strong enough to swallow him up. His powerful sense of design, of form and picture construction, prevented him from accepting the formlessness of Impressionism, or its literal intent.

Cézanne set out to "make of Impressionism something solid and enduring like the art of the museums." And how gloriously he succeeded!

Once turned in a direction more congenial to his nature, Cézanne's art developed rapidly and improved steadily until the end of his life. It was in this second, mature period that practically all of his great paintings were produced. Later in life, he produced many charming and interesting water colors in addition to his oils.

10   What Cézanne Tried to Do

Monsieur Vollard's well-meant but misleading anecdotes to the contrary, Paul Cézanne was a keenly alert, intelligent man who knew precisely what he was doing—that is, within certain perfectly natural limits.

He rightly sensed the importance of his art, but thought of it, however, only in terms of his own time. Consequently, he never quite appreciated how daring and revolutionary were some of the artistic innovations he instituted as he tried to "realize his sensations." He never suspected how enormous would be the influence of these innovations on artists to come, nor in what direction that influence would lead.

Nor did he seem to fully understand, in introducing design into his pictures, that he *was* designing. He arrived at his design not directly and consciously, as did many other modern artists, but by an indirect and tortuous path of his own—by feeling it out by sheer force of aesthetic emotion, wresting it from nature, as it were, the hard way.

He sought, though he might not have used the word, for *expressiveness*—a particular kind of expressiveness all his own. It was akin to the expressiveness we have already mentioned in connection with Michelangelo, Rembrandt, and El Greco, yet it took an entirely different turn, because Cézanne lived and painted in an entirely different world from that of the older masters. Curiously, *Cézanne's* expressiveness led directly —though painfully and haltingly at times—to classic *design*.

Cézanne painted still lifes, landscapes, portraits, and a few figure groups (usually entitled "bathers"). The subjects, as such, were unimportant. What were important to him were what he called his "sensations"— actually his aesthetic emotions—as he viewed his "motif," or subject. He tried to "realize his sensations" on canvas when he painted.

Confronted with the bewildering maze of details that constitutes outdoor nature, he sought first to analyze, to simplify mentally the confusing scene before him, and second to synthesize, to recreate or "realize," the mentally simplified scene on his canvas. In both processes, analysis and synthesis, his aesthetic emotions guided his thinking; his strong natural sense of design dominated the creative rebuilding of the scene in his picture.

He disdained to *copy* ("imitate," he called it) the nature before him. He tried to capture the *essence* of what he painted.

In the first operation, that of analysis, Cézanne's eyes saw not the natural objects themselves but rather the *forms* of the objects. He saw, not a tree-trunk, but a *cylindrical form* that happened to look like a tree trunk; not an apple or a head, but a more or less *spherical form. He was not interested primarily in trees, or faces, or apples, but only in colored forms.* "Treat nature by the cylinder, the sphere, the cone . . ." he wrote to Émile Bernard.

That is why, as Meier-Graefe points out, "it is impossible to climb up any of Cézanne's trees, nor can one touch any of his figures, and nothing is less eatable than his fruit." Which is exactly what was intended. What Cézanne wanted to portray was the *roundness* of his fruit, not how appetizing it looked.

Cézanne did not stop at simplifying the forms of nature. As he transferred the forms to his canvas, he changed them slightly, recombined them, added a bit there, subtracted here, *distorted* if need be, to make a more perfect picture, a strong picture, an architecturally "constructed" picture. And incidentally, though it has taken most of the world nearly fifty years to see it, *a more beautiful picture!*

Unlike his impetuous contemporary, Van Gogh, Cézanne worked very slowly and thoughtfully. He worked from long meditation, "brush in hand," rather than from sudden flashes of intuition. He painted emotionally—but his emotion was a sustained, deeply felt emotion, tempered by the judgment of a sound and keen intellect.

And now we come to the second of those peculiar contradictions, those conflicts that add so much to the interest of Cézanne's art. As Cézanne analyzed and then synthesized nature to make his paintings, he was, in fact, destroying nature to make a design. But he didn't *want* to destroy nature. He had an immense respect for nature, and he hoped to capture its *essence* in his pictures. Yet he refused to *copy* nature.

Here again, Cézanne's intentions and Cézanne's inner nature tended to pull in opposite directions. On the one hand, while he shocked realism-loving critics by the most daring distortions (needed to achieve and complete his designs), he nevertheless clung tenaciously to the natural appearance of what he painted. Today, when his paintings are compared with photographs of his subject matter, the resemblance is striking *in spite of all the distortions and the liberties he took.*

At all times, his design derives closely from the forms of nature; never does it wander away into the realms of free imagination.

This is a hard way to paint. It is designing in a strait jacket. But Cézanne insisted on doing it that way. And again, though it made Cézanne's life miserable, the result was to enhance his art, to give his pictures a strength and solidity, an integrity of character, beyond those of any other modern.

The art of Cézanne is important in two respects—for itself, and for its enormous influence on the modern art that followed it.

In his own right, Cézanne's position is assured. He ranks, in the eyes of intelligent critics, among the great artists of history. His influence on the development of modern art is no less remarkable—both for its extent and for its nature—for the surprising directions it took. From the influence of Cézanne came both the Expressionism of the *Fauves* and the Cubism of Picasso and his followers. In terms of later art, it was not only the fact of Cézanne's injecting design into pictorial painting that had profound influence, but it was also the type of his design, its approach, its radical innovations, even its mannerisms, that impressed his followers.

The same two factors that link Cézanne to the old masters were passed on from him to the later modern artists—the factors of *design* and *expressiveness.* At times, in modern art, one or the other is emphasized, but neither are ever totally absent.

In Cézanne, design and expressiveness are closely intermingled. In reaching for greater expressiveness, he resorted to design. And in striving for expressiveness, he also achieved design. All of which, though it may sound a bit confusing, would be the natural course of events with an artist so essentially *classic* in inner spirit (if not outward form) as Cézanne. Beautiful design coincides with the highest artistic expressiveness in classic art, whether it be the art of Cézanne, the art of the Greeks, or the art of the Byzantines.

If we hearken back to the discussion of *expressiveness* in Chapter 6, we will recall that "expressiveness" was defined generally as the *personal creative touch* of the artist (that extra something a Fritz Kreisler would give to the playing of a homely melody). The personal touch of Cézanne is unmistakably stamped on everything he drew or painted, even on his copies of other masters. It was, indeed, such a powerful personal touch—

powerful enough to arbitrarily distort forms—that it sharply startled the nineteenth century world of art.

That an artist should paint so personally, so arbitrarily, so flagrantly in defiance of tradition was seen at once as a revolutionary idea; as a dangerous idea to the conservatives, but as a happy declaration of independence to those other artists who wished to express *themselves* in their art and not be slaves to their subject matter.

A new turn was given to the rapidly evolving modern art. A new word was coined to describe it, *"expressionism."* The term *"expressionism"* is sometimes used generally to include all of modern art, and sometimes particularly to describe that sector of modernism that emphasizes mystic, intuitive, highly personalized expressiveness. In its simplest form, *expressionism* means that movement in art which places the *artist's expression of his own aesthetic emotions* above all else. To an expressionist, it is no longer the subject matter that counts, but only what the artist *feels* (and expresses) about it.

That mirror for "holding up to nature" that artists had been lugging around for centuries was at last hung up on the wall so that the artist could see himself in it.

Cézanne, of course, did not carry the expressionist idea to nearly its full possibilities or its logical conclusions. That was reserved for later modern artists. Nor could Cézanne be credited with being the originator of

the idea; it had its real origins in the individualist philosophy of the romantic movement in the early nineteenth century.

Nevertheless, Cézanne's statement of the concept in his art was so unmistakable, so uncompromising and complete, that the long pent-up demand for untrammeled individual expression in art could no longer be denied. *Expressionism*—artist above subject, emotion in paint, feeling over description, creation instead of imitation, spirit over fact—had come to stay.

11   The Timid Revolutionary

The mature Cézanne was a timid, conservative little man. He was conservative in his politics, conservative in religion, and quite conservative in many of his intentions toward his art. He was anything but the revolutionary type. Nevertheless, this timid soul managed to institute a series 55   of painting devices and distortions that were, in their implications at least, the most revolutionary innovations the art world had seen since the days of Masaccio and Paolo Ucello.

The point is not that there *were* distortions (that is not revolutionary), but that the distortions were so deliberate and purposeful; that they were so boldly flaunted and not concealed; that they were part of a "system," some of the connotations of which reached down to the very roots of art. These distortions were not haphazard in any way (there is *nothing* haphazard in Cézanne's painting). Every one was studied and premeditated to the nth degree.

Cézanne distorted realistic forms for a number of reasons, but behind the great majority of these changes was his never-ending effort to solve one major problem. It was the problem *of reconciling the realistic, pictorial appearance of nature with the aesthetic requirements of the designs his inner nature urged him to construct.*

And the essence of the problem lies in the fact that the world of nature, as every good artist knows, is *three*-dimensional, whereas the world of design tends naturally to be *two*-dimensional.

This does not mean that *three*-dimensional designs are impossible. It means simply that the natural *tendency* of design—in painting—seems to be toward flatness, two-dimensionality.

Also, we *read* a design two-dimensionally. And finally, it is much easier for the artist to design *in the flat.* Designing grows progressively more difficult as the artist injects more and more *three*-dimensional *depth* into his picture. He finds himself emulating the juggler who attempts to keep more and more plates whirling in the air at once.

It is quite different with the painting of a nature-copying picture. It is not at all hard for a good artist-craftsman to paint a three-dimensional-appearing picture. Without *too* much difficulty, he can suggest a horizon that seems miles away, trees and figures that look round and solid, buildings that stand up, mountains that are massive, objects that are near and objects that are distant.

Good *drawing* is always cognizant of the roundness or solidity of things, of surfaces that come forward or go back, of the space around things, of distances, of masses and planes. The artist, if his mind's eye is good and his hand skillful, can reproduce these effects at will.

Another fact throws light on this situation—a fact that helps to explain the designer's difficulties in creating a design in more than two dimensions and also that explains the relative ease with which the pictorial artist reproduces a natural scene with an effect of depth. It is the fact—so often forgotten—*that a picture is only an illusion.*

A picture is only pigment on a piece of canvas or a piece of paper. Just a perfectly flat surface with some coloring brushed on it. The lifelike faces and figures we see, the distant hills and flaming sunset, the pretty flowers, are merely illusions created by the painter's artistry.

And most particularly, *all effects of solidity and distance are illusionary,* the result of that same professional legerdemain.

Monet: *Lady in a Garden*, 1881. 26 1/2 x 33 1/4 inches, canvas.

Cézanne: *La Montagne Sainte-Victoire,* 1903-04. 25 5/8 x 33 inches, oil on canvas.

The artist's skill succeeds in making these illusions seem very real, very convincing. He is aided, too, by the fact that our eyes are glad to deceive us. A thousand experiences and memories, habits and predispositions, plus certain tricks of optics, all conspire to increase the semblance of reality.

That is why the pictorialist "gets away with" reproducing the third dimension—depth, solidity, distance—without great difficulty. The designer, on the other hand, does not have such an easy time of it. With an abstract design, he gets little help from the observer's memories and experiences. To suggest depth at all, he must borrow some rather mechanical tricks from realistic art. And then, what is even more disconcerting, he discovers that the use of these devices to suggest depth (perspective effects, light-and-shade modeling, and the like) speedily interferes with the aesthetic integrity of his design. The devices tend to "pull his design apart," disturb its unity, its balance, its feeling of "pattern."

Cézanne's perceptions, his sense of aesthetic fitness, his design intuitions, were very acute. He understood—or perhaps felt instinctively—the conflict between three-dimensional naturalism and the aesthetic requirements of good design. Yet he did not want to work only in two dimensions. He wanted to preserve the three-dimensionalism of nature, which he perceived, also, very sensitively.

His distortions, his peculiar use of color, result from his efforts (on the whole, successful) to maintain the three-dimensional appearance of nature without damaging the aesthetics of his design. He effected a compromise by eliminating from his pictures, as far as possible, those traditional depth-suggesting devices which interfered with design, and he substituted for them *other* devices, which gave an impression of depth more or less adequately, but which were much less harmful aesthetically. This, at times, involved some changing—some distorting—of the natural motif he painted from.

What was this aesthetic requirement of design that Cézanne was so insistent about maintaining—this quality of "pattern"? It was his feeling that a good design should be a *continuous* entity from frame to frame of the picture—that it be knit together all in one piece, like a sweater, without gaping holes, unsightly bulges, or unfinished edges. Even though the design might be made up of many parts of varying importance, these parts should relate harmoniously to one another, should all be of one family.

In Cézanne's pictures, this pattern of design is two-dimensional in spirit. It exists on the surface of the canvas—in the "picture-plane" (that is, the picture surface), as it is called technically. Any object in the picture that is modeled too sculpturally, that is too strongly defined by dark-and-light shading (*chiaroscuro*), can appear to protrude from the picture surface. It then disturbs the frame-to-frame *pattern* feeling of the design.

And similarly, any object or device that too insistently carries the eye too far *into* the distance—*into the picture*—also disturbs the design pattern. *It makes a hole in the design*, as it were. The most frequent and disturbing instance of this is the familiar road leading off into the distance, with its strong perspective lines—lines that pull the eye irresistibly into a "funnel" into the picture.

DISTURBING EFFECT OF MODELING in a two-dimensional design. The modeled objects seem to protrude from surface, interrupting uniformity of design pattern throughout picture.

LINEAR PERSPECTIVE MAKES A FUNNEL INTO THE PICTURE. The powerful lines of linear perspective pull the eye into the picture—lead it to a "hole" in the picture's design. It is difficult for design to guide the eye *around* a picture when perspective pulls so strongly in *one* direction.

HOW CÉZANNE AVOIDED LINEAR PERSPECTIVE. Whenever possible, he avoided "vanishing point" linear perspective by preventing his roads from becoming triangles. He frequently tucked them behind buildings or blocked them off. This often involved distortion of the realistic scene.

HOLES IN THE DESIGN. The dark spots give effect of "holes" in the design. Lines that converge to a point have a similar effect.

THE WINDING ROAD IS A GIMLET boring into the picture. Perspective includes curved as well as straight lines and in either case has the same disturbing effect to the designer.

LANE AND TREES. Looking straight down a lane between trees, the pull of perspective is enormous. Cézanne counteracted it by throwing strong horizontal shadows across the road and by leading the eye, not into a "hole" of distance, but into a maze of lines and forms which guide the eye *up* into the picture.

DISTANCE WITHOUT PERSPECTIVE. To avoid the usual linear and aerial perspective devices, Cézanne often relied on "overlapping planes" to give an effect of distance. This is a weaker method of suggesting distance than linear perspective, but it also side-steps the design difficulties created by linear perspective.

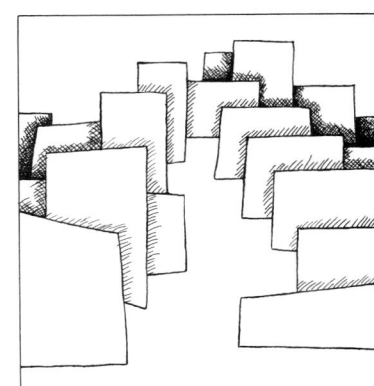

With considerable ingenuity and originality, Cézanne found ways to achieve his design without total loss of pictorial depth.

The protruding effect of sculptural modeling he avoided by a unique use of color, which replaced (not entirely, but sufficiently for Cézanne's purposes) the objectionable light-and-shade modeling.

The funneling into the picture of linear perspective he avoided by suppressing linear perspective as far as possible. (This resulted in occasional distortions, causing academically trained critics to say that his pictures were out of drawing.) He also suppressed aerial perspective. Distant objects, for example, are not allowed to fade away, but are painted strongly, and sometimes increased in size or lifted higher in the picture.

A familiar instance is the famous *Mont Sainte Victoire* that Cézanne painted so often. In nearly every case, the distant mountain is strongly defined and looms up larger than it would in normal perspective. Even the sky in back of it is given an opaque, "gun-metal" quality to keep it from dropping back into the distance (which, also, deliberately violates the canons of recent academic art).

To compensate for the loss of perspective, and to keep his volumes in place in the picture, Cézanne substituted a weaker, but reasonably adequate, way of indicating distance *by a series of overlapping planes* (suggestive of the overlapping scenic wing "flats" sometimes used on the stage). This device, so often used in Chinese and other Oriental art, made possible the *suggestion* of deep space without breaking up the design pattern. (See diagram above.)

Wen Tung: *Landscape: Late Autumn*. Design-conscious Chinese art has for centuries used the "overlapping planes" method to depict distance. Linear perspective is only important when art *insists* on being totally realistic.

The total effect of these devices is to flatten the depth of Cézanne's pictures—to collapse it like an accordian. The sculptured roundness of objects squeezes into a kind of bas-relief. The picture becomes a tapestry or *curtain—not* an open window looking out into the distance. Because of this flattening, the two-dimensional life of the underlying design remains unfettered.

Nevertheless, so skillfully are Cézanne's compromises effected that we are not particularly aware of the loss of depth; the pictures still maintain an illusion of three-dimensional distance, but not quite so strongly as before. Buildings, rocks, objects are still *felt* as solid masses, as volumes; they are still surrounded by space; yet there is nothing in their depiction that disturbs Cézanne's design pattern.

Also the buildings still look like buildings, in spite of the fact that the lines of their edges may violate some of the rules of academic perspective. When compared with photographs of Cézanne's original "motifs," the paintings are seen to give a remarkably convincing impression of the scene depicted. One may find it surprising—after becoming really acquainted with Cézanne pictures and experiencing their charm—to discover how *unimportant* perspective sometimes turns out to be.

Color is also used by Cézanne to help reconcile the depth of nature with the flatness of design. He developed a way—obviously suggested by the "blackless" coloring of the Impressionists—of substituting color changes for the old light-and-shade modeling, which he found undesirable. As the planes, the surfaces, of objects changed their positions, either faced the

61

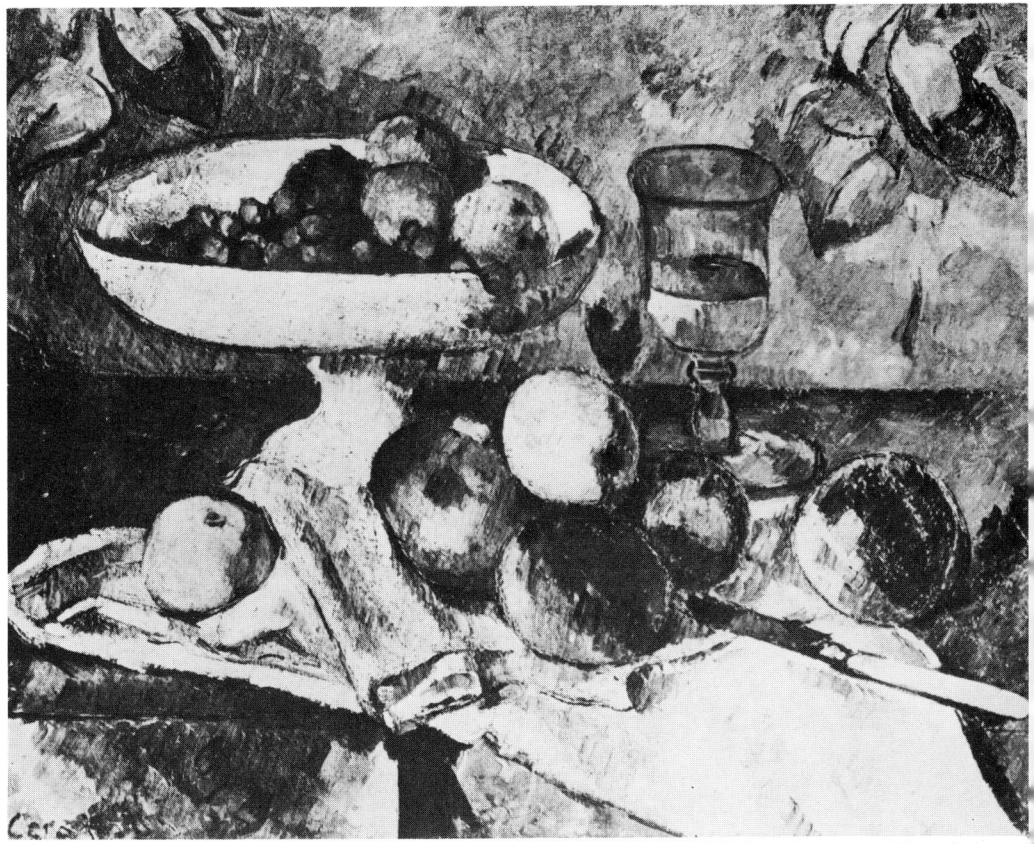

The approximate shape of the top of the fruit bowl as pictured by Cézanne, and as it would be if depicted normally.

AS DISTORTED BY CÉZANNE

NORMAL SHAPE

Cézanne: *Still Life with Fruit Dish.* This picture illustrates an interesting distortion frequently resorted to by Cézanne for aesthetic purposes. Instead of being a thin oval (as seen in perspective), the top of the fruit bowl has been broadened out almost into an oblong with rounded corners. This is done to harmonize better with the ample spherical forms of the fruit—to maintain a unity of design.

The near-oblong shapes of the tops of the fruit dish and wine glass are emphasized in the diagram. Grave, full, rounded, circular, or rectangular shapes predominate in the picture. A thin, "shrill," though elegant oval would be out of harmony, and hence was altered by Cézanne to fit the spirit of his design.

observer or turned away, Cézanne gave them a difference, not in light-and-dark shading, but in *color*.

Furthermore, he made use of the *advancing* effect of warm colors (such as yellow, orange, red) and the *receding* effect of cool colors (green, violet, blue) as substitutes for dark-light shading. Here again, these color changes helped maintain the required design flatness of the picture, and yet permitted a reasonably adequate pictorial representation.

This *constructional* use of color has fascinated many critics and they have made a great fuss about it. Nevertheless, another aspect of Cézanne's color should be of more interest to the average person—its quality of charm. Because it is such quiet, unpretending, *understated* color—Cézanne's coloring sometimes disappoints on a first look—it seems thin, flat, lifeless. But as one grows more familiar with the pictures, he comes to like this understatement—finds that it wears well. In time, he senses a special feeling of pleasantness about this coloring that doesn't fade away. (This pleasantness is due to Cézanne's impeccable color sense.) The color that at first seemed thin and lifeless is finally found to be increasingly interesting, lively, and richly satisfying.

The conflict between Cézanne's nature's *three*-dimensionalism and his design's *two*-dimensionalism is the third of those peculiar conflicts that characterize his work (the others being the conflict of classic versus baroque, and the conflict between Cézanne's respect for nature and his desire for nature-destroying design). These clashing aims led to distortion at times but also tended to enrich his work, adding to its interest and personality.

Other distortions in Cézanne's work are caused purely by the needs of his design. For example, in the *Still Life* reproduced at the beginning of

Chapter 8 (page 47), the two sides of the decanter are obviously distorted out of shape. They were distorted because the aesthetic and imaginative requirements of the picture's underlying design required them to be distorted. (Turn the picture and diagram upside down and look at them that way.)

Roger Fry has noted another interesting distortion (see pages 62-63), in which the thin oval shapes of the tops of bowls or dishes, as seen in perspective, are opened up to make them look almost like oblongs with rounded corners. This distortion occurs because Cézanne's design is, in spirit and fact, a design of rectangles and circles. The sentiment, the feeling, of the thin oval form is alien to the gravity, the amplitude, of the circle and rectangle. Hence, to keep the feeling of his design uniform throughout, Cézanne distorts his ovals into more nearly circular or rectangular shapes.

Fry also calls attention to the way Cézanne places objects in the middle of the picture and parallel to the picture surface. Cézanne's composition is here simple, grave, primitive, and architectural, and contrasts sharply with baroque ideas, which delight in leading the eye back into the picture (which, of course, Cézanne did *not* want).

Cézanne's practice of arranging his objects flat-on facing the canvas sometimes got him into difficulties. On occasion, he found his design becoming too rigid, too static. To overcome this, he initiated another kind of distortion—he tipped his buildings, models, bottles, and so on, slightly off-center to make the composition more dynamic. (See *Portrait of Joaquim Gasquet,* above.) This device was viewed with horror by all of the unsympathetic critics. But actually it is very easy to get accustomed to, and if one is not prejudiced and knows the reason for the distortion, he

65

CHANGED EYE LEVELS. Cézanne: *Still Life with Fruit Basket.* The left side of the picture appears as if looked down upon from above, the right side as if seen from a lower eye level.

By introducing more than one eye level in the same picture, Cézanne violated academic rules, but did it because he believed he could achieve a more interesting picture, as well as add interest to his *design.*

very soon does not notice the distortion at all. It is the final effect produced by the distortion that is important, not the distortion itself.

One of the most interesting of Cézanne's distortions is his method of showing different parts of the same picture as if seen from different angles, different eye levels.* For example, in the *Still Life with Fruit Basket* (opposite), some of the objects may be seen as from the front, others as from above. The surface of the table may tip down at one side of the picture and be in an entirely different plane at the other side. All of which is quite unconventional and never happens in academic pictures seen from a single viewpoint.

However, many a painter, academic or otherwise, has often wished he could incorporate two viewpoints in the same picture. From one point of view he finds one part of his subject particularly interesting, the other part not so interesting. By moving around to another point of view, he finds the second part can be seen to better advantage, but not the first. Unfortunately, because of changed perspective and angle, he finds himself unable to paint both views at once, and probably, if he is an academic, he gives the whole thing up and moves on to another site.

Cézanne, not obliged by any self-imposed rules to stick to pure realism, solved this problem—naïvely perhaps, but boldly and directly. He painted both views in the same picture and let perspective fend for itself. He was not painting perspective, he was painting an interesting picture the way it seemed *most* interesting to him. (Later, Picasso was to carry this idea to an extreme by painting front and side of a face together in the same picture.)

Design considerations also entered into these "split-level" or "changed eye-view" distortions. They helped break up too much regularity, too much static parallelism to the rectangular frames of the picture, when the still-life table was painted face-on.

Cézanne painted with short, rectangular brush strokes that were often parallel or that often crossed objects instead of following contours. At the same time, he tended to block out curving forms into planes or facets, making them look as if they were hewn instead of painted. (This practice, incidentally, gave Cézanne's forms a "surface," thereby further enabling him to delineate form without resorting to light-and-shade modeling).

This breaking up into planes is more pronounced in some pictures than others. In some extreme cases, the effect is almost exactly like the Cubist abstractions of another, later day. Or perhaps it should be stated the other way around, for the Cubist abstractions were precisely derived from these more angular pictures by Cézanne.

Even the Cubist painting device called *passages* is found in Cézanne's angular pictures. A *passage* is a shaded area that is sharply defined by a line, or linear edge, at one side, but which fades into the background at the other side.

It should be clear now that the art of Cézanne—which at first glance seems so crude, so primitive and elemental—is actually interwoven with

* For a more comprehensive discussion of Cézanne's compositional devices, the reader is referred to Erle Loran's *Cézanne's Composition*, a most valuable contribution to the subject, and a source to which this author is gratefully indebted.

complex theory, is controlled by delicate aesthetic considerations, and includes daring technical innovations that influenced other artists for decades to come.

Yet, no one of these points—nor even all together—answers the question about Cézanne's pictures: *"Is it art?"* In the final analysis, that is a question that must be answered personally, by you and by me. It is helpful to know that Cézanne attempted to achieve the art qualities that seem to characterize the great art of the past, namely, *design* and *personal expressiveness*, and that, apparently, he succeeded. But, finally, the answer must come from *our* judgment of Cézanne's pictures themselves. Do they stand up? Do they thrill us as great pictures should?

This can be said: While many people find difficulty in appreciating Cézanne's pictures at first, more and more people are finding that his pictures become increasingly interesting and satisfying on longer acquaintance. These paintings do not wear out; they grow and grow as one discovers more and more about them. The little oddities, the distortions, the seeming crudities, vanish from our consciousness, and we become, at last, fully aware of the inner beauty, the harmony, emotion, and character, the symphonic grandeur that makes these pictures what they are indeed —*great art!*

Cézanne: *Provençal Landscape*. Note how the landscape forms are blocked out into angles and planes. In breaking up his picture into planes, Cézanne influenced the thinking of later artists.

CUBISM. Léger: *Village in the Forest, 1914*. The methods and mannerisms of Cézanne's painting influenced the development of *Cubism*, years later. The "planes" and the angularity of Cubism derived from Cézanne.

ALBRIGHT ART GALLERY, BUFFALO, N.Y.

12 Vincent van Gogh

Two artists could not be more strikingly opposite in almost every way than Paul Cézanne and Vincent van Gogh. Cézanne's life was as quiet and uneventful as a lowlands stream—it had little bearing on his art. Van Gogh's life was an ever-gathering storm, turbulent and tragic. With him, life and art were one and the same thing. In person and art, Cézanne stood for everything that was Latin and Mediterranean. Red-haired Vincent van Gogh came down from the cold North; he was as thoroughly northern, as thoroughly Teutonic, as Beowulf or Siegfried.

Cézanne painted slowly and carefully, with a classicist's ingrained respect for order and aesthetic rightness. Vincent painted at a furious speed, careless of detail, and utterly without premeditation. His colors were brassy, raw, intense, whereas Cézanne's were restrained, quiet, understated. The cube and the sphere epitomize Cézanne's classic design; the spirit of Van Gogh is best expressed by the leaping flame—the shape taken by his dark cypress trees.

The rift in the thought, the feeling, and the vision of these two men was a world wide. But because it was so divergent, modern art today is vastly richer and broader than it would have been otherwise. Each of these artists was a cornerstone in the edifice of modernism—but at diagonally opposite corners. All the rest of modern art lies in between.

From this dual source, two streams of influence—sometimes opposing, sometimes intermingling—flow up through all post-Impressionist (modern) artistic effort. The Cézanne stream favors orderliness, studied aesthetic balances, and divisions of space; stability and clarity; gravity and calmness of line and form; emphasis on *design*. The Van Gogh stream leans to uninhibited disorder; to highly personalized and unbridled emotion; to movement, unbalance, indefinite statement; to lines that wriggle and twist and curve; to the kind of abstraction that tends toward mysticism rather than geometry—to emphasis on personal *expressiveness* above all else. From the Cézanne spring came Cubism and geometric abstraction; from the Van Gogh fountainhead, the Expressionists.

Vincent van Gogh's life was a miserable one, and a short one. It ended in 1890 at the age of thirty-seven. Though marked by failure after failure, it nevertheless finally presented to the world a tremendous gift of achievement.

There was nothing petty or merely unlucky about Vincent's struggle and downfall—it was heroic tragic drama. Indeed, it resembled a great Shakespearian tragedy in the remarkable perfection of its motivation, its ominous march of events, and the relentless acceleration with which it rushed to its inevitable doom. So perfect is the plot that it seems as if, with very little editing, it might easily be presented on a stage or written into a novel. (In fact, several such presentations have already been attempted.)

Furthermore, the whole story has been richly documented in Vincent's numerous letters to his brother Theo—a correspondence that fills three fat volumes and covers almost the entire span of Vincent's career.

In Van Gogh's troubled life there are actually several separate dramas: Vincent against himself. Vincent the individualist against the world. Vincent as a hero in revolt against the bourgeois civilization of the nineteenth century. Vincent the saint who tumbled in the mire. And Vincent the artist who at the age of twenty-seven did not know how to draw, but who by sheer persistence, in ten years, made himself into one of the great painters of all time—though he sacrificed mind and life in the process.

Or again, Vincent van Gogh's life can be looked at in an entirely different way, as a study in psychology. From his obviously spoiled and ill-disciplined childhood, through his unhappy youth with its succession of frustrated love affairs, his struggle with family and society, on to the final epileptic madness and suicide, there is a wealth of provocative material to intrigue the modern psychologist, whether amateur or professional.

Either way, whether seen as tragic drama or psychological study, Vincent's career has the fascination of a meteor plunging down across a dark autumn sky. Yet somehow, out of this ill-fated career, came a flood of sunny, smiling pictures, to make *our* world a little happier.

Roger Fry has summarized Vincent van Gogh's character as pointedly as anyone. He wrote: *

> He was, of course, a modest, retiring young man; but he was also a saint. He was the victim of the terrible intensity of his convictions—his conviction that somewhere one might lay hold of spiritual values compared with which all other values were of no account.
>
> This obsession drove him out of Goupil's, drove him to the Gospel and into a seminary for Protestant pastors; out of that again—for he made the fatal mistake of carrying out Christ's teachings literally—into sheer vagabondage and art; and then the terrible pressure of the obsession and his growing violence of character drove him into the madhouse and at last to suicide; but not, fortunately, until, with incredible determination and courage, he had taught himself to find an expression in paint for the desperate violence of this spiritual hunger and left a body of work the mere bulk of which might well have occupied a lifetime, though there were barely ten years between his beginning painfully to teach himself to draw and the fatal pistol-shot.

This is the comment of a famous art critic. More personal is the complaint of the long-suffering, all-understanding brother Theo, the co-hero of the Van Gogh epic: †

> It seems as if he were two persons in one, one marvellously gifted, tender and refined, the other egotistic and hard-hearted. They present themselves in turns, so that one hears him talk first in one way, then in the other, and always with arguments on both sides. It is a pity that he is his own enemy, for he makes life hard not only for others, but also for himself.
>
> Then there is something in his way of speaking that makes people either like or dislike him strongly. He has always people around him, who sympathize with him, but also many enemies. It is either the one or the other, even to those who are his best friends it is difficult to remain on good terms with him, as he spares nobody's feelings.

Vincent was an idealist, without compromise. He mistook ideas for facts—seemed utterly blind to life as it is. He had an overwhelming urge for the absolute, and the fantastic actions of his life resulted from his determined efforts to enforce the absolute in actual practice.

Of his passion for humanity, Roger Fry wrote:

> In all the turmoil of his inner life the one dominating supreme impulse was a passion of universal love. It was the Christian idea of a love so all-embracing that it could scarcely attach itself to any individual; it was for all men and all things. And the tragedy of his life lay

* *Transformations.*
† Editor, J. Van Gogh-Bonger, *The Letters of Vincent van Gogh to His Brother.*

precisely in this, that only in his painting could he find any sort of expression for this love. When he approached people the very intensity of his feeling obstructed and distorted its expression, and instead of attracting and soothing them he infallibly irritated and repelled.

It was only natural that Vincent should feel a great desire to preach. And preach he did—in business, in religion, in social reform, and in his art.

In the emotional zeal that swept him along, Vincent developed a tendency toward exaggeration, both in life and in art. This exasperated his teacher Mauve and the academic artists, but it also helped make Vincent's art expressive and great. In life, however, the exaggeration (coupled with his constant demand for the absolute) led him into many absurd situations.

For instance, when he went to preach the Gospel to the poor coal miners in the gloomy *Borinage* district of Belgium, he was not content merely to preach. He had to make himself more miserable than the Borains themselves, exchanging his good clothes for rags, living in a hovel, and even smearing his face with coal dust to make him look as black as the miners. And of course he could not wait to go down into the Marcasse, the oldest and most dangerous mine in the district.

Later, out of pity, he befriended a prostitute—an ugly, foul-spoken woman, who was about to have a child by another man. It was not enough that he took her in and provided for her—he wanted to marry her too. The affair, however, finally came to an end, as much because of its sheer absurdity and impracticality as anything else.

There was yet another facet of Vincent's character—his grim stubbornness about everything he considered important. This tenacious persistence, misapplied, made his life a thousand times more difficult than it would have been otherwise. But it was also the making of Van Gogh the artist. Any other man would have faltered in the path he set for himself.

Vincent van Gogh was born March 30, 1853, in the little Dutch village of Groot-Zundert, the eldest of a poor pastor's family of six children. From his father, Vincent apparently inherited an interest in religion and the desire to preach.

As a boy, Vincent was uncommunicative and solitary. He loved nature and liked to wander about the countryside, always alone. His rather sketchy education was completed at the age of sixteen—although he later supplemented it somewhat by considerable reading. He could speak and write both Dutch and French fluently, and was able to deliver a sermon in English (although, he admitted, with a bit of an accent).

At sixteen, when it was time for him to go to work, family connections found him a place with Goupil's, one of the leading print and picture houses in Europe. At first he did very well there. Then the perversity of his character began to make trouble. A growing religious fervor seemed to swallow him up, and he became self-righteous to the point of rudeness. First he insulted his customers, and then his employers.

Dismissed, family influence procured him another chance in the Lon-

Gauguin: *Poor Fisherman,* 1896. 25 3/4 x 29 5/8 inches, canvas.

don branch of the firm. But there he became involved in a futile love affair with a girl who was already engaged—with the result that he became more morose, more religious, and more boorish than before. His attempt at business ended in complete failure.

Next Vincent decided to study for the ministry at Amsterdam, but despite all his diligence and persistence, he proved a poor student, and finally he failed at this, too. His religious fervor had not abated, however, and he was still determined to preach the Gospel. So, after a brief course at an evangelists' school, he managed to get a trial commission to preach as a lay evangelist in the economically depressed Borinage coal-mining district of Belgium. At first, practical and happy, he preached and nursed the sick and injured. Then, according to his sister-in-law: *

> Soon, however, he falls back to the old exaggerations—he tries to put into practice the doctrines of Jesus, gives away everything, his money, clothes and bed, he leaves the good boarding-house at Denis, in Wasmes, and retires to a miserable hut where every comfort is lacking . . .

And so on, to the limit. But Vincent's "excess of zeal" was not looked upon with favor by the committee who had sent him there, and after the trial period of six months, he was not renominated.

This fiasco was followed by a most unhappy period of sheer vagabondage (the winter of 1879-1880). Vincent was then twenty-seven years old. Two important things occurred in this period. First, the formerly overwhelming religious enthusiasm began to fade; religious reflections and Bible texts gradually vanished from his letters. Second, he began to draw. Vincent van Gogh the evangelist was at last replaced by Vincent van Gogh the artist.

Up to this time he had not even shown an interest in drawing, and certainly no ability or talent. Nevertheless, he felt that his decision to draw was like a "cry of deliverance." His brother Theo, who was beginning to do fairly well at Goupil's, decided to aid Vincent by paying him a small allowance monthly. This arrangement was continued up to Vincent's death.

With grim determination, Vincent set out to teach himself to be an artist. From a borrowed anatomy chart, he learned anatomy, bone by bone, and muscle by muscle. He struggled with perspective, picked up a scrap of criticism from one artist here, another there. He haunted the studio of his artist cousin Mauve, who helped him considerably.

Vincent drew painfully and amateurishly at first, but steadily improved, advanced slowly from drawing to water-color painting to oil painting, until, after five years, his work began to attain professional character. But it failed to please according to academic standards ("lacked charm"), and he made no sales.

During this period came another unhappy love affair—this time with

73   * *Ibid.*

his cousin "K.", who, however, had just lost her husband to whom she had been very devoted. She was in no mood to accept Vincent's proposal of marriage, in spite of his determined efforts to win her. She literally fled from him and, eventually, he had to give up.

It was on the rebound from this, perhaps, that he became involved with the woman he called "Sien." Vincent had set up a small studio in The Hague to be near the friendly painter Mauve. One day Theo received the following somewhat startling news: *

> They suspect me of something—it is in the air—I keep something back—Vincent is hiding something that cannot stand the light.
>
> Well, gentlemen, I will tell you, you who prize good manners and culture, and rightly so if it only be the true kind, which is the more delicate, refined, manly, to desert a woman or to stand by a forsaken woman?
>
> This winter I met a pregnant woman, deserted by the man whose child she bore.
>
> A pregnant woman, who in winter had to walk the streets, had to earn her bread, you know how.
>
> I took that woman for a model, and have worked with her all the winter, I could not pay her the full wages of a model but that did not prevent my paying her rent, and, thank God, I have been able thus far to protect her and her child from cold, by sharing my bread with her.

Her name was Christine, but Vincent liked to call her Sien ("his own"). She was described as ugly,

> . . . a coarse and uneducated woman who speaks with a low accent and has a spiteful character, who is addicted to liquor and smokes cigars, whose past life has not been irreproachable, and who draws him into all kinds of intrigues with her family.†

Nevertheless, Vincent wrote a little later:

> As soon as she comes back from Leyden I will marry her, without telling anyone, quietly and without fuss. Then we would be glad to have that house and we are prepared to live as simply as possible.

But the marriage never took place. Whatever happiness might have existed in the arrangement faded entirely before long. Vincent found his small allowance inadequate and his opportunity to paint curtailed. Finally, the two separated by mutual agreement.

Living again with his family in Holland, Vincent worked harder than ever on his drawing and painting. Here, finally, occurred one more ill-fated

* *Ibid.*
† "Introduction," *The Letters of Vincent van Gogh to His Brother.*

incident with a woman, one more hopeless attempt at matrimony. This time the girl, one of three unmarried sisters, became deeply attracted to him and he intended to marry her. But the girl's family vehemently opposed the idea, and violent scenes took place between the sisters. One of these scenes so excited the woman that she attempted to commit suicide.

The attempt failed, but her health was so damaged that it was necessary for her to convalesce for six months before recovering. The romance was ended, of course. The antagonism of the Dutch villagers, who unfairly blamed Vincent for all this, forced him to move again. After a short stay in Antwerp, he joined his brother Theo in Paris.

At Paris (1886-1888), Van Gogh, now no longer amateurish, but still painting in a dark, crude style, came under important influences which radically changed his art. The decorative influence of Japanese prints brought cohesion to his compositions, while the impact of Impressionism chased the gloomy darkness from his palette and helped him to form the style that is today associated with his name.

At Paris he met the advanced artists of his day—Seurat, Toulouse-Lautrec, Gauguin, Pissarro, Sisley, Signac, Renoir, Bernard and, according to legend, on at least one occasion, Cézanne. (Vincent bought his paints at the same Père Tanguy's shop frequented by Cézanne. Meeting there one day, Vincent insisted on showing his canvases to Cézanne. Cézanne's considered comment was, "You paint like a madman!") Vincent sided with these radical artists because they were in critical disfavor, underdogs in the world of art, and he always sympathized with the underdog in opposition to the powers that be.

The two years in Paris represent the consolidation of his powers, the budding of Van Gogh's genius. The bud burst into full flower when, in 1888, dissatisfied with Parisian life, he went to Arles in the south of France. The brilliant sunshine of Arles seemed to penetrate both into his soul and into his pictures. It heightened his inspiration and brightened his colors. It cleared his vision and brought out the best in his style. Apparently happy at last, he produced an enormous quantity of fine canvases in rapid succession. One a day, two a day they came, day after day. He painted in the hot sun, as rapidly as possible, because he was afraid that bad weather or the fiercely blowing *mistral* would cut down on his painting time. He was in an exalted mood. One day bad weather did come—and he slept for sixteen hours continuously, he had so overworked himself.

Near the end of the year he prevailed upon Paul Gauguin to come and visit him. The relations of the two artists, though friendly enough, contributed to the tension and strain Vincent was piling on himself. Both men were strong characters, opinionated, given to argument, and between them ran a natural undercurrent of rivalry. Each tried to teach the other. (Each *did* teach the other, in fact.) Vincent wrote:

> Our arguments are terribly *electric*, we come out of them sometimes with our heads sometimes as exhausted as an electric battery after it is discharged.

75

Sharaku: *Danjuro V in Role of Ko no Moronako.*

Kiyonaga: *A Standing Woman, in the Costume of a Daimyo.*

JAPANESE PRINTS. These importations from exotic Japan, newly opened to the western world, made a tremendous impression on Parisian art circles in the 1870's and 80's. Many artists were influenced by them, including Van Gogh, Gauguin, Toulouse-Lautrec, and Whistler. Their decorative qualities, their strong design, inspired Van Gogh to develop his own design.

Hokusai: *The Great Wave at Kanagawa.*

Gauguin wrote:

> Between two beings, he and I, he like a Vulcan, and I boiling too,
> a kind of struggle was preparing itself . . .

Finally, just at Christmas time, the sustained, tremendous overwork, the diet of absinthe and coffee, the incessant smoking, the prolonged arguments, the tension of Gauguin's presence, the general emotional turmoil, proved too much for Vincent. He began acting strangely. Suddenly he threw a glass at Gauguin. A little later, in the darkness, he followed Gauguin, razor in hand. When Gauguin turned about and spoke his name, he fled to his room, while Gauguin, for his own safety, took a room in the inn. That night, Vincent cut off part of his ear and sent it to a girl in a nearby brothel. He was found unconscious and bleeding in bed the next morning, whence he was removed to a hospital.

Theo was summoned and stayed over the holidays at Arles. After a few days, Vincent began to recover his reason, and feeling that he was in good hands, Theo and Gauguin returned to Paris together.

Critics unfriendly to Gauguin have charged him with the blame for bringing on Van Gogh's "madness." He is alleged to have baited Vincent, toyed with him as a cat toys with a mouse, to have taken advantage of him by pitting his "cool intelligence" against Van Gogh's "childish emotion," to have, as it were, cast the "evil eye" on him—and then to have lied about it afterward.

Such charges need better proof than is now available. Actually, all the more reliable evidence tends to lean the other way—to remove blame from Gauguin. Nothing in Van Gogh's character or history indicates that he would be a soft touch for Gauguin or anyone else. Vincent had very much of a mind of his own, and a strong one. He was quite as intelligent as Gauguin, if not quite as cool, or as logical or analytical a thinker. In fact, it is some tribute to *Gauguin's* strength of mind that *he* was not overwhelmed by Vincent.

Then again, Gauguin went back to Paris with Theo, apparently on friendly terms. (The sensitive Theo would have quickly detected anything sinister in Gauguin's relations with Vincent, had there been any such thing.) Furthermore, Vincent and Gauguin continued to correspond and even to exchange pictures. The story of the actual incident comes from Gauguin, yet there is nothing in the subsequent history of Vincent's illness to indicate that Gauguin was lying at any time.

Vincent appeared to have recovered, then suddenly had another attack and had to return to the hospital. Between the attacks, he was perfectly normal, in fact, able to paint the strong portrait of himself with the bandaged ear. The attacks of irrationalism, distress, hallucinations, and finally unconsciousness recurred again from time to time.

Because of these unexpected recurrences, and also as a result of an unfortunate scene with the street urchins of Arles, Vincent decided to go into the asylum of Saint-Rémy in the hope of effecting a cure. Vincent's illness (controversy over it still continues) apparently was not insanity at all, but a form of epilepsy (said by some authorities to be curable today). Between the attacks, which recurred at intervals of several months, he was entirely normal, though of course often badly shaken and frightened. In the intervals between attacks he painted, but not as rapidly as before. In many respects, the artistic quality of his work actually improved, although it frequently showed signs of his nervousness and apprehension.

Vincent remained at the hospital of Saint-Rémy for a year. At first restful, the atmosphere of the madhouse began to disturb him, and in May, 1890, he arranged to leave. He met Theo and Theo's wife Johanna at Paris and then found a place to stay at Auvers, nearby. Here he was to be under the care of Dr. Gachet, a somewhat eccentric but art-loving physician who also knew Cézanne and many other struggling artists.

For a while, all was well. Vincent painted happily. Then one hot day in July he felt a premonition of another of the dread attacks coming on. In an impulse of despair, he borrowed a revolver and shot himself, although he did not die until two days later, in Theo's arms (July 29, 1890). Emile Bernard, Dr. Gachet, Père Tanguy, Albert Aurier, and Henri Rousseau were among those who attended the funeral. Dr. Gachet planted sunflowers on the grave. The following spring Theo died, too, and was buried beside his brother in the little Auvers cemetery.

There is more than a little danger that the sheer drama and story interest of Vincent's life may fascinate us to the extent that we forget about his *art*. But his art, after all, was the real crowning glory of his life. The events of his life helped mould his character, and this peculiar character in turn expressed itself in his paintings. Because his ideas were original, because his emotions were titanic, the expression of these ideas and emotions in his art could not fail to be interesting. Because, somehow, all that was fine and sweet in his character seemed to distill itself into his pictures, these pictures, in spite of the clamor of their color and the roughness of their technique, are seen to be appealingly beautiful.

13   Suns, Spirals, and Flames

The total span of Van Gogh's artistic effort was just ten years. All his greater pictures were painted in the last three years of the ten. But in those three years his production was greater than that of most other men in a lifetime. When Vincent van Gogh started to find an expression for his troubled spirit in art, he was no artist at all. He couldn't draw. He had not even displayed a real interest in drawing until he was twenty-seven years old. Yet, because he was the kind of man he was, he became a great artist.

Because of his grim persistence—working unceasingly year after year, eagerly clutching at the slightest bit of guidance or information that might

Van Gogh: *The Arlésienne*. This interesting pic
ture clearly shows the influence of Japanese print
on Van Gogh's painting. (See prints on page
76 and 77.) The plain background, the interes
ing silhouette outline of the figure, the larg
simple areas of color, and the decorative distribu
tion (patterning) of darks and lights, all deriv
from Japanese inspiration.

help him—he was able first painfully to master the most elementary principles of drawing and then to move on to become an accomplished painter.
Actually, thanks to his Dutch tenacity and thoroughness, he trained himself very well. What is not always realized, the mature Van Gogh was
well grounded as a craftsman; his technical equipment was excellent (far
better than Cézanne's). In 1888, when Vincent started to paint his great
Arles pictures, he had a masterly command of painting technique.

Indeed, as some of his Paris pictures suggest, he probably had the
technical ability to be an outstanding academic artist, if he chose. But his
nature would never permit him to be an academic artist. "I am Vincent
the Dutchman!" he roared back at an indignant Antwerp instructor—and
"Vincent the Dutchman" he remained all his life.*

Because he was the kind of man he was, Vincent utterly abandoned
himself in his art, threw every inch of his personality into every sketch and
painting. Heroically emotional, his emotions poured freely into his pen
and brush. Even the amateurish early sketches show signs of his militant
personality bursting through the barriers of realistic drawing.

* His canvases are signed "Vincent." The reason for doing this is given in a letter
to Theo: "But though it doesn't in the least matter this time, in future my name ought
to be put in the catalog as I sign it on the canvas, viz. Vincent and not Van Gogh, for
the simple reason that they do not know how to pronounce the name here."

Because he was Vincent van Gogh, his art is full of a kind of preaching; full of his love for the underprivileged; full of his love for everything. He was the first—and probably the best—of those recent artists who depict scenes of "social significance." The sentimental, "glorified" stage-peasants of Millet turn to tinsel when compared with Vincent's gnarled farmers, weavers, and "potato-eaters."

Vincent paints a pair of worn shoes with such sympathetic tenderness that they have the appearance of a couple of dear old friends. When he wishes to depict sunshine, he inundates his canvas with blazing yellow, even puts the incandescent disk of the sun itself in his sky. To match the intensity of his feeling, he squeezes raw color straight from the tube on to the canvas. His paintings are fiercely intense, tremendously alive, utterly personal, uncompromising, yet deeply tender, loving and friendly, because that was the kind of man Vincent was. He could be no other kind, he could paint no other way.

From his first faltering sketches of miners in the Borinage to his last paintings before his death, Van Gogh's art constantly improves; his pictures grow steadily better throughout his life. The arms and legs on his first sketches look like sticks. Gradually, step by step, the sticks acquire form and roundness, the figures become more lifelike. Then the pencil gains more freedom; the figures, more animation.

81

His first paintings, influenced perhaps by Dutch traditions, are dark and gloomy in color. But as he moves southward, from Holland to Antwerp and Paris, his palette grows progressively lighter.

The Parisian period of about two years was, in a sense, the most important in Vincent's artistic life—the formative period of his genius. Here he came face to face with Impressionism and promptly submerged himself in it. He also found himself surrounded by the radical artists of the day, and their sharp criticisms, their bubbling ferment of new ideas, did much to give his own art the polish it needed.

With typical determination, he learned to paint in the little multi-colored brush strokes of Impressionism, and with typical independence, he soon burst through the rules of Impressionist theory. The little dots lengthened into long, impatient streaks, and the indefinitely delineated forms soon regained their solidity. But Impressionism left its mark on him in the lightness and brilliancy of his color, and also in the skill with which he manipulated the little wiggly brush strokes to give his paintings life and interest.

At this same time, his pictures became better organized, began to show evidences of *design* in their conception. The inception of the trend toward design, which continued and increased from then on, can be ascribed to two sources:

First, the influence of Japanese prints, which not long before had been introduced into France for the first time (Japan itself had been opened to Western civilization by Commodore Perry in 1853, only a few years earlier). These prints, the somewhat postery, but strongly designed and highly decorative creations of Hokusai, Hiroshige, and others, made a tremendous impression on the artists of Western Europe. (See page 76.)

(Left) Van Gogh: *Country Road by Night.* The tree is a flame; moon and stars grow into spirals, the road is a sinuous ribbon. Why? Partly because Van Gogh *felt* that way about the scene before him, and partly because the picture's design—*a design of motion*—called for these curving and spiraling shapes.

(Right) This simplification of the picture shows the basic design pattern. (Compare with design diagrams of Cézanne's pictures, pages 46 and 47, and Michelangelo's picture, page 23.) The over-all space from frame to frame is divided into a few, large, simple color areas. But movement is the real basis of Van Gogh's design: the swirling lines carry the eye round and round the picture; the entire canvas is restlessly alive.

They influenced not only Van Gogh, but also Gauguin, Toulouse-Lautrec, Whistler, and many others.

Second, the influence of the artists he met in Paris and the influence of their pictures. He saw a number of Cézannes and admired them. He was the friend of Gauguin, Seurat, and Toulouse-Lautrec, and these men not only helped him to see with a new vision, but also supplied a critical viewpoint toward art that Vincent himself utterly lacked.

At Paris, Vincent prepared himself for greatness. In his next, his Arles period, he demonstrated that greatness.

At Arles, Van Gogh reached his maturity as a painter. He was no longer a beginner learning to draw, an amateur learning to paint. His practiced brush responded easily to his will, and, unhampered by inhibitions, he was able to pour his flood of feeling freely onto the canvas, finishing a masterpiece in a few hours.

Art has a way of rewarding those who approach her with simplicity and honest emotion in their hearts, and who quickly and courageously transfer that emotion to canvas, just as she often penalizes those who, too coldly and intellectually, try to outwit her. The humble emotionalist usually makes better pictures than he realizes; the intellectual schemer, poorer ones.

The intensity of Vincent's emotion, the natural poetry of his feeling, imbued his paintings not only with life and animation, but automatically supplied the structural *design* that was needed to give his art real greatness. It is natural to design—more natural than to draw (that is, copy). The art of primitive peoples is all design. Indeed, when, idly waiting in a telephone booth, our super-civilized pencil "doodles" on the pad, it usually "doodles" a design, seldom a drawing.

STATE MUSEUM KROLLER-MULLER, HOLLAND

Design is order, taste, rightness, but it is also movement, life, rhythm. Van Gogh, restless, spiritually champing at the bit, could not keep movement out of his pictures if he wanted to; nor could he keep out design. It flows through his Arles pictures, and shows itself particularly in a marked simplicity of composition and a new over-all feeling for pattern.

The final period of Vincent's life, the two years between his first epileptic attack and the final suicidal shooting, marked no let-down in the quality of his work. It shows no signs of approaching "madness"—as some now-outdated critics once claimed—no "darkening" of the mind. Vincent's illness had no *direct* effect on his work—he painted in the months-long perfectly sane and lucid intervals between attacks—but the illness *did* have some *indirect* effects. Nervous, distressed, and deeply shaken by the terrible attacks and the fear of impending repetitions, he could not keep his unhappiness out of his work; his painting lost its gaiety and bravado, became less cheerful, and also, at times, a bit careless, a bit less meticulous in detail.

But artistically it improved. The feeling for design grew, and his compositional design patterns became more interesting, his pictures more

Van Gogh: *The Yellow Chair*. It would not be too difficult to imagine a similarity between the legs of this chair and say, perhaps, the outspread legs of a man, standing squarely on the floor. Van Gogh's inanimate objects often seem "alive," seem to suggest attributes of animals or human beings.

abstract, but structurally more creative and original, more modern. One wonders what he might have created if he could have been cured.

What did Van Gogh try to do? Why did he paint the way he did?

He tried to paint the feeling of things—the feeling he felt for them within himself. He did not mind if they were not photographically accurate representations of the subject; that was not important, and he knew it. Vincent loved everything, and he wanted his pictures to shout his love. He loved yellow (and blue), and so he made his pictures scream with yellow. He felt an intimate brotherhood with laborers of all kinds—he always thought of himself as "a laborer"—so he painted laborers who looked as if they had really labored for a hundred years.

He looked up at the stars, brilliant in the southern sky. "A star-spangled sky for example, that's a thing I would like to try and do . . . ," he wrote. And he painted the stars blazing in spirals swirling like fireworks. We are not sure that the stars *looked* that way, but we know exactly what Vincent *felt* about them.

This is not the same kind of approach to art as Cézanne's, for instance. It is something entirely different. And because it is so different, the modern art of today that has its roots in the art of *both* Cézanne and Van Gogh is broader and bigger. From Cézanne, aesthetics, *design*. From Van Gogh, the subjective and the personal, sheer feeling—*expressiveness*.

There is a curious note of mystery about Van Gogh's paintings. A vague suppressed hint of some inner significance. A baffling personal touch in the forming of the shapes, the surprising selection of color, a "subterranean life." This, of course, is simply the reflection of Van Gogh's powerful personality, impressed by him on the face of his paintings. We see it particularly in the way he "humanizes" inanimate objects in his pictures.

The legs of *The Yellow Chair* (page 84) could easily be imagined to have a strong resemblance to the outspread legs of a man standing squarely on the floor. By using more of the same kind of imagination, we can see his *Still Life* of teapots, cups, and the like, as a parade of well-washed people on their way to church of a Sunday morning. Or we can fancy one of his "bowls of potatoes" to have a rather close resemblance to a cuddled litter of kittens. The limbs of trees often look like outstretched arms; the windows of houses may be seen as peeping eyes; his old shoes look as if they wanted to talk.

It is not caricature—it is nothing like caricature. It is a part of Vincent himself. It is not actually seen, it is felt; it is haunting and mysterious; it is the deeply personal expression of Vincent's sympathies and inner feelings. This mystery, this haunting visual echo of the man himself, contributes much to the interest and durability of Vincent's paintings as works of art. It is an important part of his genius and greatness.

What about Van Gogh's color? Let him answer in his own words:

And I should not be surprised if the Impressionists soon find fault with my way of working, for it has been fertilized by the ideas of Delacroix rather than by theirs. Because, instead of trying to reproduce exactly what I have before my eyes, I use color more arbitrarily so as to express myself forcibly.

. . . I am going to give you an example of what I mean.

I should like to paint the portrait of an artist friend, a man who dreams great dreams, who works as the nightingale sings, because it is his nature. He'll be a fair man. I want to put into the picture my appreciation, the love that I have for him. So I paint him as he is, as faithfully as I can, to begin with.

But the picture is not finished yet. To finish it I am now going to be the arbitrary colorist. I exaggerate the fairness of the hair, I come even to orange tones, chromes, and pale lemon yellow.

Beyond the head, instead of painting the ordinary wall of the mean room, I paint infinity, a plain background of the richest intensest blue that I can contrive, and by this simple combination of the bright head against the rich blue background I get a mysterious effect, like a star in the depths of an azure sky.

Oh, my dear boy . . . and the nice people will only see the exaggeration as caricature.

At another time Vincent writes:

Painting as it is now promises to become more and more subtle—more like music and less like sculpture—and above all it promises *color*. If it only keeps this promise.

And again:

I am always in hope of making a discovery there, to express the love of two lovers by a marriage of two complementary colors, their mingling and their opposition, the mysterious vibration of kindred tones.

Yellow and blue, Vincent loved, and he used them to express the beautiful. But he did not always seek "the beautiful." Speaking of his now famous interior scene of a night café, he wrote:

. . . the picture is one of the ugliest I have done.
I have tried to express the terrible passions of humanity by means of red and green. . . .

And finally, and more generally, he sums up:

It is color not locally true from the point of view of the stereoscopic realist, but color to suggest any emotion of an ardent temperament.

TEXTURES. In art, any patterned area is called a *texture*.

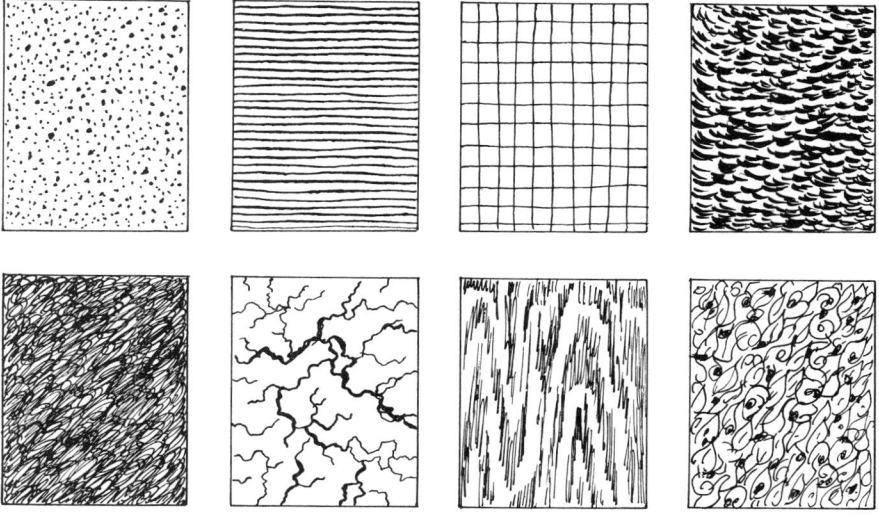

Vincent's design, derived from the postery Japanese prints, consists primarily of large simple areas of color, conceived flatly, and sometimes bounded by lines. (The idea of using a red boundary line, he borrowed from Rubens.)

Somehow, under the stress of Vincent's emotion and the fluidity of his expression, these broad areas seem to fall into place naturally and correctly, and above all, interestingly. Unlike Cézanne's studied aesthetics, Van Gogh's design just seems to happen. And it has a peculiar vitality of its own, though it is quite different and admittedly less profound than Cézanne's more revolutionary design.

Van Gogh's design has another characteristic besides the division of the picture into large color areas, namely, the extremely important use of the individual brush strokes for design purposes. For example, Vincent depicts a field of wheat (predominantly yellow or ochre in color) with numerous, separately defined brush strokes which both (a) adequately suggest stalks of wheat and (b), from a *design* viewpoint, *break up the flatness* of the unrelieved yellow area—in other words, fill it up with what in art is now known as a *"texture."*

The concept of *texture* is an extremely significant one in modern art—it occurs again and again—and this application by Van Gogh is its first

Van Gogh: *The Asylum at Saint-Rémy*. In Van Gogh's later pictures, the small brush strokes become more active, take a more important part in the picture's design. Here the brush strokes have burst the bounds of the usual color areas and they swirl across the entire picture.

important use. In art, the word "texture" has a somewhat broader meaning than the one to which most people are accustomed. For instance, in general, texture is often thought of as a surface that can be *felt* by the fingers, such as the weave of a piece of cloth. A *rough* texture, a *smooth* texture. In art (perhaps because there was no other word available), the word "texture" has been extended to include any visually broken-up area.

An artist calls a mottled area in a painting a *texture*. Or an area of polka dots, or cross-hatched lines, or varied brush strokes.

Textures are very useful to artists. Both realistic and modern artists use textures to give roundness to forms (Cézanne's use of color *planes* to round his forms is actually a use of texture). A texture gives the solid form a "surface"—makes it more convincing.

The very nature of oil paint necessarily creates a need for some kind of textural handling, because the oil paint in a picture is not very different from ordinary house paint. If you paint a wall with house paint, you get a flat, even area of color, unbroken by any variation of any kind. The same thing happens on a canvas. On a wall this may be quite desirable, but in a picture it is quickly seen to be too flat, boring, and unsatisfying.

So the artist "breaks up," enlivens the flat, even expanse of color—gives it a texture of some sort. He subtly varies his color, or he may use thick

pasty paint and heavy visible brush strokes to break up the monotony. If he is a modern artist, working decoratively rather than realistically, he may build the texture into a design pattern.

Van Gogh was the first of the moderns to use texture in a modern way. His use of it was partially representational, partially for design. Other modern artists, later, were to use it *entirely* for design.

Van Gogh was fascinated by the different effects created by different types of individually defined brush strokes. He continually experimented with brush strokes and varied effects of heavily piled-up paint on the canvas.

An important development in his use of brush strokes takes place from the Arles period to the end of his life. The straight simple brush strokes simulating stalks of wheat or grass, or the leaves of trees, began to grow curly and animated; they became imbued with an interesting life of their own, and swirled and spiraled across the canvas. In the Arles period, the brush strokes generally remained within the bounds of the major color areas, but later, at Saint-Rémy and Auvers, they began to romp all over the picture. (See illustration, page 89.)

The result of this development was a far-reaching change in Van Gogh's design. Instead of the brush strokes remaining merely a texture filling an area, they now become an integral part of the design. The effect was to make the whole design more complicated, more subtle and interesting, and also somewhat more abstract. Furthermore, because these wriggly, curving brush strokes were alive with motion, they increased the activity and movement of the entire picture. It is this extremely interesting development in design that lifts Van Gogh's art to its highest peak.

In some of his pictures, Vincent painted cypress trees. He painted them dark, bluish-green in color, but their shapes were like flames, licking upward. These nervous, undulating, upward-swirling flame shapes seem peculiarly and fittingly symbolic of Van Gogh's art. The flame, reaching for the stars. The flame, active, restless, nervous, alive. The flame, self-consuming. The flame of a second Prometheus.

Van Gogh's art is a tremendous effort to put living life into a picture. It is close to the art of Rubens and Delacroix in its love of restless movement—akin to Rembrandt in its sympathetic love of humanity. Even more than Leonardo and Michelangelo, and perhaps as much as El Greco, Van Gogh's painting typifies, supremely, the intense personal *expressiveness* of an artist's feelings.

Though painted by a man whose personal life was one of the most miserable, most tragic in the history of art, many of Vincent van Gogh's pictures are among the happiest, sunniest canvases we know; they literally smile at the beholder. Because of this sincere friendliness, perhaps, Van Gogh, of all the modern artists, seems to have been the first to find real favor with the general public.

Again the question—is it art? Van Gogh's pictures, looked at too much, would not wear as well as Cézanne's. The enthusiastic, raw colors might occasionally come to offend. The design, certainly, would not be so profound or lastingly intriguing. But the Van Goghs would be too vital to die. They are great pictures, too.

More and more people are finding Van Gogh's pictures very pleasing. Not so much because they are a tremendous expression of a man's heroic feelings, but because, shining through the rough paint and distorted forms, there comes to us something that can't be hidden, the true sweetness and beauty of Vincent's character, with all the dross burned out. It is what the dwarf Toulouse-Lautrec sketched in a marvelously sympathetic portrait of Vincent. It is what Theo saw in Vincent. Now the world is beginning to see, too.

14   Sheep in Wolf's Clothing

At this point, someone might well say—someone who has heard something of the lives of the modern painters—"We have had the 'saint,' Vincent van Gogh; now we shall hear about the devil, that black fiend Gauguin!"

But alas, we shall do nothing of the sort. Because that fabulous diabolical creature, that sinister superman of evil, never lived.

There were two Gauguins: the legendary one, cold, evil and inscrutable, and a very different, very human *real* one. Both Gauguins, the real and the legendary, led fantastic lives. Both, after many colorful incidents, ended the tragic drama of those lives miserably in a squalid native hut on a lonely South Seas island. The true story is not less interesting than the false one, but the legend has had the greater publicity, and the legendary version is the one with which the American public is more familiar.

The main point of difference between the two versions is that, in the legend, Gauguin is simply portrayed as an out-an-out villain, whereas in real life Gauguin was no villain at all, merely an everyday human being struggling manfully against his fate.

Every twist and turn of the legendary version finds a way to emphasize Gauguin's alleged villainy. He becomes a sort of fictional automaton, whose thoughts and movements are controlled to suit a prearranged plot. It is as if Gauguin's enemies (he had many, as well as many friends) had deliberately concocted the story to blacken his character. In fact, that is very probably how the legend *did* start.

According to the legend, Gauguin was cold, callous, selfish, cruel, a sort of monster who preyed on his fellow men. He was pictured as a "monstrous egotist" and a prodigious liar. Actually, of course, Gauguin was not at all like this. He was on the whole emotional, generally kindly, sincere, and generous. But he had his minor faults, greatest of which were his capacity for sarcasm and his tendency to act in an irritating, if not insulting, manner toward those he did not like. It was probably because of his own sins of the tongue that Gauguin suffered so much from the spiteful tongues of others.

91

The legend has gained undeserved strength from the popularity of W. Somerset Maugham's novel, *The Moon and Sixpence*, the material for which, whether by accident or design, seems to more or less coincide with the malevolent Gauguin fable. Many people, reading this book, have innocently believed it to be an authentic picture of the *true* Gauguin, which it certainly is *not*.* Gauguin's wife, surely an authority on the subject, could not find a single trait of Maugham's character *Strickland* which had anything at all in common with her husband.

An unhappy by-product of the malevolent legend is the cloud that still hangs over Gauguin's reputation as an artist. It has become somewhat fashionable to cast slurs on his artistic ability—to rate him as a second- or third-rate artist. (Maugham, in the catalog of an important 1946 exhibition, wrote: "I should not say that Gauguin was a great painter.") Even among sympathetic modern critics, who should know better, the greatness of Gauguin's art is still not yet fully appreciated.

Over the years, Gauguin the *man* has been constantly *over*estimated, whereas Gauguin the *artist* has been just as frequently *under*estimated. It is clear that critics have not devoted enough careful study to his pictures, and that they have been entirely too much intrigued by his colorful life. One result is that Gauguin's art has been judged only superficially and that therefore the real importance of his art remains to be discovered by a considerable portion of the critical fraternity.

Gauguin the *man*, however energetic and clever, was one of the multitudinous little people of the world. On the other hand, Gauguin's stature as a creative *artist* is enormous. He is a giant, by no means inferior to Cézanne, Van Gogh, or any other artist of his time.

In endeavoring to estimate Gauguin as a person, one has to steer a nice course midway between Scylla and Charybdis. Gauguin's enemies tried to paint him as a monster. His friends and relatives saw him as a kind of superman who could do anything he set his mind to. Both viewpoints are equally misleading, because Gauguin was neither a monster nor a superman, and he could not accomplish everything he set out to do. Apart from his artistic genius, he was just *an everyday human being* who happened to live an extraordinary life. He was an intensely *human* person, with very human faults and very human virtues, and plenty of both. He possessed an alert, imaginative mind, a rather remarkable store of energy, and very strong emotions. But it was his essential *humanity*—coupled with his great love of art—that provided the key to his character and career.

His life was a tragedy: drama of a somewhat different nature from the onrushing drama of Van Gogh's unhappy life, but drama nevertheless. Gauguin's tragedy lacked the dramatic sharpness, the brevity and clarity of Vincent's meteoric career. Indeed, many years elapsed before Gauguin succumbed to his inevitable fate; but it *was* inevitable, a fate that he brought upon himself, and the saga of his life was fraught with dramatic

* In his book, Maugham makes no claim that Strickland *is* Gauguin. Therefore he was under no obligation to follow the real life of Gauguin.

struggle against his destiny from the beginning. He challenged the gods of his day, and he failed in the end because his frail humanity was not strong enough to overcome the Olympian forces arrayed against him. His own weaknesses precipitated his downfall.

More than Van Gogh—perhaps more than any other artist of the time —he set himself in opposition to the prevailing trends of nineteenth century civilization; he eagerly accepted the gage of battle and dedicated his life to an unceasing guerrilla warfare against middle-class culture. In a foreword, Frederick O'Brien wrote:

Gauguin's whole life as a painter was an outcry, almost a curse, against materialism, against accepted success; against laws, morals, money, critics and clerics.

Gauguin hated what life has come to mean in civilization. He spilled his energy in bitter blows against the steel shield of society and bruised his spirit continually in vain struggles against realities, which he tried to prove ghosts.

Gauguin's war against the nineteenth century was not entirely one of his own choosing. It was forced upon him by the many frustrations, the many rebuffs and defeats he suffered when he tried to express himself as a creative artist. Particularly galling to him—and a very personal source of distress—was society's economic neglect of its artist class. Gauguin himself wrote: *

I believe that every man has the right to live and live well in society, proportionately to his work. The artist cannot make a living, therefore society is criminally and badly organized.

Gauguin did not win his war with society. Far from it, he failed at every turn. He failed even to live his own life successfully, in spite of all his cleverness and energy. The end of his struggle was his own miserable death—an unmarked grave in the Marquesas Islands.

A wiser man might have done better. But Gauguin was not a wise man. He was just an everyday human being.

Gauguin's greatest weakness was that he was a clever, but an ignorant, man. He lacked proper educational background and the philosophical soundness and good judgment such a background might have given him. Yet, he was intelligent. His mind was keen and alert. He learned easily, but judged badly. In this dangerous combination of cleverness and ignorance can be found the source of many of his other failings.

To make matters worse, he also lacked an adequate sense of humor (he constantly tended to substitute sarcasm for humor). This, together with his essential ignorance, trapped him into pitfall after pitfall; permitted him to make himself foolishly conspicuous in public, to become a *poseur*; caused him to be insultingly intolerant of fools and bores; led him, unnecessarily, to arouse antagonism in others, to make a host of enemies—enemies whose

* Robert Burnett, *The Life of Paul Gauguin.*

relentless hatred eventually came back to him in a whirlwind of spiteful retribution.

Gauguin was not a good business man, nor a good manager of personal finances. This can be said in spite of his quite successful interlude as a stockbroker (it was, after all, only an interlude between his earlier career as a sailor, and his later one as an artist). Fortune smiled on him while he worked in the stockbroking firm of Bertin's—fortune, and a rising stock market due to the recovery of France from the War of 1870. At many other times during his life, however, he demonstrated a lack of real capacity for business in general.

Money slipped through his fingers. He lived in almost continual poverty, not because he never received any money, but because he was prodigal and wasteful when he had it. Blindly optimistic about the future, when he had money, he promptly spent it. Hence, he was most of the time without enough to live decently.

Another complicating factor in Gauguin's life was his erotic nature, which seemed to become intensified as a result of his long and unwanted separation from his wife. An acquaintance stated:

As for love, it was his great passion, the one that dominated him all his life, and which, at first enclosed and repressed, became from

day to day more despotic and ardent. . . . During the time at Le Pouldu, he submitted it again to a comparatively strict discipline. But he regretted freely not having practised in his youth the free life of the Quartier Latin; and, perhaps to atone for this omission, he already dreamed of emigrating to Tahiti. . . .

Gauguin's naturally sensuous nature affected his philosophy of life at all times, and, in particular, brought him more than once into sharp conflict with nineteenth century prudishness. Burnett wrote:

The attitude of the world to sex had always been of profound interest to Gauguin. His own interest in it he had placed among his three cardinal occupations and like many who possess a physical necessity in excess of their neighbors he had also a greater understanding and tolerance for its many manifestations than those sections of the world whose interest is secondary or minimal.

Gauguin's second great addiction was tobacco—he was an incessant pipe smoker. But alcohol played little part in his life. He was a very light drinker (the legend to the contrary) and only occasionally partook of a small glass of cognac to be sociable. In his tragic last years in Tahiti,

95

it is probable that his drinking increased and that he indulged in an occasional drunken spree, but for that—for a lonely and disappointed white man, painfully ill in the tropics—there was much provocation.

Much has been said of Gauguin's vanity and egotism, and there is no doubt that he was guilty of both, though not to the abnormal extent claimed by some commentators. As for the personal vanity, it may have been a quite natural result of his having been a tall, handsome, and rather dashing youth, further gifted with considerable physical strength and dexterity.

Gauguin's so-called "egotism" was largely a rightful self-respect he owed to himself and an honest pride in his work. Should he be blamed for considering his own work better than that of some of the weak and dilettante artists who surrounded him? Time has found him a far greater artist, and the others far poorer, than any of them dared imagine at the time.

The more we consider the "faults" of Gauguin's character, the more we recognize them as the kind of faults we see daily in people about us—not heinous crimes, but the *little* failings of human nature. If, at times, they seem to become intensified in Gauguin—if he becomes extreme in his bitterness toward his wife, for example—the cause will be readily found in the physical suffering and emotional torment that was his lot.

And also, if there were faults, there were virtues, too. There were his amazing patience, his optimism in the face of crushing adversity, his generosity, his independence and tolerance, and his kindness. If he had enemies, he also had friends. And he had courage—great courage; he was one of the most courageous men of his day.

There was something else. Our ungrateful society would do well to consider it a virtue, and a very precious one.

Paul Gauguin was a great artist. He gave the world many beautiful pictures to be enjoyed by all for years to come. The rich beauty of these pictures was nourished by their creator's unhappiness.

15   From Yellow Christs to the House of Carnal Pleasure

In the restless year of revolution—the Revolution of 1848—Paul Gauguin was born. Gauguin's mother, Aline-Marie-Chazal, a woman of considerable charm, was descended from a rich and erratic Spanish family in Peru. His father, Clovis Gauguin, was an obscure political journalist of liberal and republican leanings.

When the *coup d'état* of Louis Napoléon in 1851 put an end to democratic government in France, journalist Clovis Gauguin found himself without a job. He decided to emigrate, with his wife and two children, to Peru, where he hoped to start a newspaper.

But on the way, at Puntas Arenas, Clovis Gauguin died suddenly of a heart attack. His wife, Aline-Marie, went on to Lima, where she was welcomed by her near-fabulous family, which was headed by her great uncle, Don Pio, said to be 108 years old at the time, who had taken a new young wife at the advanced age of 80 and who had had several children by this marriage.

The family was wealthy and influential—a cousin was the President of Peru—and they lived well. The children, young Paul and his sister, were particularly happy. They were given a little Negress as a playmate and companion, who walked in front of the family on the way to Mass in the Cathedral, carrying the little carpet on which they knelt.

According to custom, as a form of taxation, the family supported a madman who was kept chained to an iron ring on the flat roof of the house. One night the children were awakened by the appearance of the madman in their room. He had broken his chain. He peered at them for a terrifying, breathtaking moment, then returned quietly to his roof.

In his *Intimate Journals*, Gauguin wrote of another childhood incident:

> Another time I was awakened at night and saw the superb portrait of my uncle, which hung in the room, with its eyes fixed on us, *moving*.
>
> It was an earthquake.
>
> Brave as you may be, wise even as you may be, you tremble when the earth trembles. That is a sensation common to everybody and which no one will ever deny.

Aline-Marie Gauguin hoped to remain in Peru for the rest of her days, but the necessity of settling the estate of her father-in-law required her to return to France, taking the children with her on the long sea voyage. But once there, news came from Peru that old Don Pio had died, and that his other heirs had so twisted the execution of his will that she was left nothing.

Madame Gauguin was forced to remain in France, and the family lived with her brother-in-law, Isadore Gauguin, whom the children called "Uncle Zizi." Young Paul went to a boarding school, at the age of eleven entered a seminary, and then attended the *Lycée* at Orleans until he was seventeen.

He wanted to become a sailor. Being unable to pass the examination for the *Ecole Navale*, which would have prepared him to become an officer in the French Navy, he entered the Merchant Service as a *pilotin*, or apprentice. His first voyage was to Brazil in the *Luzitano*, a 1,200 ton sailing ship. As far as Gauguin was concerned, the voyage was uneventful save for an amorous adventure in Rio de Janeiro with a Madame Aimée, a charming singer of light opera, and another adventure on the return trip with a passenger, a wealthy Prussian woman.

In 1868, at the age of twenty, he gave up hope of a successful merchant marine career and joined the French Navy as a third-class seaman.

The Franco-Prussian War he spent on the cruiser *Jérôme Napoléon* in the North Sea and later at Copenhagen. After the war he was given an honorable discharge, and at the age of twenty-three his six-year career as a sailor was finished.

He had traveled over a great part of the world, and had made a visit to India. While he was at sea his mother had died, and her family possessions had later been destroyed by fire in the Prussian bombardment of Paris.

Fortunately, at this time, a friend of his mother, Gustave Arosa, who had been appointed guardian of the children, found Paul a position in the office of a stockbroker named Bertin. Gauguin quickly showed an aptitude for this kind of work, advanced rapidly, and soon was able to speculate successfully himself. He earned an excellent income for a man of his age.

One day, in a restaurant, he met an attractive young Danish woman, Mette-Sophie Gad, who was then visiting Paris. He fell in love with her instantly, courted her, and on November 22, 1873, married her. The marriage pleased Mette's Danish bourgeois family, which put great stock in respectability and security, and Gauguin, with his promising financial position, seemed to offer these in abundance.

The first years of their marriage—in fact, practically all of it while they were together—were very happy. Gauguin was devoted to his fair wife. They had five children—four sons, Emile, Clovis, Jean, and Paul (or Pola), and one daughter, Aline.

Almost immediately after their marriage, Paul began to develop a hitherto unsuspected interest in art and painting. The beginning may have been entirely accidental—perhaps it was suggested by seeing the small collection of Impressionist pictures owned by his family guardian, Gustave Arosa. Later, Gauguin began to make a similar collection himself.

From the beginning, this collection was an extremely discriminating one, which casts some light on Gauguin's character. He apparently had been gifted with a natural sophistication—especially in matters aesthetic—that was not given to the rustic Van Gogh or the provincial Cézanne. It was this sophistication, perhaps, which later enabled Gauguin—in spite of his inconsequential education and his desultory reading (limited to bits of the Bible, Dumas, Edgar Allan Poe, Loti, and Lamartine)—to write for publication with an accomplished and colorful literary style.

It was this sophistication, too, that may have been responsible for making his path to painting a surprisingly easy one—far different from the early struggles of Cézanne and Van Gogh. Once he began to draw and paint, Gauguin advanced with amazing speed. Only three years after his marriage, he painted, in the academic tradition, a landscape of sufficient merit to be accepted by the Salon of 1876. He also attempted sculpture with considerable success. Save for the occasional and incidental guidance of his artist friends he was truly self-taught.

In the meanwhile, his brokerage business prospered, and in his best years his income approached $7,500 annually (a much more formidable sum in those days than it would be today). He spent $3,000 on his collection of pictures, which included paintings by Manet, Renoir, Claude

Monet, Cézanne, Pissarro, Guillaumin, Sisley, Jongkind, and two drawings by Daumier. He lived comfortably in a fashionable house with a garden and a large studio.

Through his collecting activities, Gauguin soon became acquainted with the artists of the Impressionist group and joined their famous café meetings. He met Manet, Monet, Cézanne, Degas, Guillaumin, and Pissarro. These men encouraged him in his painting, particularly Pissarro, who acted as a mentor for Gauguin, just as he also did for Cézanne and Van Gogh. In 1880, Gauguin began to exhibit with the Impressionists in their group exhibitions.

In 1881, one of Gauguin's nudes, exhibited in the Sixth Impressionist Exhibition, won extravagant praise from the critic Joris-Karl Huysmans. It was a strongly modeled figure in the *realist* manner, very different from Gauguin's later pictures. It probably appealed to Huysmans for its bald, unsentimental realism. The next year, when Gauguin's style became more strongly influenced by Impressionism, Huysmans was not so complimentary.

At home, Mette Gauguin watched her husband's hobby grow ever more important, but she did not seem in the least concerned. In fact—and it is a significant fact, attested to by her children—she did not ever display any great interest in her husband's art. Her family—and the friends whom she entertained, for she was sociably inclined—were her absorbing interests. The Gauguins' home life continued to be happy.

But Paul Gauguin was becoming more and more bored with his stockbroking business, and more and more excited about painting, to which he could only devote his Sundays and holidays. Gradually, the desire grew in him to become a full-time painter, and his business career became increasingly distasteful. He had money saved up, and the fateful step did not seem too risky; his paintings had been praised publicly, as well as privately by his friends, and an acquaintance had already given up finance for full-time painting.

The project was discussed at length with intimate friends and, of course, with Mette, who could not have been very enthusiastic about it, but who knew she must acquiesce if her husband insisted.

It was not a hasty decision. Gauguin was nearly thirty-five years old, had been married for ten years, during all of which time he had been painting. But Gauguin was a born artist, not a stockbroker, and the final decision was inevitable. In January, 1883, Paul Gauguin gave up his work as an Exchange broker to become a full-time painter.

"From now on," he told his friends, "I am going to paint every day."

The heavens trembled.

Gauguin did paint every day, industriously. But his paintings did not sell. ("The paintings did not sell"—that same terrible refrain that meant tragedy to so many of the early post-Impressionist painters.)

After a while the Gauguins moved to a smaller house. In eight months nearly all the money they had saved was spent. Then Mette and Paul Gauguin made another mistake. They went to Copenhagen, where they hoped that Mette's family might help Paul find an occupation that would enable them to live, yet permit him to paint. He accepted a commission to sell French awnings to the Danes.

Gauguin was received coldly by the Gad family. To this wholeheartedly bourgeois family, with its almost fanatical worship of security and financial standing, he had already committed one unforgivable sin by relinquishing his profitable work as an exchange broker. He quickly committed other sins—first, by failing to secure any orders for awnings, second, by insulting some of his customers, and third, by insulting his wife's family.

The feud with the Gad family, undoubtedly provoked at first by their utterly unsympathetic attitude toward the artist, was fed by his Latin sensitivity, his touchy pride and unfamiliar manners, and quickly grew to a determined hostility. His mother-in-law and sisters-in-law became Gauguin's enemies and did everything in their power to arouse Mette against him. Soon she began to side with her family against her husband.

Gauguin, on his part, aggravated the situation by making inexcusable scenes. Meanwhile, Mette tried to earn some money by teaching French to diplomatic students. Finally, conditions became so impossible that the only sensible solution was for Gauguin to return to Paris. He had very little money, so Mette and he decided that he should go on alone and leave Mette and the children in Copenhagen. Later, when he had found work, he would send for her and the family. He hoped his pictures would soon begin to sell and expected that the separation would only be for a few months.

According to Gauguin's biographer, Burnett: "In June of this year, 1885, Gauguin left Copenhagen by train for Paris, taking with him his second son, Clovis, now just six years old. He gave Mette all his property and the money he had received from one of his brothers-in-law who bought his collection of pictures."

This is the true story of how Gauguin came to be separated from his wife. Their separation was to be permanent, although neither of them suspected it at the time.

Throughout the rest of his life, Gauguin lived more or less chronically in want, but the eight months after his arrival in Paris were the worst of all.

For his room in the Impasse Frémin he was able to hire a small bed for the boy and a mattress for himself, but when the winter came he had no spare money for the purchase of blankets or coal for the heating of the room. "We freeze at night . . ." he wrote to Mette. "For a month it has been cold again, snowing. I sleep on a plank, wrapped up in a traveling rug." *

Meanwhile, Mette had her hands full with her four other children in Denmark. As the separation from her lengthened, and as his own disappointments and frustrations increased, Gauguin's letters revealed a growing strain of bitterness toward his wife. In his mind, the faults of her sister and mother became fixed on her, and he upbraided her harshly

* Burnett.

in unjust, cynical messages. Yet he did not cease to love her and hope for their reunion.

Two years after their separation, just before Gauguin sailed for Panama and Martinique, they saw each other again, briefly. Mette came to Paris to take the boy Clovis back to Denmark with her. The meeting was short and did little to bring them together permanently.

After his difficult winter in Paris, Gauguin went to Pont-Aven in Brittany, where there was an artist colony, and where the cost of living was reputed to be very low. He stayed at the famous *pension* of Madame Gloanec, who charged her guests 55 to 70 francs ($10 to $15) a month for bed and board.

It was here in Brittany that Gauguin's mature painting style began to take form. Having immersed himself in Impressionism (as had Cézanne and Van Gogh), and finding it not quite satisfying, he began to change it to suit the aesthetic needs of his own personality. The direction he took was different from that taken by Cézanne or Van Gogh, with the result that he, too, made an important contribution to the growing structure of modern art.

Living in Brittany may have been cheaper than in Paris, but there was still the cold winter to reckon with, and he thought of going to some other part of the world where expensive coal would not be required. Gauguin did not have the average Frenchman's fear of travel. Having been a sailor for years, a long ocean voyage held no terrors for him, and it seemed quite natural for him to seek an answer to his economic difficulties by traveling to a distant spot. He decided to go to Panama, where a French company was trying to build a canal, and where work was available.

On the way to Panama in 1887, accompanied by his friend Charles Laval, Gauguin stopped briefly at Martinique, which delighted him so much that he wanted to return. On his arrival at Panama, he found that living costs were considerably higher than he had expected, whereupon both he and Laval quickly determined to return to Martinique.

To pay their fare, they secured work at the canal as laborers, digging from 5:30 in the morning until 6 in the evening under a tropical sun. At night they were devoured by hordes of mosquitoes. But the pay was high, and after two months they were able to take passage to Martinique.

For a brief time, they found happiness there. The luxuriant colors of the island inspired Gauguin and brightened his palette. But in the heat and humidity, both he and Laval suffered miserably from the malaria they had contracted in Panama. Laval, in a fit of depression, attempted to commit suicide—an attempt that was frustrated by Gauguin. Gauguin himself was attacked by dysentery. Unable to overcome the climate and illness, the two artists were forced to return to France after an absence of nine months.

Not long after, with the help of Theo van Gogh, Vincent's brother, Gauguin was permitted to have a one-man show in Goupil Galleries (now changed to Boussod and Valadon) and sold enough canvases to bring him a little money. He apparently hoped to get Mette to rejoin him with the children, and made a trip to Copenhagen to see them.

101

Of this visit, Robert Burnett writes:

Whatever opinion Gauguin may have had of his mother-in-law—
we know that it was very definite—he could not have expected the icy
reception that he received. It was three years since he had left
Madame Gad's house to his own, and to everyone's relief. He had seen
Mette in Paris when she had come to fetch Clovis, and although they
had not met without some recrimination, Mette had not shown the
aloofness that she now displayed.

The fear of the effect that his visit to his wife might have had
induced Mette's family to renew the pressure on her that they had so
successfully exercised three years before. Her mother, in particular,
succeeded in making her fear rather than look forward to Gauguin's
arrival, and when he arrived she received him very coldly. Gauguin
found it impossible to see her alone, for the uppermost fear in her
mother's mind was, it seemed, that as a result of this meeting another
child might be born to them and add to the expenses of the household.

The reunion with the children, who had almost forgotten him,
gave Gauguin great pleasure. But—"Mette had merely repeated during this visit that she would not come to him unless he were able to
promise her and her children a suitable home."

Gauguin: *Girl from Brittany in Prayer*. Gauguin's best Breton pictures rank equally, artistically, with those he painted in Tahiti. Both strong design and personal expressiveness are clearly apparent in this interesting painting.

Gauguin went away with a still greater hatred for her family. He still hoped for some years more that she would rejoin him in Paris, but the reunion never occurred, and it became clear eventually, even to Gauguin, that the family was broken up forever. He corresponded with Mette until near the end of his life, until finally there came one of his letters so bitter that no further answers could be forthcoming.

There is one more bit of testimony on this subject that should be cited, Mette's own statement, made many years after Gauguin's death: "I could not understand his taking up art, though now I understand that he had a right to act as he did. But surely no one can be surprised that I refused to accompany him and bear him more children in an existence which to my mind was a mad and hopeless adventure." [*]

The three and a half years between Gauguin's return from Martinique early in 1888 until his departure for Tahiti were spent almost entirely in Brittany, first at Pont-Aven and later at Le Pouldu. The breaks in this stay were his famous three months' sojourn with Van Gogh in Arles, and occasional visits to Paris.

It was in this second period in Brittany that Gauguin's now mature painting reached its full development, and he began to produce what

[*] Pola Gauguin, *My Father Paul Gauguin*.

are today regarded the first of his masterpieces. He had broken entirely with Impressionism and was now painting in his typical style, with its decorative compositions, its broad, flat, simplified areas, and its growing emphasis on design at the expense of realism. This was to continue. The difference between his Breton pictures and his later Tahitian paintings is largely a matter of subject matter—the Tahitian subject matter was more exotic, but the painting approach was much the same.

At Madame Gloanec's *pension*, there were two groups of painters, the larger group of academic painters, and the smaller group of insurgents who came to be more or less headed by Gauguin. The academic painters unanimously hated the independents—that "pestiferous set"—and called them lunatics. Perhaps to keep the peace, the smaller group ate in a separate room leading out from the main dining room of the pension. It was probably in this strained atmosphere, which Gauguin's humorless and sarcastic personality did nothing to allay, that the spiteful Gauguin legend had its inception.

Gauguin came to be considered the master of the insurgent group who called themselves *Synthetists* and their art *Synthetism*. In its essence, Synthetism apparently meant simplification. As a movement, Synthetism is now seen to have been of little importance in the history of art. It was a word to bandy around for a while, and Gauguin himself, who was always impatient of labels and theories, tired of it and denied that it was of any lasting importance.

Later, Gauguin's art was coupled with the term *Symbolism*, the watchword of which was: "Suggest, do not state." But Symbolism was essentially a literary movement, headed by the poet Mallarmé, and had little to do with painting. Here again, Gauguin, though friendly enough personally with Mallarmé, soon renounced any connection with Symbolism.

Not long after his return from Martinique, Gauguin was invited by his friend Van Gogh to come to Arles. Van Gogh knew that Gauguin was ill and poor, and thought the two of them might do better by consolidating their resources. The trip to Arles was expensive, so Gauguin suggested that Vincent join the group at Pont-Aven. But this did not appeal to Vincent, who had heard of the endless discussions and enmities of the Pension Gloanec, and who had, moreover, fallen in love with the brilliant sunshine and brighter color of Southern France. Eventually, Vincent prevailed—with financial help from brother Theo—and Gauguin went to Arles.

The story of the visit and its tragic ending is told in the chapter on Van Gogh. In spite of some petulant and ill-considered remarks in his writings, it is clear that Gauguin was deeply upset by the Arles incident, that he had a real affection for Vincent, and felt a serious loss in the unhappy termination of their venture together. At one time, long after, Gauguin wrote:[*]

It has been that way my whole life; I stand at the edge of the abyss, yet I do not fall in. When Van Gogh went insane I was just

[*] *The Letters of Paul Gauguin to Georges Daniel de Monfreid.*

about done for. Well, I got over it. It forced me to exert myself. All the same my life has been a queer mix-up.

And again he said: "In spite of what the public may think, two men did tremendous work there, useful to both of them; possibly to others. Certain things bear fruit."*
It was the truth.

In Brittany, after the Arles incident, Gauguin painted some of his most famous Breton paintings, among them "La Belle Angèle," the "Yellow Christ," and "Jacob Wrestling with the Angel." "La Belle Angèle" was a portrait of a certain Madame Satre, a friend of some of the painters at the Pension Gloanec. She refused to accept the picture when Gauguin offered it to her as a gift. Later, the picture was purchased by the painter, Degas. Today it hangs in the Louvre.

The trip to Panama and Martinique had not quenched Gauguin's desire to seek a warmer, cheaper, and friendlier climate where he could paint as he pleased and get away from the convention-bound European "imbéciles" (academic artists, unfriendly critics, prudish moralists, stupid bores, and arrogant officials). Just about this time, possibly at the Universal Exhibition, he came across a pamphlet that described Tahiti in glowing terms. He had also been reading the books of Pierre Loti. These together, perhaps, gave him the idea of going to Tahiti. He wrote:

> My mind is made up: I want soon to go to Tahiti, a little island in Oceania, where material life has no need of money. A terrible epoch is being prepared in Europe for the coming generation: the reign of Gold. Everything is rotten, both men and the arts. Here one is incessantly distracted. There, at least, the Tahitian, under a summer sky and living on a wonderfully fertile soil, needs only to put out his hand to find food. Consequently, he never works. Life, to the Tahitian, consists of singing and making love, so that once my material life is well organized, I shall be able to give myself up entirely to painting, free from all artistic jealousy, and without any necessity for shady dealing.

To finance the voyage, a public sale of Gauguin's pictures was held at the Hôtel Drouot. Thanks to a laudatory article in the *Echo de Paris* by the critic Octave Mirbeau, public curiosity was aroused and the sale was a success. A benefit performance at the Théâtre d'Art was also held, but did not prove so successful financially. Before leaving, Gauguin was given a farewell dinner by his friends. Among the thirty guests present were Eugène Carrière, Odilon Redon, Albert Aurier, Jean Dolent, Charles Morice, Saint-Pol Roux, Julien Leclercq, Edouard Dubus, Adolphe Retté, Alfred Vallette, Jean Moréas, Dauphin Meunier, and Madame Rachilde. Mallarmé, who was ill, sent a note of regrets.

Gauguin sailed from Marseilles on April 6, 1891. He arrived at Papeete early in the morning of June 9, having remained on deck all night.

105   *Burnett

Gauguin's first visit to Tahiti lasted two years. It was the golden period of his life—to him what Arles was to Van Gogh. In good health and as near happy as he ever could be, he painted industriously, completing 66 canvases, including "Ia Orana, Maria" and "The Spirit of the Dead Watches."

He lived like a native at Mataiéa, a beautiful spot some distance away from the Europeanized Papeete, which Gauguin could not stomach. He lived in a native hut, dressed like a native, learned the native language. Burnett describes the place:

> In front of his hut lay the sea and the white foam on the coral reef bordering the lagoon, the enclosed expanse of water between the reef and the shore. Behind, the rich sloping land rose until it met the mountains, which at this point were splayed open into a deep chasm with a vast group of mango trees growing against the rock face. The earth was a deep purple, covered in places with the metallic yellow leaves of a trailing creeper.
>
> At Mataiéa Gauguin found a physical peace, the existence of which had been unknown to him during his (temporary) stay in Papeete. He felt far from the Europe that he had known and that now seemed like a prison to him. There was a silence at night, accentuated by the occasional playing of the *vivo*, the flute of the Tahitians. In Martinique, the night had been a signal to the insects to begin their grating bedlam, but in Tahiti, when the *vivo* was silent there was true silence.

A very young native girl, named Tehura, came to live with him as his "Tahitian wife." She was a good companion for him, and the arrangement proved a happy one for all concerned.

Gauguin's taste of South Seas paradise was not destined to last forever. The grim specter of finances intervened. With his usual prodigality, Gauguin failed to make his funds last. And while he was away from Paris, no one was buying his pictures, or, if a picture *was* sold, the purchaser did not pay him. At last, Gauguin was forced to return to France, borrowing to pay his fare. He arrived at Marseilles with four francs in his pocket.

The wheel of fate spun again, bringing a windfall to Gauguin. But in the windfall were the seeds of death—the slowly unwinding drama of Gauguin's life was climbing to its climax. First would come a giddy moment of doubtful glory and then the tragic denouement.

Almost at the same time that Gauguin was arriving, practically penniless, in France, his Uncle Zizi died, and Gauguin inherited Zizi's estate of from 10,000 to 13,000 francs. As a result, the next two years were a particularly fantastic interlude in an already strange life.

To shock the *imbéciles*, Gauguin dressed oddly, in "a long blue frock coat with buttons of mother-of-pearl over a blue Russian shirt bordered with yellow and green embroidery. His trousers were of putty-colored cloth.

"He had a large gray felt hat with a sky-blue ribbon, white gloves and a walking stick, the handle of which he had surmounted with a blister pearl and carved into the form of a male and a female figure in an intimate embrace. He wore the special Breton sabots that he had carved and decorated himself." * He is said to have carried a green parrot, or his pet monkey, around on his shoulder.

He moved into a large studio, exotically decorated with chrome yellow walls and a collection of Oceanic boomerangs, lances, and axes.

Apart from the easels, the furniture in the studio was limited to a Persian carpet, a somewhat shabby sofa from the period of Louis-Philippe, a piano, and a large camera mounted on legs. On the chimney-piece that was never used were displayed a variety of mineralogical specimens and tropical shells. A pet monkey lived among the easels.

Gauguin's chief and most surprising decoration was, however, his mistress, a half-caste Javanese who opened the door when a feeble tinkle from the hand bell announced a guest. Her name was Annah and she had come originally to Gauguin as a model. She was small, and when walking with Gauguin dressed in his new clothes, she made him appear far taller than he was. The impression which Gauguin wished to give was more astonishing and prosperous than was the one which was received by the majority of his friends.†

It has been suggested that Gauguin's posturing was purposeful—even that it had been prompted by his friends—a means of arousing the curiosity of the Parisian public and thus of helping to sell his pictures. If so, it failed, but it undoubtedly gave pleasure to Gauguin, whose natural vanity made him forever eager to indulge in self-dramatization.

An unending procession of writers, sculptors, and artists came to his receptions at the studio, among them Rodin, Maillol, and August Strindberg. During this period, Gauguin made a trip to Belgium to see the Flemish paintings, and another trip to Copenhagen to see Mette and the children. Whatever was said there, they remained at Copenhagen, and it became clear to him that the family would never be reunited.

Gauguin's entertainments, and the extravagant purchases of Annah, quickly frittered away his legacy. In the interests of economy, he again went to Brittany, where his strange appearance surprised and irritated the Breton peasants, and the presence of Annah scandalized them.

One day, as a result of remarks passed about her, he became involved in a fight with a group of sailors. Though he was an expert boxer, Gauguin was outnumbered, and finally one of the sailors, approaching from behind, kicked him violently on the ankle with his sabot, shattering the bones. Gauguin was taken to Pont-Aven on a stretcher. The broken bones never healed properly, causing Gauguin great discomfort the rest of his life. While he was helpless, Annah, the cause of the brawl, fled to Paris where

* Burnett.
† *Ibid.*

107

she ransacked the studio of everything she considered valuable and disappeared.

Finally, to cap all other misfortunes, Gauguin contracted syphilis from a casual meeting with a Parisian prostitute—a disease that added to his later miseries and probably hastened the collapse that ended his life nine years later.

He was now depressed and disgusted, both with himself and with Europe. His Tahitian paintings had not made the sensation he had hoped for. He decided to leave France forever and spend the rest of his days in Oceania. Again there was a sale of pictures, and in 1895 he sailed again for Tahiti.

The last eight years of Gauguin's life were spent in Oceania, the first six in Tahiti and the last two on the island of Hiva-Oa in the Marquesas. They were years of constantly increasing misery. His shattered ankle caused him great anguish, and in addition, perhaps from overexposure to the sun, he contracted a chronic eczema on the legs. His infection of the blood remained uncured and advanced from stage to stage. Near the end, his eyes were seriously weakened.

His financial difficulties seemed to grow ever more complicated. Money was forthcoming to him from time to time but never seemed to reach him. Finally, at one time, when his health had taken a turn for the worse and he was almost penniless, he attempted to commit suicide. He sought a lonely place in the mountains, where he thought the ants would quickly eat his body, and swallowed a quantity of arsenic. But the dose was either too large or too small; his violent vomiting freed his body of the greater part of it, and he spent a frightful night on the mountain, but did not die. During the next months his other sufferings were intensified by the effects of the poison. Ironically, the next mail boat brought him some money, and he did not again consider killing himself.

Gauguin became involved in constant controversy, with the government of the islands, in which he defended the natives against abuses, and with the missionaries, whom he considered an undesirable influence. In Tahiti, the Protestant missionaries had the upper hand and drew his attack. When he moved to the Marquesas, his feud was with the Catholic Mission, which was dominant there.

This latter mission was scandalized because a native girl took up her abode with him to act as wife, cook, and companion. When the mission attempted to interfere, Gauguin protected himself by decorating his hut in such a way that the reformers would not come near it. As described by Burnett:

> For the decoration of his hut he had carved and colored two panels, placing them on either side of the door. They showed nude female figures and held, for the encouragement of his visitors, inscriptions which he had once before carved on panels that he had done in Brittany. "Be mysterious—you shall be happy" was inscribed on one; "Be amorous—you shall be happy" was the recommendation of the other.

The spaces between the panels and the ends of the front of the hut were occupied by two large canvases of figures in Polynesian land-scapes. He now carved two statues in *bois de rose*, placing them in front of the panels. One represented a horned priest with satanic features, the other a young girl whom he named "Therese." She was without clothes, but she had a certain number of flowers in her hair and was partially covered elsewhere with garlands. [All of which was a rather pointed allusion to a rumored love affair of the missionary bishop.]

Gauguin was not yet, however, satisfied that he had sufficiently manifested his defiance. He decorated the alcove inside his hut with a series of lickerish and indelicate photographs which he had bought at Port Said. As he intended—these obscene photographs, the insulting decorations, and the name of his house, carved on a plaque above the door—"The House of Carnal Pleasure"—amply sufficed to keep the missionaries from visiting and annoying him.

In his last years, Gauguin's feuds with the civil authorities grew in intensity and bitterness, until finally he made so damning an accusation against one minor official that it could not be ignored. To vindicate the official, Gauguin's accusations were held to be untrue and libelous, and a prosecution was instituted against him. He was promptly sentenced to three months' imprisonment and a fine of a thousand francs.

The sentence came as a terrible blow to Gauguin—a blow from which he never recovered. The new anxiety, piled on his complication of physical illnesses, was to prove fatal. While the sentence was suspended, pending an appeal to Papeete, he became seriously ill in his hut, where he was attended only by an old native ex-cannibal and by the young Protestant pastor of the valley, a neighbor, with whom, rather surprisingly, Gauguin was on friendly terms.

On May 8, 1903, the old native, Tioka, came to fetch the pastor. Gauguin had had a heart attack and "did not know if it were the morning or the evening, the night or the day." After attending him for a time, the pastor went away, but was recalled at 11 o'clock in the morning and found Gauguin dead.

In a letter to Daniel de Monfreid, the pastor Vernier wrote:

I tried myself the rhythmical moving of the tongue and artificial respiration, but it was useless. Paul Gauguin was dead, and all signs point to the fact that he succumbed to a sudden failure of the heart.

I am the only European who saw Gauguin before he died.*

There was a curious anticlimax. When the Protestant pastor, Vernier, again arrived at Gauguin's hut, he found the Catholic Bishop and his assistants there preparing to bury Gauguin the next day with full Catholic ceremony. Vernier intended to attend the removal of the body, but when he arrived at the appointed hour on the following day, he found that the time had been set ahead and the burial completed. The mission had enjoyed a final triumph.

* *The Letters of Paul Gauguin to Georges Daniel de Monfreid.*

Gauguin's grave was left unmarked. His possessions were seized by the authorities, in settlement of the unpaid fine, and auctioned off to souvenir hunters.

Years later, when Gauguin had become world-famous, an elegant white slab was placed over his supposed grave. But native gossip has it that the true site was missed by a considerable distance.

16   Gauguin's Art

The character of Gauguin the artist contrasts sharply with that of Gauguin the man. The whole career of the man was a fumbling-bumbling thing, full of mistakes, misjudgments and defeats, ending in tragedy. The career of the artist, as an artist, was a bright and shining triumph, unmarred by indecision, false starts, or errors of judgment. It was an unswerving arrow-flight to artistic greatness.

Gauguin: *Maternity*. One of Gauguin's greatest paintings. A masterpiece of design, blended into the subject matter of the picture. Poetry in paint.

A natural artist, Gauguin developed easily and quickly, passing through a logical series of consecutive stages—stages of Academicism, Realism, and Impressionism—until finally he attained the sumptuously rich, lyrically decorative style in which his own aesthetic personality best expressed itself.

It is rather amazing that such an individual as Gauguin the man should have created an art so spiritually honest, so deeply sincere, as that produced by Gauguin the artist. Everything was against it. There was every temptation in the world for Gauguin—clever, sophisticated, and facile as he was—to paint pictures that might easily have been slick and pretentious, showy and false. Yet the idea of painting such slick, easily salable pictures never seems to have entered his head.

He did not have to go through the racking struggles of a Cézanne or a Van Gogh, yet his art is not below theirs in integrity. Never once, in his art, is Gauguin untrue to himself.

This is the miracle of Gauguin. Perhaps it was the result of a rigorous aesthetic conscience. Or it may have been caused by a sheer, fanatical devotion to art—a love that placed art before all else. But in any case, the miracle was accomplished, and its effect was to give strength and greatness to Gauguin's painting.

Gauguin rose above the influences that helped give form to his style.

This diagram shows the pattern of lines and values in "Maternity." Note the sinuous movement of the lines, how beautifully they flow into each other, weave together. Also note dark and light values, how they are distributed over the canvas according to a definite design pattern.

His greatness, for example, did not depend on his having painted in Brittany or in Tahiti.

Outwardly, at first glance, the work of the two periods (Breton and Tahitian) seem to be different in style. Actually, however, it is only the subject matter that is different. All the purely *artistic* qualities—design, color approach, drawing, and the like—are much the same in both the Breton and Tahitian paintings.

This was noticed by Charles Marriott,* who wrote, somewhat tartly:

> This applies with particular force to Paul Gauguin, whose artistic meaning and importance have been entirely obscured by the fact that he found Tahiti more congenial than Europe.

> Incidentally, it may be remarked that it is precisely the morbid character of civilization, in the sense of overcivilization, which makes too much of the Tahitian subjects of Gauguin. Their artistic value, as distinct from their purely circumstantial interest, is that they supplied him with splendid physical types, peculiarly well adapted to his aims in painting. Exactly the same virtues are to be found in his Breton pictures.

> They are an extraordinary power of simplification in drawing combined with capacity to design in bold patterns of color.

Gauguin was in no sense a *primitive* artist, nor was he influenced any more than slightly by the primitive native art of Polynesia. Aesthetically, he was very much a European, and his art was thoroughly civilized, complex, and sophisticated.

This was in spite of his professed admiration for native ways of living and, more important, it was in spite of his quite clear and sympathetic understanding of the primitive Polynesian art he had the opportunity to see at first hand. He liked and appreciated this highly designed native art, yet little if any of it "rubbed off" on his own work. The reason is not far to seek. With his own highly developed, strongly designed, personal art, he had no need for inspiration from native design sources. Furthermore, the spirit of Polynesian design was quite alien to Gauguin's natural aesthetic approach and offered him little that he could use.

Many critics, theorizing on the development of Gauguin's art, have ascribed the origin of his inspiration to various sources. But no two critics cite the *same* sources. Among the influences mentioned, at one time or other, have been:

medieval stained glass	Egyptian art
medieval enamels	Gothic statues
Near East textiles	Hindu statues
Japanese prints	Persian pottery
ceramics	primitive arts

* *Modern Movements in Painting.*

It is rather curious that so many critics have tried to place the source of Gauguin's inspiration outside of himself. It is also interesting that they have not agreed on which outside influence it was.

As a matter of fact, all the forms of art listed above have one thing in common—something they also happen to share with the art of Gauguin. They are all arts of *design*. Gauguin was a natural designer, and it is not surprising that his painting has a kinship with other designed work. It was not necessary that his art be derived from anywhere outside of himself. The urge to design springs from within. If Gauguin's "religious" pictures painted in Brittany have a resemblance to medieval statues, it does not follow that he copied medieval models. What is more likely is that, design-minded, he approached his subject in a manner somewhat similar to the artistic approach of the medieval craftsmen, and hence produced somewhat similar results.

Some of Gauguin's Tahitian heads and figures show a remarkable resemblance to the art of the Greeks. Yet Gauguin avowedly would have nothing to do with ancient Greek art; in fact, he knew very little about it. Nevertheless, through the universal medium of design, the inner spirit of this nineteenth century Frenchman approached surprisingly close at times to that of the immortal Attic sculptors.

It is idle, however, to pretend that Gauguin's art was *totally* uninfluenced by the work of any other artists whatever. There were at least *three* very real influences that did much to give his painting its final direction.

The *first influence* was that of Impressionism—the influence of Pissarro —which served to free the young Gauguin from the academic-realistic way of looking at things. It led him also to the "arbitrary" use of color described by Van Gogh. But Gauguin's innate urge to design would not allow itself to be fettered by the doctrines of Impressionism, and he broke away from Impressionism almost completely—more completely than did any of the early modern artists.

The *second influence* was that of the Japanese prints, an influence that affected Gauguin as much as, if not more than, Van Gogh. From the Japanese masters, Gauguin learned to divide up his pictures into broad, flat, decorative areas. Rather than fill these areas with brush-stroke textures, as did Van Gogh, Gauguin preferred to depend on exciting combinations of color to keep his pictures interesting.

Gauguin handled these large areas more decoratively than did Van Gogh—more, indeed, as the Japanese themselves had handled them. In the developing of a system of design along these lines, Gauguin also may have been influenced by such old masters as Botticelli and Fra Angelico (prints of whose pictures hung in his room in Brittany).

The *third real influence*, and perhaps the greatest of all, was that of Cézanne. When Gauguin sold his picture collection, he kept out a favorite Cézanne for himself. He copied and imitated Cézanne—in fact, incorporated partial copies of his Cézanne picture in some of his own paintings. (This in spite of the fact that, personally, he was not on good terms with Cézanne. In letters, Cézanne accused him of "stealing his thunder." Gauguin would not permit *his* children to play with Cézanne's son.)

113

Gauguin followed Cézanne's lead in a number of important respects. Like Cézanne, he employed a process of first simplifying and then re-creating nature. The essential nature, however, both of Gauguin's simplification and of his reconstruction, was quite different from that of Cézanne. Cézanne simplified nature into its basic *solid forms*, whereas Gauguin's simplification was confined rather to *areas* of surface, areas which would be useful to him in the development of designs.

In the reconstruction, even in designing, Cézanne tried to maintain a semblance of three-dimensionalism throughout his picture—tried to base his picture solely on nature. Gauguin, on the other hand, better able than Cézanne to "imagine in paint," did not share Cézanne's pious respect for nature as such. Nor was Gauguin too much concerned with maintaining three-dimensionalism in all parts of his pictures.

In certain other respects, the two artists were in accord. They shared a desire to keep the picture an aesthetic unit from frame to frame. Gauguin disliked "holes" in his canvas even more than did Cézanne. Each wanted his paintings to succeed in design—to "come off," as it were—to be "realized."

Gauguin's refusal to subscribe to Cézanne's wholehearted respect for three-dimensionalism resulted in an important structural difference between the pictures of the two men. Cézanne required himself to maintain the illusion of three-dimensionalism throughout the canvas. But Gauguin was satisfied if the large foreground figures (and even they were subtly flattened) retained a semblance of three-dimensional solidity. He was quite content to let the background flatten entirely into a tapestried curtain or backdrop. And if distant forms became unrecognizably distorted into flat, decorative areas, so much the better.

In so painting, Gauguin flattened his picture even more than did Cézanne, emphasized design as design to an even greater extent, moved farther away from realistic naturalism, and brought his art one step nearer to present-day modern abstractionism. (Incidentally, in this, Gauguin again suggested the ancient Greeks, whose art was conceived as set against a stagelike backdrop of one kind or other.)

Was Gauguin justified in doing this? It has already been pointed out that the effect of three-dimensionalism in a picture is only an illusion. It has also been shown that Cézanne substituted some illusionary devices for others. Gauguin merely went farther along the trail blazed by Cézanne. There was a greater disintegration of realism, but there remained neverthe-less an adequate representation of nature *in the important parts of the picture*.

In Gauguin's renunciation of complete three-dimensionalism, something else, however, was gained, namely, a greater freedom to design—a greater opportunity to develop the decorative possibilities of a picture—which Gauguin exploited to the utmost degree. In casting off the fetters of the insistent three-dimensionalism that caused Cézanne so much toil and struggle, Gauguin was enabled to *design* with greater subtlety, complexity, and interestingness. It became possible for him to instill a sensu-ous beauty into his paintings—to recapture some of the flowing *grace* of the Botticelli he admired. Color, too, could be used more directly for design purposes.

In the semiflattened Gauguin pictures, design reaches symphonic proportions, and color, line, and pattern of areas are organized and blended together with great subtlety, a subtlety that one appreciates fully only after he has looked at a Gauguin painting for a considerable time. It is this more advanced development of design that gives Gauguin's art a special interest, in its own direction, beyond that of Cézanne and Van Gogh, and which, to some degree at least, compensates for the lack of Cézanne's greater structural interest and of Van Gogh's deeper emotional power.

Cézanne's design is a building. Gauguin's is a poem, rich, sensuous, lovely. Gauguin is the Keats of modern art.

There is some controversy today among "experts" on modern art over the relative merits of an art like Gauguin's and that of Cézanne. Some of these theorists would find Gauguin's art weaker because it has lost some of the three-dimensionalism maintained by Cézanne.

They forget that the *insistence* on three-dimensionalism *as a necessity* is basically an idea that belongs, not to modern art, but to traditional *realistic* art. Three-dimensionalism is a veritable necessity for realistic painting, but is there any reason why it should necessarily have equal importance in *modern* art, the first requirement of which is not realism, but pictorial vitality—design and expressiveness?

Cézanne's skillfully compromised three-dimensionalism we have found interesting; but Gauguin's lyrical design-patterns are interesting too, in a different way. One cannot safely place one ahead of the other. *Both* men produced great art.

Turn to the reproduction of *Maternity* (page 110), one of Gauguin's most beautiful pictures, and to the accompanying diagram (page 111). The diagram is intended to indicate some of the principal *lines* of the picture. Note their rhythmic, sinuous quality (check back on the picture as well as the diagram), how beautifully they seem to flow through the picture. Notice also how they divide up the rectangular surface of the picture into nicely *related* areas; in other words, how they compose the picture. Turn picture and diagram upside down and study the abstract effect of the painting's design.

Note the feeling of *aliveness* this picture seems to have in spite of the calm poses of the figures. This aliveness arises from the sensitive design, the interesting relationships of areas and values, the movement and contrast of line.

In these black-and-white reproductions, however, one of the most important elements of Gauguin's design is not evident—namely, his *color*.

Gauguin distorted (or rather, ignored) nature more completely in his color than in any other aspect of his art. In many instances, he discarded natural color entirely; nor did he choose to employ the structural color of Cézanne. Instead, Gauguin substituted the "arbitrary," emotionally selected color of Van Gogh.

Gauguin's use of arbitrary color went far beyond anything attempted by Van Gogh. The intent of the two men in employing arbitrary color was also different. Van Gogh used it for intense expression, Gauguin for design, to help knit his picture together, and for the sheer beauty of the color combinations themselves. With his color, abstractly conceived, Gauguin sought to create visual music.

Gauguin pioneered in using color abstractly. He could paint the seashore sands cerise-pink, dogs red, and horses blue or green. He also pioneered in the use of exotic colors and unusual colors, which served to enrich his pictures. Particularly notable are his daring cerises and pinks, his aqueous blue-greens, and his smoky violets. Later on, other painters—especially Matisse—were to carry on this tradition of daring color, but there is little in Matisse's color that was not foreshadowed by Gauguin.

Gifted with a remarkable color sense, he combined his exciting colors with a delicate subtlety and a consummate knowledge of the relationships of hues, values, and contrast. He tended to avoid extreme contrasts, except for accents. Indeed, Gauguin's color is perhaps the most interesting and pleasing, not only of the nineteenth century, but in the whole history of art, and he is one of the greatest colorists of all time.

A quality of Gauguin's pictures that has often been noticed is their calmness. They seem to be imbued with a "timeless immobility."

There are reasons for this calmness: the inactive, relaxed poses of the figures; the large, quiet, flat areas of soft color. But most of all, the calmness is due to Gauguin's frequent use of *strong horizontals and verticals* in his design and his avoidance of the restless and dynamic diagonals.

Verticals and horizontals in a design always create a feeling of stability and quiet (just as oblique lines suggest instability and action). By emphasizing these verticals. Gauguin keeps his pictures *as a whole* calm, while the sinuous curves of the less important shapes slyly introduce a secret life, which interests, but does not disturb.

The total effect of a typical Gauguin picture, with its flattened background, is that of a rich tapestry or painted curtain. The eye does not sink into the picture, but wanders over its surface which, in turn, is composed of a tastefully distributed *pattern* of related and harmonious areas of color.

In his development of *pattern*—as well as in his revival of lyrical, decorative qualities in design—Gauguin made an important contribution to modern art. He built higher on the cornerstones of Cézanne and Van Gogh, and added something new. If the symbol of Cézanne's art was the cube and sphere, and Van Gogh's the leaping flame, Gauguin's was the patterned flower.

As far as the two main streams of modern art are concerned, Gauguin leans toward the Van Gogh stream of personal expression—in spite of the fact that Gauguin was at the same time so deeply indebted to Cézanne. Gauguin was a designer, but his design grew essentially out of his personal emotion and was not formulated intellectually. In fact, again, like Cézanne and Van Gogh, Gauguin did not appreciate how deliberately he *was* designing. He did not think of himself as a designer, but as a painter. He did not resort to design for the sake of the design itself, but to create pictorial music any way he could. Nor are his paintings lacking in personal *expressiveness,* his pictures shout "Gauguin! Gauguin!" as loudly as Rembrandt's work shouts "Rembrandt!"

Gauguin's influence on later painters has been underestimated. The second generation of modern artists—the famous "Fauves"—was influenced more directly by him than by either Cézanne or Van Gogh, although the influence of these two was not lacking. Gauguin's influence on Matisse is most important of all, although his ideas also affected the work of Friesz, Rouault, Marquet, Odilon Redon, Bonnard, Modigliani, Hodler, and Otto Mueller. From Gauguin, Matisse inherited not only his color, but also some of his ideas about drawing, and particularly his posterlike use of large flat areas (in turn, a heritage from the Japanese printmakers).

Again comes the question about Gauguin's painting: Is it art? And again the answer: "Yes," for the same reasons as in the case of Cézanne and Van Gogh. Gauguin's pictures wear well, appear to grow more interesting as we get to know them more intimately.

At first sight, Gauguin's pictures do not, as a rule, seem quite as disturbing as Cézanne's or Van Gogh's,—but a casual first look can be quite as inadequate in Gauguin's case as with the others. Glanced at superficially, Gauguin's paintings seem oversimplified, overobvious, possibly a bit dull. It is only on longer acquaintance that their true subtlety, complexity, and rich beauty become fully apparent. Thus seen, Gauguin's beautiful, sensuous, lyrical pictures provide a just claim to artistic greatness.

17   Seurat and the Little Dots

It has already been pointed out how the characteristic little dabs of paint of Impressionism underwent significant changes when they were taken over by the pioneer modern artists—the *post-Impressionists.* In Cézanne's hands the dabs became rectangular, chisel-like brush strokes. Van Gogh's impatient emotion lengthened them out into ribbonlike streaks of pigment. For a time, before he flattened them out entirely, Gauguin used brush strokes somewhat similar to Cézanne's.

But the most remarkable change took place in the work of a fourth artist, Georges Seurat, who congealed the haphazard dabs into precise little round dots of pure color, placed side by side not unlike the tiny dots of a modern color engraving. These dots, thousands of them, patiently stippled one by one, have become a hallmark of Seurat's painting.

If the use of these dots were its *only* outstanding characteristic, Seurat's art might have achieved some notice as an artistic curiosity for a few years, and then would have been forgotten. The fact is, however, that the dotting technique, the famous *pointillism,* is now considered only a minor element in Seurat's art. His extremely interesting composition and design, his delicate sensitivity of touch, and his haunting originality are seen to be much more important, and, as a result, he is revered as one of the world's great artists. His work—like that of Cézanne, Van Gogh, and Gauguin—is richly endowed with the essential artistic qualities of design and expressiveness.

As a pioneer of modern art, Seurat stands between Cézanne and Gauguin. His pictures, the famous *Grande Jatte* especially, are organized in a manner somewhat similar to that of Cézanne. Like Cézanne, Seurat tried to reconcile two-dimensional design with three-dimensional depth. His pictures have the "constructed," "architectural" quality that is also suggested in Cézanne. On the other hand, Seurat leans toward Gauguin in a willingness to imagine and distort, and in the tendency, particularly evident in his later pictures, to flatten pictorial depth in favor of decorative design patterns.

Seurat stands out as the most *intellectual*, the least emotional, of the four early moderns. Because of this intellectual approach, his art has surrounded itself with a cloud of theories, which today tend to obscure and bedevil appreciation of his real accomplishments. These theories, for the most part, appear to be of less and less importance as time goes on. In fact, it is becoming increasingly clear that Seurat was a great artist in spite of his theories—even in spite of his intellect.

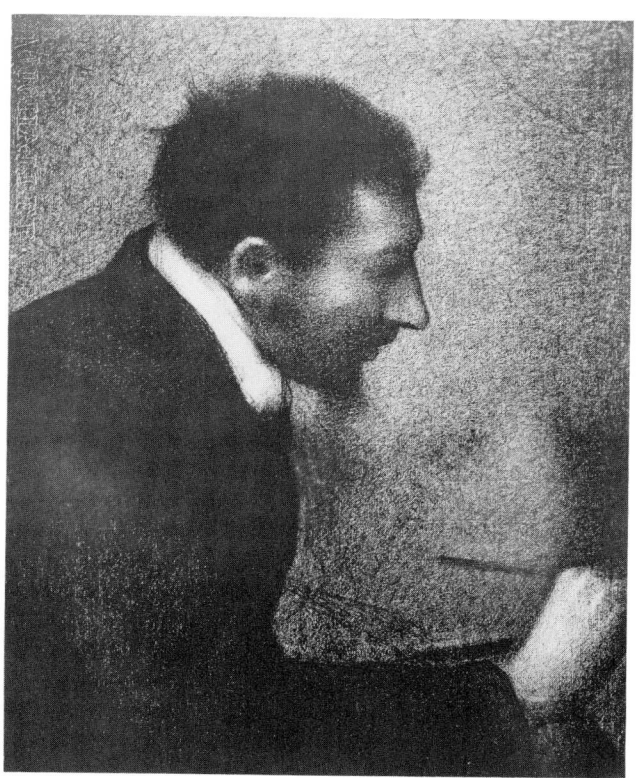

Seurat's influence on later modern artists was very great. Belonging to the orderly Cézanne stream of influence (as opposed to Van Gogh's emotionalism), he particularly served as an inspiration to the Cubists. He widened and straightened the trail first blazed by Cézanne—made it into a clear path easier for others to follow.

Cut off by an untimely death at the age of 31, Georges Seurat's life was short and uneventful. He was born December 2, 1859, in Paris. His father, a court bailiff, was sufficiently prosperous to provide Georges with an allowance all his life, so that he was never in need.

Young Seurat was given a conventional education until he was seventeen, after which he entered the *Ecole des Beaux Arts*, stronghold of artistic traditionalism. Here he studied for four years under Henri Lehmann, a pupil of Ingres. Seurat was strongly influenced by Ingres, but probably not so much because of Lehmann's teaching as because of the fact that spiritually Seurat had so much in common with Ingres and saw things in the same way.

Though not exactly a good student according to academic standards (he was too independent), Seurat had a keen mind and great intellectual curiosity. Naturally studious, he spent much time in the Ecole library, as well as in the museums. It was in this library, at the age of twenty, that he probably read the scientist Chevreul's book on color, *De la loi du contraste*

119

simultané des couleurs. This book was to have great influence on his later painting theories. Georges' education was completed with a year's term of military service ending in November, 1880.

At first, Seurat's serious artistic efforts were confined to drawings made with a soft pencil or conté crayon. One of these drawings—the beautiful portrait of his friend Aman-Jean—was exhibited in the official Salon of 1883 and won enthusiastic critical comment.

When he turned to painting as a next step, a ferment of new ideas were bubbling up in his mind. A growing admiration for Delacroix, the influence of the artist Paul Signac whom he had recently met, the scientific theories of color they had both studied, and possibly some contact with the Impressionists—all tumbled about in his brain, all gradually came to a focus in his new paintings. (At this time, he ruthlessly destroyed all earlier paintings which failed to conform to the new theories.)

Seurat's first great painting in the new style was the *Baignade* (1883), a picture of bathers lounging on the banks of the Seine on a hot summer day. This was followed by his now world-famous masterpiece, *A Sunday Afternoon on the Island of La Grande Jatte* (1884-1886), an enormous picture which required two years to complete. Later paintings of importance were *Les Poseuses* (the Models) (1888), the *Parade* (1888), the *Chahut* * (1890), *Jeune Femme se poudrant* (1890) and *Le Cirque* (1891).

Together with Signac, Seurat found himself the leader of a new artistic school, the *pointillists*, or, as they preferred to name it, the *neo-Impressionists* (not to be confused with *post*-Impressionists). For a time, Pissarro, Van Gogh, and Gauguin came under the spell of these new theories of "scientific color," color precisely "divided" on the canvas. (All three, however, soon returned to their natural styles.) Pissarro called the new approach "scientific Impressionism," contrasting it with the "romantic Impressionism" of Monet. This neo-Impressionist school tended to meet and exhibit together. They exhibited at the eighth (and last) exhibition of the Impressionists, and a number of times at the "Salon des Indépendants."

While helping to arrange one of these *Indépendants* exhibitions, early in March, 1891, Seurat developed a sore throat, followed by a fever which sent him to bed. A few days later he died—March, 29, 1891. The precise nature of his illness apparently was never ascertained (one authority says it was "septic quinsy," another "pneumonia," while Pissarro thought it was "diphtheria").

Seurat did not lack for friends among the Paris artist groups. He knew Van Gogh, who inquired about him in letters from Arles. On occasion, he accompanied the elfish Toulouse-Lautrec on nocturnal visits to circuses and music halls. Seurat took part in the neo-Impressionist group activities. But for the most part, he was a taciturn solitary, who spent most of his life alone, working even at night in the studio where he lived. It is supposed that long hours of solitary overwork may have been a contributing factor in bringing on his fatal illness.

* *Chahut* was the name of a naughty high-kicking dance something like the Can-Can.

It was not known until after Seurat's death that he had a mistress, Madeleine Knobloch, who bore him a son. This infant son survived his father by only a few days, succumbing to the same illness. Madeleine Knobloch was the model for the picture, *Jeune Femme se poudrant.*

In his manner, his dress, and in the arrangement of his studio, Seurat was always correct, orderly, and punctiliously neat. This same love of precise arrangement and formal order, so characteristic of his personality, is also indelibly impressed on his art.

The confusing jumble of theory and endless discussion of principles that surround Seurat's art can be cleared up by the simple expedient of dividing his painting into its three major aspects and by considering each one separately:

1. Theories of color
2. Composition and design
3. Personal elements in his art

The *theories of color* refer specifically to the neo-Impressionist doctrine (*pointillism, divisionism,* and so on) adhered to by Seurat and his followers. This aspect of Seurat's art has been the most publicized, both by the pointillist artists themselves and by the critics. In fact, for twenty years, until the advent of the Cubists (about 1910), this was the only aspect of Seurat's painting that received any attention at all in art criticism. Today, however, this approach is not considered as vitally important as formerly, and while it must be reviewed briefly to explain some of the oddities of Seurat's painting style, it is now seen to have little or nothing to do with Seurat's greatness as an artist.

Of vastly greater importance, it is now realized, is the second aspect, Seurat's *composition* and *design.* Little was said about this in Seurat's lifetime; and he himself, taciturn and suspicious, was not one to explain the secrets of his art at length. Not until a generation later did the eyes of younger artists discover in his paintings a powerful system of composition and design. This discovery at once elevated Seurat to a leading position in the history of recent art, and his influence on later artists, the Cubists particularly, has been enormous. Present-day criticism is now giving to Seurat's composition the analytical explanation that was once given only to his color theories.

The third aspect has not yet received so much attention, but it has not escaped the notice of the more sensitive critics, such as Roger Fry. This refers to the *personal elements* in Seurat's painting that cannot be analyzed at all—the things he did unconsciously, sometimes in violation of his own theories: his originality; his delicate sensitivity of line; the sense of mystery that pervades his pictures; his oddly individual way of seeing things (his "vision"); in short, the *personal expressiveness* that sets his painting aside from all others. This quality is not immediately discerned in his work, which at first seems cold and impersonal; but it is there and becomes increasingly apparent as one becomes more and more familiar with his pictures. It is the final assurance of his greatness as an artist.

Returning to the first category of Seurat's work, the pointillist color theories, it will be noted that these theories are in essence similar to the ideas of the Impressionists, but are codified and reduced to exact rules. *Simultaneous contrast*—the effect of a purple shadow produced by a bright yellow rock—was no longer allowed to be a matter of an artist's random "sensations"; it now became a matter of "scientific" law. Under these circumstances, the shadow must *always* be purple (and of a proper tone); it could not be anything else. To facilitate the correct contrasting of colors, the pointillist palette was reduced to a certain number of fixed colors of carefully graded tones—a so-called "color circle"—red, red-orange, orange, orange-yellow, yellow, and so on around the spectrum.

The broken-color idea which the Impressionists used haphazardly (but effectively) was also made "scientific" by the pointillists. To make green, small dots of yellow and blue were put down side by side; purple was produced by a mingling of red and blue dots; and so on. The thought here was that this "optically mixed" color would be more intense than a green or purple made by direct mixture of pigments. The idea was given support by experiments with whirling color disks, made by the American scientist Professor O. N. Rood of Columbia University.

The meticulous precision of pointillist color selection extended even to the frames of the pictures. The pictures could only be framed in neutral white, nothing else. Later, Seurat advanced beyond this and stippled his frames with dots of the proper contrasting color effect.

The pointillist color theories, based on the scientific tracts of Rood, Chevreul, and others, today interest us not so much because of their success or failure, but because of the revelation of a point of view of historic importance. Nineteenth century art and science were no longer merely brushing against each other—here they found themselves clasped in a tight embrace. The *artist* Signac personally visited the *scientist* Chevreul to ask for advice on color.

However it may be, in the case of pointillism, the liaison did not prove forever happy. Something went wrong. If we look at the neo-Impressionist pictures today, we see that their "optically mixed" colors are *not* more brilliant or more luminous than those of the Impressionists; in fact, they are actually hazier and grayer. Perhaps the artists misinterpreted the findings of science, possibly mistaking oil pigment for rays of light. Or perhaps, as later scientists have maintained, the *science* of Rood and Chevreul was itself faulty.

This theoretical imperfection, however, need not be taken to rule out the neo-Impressionist paintings as pictures. They still achieve a remarkable illusion of atmosphere, if not of brilliant color. And the pointillist dotting—even more than the Impressionist dabbing—tended to push the hand of the artist toward formal design and away from imitative realistic drawing. Even the otherwise uninspired paintings of Signac are made more charming and interesting by the degree of design forced on him by his medium of expression. With Seurat, a much more profound and sensitive artist, the pointillist method aided and abetted a naturally strong leaning toward the formalism of design. Otherwise, the pointillist color theories contributed little to his art.

Seurat's compositional devices, particularly those used in the complex picture *A Sunday Afternoon on the Island of La Grande Jatte*, have attracted the attention of numerous critics. For example, one writer is much impressed by the way the eye is led, by strong lines and areas, around the picture in a circular path, finally coming to rest in a natural center of attention, the mother and child. (See diagram, page 124.)

Another critic notices that a diagonal, starting in the lower left corner, intercepts three sets of tandem figures as it crosses the picture (while a counter-diagonal in the opposite direction intercepts somewhat similar combinations of figures. (See top diagram, page 125.) Still another commentator points out how the successive broad bands of color—the dark shadow in the foreground, the bright sun-lit middle area, and the darker band of tree foliage at the top—simplify the picture and the many smaller objects in place. (See lower right-hand diagram, page 125.)

All these things are interesting enough, and not unimportant, but their importance is really only incidental to the more fundamental design organization of the picture. That is, (a) its successful compromise between three-dimensional depth and two-dimensional design; and (b) its over-all "pattern" of many parts, all of which *relate* not only to each other, but also to the picture as a whole.

Seurat is said to have remarked that the art of the painter consists of his handling of the "space hollowed out" in the canvas. The precise meaning of the remark, of course, is not self-explained, but it *does* present the implication that the "hollowing out" of the space is under the control of the painter, for him to arrange and organize as he desires. Seurat has certainly done this in his construction of the *Grande Jatte*.

His approach is very much like that of Cézanne. The picture creates a strong illusion of depth, but the depth does not go so far back, so infinitely, that it quite permits the eye to escape in the distance (it remains *in* the picture); nor does the effect of depth in any way interfere with the abstract two-dimensional design created by the shapes and areas of the picture. This painting, like those of Cézanne, has something of the quality of a bas-relief.

In its combination of tightly knit *design* on the picture surface (or picture plane) and its illusion of considerable depth and distance, both occurring at one and the same time, the *Grande Jatte* is an eminently successful example of a type of picture construction sought by both Cézanne and Seurat. In the *Grand Jatte*, each figure is in its right place, as if on a chess board. We think of the figures as solid, yet if we observe their drawing closely we note that they are drawn almost as flat as pieces of cardboard. The effect is not too much unlike that obtained by looking in an old-fashioned stereoscope.

This in itself is interesting, but what is more interesting, from the standpoint of modern art, is the great degree of *design* made possible by Seurat's deliberate approach. Quite unlike Cézanne, Seurat had no inhibitions about deforming "nature" if that suited the purposes of his design, and Seurat altered natural objects far more profoundly, more completely, than did Cézanne. Furthermore, Seurat did not have to sit in front of nature and paint it, point by point, as did Cézanne. Gifted with greater

123

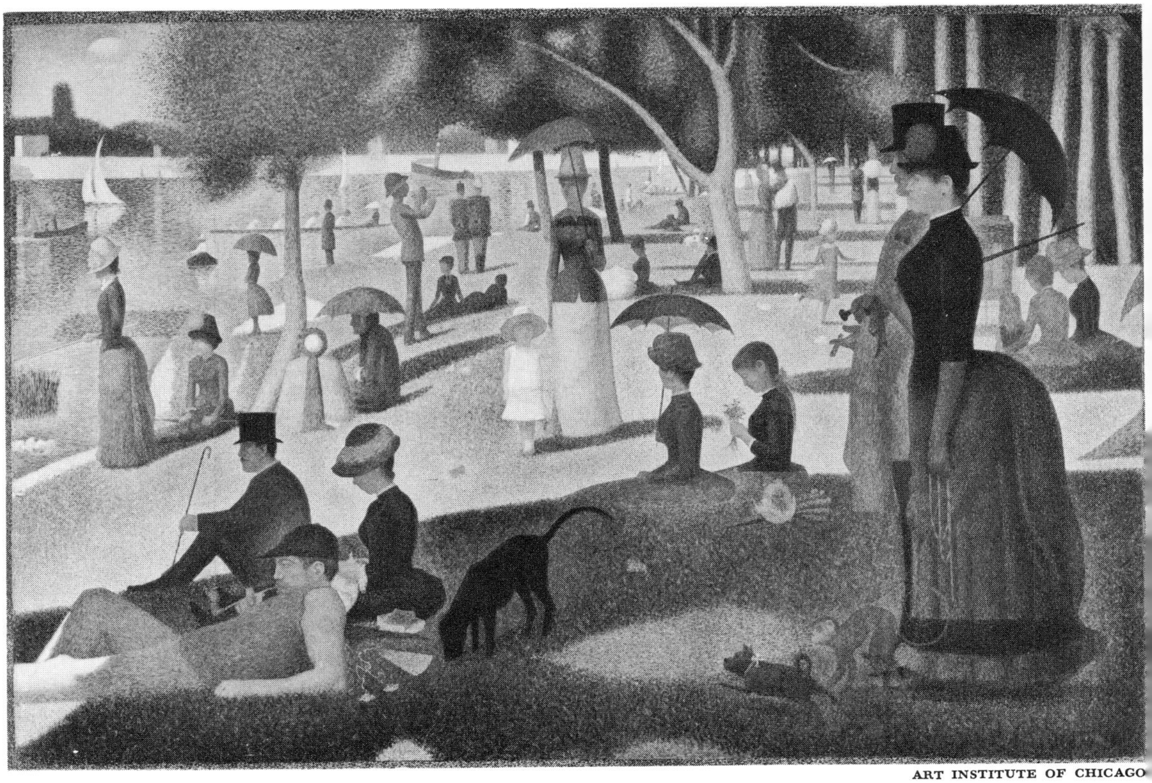

ART INSTITUTE OF CHICAGO

COMPOSITIONAL DEVICE. The eye is led *around* the picture by leading lines and by the pull of strong dark-and-light areas. The eye finds a final resting place near the middle of the picture at a center of interest, the mother and child.

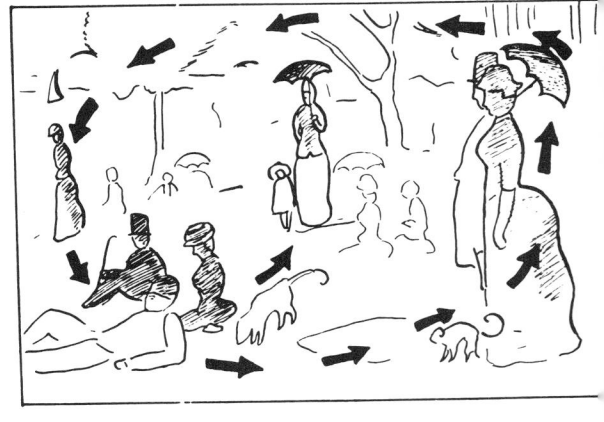

Seurat: *A Sunday Afternoon on the Island of La Grande Jatte*. Seurat's largest and most famous picture took two years to complete. The figures are formalized, designed. The whole picture is a design, yet at the same time it conveys an adequate illusion of three-dimensional depth.

COMPOSITIONAL DEVICE. Note how a diagonal (a, b, c) intercepts three sets of tandem figures, and how a counter-diagonal (1, 2, 3) intercepts three similar combinations.

COMPOSITIONAL DEVICE. A dark band of *shade* crosses the foreground of the picture. Above this is a lighter band of bright sunlight. Near the top is another band of shade caused by the dark foliage of the trees. The division of the picture into these three broad areas tends to simplify the otherwise complex composition—helps organize the many scattered details into simpler larger groups.

visual memory and imagination, Seurat painted his pictures as he pleased, in his studio, using sketches made from nature only as notes (a method used by many other artists, before and since).

It is not quite true, as one writer has stated, that Seurat's figures look like "dummies full of stew," but they certainly do not look like realistic human beings. They are frankly simplified, distorted, changed. They are not representations, but they *are* designs, and part of the larger design of the picture as a whole.

Seurat's design is more completely design, in a technical sense, more deliberately design, than is Cézanne's. It can be called *tight* design, in contrast to Cézanne's *loose* design. This does not make one painter better or worse than the other. It is just a personal variation in emphasis. It may be said, however, that as a modernist Seurat advanced beyond Cézanne; that he progressed farther along the path that future modern artists were to follow.

We have used the word "pattern" in connection with the paintings of both Seurat and Gauguin. It is a word that comes up again and again in discussions of modern art, because it describes a fundamental concept in the point of view of modern picture makers. Let us examine this concept of *pattern* a little more closely.

Consider only the flat surface of a picture and its four edges. This forms a flat rectangular plane called the *picture plane*, or the picture surface. For the time being, think of this two-dimensional rectangle only, forgetting entirely about considerations of depth or the possibility of a third dimension. Note the figures in the diagrams below.

In the rectangle at the left, a haphazard grouping of lines will be found. Suppose that the lines can move about freely. Then suppose that all of these lines, and also the four lines that form the edges of the picture, were suddenly charged with static electricity so that each line repelled the other line. Let us assume that the lines, being free to move, would distribute themselves about the rectangle as in the figure (b) at the lower right. When the lines, acting under the electrical force, finally stopped moving, they could be assumed to be in a state of perfect balance or equilibrium.

The lines form a *pattern* over the face of the rectangle, each part in balance against the next part. Instead of the lines, we can also imagine the same thing happening with *areas*. The areas, too, can form a pattern under "tension."

All of this is imaginary. It is a fanciful way of illustrating the idea of *pattern* in a design. In a good design, the elements—the lines, the areas, the "weights" of black-and-white or of color—should distribute themselves about the picture as if there were a *feeling* of balanced tension between the different parts of the picture, especially those parts left free to move in space. Unless anchored down by its own lines, the parts of a design should be thought of as freely movable—and as if under some sort of pressure or tension—like particles in an electrified or magnetized field. This imaginary conception should help one sense the aesthetic feeling of *pattern* in a good design.

A picture is said to achieve a feeling of "pattern" if every individual part of that picture, from frame to frame, corner to corner, seems to be in exactly the right place aesthetically. Also if every single part seems to be in just the exactly right aesthetic relation to its neighboring part (which may happen to be one of the *lines* that form the edges of the picture). And if, finally, the whole broad area of the picture surface is filled with its component parts in a harmonious manner, evenly, without disturbing gaps or congestions, from edge to edge of the picture.

In other words, to form a completed design, every part of the picture included in its four edges should be *organized* in some emotionally felt, aesthetically satisfying arrangement. Not only do the lines and areas partake of this organization, but also the space between them. Every good design—every *designed* picture—should have this pattern feeling. It need

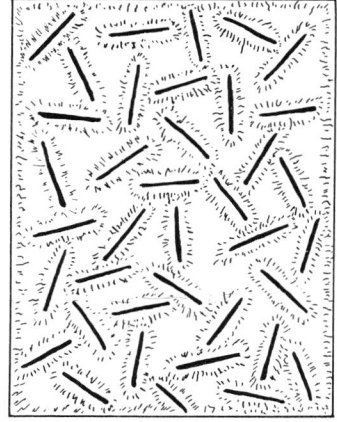

not, however, be a pattern merely of small lines or areas spread evenly over the picture rectangle, like a piece of ornamental wallpaper. The design can consist of *a few large areas,* or of areas of different sizes—but organized, not haphazard; in equilibrium, not floating loose; in balance, not off-balance. This is what is meant by *pattern.* It is an essential characteristic of modern art and will be referred to again and again.

The paintings of Seurat display this feeling of pattern to a marked degree, particularly the *Grande Jatte.* Every element in a Seurat picture is just exactly the *right* distance from the next element. Every bit of picture area is filled precisely right aesthetically. Throughout a Seurat picture there is a subconscious sense of resolved tension, of many parts in perfectly balanced equilibrium. This is pattern. It is a notable characteristic of Gauguin's pictures also. (Though also inherent in Van Gogh and Cézanne, it is not so obviously apparent or so deliberately expressed as in Seurat and Gauguin.)

A Sunday Afternoon on the Island of La Grande Jatte is Seurat's most ambitious picture and his most famous masterpiece. But from the standpoint of the development of his style, it is an "early picture," painted by a young man. As Seurat grew in power as a painter, his ideas of design and

128

Seurat: *The Parade*. This is one of Seurat's later pictures. Notice its increased flatness, its sacrifice of three-dimensional solidness and depth for purposes of design. An air of mystery pervades this picture.

GEOMETRIC DIVISION OF THE PICTURE AREA. Note the emphasis on horizontals and verticals, which acts to divide the large rectangle of the picture itself into smaller rectangular shapes. In this type of design composition, Seurat anticipates the ideas of many later artists, such as Piet Mondrian and also the geometric Cubists.

composition developed likewise, and his later pictures show important differences from the approach of the *Grande Jatte*.

In a typical later picture, *The Parade* (above), we find the depth of the picture subject greatly flattened, almost to a flat plane. The artist, apparently, is no longer interested in the depiction of deep space. Pictorial elements in the picture have become deliberately debased, design elements correspondingly emphasized. Seurat was becoming more of a *modern*.

In this and other later pictures, he becomes less and less interested in realistic drawing—his formalized figures become less human beings and more design elements. And we must not forget that this was entirely intentional. There was no question of Seurat's ability to draw. He had proved himself one of the outstanding realistic draughtsmen of his day; had won critical praise for his fine drawing exhibited in the official *Salon*. It was interest in expressive design that led him to distort, to bring his pictures closer to the abstractions of a later day.

Cut off as he was by death at the age of thirty-one, there is cause for much speculation as to what Seurat might have done had he lived longer. At the time he was developing rapidly, and the world undoubtedly suffered a great loss in his untimely passing.

An interesting feature of the *Parade* is the dividing up of the picture area into geometric rectangular segments by means of vertical and horizontal lines (see diagram). This geometric division was to be repeated later in the works of the geometric Cubists, and it even foreshadows, to some extent, the ideas of such an artist as Piet Mondrian.

Is it art? The question has now been asked four times—with Cézanne, with Van Gogh, with Gauguin, and again with Seurat. Any answer we might give could not be proved, in words, by analysis or logic, because the word *art* itself is simply not definable in precise terms (a fact demonstrated by the innumerable attempts to make such a definition—all of them obvious failures). One can only fall back on the most reliable authority we have—the test of time. Thus far, Seurat's work has stood the test of time magnificently.

Again, one can make the observation that of the pictures that mankind accepts as "great art" *all* abundantly possess the qualities of *design* and *personal expressiveness*, and that there is *no* painting lacking in these qualities that is universally considered "great."

The paintings of the four early moderns *do* possess the qualities of design and expressiveness. This may not automatically guarantee their greatness, but it is at least an indication of it, and of the fact that they *do* fulfill what seems to be an essential requirement of greatness in art.

Thus far, in Seurat's case, we have considered only the quality of design, and have not as yet looked into the matter of expressiveness. Before doing so, however, we might well examine a question that is suggested, in part at least, by the peculiar nature of Seurat's painting. *Does design alone—without personal expressiveness—provide assurance of greatness in art?*

The answer is near at hand. On many household objects, on draperies, on floor coverings, on dress fabrics, on countless other utilitarian items, can be found designs. Some of these designs are interesting (and more are getting to be), but unquestionably the great majority are not. The chances are that *most* of these things we see are dull, uninspired, unoriginal, the work not of artists but of unsensitive and indifferent hacks serving the purposes of cheap, commercial, quantity production. This is design without art.

The same thought can be carried over into the painting of pictures. The design in a picture can also be dull, uninspired, unoriginal, when produced by a painter who lacks the personal touch, the originality, the sensitivity and inspired artistry—namely, the *personal expressiveness*—of a true artist. Hence, the mere presence of design is not enough; it must be interesting design, expressive design. This may seem a small point, but in modern art it is vitally important, particularly today when the art schools are turning out hordes of abstractionists, not all of them gifted with any great degree of originality or creative inspiration. The point is also important in the case of Seurat, whose work appears to emphasize problems of design before all else.

130

Fortunately, personal expressiveness is amply present in Seurat's painting, even though he himself seemed to try consciously to stifle it, and even though it is not quite as apparent to the onlooker as in the paintings of Van Gogh or Gauguin or Cézanne.

The impression *first* given by seeing a Seurat painting (a final version, not one of the preliminary sketches) is a feeling of coldness and stiffness, of impersonality, of an obvious intellectualism that startles but does not convince. One senses the influence of theory in the making of the picture and is not surprised to learn that the artist has painted by the "laws of science" rather than by emotional sensation. The tightly designed forms, the patiently applied little dots, the definite lines, all indicate a love of precision and order, which is as Seurat *consciously* intended it.

The muse of Art, however, is a sly minx. When a born artist comes into the world, she is not one to let him escape her dominion, even though he, himself, does his best to become a scheming scientist first and an artist second. With a touch of her magic wand, she makes her erring son an artist in spite of himself, and sooner or later the world finds him out, all his efforts to the contrary. Such was the case with Seurat.

His theories could not conceal the exquisite delicacy and sensitivity of his line, nor could his natural decorative sense be quite suppressed, nor his moody originality of conception. Nor his quaint, whimsical sense of humor, so different in form of expression, yet so alike in spirit to that of his impish friend, Toulouse-Lautrec. Cold and forbidding on first appearance, Seurat's pictures conceal an inner cheerfulness which shines through on longer acquaintance. The more we see of Seurat's work, the more we find him "giving himself away," revealing unsuspected emotional values.

His poetic, tensely sensitive *line* is one of the glories of nineteenth century art. Seurat was pre-eminently a *line* artist. He belonged to that breed of artists who see forms in terms of *contour* first, who treat line as a living thing in its own right. (The opposite category is that of the *mass* artists, who seem to forget all about contour in their efforts to emphasize the bulk, the roundness, and the weight of their forms. Renoir is an excellent example of this group.) If we examine Seurat's figures in his finished pictures we find that while, as a competent draughtsman, he has a perfect understanding of form, he constantly flattens it. Contour, on the other hand, is never neglected.

It is curious that in his black-and-white drawings Seurat consciously attempted to suppress his own linear predilections by rendering with soft edges; but even in these lineless creations there is an evident awareness of a place where a line should go. Though drawn without a single linear edge, line is *implied* everywhere.

Seurat gives himself away, also, in the many charming oil sketches, loose and spontaneous, that he made as preparation material for his more austere finished paintings. Ingratiatingly friendly, these sunny *croquetons*, as he called them, reveal a warmth of personality that is largely concealed in the rigidly stylized completed paintings.

131 Nevertheless, charming as the sketches may be, they lack the design

interest, the depth, and the content of the final versions; and in due time, one will discover in the finished paintings not a little of the same charm that makes the sketches so attractive.

Seurat's painting is perhaps the most original in the history of art. No one before him painted with such an original approach; few conceptions are as oddly individual as his. But particularly his own is the strange sense of mystery that characterizes his art, that is so haunting in a picture like the *Parade*. Emotion, personality, *expressiveness*—even though unintentional—finally triumph over intellect.

Today, Seurat's art is both overestimated and underestimated. It is, perhaps, overvalued by the international art market, which speculates on the scarcity of Seurat's output (only seven fully complete figure paintings). A syndicate of dealers is said to have offered in vain a sum like $500,000 for the *Grande Jatte*. But this has nothing to do with art, or the *artistic* value of Seurat's painting.

Again, certain elements in Seurat's art tend to be overestimated by certain present-day theorists. Seurat's compositional devices are now getting the acclaim that was once accorded his color theories, yet these compositional devices are no more positive guarantee of the artist's greatness than was the earlier theorizing. They are only a *part* of the whole.

It is perhaps the *under*estimated quality—that of the concealed *personality* in his pictures, the element of *personal expressiveness* (combined, of course, with his powerful *design*)—that will best assure Seurat of a permanent niche in art's everlasting hall of fame.

It is now time for a brief recapitulation. With the completion of our study of the four "pioneers"—Cézanne, Van Gogh, Gauguin, and Seurat—we come to a turning point in the history of modern art. The works of these four artists constitute the foundations of modern art—they are the roots of the tree, the sources of the stream. No sooner had these masters laid down the general directions the new art was to take, than other artists came forward with new variations, new contributions, and new ideas. Immediately, the tree began to develop, the stream, to swell and grow.

Behind the dynamic character of artistic modernism were strong propelling forces deriving from the history and culture of the nineteenth century. The cultural calm that might have attended the bourgeois triumph was periodically disturbed by a steady ground swell of unrest, itself the aftermath of the hurricane of the French Revolution. But even more disturbing was the relentless march of the new industrialism; the onrush of the new science.

The prevailing unrest transmitted itself to the realm of art and led to an artistic revolution that paralleled the political and industrial revolutions and, like them, succeeded in upsetting centuries-old traditions. In the early part of the nineteenth century, artistic unrest manifested itself in a series of successive steps: first reactionary neo-Classicism, then Romanticism, Sentimentalism, and Realism. In the second half of the century, officially sponsored academic realism achieved a brief period of uneasy triumph, only to be attacked again by the restless forces of revolution.

Impressionism was the first wave of attack; modernism was the attack in force. The first moderns rejected the slavish respect for near-photographic realism and the emphasis on story-telling that characterized academic-realistic art. The pioneer modern artists, seeking something new and vital, something more permanent, something that had been forgotten in art, turned back to the old masters. This is an important point to note at this time. For while Cézanne, Van Gogh, Gauguin, and Seurat looked chiefly to the museums for instruction and inspiration, their followers extended the search to other and quite different sources, and by so doing, vastly expanded the development of modern art.

Although their paintings differed widely in general appearance, the four pioneer moderns succeeded in creating a new art of great vitality which had certain qualities in common. The most important of these qualities, we have arbitrarily labeled (for want of better terms) *design* and *personal expressiveness*. These qualities are also present in the works of the greatest old masters.

In achieving these qualities, the early moderns rudely violated the pat rules of academic-realistic art. They wandered away from strict realism, "distorted" nature, flattened pictorial depth, and interested themselves in expressive design rather than in accurate representation or in the depiction of story-telling subject matter. The new paintings became more and more expressions of the *artist's* aesthetic feelings, at the expense of faithful imitation of "nature." This was the beginning of modern art. Its justification was that it produced pictures of great interest and lasting vitality.

Contributions to the stream of modern art began immediately. Indeed, some of the first contributions came from contemporaries of Cézanne, Van Gogh, Gauguin, and Seurat. The work of the contributing artists was not, as a whole, quite as fundamentally modern as that of the original four, but it nevertheless contained elements of great value to the development of modernism. Renoir and Toulouse-Lautrec were two such contributors, and their most important contributions were in the field of *drawing*.

18   Renoir and the Problem of Drawing

There exists a distinction between *drawing* and *painting*. Sometimes beginners who cannot "draw" at all can paint surprisingly well. And on the other hand, accomplished artists who can draw with feeling and skill sometimes find it difficult to express themselves in paint.

Generally speaking, drawing is concerned with the delineation of shapes and forms on paper or canvas, whereas painting has to do with the manner in which color and pigments are applied. Of course, all paintings include elements of *both* drawing and painting, but it is possible for one or the other to be emphasized. It is easy to think of Michelangelo, Holbein, or Toulouse-Lautrec as great draughtsmen, or of Titian and Renoir as great painters.

There is also a distinction between "*a drawing*" and "*a painting*." We think of a painting as executed in color. It may be a water color or a gouache, but *usually* when we speak of a "painting" we are thinking of an oil painting on canvas or board. Conversely, a "drawing" is usually a monotone rendering in pen, pencil, or chalk on paper.

As far as *art* is concerned, it does not matter in the least what medium or means of expression is used. Painting is not necessarily better than drawing, or vice versa. Nevertheless, in practice, the kind of medium chosen *does* have an effect on a good artist's work; his sensitive hand, his delicate aesthetic sense, respond differently to different mediums. Hence, it is not surprising that in oil paintings we *generally* expect to find such qualities as completeness of expression, and the full development of color, texture, and composition, whereas in drawings we have come to look for less completeness, but more directness and freshness of expression, more spontaneity, and more sensitive awareness of line and contour.

The drawing made for its own sake has a special advantage as far as the student of art is concerned—it is concerned *only* with the "problem of drawing" and does not introduce any perplexing questions of color or pigment. Such drawings, however, are not always available for study, and it sometimes becomes necessary to isolate, as best one can, the element of drawing in an artist's paintings.

We are concerned with drawing because it has such an enormous bearing on one's understanding of the philosophy of modern art. The modern artist and the academic-realistic artist see drawing in a completely different light. What the modern artist considers a "good drawing" is likely to be a far cry from what the academic-realist calls a "good drawing," and vice versa.

In particular, our concern is with the basic "*problem of drawing*" which all artists face but which every individual artist solves in a different way. The problem of drawing is the problem of depicting a *three*-dimensional real object on a *two*-dimensional sheet of paper.

In attempting to draw, the first impulse of the beginner is to try to visualize his subject and *then draw a line around it*. He thinks only of the outside contours, forgets that his subject has solidness and roundness that must also be expressed. Ages ago, a caveman artist held his hand against a rock and scratched an outline around the hand. An ancient Greek is said to have noticed the shadow of his sweetheart on a wall and preserved her image by tracing the outline of the shadow with a piece of charcoal. In neither case was the result permanently satisfying; the outlines were beautiful, but all else was missing.

Nearly every bright youth entering art school can draw a reasonably accurate silhouette *outline* of the figure. It is when he tussles with the third dimension—the part of the drawing that comes toward him or moves away from him—that he gets into trouble. And it can be said that he will probably have this kind of trouble for the rest of his artistic career, because the problem of three-dimensional drawing is not easily solved.

When the figure is in an active pose, arms and hands reach forward *at* you, knees and elbows bend and foreshorten in the most baffling planes and angles, shoulders and buttocks protrude, the small of the back recedes. Every part of the body varies in shape, not only in silhouette outline, but forward and backward, too. The body has roundness, weight, solidity. And all this must go down in line on the flat pad of paper. No wonder, then, that the working artist almost immediately ceases to think of the model as a person or body, but only as a complex of subtle *forms*, forms that must be analyzed, understood, and then reproduced on paper.

It might seem that, by carefully analyzing each form and transferring it to paper, the artist *might*, with patience, get the figure drawn. But there are further pitfalls. The model is not an immobile statue, but a human being—a living thing. There is certain to be a certain swing and thrust in the pose; bodily tensions, compressions, and saggings; a unity and rhythm in the entire body, all of which are speedily lost in any tedious piece-by-piece method of drawing. Furthermore, the artist often has difficulty in "carrying in his head" all the details of form at one time; if he concentrates too much on the head, he may get the legs and feet entirely out of proportion. (Indeed, a rapid free sketch, careless of detail, often turns out to be a more lifelike and convincing representation than a careful, extended study.)

And that is not all. Hold one hand a few inches from your eyes, then look through the fingers at your other hand held at arm's length. Note how much smaller the distant hand appears in comparison to the near hand. There is the effect of perspective to be reckoned with in the drawing of a figure as well as in the drawing of a house.

This "problem of drawing" has confronted artists throughout the ages. Giotto and Masaccio wrestled with it mightily. The nineteenth century academic-realistic artist faced it, too, and in a particularly embarrassing way, because he was so very anxious to achieve near-photographic realism. Hence, to overcome the difficulties of drawing, the academic realist applied a "system" which he liked to call "knowledge of drawing." He used many devices—"blocked in" the large forms of the figure, studied anatomy, studied antique statues, "idealized" what his eyes saw, and so on. In essence, however, what he really did was to memorize a more or less standard figure ("idealized," of course, and "based on the classics"), and he drew, in fact, largely from precept and memory, and only slightly from the model before him. "Anatomy" lessons taught him how to depict standard muscles in numerous convenient positions. This standardization greatly simplified the problem of drawing and made it possible to produce faultless realistic renderings, which was what the academic-realistic artist wanted.

But this standardized approach to drawing had a rather obvious fault—it could not help but produce figures that were stereotyped, impersonal, and lacking in individual character. Actually, *there are enormous differences in living human figures*, and not one real human body in a hundred would come even approximately close to the proportions of the anatomy diagrams. In trying to depict a somebody that was a summation of everybody, the academician produced a nobody.

Furthermore, in standardizing, the academic artist lost almost all intimate contact with the extremely interesting interplay of *real* natural forms, solids and planes. Though he professed to draw from nature, he was actually ignoring nature. He lost the inspiration and challenge provided by nature's perversity and variety. Leaning on precept and striving for effect, his eyes began to see form, and the relationship of forms, only dimly. Indeed, it is probably due to this strictly academic approach to drawing that traditional nineteenth century art became so sterile and artistically unsatisfying.

The early moderns, indeed *all* of the more vigorous artists of the late nineteenth century (particularly including such men as Degas and Toulouse-Lautrec), rejected the standardized academic methods and insisted on finding new inspiration from the model itself, regardless of the difficulties and complexities of the task they set for themselves.

In doing so, they sacrificed the assurance of achieving near-photographic realism in exchange for artistic values they considered of far greater importance. What these values were, precisely, varied with each individual artist, but in general, greater vitality, greater "essential truth," greater artistic strength were achieved. And in time, as these antiacademic artists struggled with the complexities of three-dimensional form, a new and richer conception of drawing arose. Drawing that not only reproduced the shape of the figure but also *commented* on it at the same time. A rather clear-cut example of this new conception is found in the drawing of Pierre Auguste Renoir.

Renoir was a thoroughly *professional* artist from the very start. As a boy he made money by painting flowers on china; later he decorated fans with copies of Boucher and Watteau. Then he painted saints on calico screens for the use of missionaries in distant lands where there were no churches, and this occupation proved so lucrative that young Renoir was enabled to take a year off to study "serious art" at Gleyre's studio in Paris.

There he met Sisley and Monet, and with them, in due time, helped to establish the Impressionist style. For a number of years he suffered the economic vicissitudes that were the lot of all the early Impressionist painters. Of them all, however, he was prehaps the first to improve his lot by actually selling pictures, and his paintings were the first to increase in price. His relative success resulted partly from his skill in figure painting and partly from the natural charm of his work—both of which together enabled him to paint portraits that were quite acceptable in certain fashionable circles. Later, his plump and pleasing nudes also found a ready market.

Renoir's life was long and, like Monet, he lived to see his pictures command higher and higher prices. His output was enormous—he is said to have painted nearly 5,000 pictures, more than any other important artist of his time. Before his death in 1919 he had been decorated by the French Government and had looked upon his own pictures hanging in the Louvre.

The taint of commercialism is not entirely absent in Renoir. The quality of his work is uneven and there are some paintings that are little better artistically than commercial "calendar art." But these are the exceptions rather than the rule, and today Renoir's greatness as an artist is practically unquestioned.

But Renoir's place in the history of art is not easy to assign exactly. He is the exponent of no one school, but is rather an outstanding individual, like Daumier. Perhaps more than any one else, perhaps even more than Monet, he was responsible for the development of the mature Impressionist style, yet he did not remain an Impressionist in the sense that Monet did. Like the moderns, Renoir did not let Impressionism destroy his sense of form.

And then again, he contributed to the modern movement, yet he could not be called a modern. That was because he was such a great traditionalist—in the great tradition of Titian, Watteau, and Boucher. Renoir neither copied nor imitated Titian, yet the spirit of his work is nearer to Titian's than many of the Venetians of Titian's own time. But Renoir had nothing in common with the academic-realistic art of the nineteenth century.

Renoir, though not necessarily the greatest artist, is surely the greatest *painter*—as a painter—of modern times. No one surpasses him in the sheer, glorious application of pigment on canvas. No other's brush caressed the canvas so lovingly, no one had more love of oil color for its own sake, no one had a more passionate desire to just paint and paint and paint. Renoir is said to have painted every day of his life that he was physically able to do so. In the hospital for an operation, he painted the flowers sent to him. In his later years he was almost completely paralyzed by arthritis. Unable to hold the brush in his fingers, he had it strapped to his wrist; an elaborate device lifted his wheel chair so that he could reach far corners of the canvas. Under these difficult conditions, he painted some of the greatest masterpieces of his career.

However magnificent Renoir's achievements as a *painter* may be, it is not his painting that is of special interest to us in our study of modern art. Rather, it is his *drawing*.

Curiously, the academic critics of Renoir's time could find only fault with his drawing. His painting they could stomach begrudgingly, considering it "crude" and "rough," but they were sure that he could not draw. Indeed, they felt the same about *all* artists who refused to follow academic traditions of near-photographic realism. It never occurred to these critics that there was any other approach to drawing than that of painstaking imitation of nature.

Actually, Renoir's draughtsmanship is scarcely less competent than his painting. From a purely *modern* point of view, it is even more interesting than his painting, because Renoir's drawing not only reproduces the forms he saw before him, but also includes his reactions to those forms.

On page 139 we see a Renoir drawing of a nude, his favorite subject. Note the plumpness, the roundness, the *largeness* of the figure. One could well have the feeling that the flesh of this body might be three feet or more in thickness. In many of Renoir's drawings, his females look like titanic Amazons.

137　　　It might be assumed that Renoir liked to picture enormous women.

In that case, however, he would have selected Amazon-like models. Actually, his models (a number of whom have been photographed) were usually on the "petite" side, healthy but trim and neat; small rather than large. No, Renoir did not paint his models this way because he liked fat women, or big women.

He painted as he did because of his sensuous love of *form* for its own sake. He was sensitively aware of the roundness, the thickness, the bulk of form, and his foremost desire as a painter (or draughtsman) was not only to recapture these three-dimensional qualities on a two-dimensional canvas, but to *emphasize* them, to convey to others some of his own loving admiration for the monumental bulk of a thigh or torso, the roundness of a head, the cylindrical fullness of an arm or leg.

The female figure provided endless variations of the rich, round form that Renoir wanted to *draw*. (It also provided the subtle flesh *colors* he loved to tell about in *paint*.) It is for this reason he painted so many nudes. For such a painter there could be no better theme. Renoir's aesthetic approach to his art was intensely sensuous, but sensuous in the broad, general sense; there is a healthy awareness of the charm and charms of femininity, but there is no trace of the pornographic. He painted a bowl of flowers, the flashing waters of a river, or a nude female with the same joyous gusto.

Renoir: *Baigneuse*. This nude figure displays magnificent roundness and massiveness. It is sheer *form*, expressively depicted by the painter. In making us aware of this richness of form, Renoir was, in effect, "commenting" on the nature before him.

In his eagerness to convey his aesthetic feelings about the forms he painted, Renoir paid little heed to realistic accuracy in his drawings. The relatively slim models became "heftier," more massive and plump, on Renoir's canvases. And it didn't matter—except to the academic critics. The important thing was that, in his drawings, Renoir *had something to say* about the nature he painted, and that that something could be conveyed to others when they viewed his work. By thus adding the element of *comment*—interesting comment—to the process of drawing, Renoir made an important contribution to modern art.

Renoir's own "comment" was confined mainly to the massiveness and roundness of form. Later, other artists would express their feelings in their drawing about *other* aspects of what they saw. A Matisse, for example, would emphasize the decorative effect of a lock of hair, the oddity of a hooked finger, the curious planes and patterns of a seated figure. (See illustration, page 141.) Picasso would comment extensively in many drawings, acidly and brilliantly. And so would many others.

The expression of a great creative artist's feelings, injected into his drawing, had the effect of making that drawing much more interesting than if the drawing were completely impersonal and photographic in spirit. The greater the artist, the more interesting the comment. Or perhaps it should be stated the other way around. A new and more exciting

DURAND-RUEL

Drawing by Matisse. This beautiful modern drawing includes the artist'
emotional "comment" on what he saw. He makes us feel, as he did, th
decorative feeling of the strands of hair, the hooklike connotation of th
fingers, the dramatic length of the nose and face, the set of the chin as i
buries itself in the hand, the pensive cast of the eyes. According to academi
standards of realistic drawing, this sketch may appear clumsily drawn—
"out of drawing." Nevertheless, if we look at the drawing for a while, w
become less and less aware of these academic "errors" and more and mor
aware of its beauty and inner veracity. Actually, in a few lines, it provide
a more penetrating and complete idea of the appearance of the model tha
might be given by a much more detailed but less inspired oil paintin
Furthermore, this drawing reveals an exquisite sense of *pattern* and a lovel
decorative flow of line.

conception of drawing had been created, yet to those who looked only
for realistic accuracy, such drawing seemed "crude," or "distorted," or
"amateurish."

The idea of an artist "commenting" on his subject in his drawing is a
basic concept of modern art. The modern artist does not hesitate to
depart from strict realism to express his feelings in his work; he does not
hesitate to "distort" nature, the better to express roundness, or thinness,
or tallness, or any other attribute of form, or to emphasize the decorative
qualities, the rhythms, the patterns, the movement suggested by his subject. As modern art developed, its artists became more and more conscious
of their *right* to do this— their right of expression. It was the right to be
creative instead of being merely imitative.

Another basic characteristic of modern drawing should also be mentioned—its respect for *directness* and *spontaneity*. To most present-day
artists, there is no longer anything surprising or remarkable in the idea
of making a rapidly executed, *loose, free* drawing directly from the model,
without tracing or working over. Today, even commercial drawings are
often executed that way. But we may forget that this approach is a
relatively recent development, that not so many years ago the "loose" or
"free" drawing was looked upon as merely "careless" or "unfinished."
In the late nineteenth century the aim of drawing was to be realistically

accurate, detailed, and complete, and the artist was expected to keep at it, erasing and redrawing, until he had achieved that aim.

The early moderns revolted against this labored method of drawing. One of the leaders of the revolt was Gauguin. Gauguin's ideas on the subject are brilliantly expounded by Jan Gordon: *

His line, too, opens an interesting question in the art of drawing. Gauguin's custom, at last, was not to alter a line once he had put it down. He said that before the line was drawn an artist had a mental conception of what he wished to put down, but that once the line was upon paper, that which had been drawn, however imperfect it might be, had destroyed the conception which lay in the mind of the artist: that any alteration of this first drawn line could not really represent genuine correction, but only the fumbling after an ideal which had been lost; that thenceforth the artist was, as it were, but stumbling about in the dark, hoping by luck to recapture something which had escaped from him.

If we persist in considering drawing merely as copying a fact, this idea is of course absurd. But a large truth lies behind, if we think of

141   * Jan Gordon, *Modern French Painters*.

it as representing an image which exists in the mind alone, and only based on nature. In this case the drawn expression does destroy, or does materially alter the mental image, and an attempt to correct usually spoils, without recapturing any more than that which we had at first seized.

An important idea—and a fundamental part of the philosphy of modern art. Spontaneity, freshness of conception, were highly desirable, were to be eagerly sought regardless of the danger of what the academics called "errors of drawing." This idea, in its infancy in the 1880's and '90's, was not to attain its fullest implications until well along in the twentieth century. And similarly, the full development of an artist's emotional "comment" on and in his drawing, the approach so well exemplified by Renoir, also did not come until a later generation. Both ideas—that of "comment" and that of "spontaneity"—came to a focus in the drawings of Matisse and Picasso.

19   The Naïve, the Sophisticated, and the Primitive

As midnight approached, on the night of December 31, 1899, the whole world was waiting up, eager to greet the arrival of a new century. It was indeed a time for noise and fireworks and bubbling champagne by the magnum.

On the surface, things looked very good at the turn of the century. At this moment and in the decade following, probably more people were enjoying a greater degree of happiness—in a contented, complacent sort of way—than ever before, and alas, it appears, ever since. Outwardly, all was right with the world. Science had been bestowing her largesse with a lavish hand. The telephone, the incandescent lamp, the horseless carriage, the wireless, and a host of other inventions brought the promise of an easier, more abundant life. And new discoveries in medicine promised more years to enjoy this happier life. Blessed science!

The First Industrial Revolution—the Age of Steam—had been replaced by the Second Industrial Revolution—the Age of Electricity and Gasoline. Marvelous automatic machines had been invented, machines that did almost everything without the aid of a human hand. And there were other machines that made more machines.

Bourgeois society had become richer and more specialized. There were now the great bourgeoisie and the petty bourgeoisie. The great bourgeoisie were the fabulously wealthy merchant princes who could now afford to be philanthropists also, who could give to the public pretentious museums and libraries. The petty bourgeoisie—now the real middle class —were the clerks, the small shopkeepers, the technicians, the professional people, the small farmers. The engineers who designed the machines belonged to the petty bourgeoisie. The artists, too, came from this class.

At the bottom of the economic heap, as always, remained the laboring class, "the proletariat . . ." which, however, had already begun to revolt against its unhappy lot.

It was an era of intense national pride. A wave of nationalism and patriotism swept over the world, originating in the great industrial powers but reaching even the small "backward" countries as well.

On the surface, life in the days of the "gay nineties" and the first decade of the new century was delightfully prosperous and contented. But under the surface, trouble was brewing. Beneath the pleasant veneer of well-to-do life growled a sullen undercurrent of mysterious forces. Though it certainly was not apparent to the "average man" of 1900, these underground forces were rapidly gathering in strength, and a cauldron of revolutionary disturbance, after simmering for years, was now boiling up to a climax.

One of these gathering forces was the not-to-be-denied upsurge of the laboring classes, which had not only developed a class consciousness, but were now beginning to organize in strength. Economically, this organization was expressed in the trade unions, speedily growing in prestige and effectiveness. Politically, there was the trend toward a new and more violent form of socialism—the *revolutionary* socialism of Karl Marx. A significant aspect of this credo was its marked impatience with peaceful methods of curing the workingmen's troubles, its insistent demand for bloody revolution.

Another ominous portent of coming troubles lurked in the military preparations that underscored the proud nationalism of the great nations. Already, the Krupp factories were fashioning siege guns to demolish the turrets of Namur and Liege. But of this, the average man knew nothing at the turn of the century.

At the beginning of the new century, science and its machines had not yet opened the Pandora's box of economic troubles that were to plague the world a few years. "Technological unemployment" was relatively unimportant. But the machine age—with its new creature comforts—had already spawned one Frankensteinian offspring that was destined to stir up more difficulty in the new twentieth century world. This was the rapidly growing spirit of *materialism*. It, too, seemed a little thing at first. But its expansion had been relentless. And it is only today that men are beginning to appreciate how overwhelming has been the influence of this materialistic spirit, how corrosively destructive its power. Desirable or not, it became the keynote of recent times.

If the progressive artists had found themselves forced by circumstances into opposition to the materialism of the 1870's and 1880's, they now found themselves in even more violent opposition to the greater materialism of the new era. All the disturbing conditions that had surrounded the artists for the past thirty years were not only continued, but sharply accentuated.

The economic dislocation of the genuine creative artist remained unrelieved (his problem has not been satisfactorily solved today). There were jokes about artists starving in garrets, but it was no joking matter to the artists themselves. Forced to live very cheaply, the artists found themselves thrown in with the poor, the disillusioned, and the discontented; their nearest neighbors were often radical intellectuals already wholeheartedly in revolt against bourgeois society. It was only natural that artists should absorb some of this spirit of revolt.

Also, incidentally, it should be remembered that the capital of the art world was Paris, and Paris was in France. Of all the important western nations, France had shown the least enthusiasm for the changes of the industrial revolution, accepting them only as a matter of necessity and maintaining as much of the old individualism as possible. The bourgeois class and the machine age triumphed in France, as elsewhere, but the triumph was more hardly won and the spirit of dissent was never completely subdued. This background of French thought affected the ideas of the artists working in Paris; it helps to explain, in part, why the artists of France tended to embrace radical artistic innovations so much faster than the artists of England, Germany, and America—countries where the machine-age civilization had been accepted with a much more eager and thoroughgoing enthusiasm.

Whatever the causes, however, it is notable that about the year 1900 there was a strong trend in art in direct opposition to the prevailing materialism of middle-class thought. Furthermore, it was an opposition—a revolt—that was becoming definitely conscious of itself. Cézanne, Van Gogh, Gauguin were revolters, but they revolted blindly as individuals without a clear understanding of the historical significance of their revolt. The new generation of artists—that of Matisse and the "Fauves"—had a much clearer sense of the existence of their revolt, of its direction, and of what they were revolting against.

Of course, these young artists saw the traditional academic-realistic art of the day as the unquestioned expression of bourgeois culture. Academic-realistic art—the art of Cabanel and Bouguereau—was the kind of art purchased by bourgeois merchant princes and by the bourgeois-controlled salons and museums. And when the defenders of academic realism glibly tied their stilted, strictly nineteenth century art to the great traditions of the Greeks and the Renaissance, the young revolters not only hooted their derision at this impudence, but grimly shifted their attack to an assault on traditionalism itself.

It was in this atmosphere of increasing revolt that *primitivism* was born. The urge to turn to the primitive in art was no sudden caprice; it was the result of deep-seated causes, of powerful forces arising naturally out of the cultural history of the times. And having started on this path, the primitivising influence set off an artistic chain reaction of amazing effects that continued for years to come.

The typical well-to-do man of 1900 believed that his time represented the peak of civilization *in every way*. History, as he saw it, was a long climbing stair of progress with himself, and the people of his time, at the very top.

As far as science and scientific invention were concerned, he was obviously right. The facts were there to prove it. In other directions, he could *assume* that he was right because, as yet, no facts had appeared to prove otherwise. The great wars, and the great, prolonged economic depression of the 1930's, which did so much to create doubts as to the ultimate worth of mechanistic bourgeois civilization, were not even dreamed of at the turn of the century.

In art, the bourgeois critic may have had some qualms at times about claiming that the art works of his time surpassed those of the Renaissance masters or of the Greeks, but he could always salve his conscience by insisting that nineteenth century art (academic-realistic) was *at least as good as* that of the Greeks, the Florentines, and the Venetians, if not *possibly* better.* After all, wasn't the official nineteenth century art just as *realistic* (if not more so) as that of its classic predecessors? And wasn't traditional realistic art the only contemporary art that counted (to the late nineteenth century bourgeois, that is)?

To the conservative nineteenth century man, the arts of uncivilized peoples—such as the African savages or the natives of the Pacific islands—were not to be considered art at all. Nor was the art of "backward" peoples—such as the Chinese, the Japanese, or the Hindus—to be taken seriously as art. And surely, by the same token, prehistoric people, at the bottom of the ladder of progress, were not to be thought of as artists either.

Behind this late-nineteenth-century attitude toward other arts than its own were three basic ideas: First, that backward or *primitive* peoples lacked mechanical scientific knowledge and hence lacked "civilization," and therefore, also, lacked "art." Second, that since nineteenth-twentieth century culture was the pinnacle of all civilization, all previous artistic achievements must be incomplete or inferior. This applied particularly to archaic and prehistoric arts. And third, that the arts of primitive peoples obviously could not be considered mature "art" because of their lack of naturalistic realism. The primitives "did not know how to draw," or so it seemed.

Today, a half-century later, we know that this A.D. 1900 attitude was faulty, both in its reasoning and in its conclusions. Bitter experience is teaching us that scientific progress is no guarantee of man's progress in any other direction. We have discovered that the works of primitive man rate very high indeed in real artistic quality, whereas, conversely, the "civilized" late-nineteenth-century art is no longer considered the fine thing it was once touted to be.

Nevertheless, it is important to note that the prosperous, respectable, comfortable middle-class man of 1900 thought of his academic-realistic art as a laudable expression of his own "highest-on-earth" civilization. It is also important to note that he considered the arts of primitive people as crude, imperfect, and ugly—the feeble attempts of savages.

This viewpoint has particular importance because of the violence with which it was opposed and rejected by the young modern artists of the day. They were now embattled not only against academic-realistic art, but also

* Tell-tale evidence of such a curious viewpoint is at least implied in F. W. Ruckstull's fantastic diatribe against modern art, *Great Works of Art and What Makes Them Great.*

against bourgeois civilization itself, with all its traditions. In fact, they saw themselves forced into the position of being against "civilization"—against "tradition." The area of attack had been widened. This was the natural result of bourgeois civilization's shabby treatment of the artists and their art. It resulted in the stream of art turning in a new direction in search of a new source of inspiration.

The inspiration that the earlier moderns—Cézanne, Van Gogh, Seurat, and others—had found in the old masters was no longer considered quite sufficient by the younger generation of artists. The old masters could give something, but not enough. It was necessary to go farther back—to get away from the traditions of hated "civilization"—to find something in art that was *simple, fundamental, unspoiled,* yet something that was strong in emotional power; something spiritual and *antimaterialistic*; something the artist might draw out of his own inner consciousness.

The art of primitive peoples, the drawings of children, and provincial folk art seemed to have these desired qualities. Furthermore, these primitive arts were then being brought to public attention through the recently founded ethnological museums. Here was a guiding light the discontented artists could not ignore, and the advance guard of art was irresistibly drawn in a new direction, toward the *primitivistic.**

The words *primitive* and *primitivistic* do not mean quite the same thing. "Primitive," in art, refers to the work of a primitive, aboriginal people. "Primitivistic" describes the art of a modern, civilized people influenced by a desire to recapture "primitive" aesthetic emotions. Neither of the words should be thought of as having anything to do with the relative excellence or crudity of the work done.

Primitive and primitivistic arts fall into a number of different classifications, such as, for example:

Prehistoric art
African aboriginal art
Oceanic aboriginal art
American Indian aboriginal art, etc.
Archaic Oriental art
Medieval European art
Folk art
Child art
"Modern-primitive" art
Art of the insane
Primitivistic art—influenced by any or all of the others

Generally speaking, however, there are but two classifications of these arts that are of immediate interest to us, namely:

1. Genuine primitive art of primitive peoples:
    (a) Prehistoric art
    (b) African, Oceanic, Amerindian art, etc.

* The word is Robert J. Goldwater's, whose *Primitivism in Modern Painting* traces the development of primitivism in considerable detail.

2. The primitivistic art of civilized peoples:
   (a) Child art
   (b) "Modern-primitive" art
   (c) Primitivistic art

Curiously, the arts of primitive peoples are *not* crude, incompetent, or unfinished. They are, in fact, as will be shown presently, *highly sophisticated arts*, comparable in artistic quality to the best art civilized man has ever produced. If these native arts have seemed crude to us in the past, it is only because *we* have misunderstood the intent and achievement of the native artist.

Curiously, too, on the other hand, elements of apparent "crudity" and naïveté do characterize the *primitivistic* art of civilized peoples. Yet again, before passing judgment on any question of artistic quality or competence, one would do well to examine carefully the artist's intent and also his achievement (which in some cases might even be arrived at quite *unintentionally*).

That a civilized man should produce, under certain circumstances, art that is crude in appearance and naïve, and a primitive man produce art that is polished and sophisticated, might at first seem strange to us. But we must remember that *there is no pattern of progress in art as there is in mechanical science.* Art does not get better throughout time. It merely changes its outward appearance from time to time under different conditions and stimuli, just as fashions in clothing change. This is strikingly exhibited in a brief consideration of prehistoric art.

20   The Talented Troglodytes

Ages ago, long before the first farmer had appeared in this world, before pottery was known, before the dog and the horse had been domesticated, perhaps even before the bow and arrow had been invented, man had created great art. The artists were members of the Cro-Magnon race, the earliest known representatives of true man—*homo sapiens*—on earth. It was the Cro-Magnon race who chased into oblivion the apish Neanderthalers, shuffling creatures who could not stand fully upright and who had gorillalike bony ridges over their eyes.

Cro-Magnon man lived in the Upper Paleolithic era—the Old Stone Age. His art and culture reached its climax in the Magdalenian culture period, about 18,000 years ago.

Though the harsh post-glacial climate later whittled him down somewhat, the Cro-Magnon was a splendid physical specimen when he first appeared on the world scene—6 feet 4 inches or more in height, broad-

PREHISTORIC MAGDALENIAN CAVE ART. Magdalenian art, produced about 18,000 years ago, is the art of the Animal Age. Only animals were depicted, never vegetation, rocks, and the like. Men were rarely shown, and then only in disguised "grotesque" form. This art is characterized by its extremely vital and sensitive drawing, by its feeling of rhythm, by its gravity and seriousness, by its solemn air of profound mystery, and by its feeling for design, which is never absent.

chested, remarkably fleet of foot, and possessing a brain capacity slightly larger than that of modern man.

He lived by hunting, using chipped flint weapons as well as ingenious traps and pitfalls to snare the larger animals. Among his animal contemporaries were the now-extinct woolly rhinoceros and the woolly mammoth, as well as wild cattle, wild horses, and great herds of bison and reindeer.

His life was seminomadic in a steppelike Europe that was open and free of heavy forests at the time, but cold in climate. When shelter was necessary, he sought it at the mouths of the great caves or grottoes (or possibly in some rude, temporary shelter he himself may have constructed). But generally, he preferred to live in the open, following the wild herd animals that provided his food.

The most amazing thing about Magdalenian Cro-Magnon man was his art. His pictures were scratched on reindeer bone or on the stone walls of caves with sharp, skillfully made flint graving tools. Or the pictures were painted in several colors by a process that is strikingly similar to modern oil painting. A number of simple earth pigments—ochres and oxide of manganese—were ground to a fine powder in stone mortars and mixed on a palette of stone or flat reindeer bone with animal oils or fats. The pigment was carried in "tubes" made of the lower limb bones of the reindeer. The colors have proved remarkably permanent, and in such a cavern as that of Altamira, the entrance of which was hermetically sealed by a prehistoric landslide, the coloring is almost as fresh and brilliant today as when originally painted.

Magdalenian Paleolithic art was single-minded about subject matter. There was one subject—animals. Animals, particularly *food* animals—reindeer, bison, wild cattle, mammoth, wild horses (which were eaten, not ridden)—were pictured again and again. Vegetation, rocks, mountains, and so forth, *were never depicted.* Human beings were rarely shown at all, and then in a grotesque *masked* or *purposely disguised* form. But the animals were drawn, not only with great skill and accuracy, but also with a wealth of sensitive artistic feeling.

It has been said that the Magdalenians were the Paleolithic Greeks. The wild horses of the Magdalenians are depicted, in their own way, more understandingly than the horses on the Greek vases. It is remarkable, too, that this particular style of cave-man art constitutes what is perhaps the most naturalistic "period" of art before the advent of the Greeks themselves. It is less stylized than both the later prehistoric and the Egyptian arts that followed it.

But though naturalistic in a marked degree (for primitive people), it is also full of design; it is by no means photographically realistic in the sense that nineteenth century academic art is realistic. These cave drawings have a haunting inner vitality. Though the poses of the animals are relatively quiet, a rhythmic movement flows through every contour, and the undulations of line are so sensitive that at times they seem to quiver with real life. Then too, the juxtaposition of the animals, sometimes overlapping one another, is controlled by a sure design sense.

150

Certain peculiarities of Magdalenian art are worthy of special notice:

1. It is an art of contour. Though rounded form is clearly felt by the Paleolithic draughtsman, he makes little attempt to emphasize three-dimensional roundness, and he avoids modeling. This is because he simply was not interested in three-dimensionalism, and his art had little need of it. He wanted to capture the "look" of the animal, its life spirit, its movement; he was not interested in its "roundness" or its "feel." Furthermore, he had no architecture to suggest the advantages of three-dimensionalism. He visualized in terms of a flat cave wall, or of a distant vista of herd animals outlined against the horizon.

2. An immense knowledge of animal life is shown in these pictures. The poses are animal-like; not manlike. Paleolithic man knew more about animals than any man has since; he lived in the Animal Age. Never before or since have wild animals been quite so important to mankind.

3. The animals are always shown in the side view, practically never front or rear. This in itself indicates *another purpose* than that of merely making a picture of animals. The cave man wanted specifically to *identify* the animal for a purpose, and hence depicted the animal in its most important (and to him, most useful) view.

4. These cave pictures were made over a period of many thousands of years. Yet, while some drawings seem a little rougher or "cruder" than others, and others more polished, there is surprisingly little variation in style. This would seem to indicate that a strong traditionalism helped to guide the artist's hand. Yet again, in spite of this, miraculously there is no loss of freshness or vitality of drawing and little trend toward stylization.

5. A solemn, reverent spirit pervades all of this art. There is nothing trivial or meaningless. A poetry of emotion, hymnlike in quality, touches every drawing.

6. As previously stated, *men* are not shown, except disguised as grotesques. In addition to the engravings and paintings, small figurines, sculptured in the round, have been found. These female figures, such as the famous "Venus of Willendorf," are always fat and pregnant, with all parts of the body having to do with maternity accentuated. But the faces are always left blank. There are no features.

7. Paleolithic man lived *near the entrances* of the great grottoes, avoiding the damp, dark, and dangerous interiors. The paintings, however, are found in dark and remote caves with small openings, often barely large enough to admit the body of a man.

Obviously, the *purpose* of the cave man in making his animal paintings was a *religious-magic* one. Most authorities are agreed on this. The naturalism of Magdalenian art (so different from the highly abstract nature of most other primitive art) was probably due to a desire to increase the efficacy of the magic. *It is most unlikely* that this naturalism was due to any purely *artistic* desire to imitate nature. It is probable that these pictures were intended in some way to insure the continuance of the food supply of the tribe or clan.

The pictures *may* have been intended to propitiate the spirits of the animals killed or intended to be killed. And obviously there was some sort of taboo against identifying the human image, as certainly the skilled Paleolithic artist was *capable* of creating human images, if he so desired. Totemism, or other elaborate symbolisms also may have been involved in these pictures, particularly in that masterpiece of all, the mysterious "battle of the animals" on the ceiling of the cave at Altamira in northern Spain—the "Sistine Chapel" of prehistoric art.

None of these magic-religious intentions on the part of the Magdalenian man in any way destroy the value of the drawings and paintings as *art*. Regardless of his purpose, the cave man, working sincerely and emotionally, created great art—great because it is so vital, so inwardly poetic, so sensitive, so deeply felt and brilliantly expressed in terms of what was intended to be expressed.

Modern critics who write of primitive man's "sympathetic magic," as it is called, as a purely utilitarian practice ("primitive man's science"), are surely missing an important point—are thinking in terms of their own materialistic civilization rather than in terms of the early man's undoubtedly more spiritual culture. This religion-magic may have had a utilitarian purpose in one sense, but it certainly was not lacking in reverent religious values in other ways. Mystery and awe attended the magic rites of cave painting. Artist was priest, and priest artist. It was not that art was the handmaiden of religion, or vice versa. Art *was* religion! And why not?

The urge to create art—to create out of the joyousness of the spirit—is closely akin to the religious spirit. Both represent an uplifting of man out of himself and his material world, a reaching for something higher and better, an expression of the emotional, spiritual nature within. Both are a negation of the animal and the mechanical—both are a climbing to the stars.

That is why—throughout the ages, in all parts of the world, regardless of creed or even lack of creed—art and religion have gone hand in hand. Not, as the skeptics would have it, because they are useful to each other, but because both *are* each other, belong to each other.

Certain thoughts may be suggested by this study of prehistoric Magdalenian art. One is that one should take the precaution of investigating an artist's *purpose* before judging the value of his art. The purpose defines the achievement. Throughout the ages, there have been many different kinds of arts because they were created out of many different purposes.

For example, there exists another type of prehistoric rock painting, produced at almost the same time, whose characteristics are just about the exact opposite of Magdalenian art. This other type—the *Levant* style found in southern Spain and Africa—is characterized by *violent action*, the antithesis of Magdalenian calm and solemnity. Furthermore, Levant art is much more interested in *men* than in animals, and is more concerned with depicting what the men and animals are *doing* than with showing what they looked like. Hence, the Levant figures are stylized—almost pictographic—rather than naturalistic. Levant and Magdalenian (or "Franco-Cantabrian") arts are not only strikingly different, but the very nature of their differences indicates the obviously different *purposes* of their respective creators. Yet each art, in its own way, is high in artistic quality.

Another thought of importance, arrived at from a consideration of Magdalenian painting, is that, *even in this most naturalistic of all primitive arts*, design is always strongly in evidence. And if it is so amply evident here, it is all the more so in other primitive arts, which are much more highly designed than the Magdalenian. Hence, we can state the axiom (gratefully borrowing a phrase from Sheldon Cheney) that, among primitive peoples, "design is universal."

A third conclusion to be drawn—perhaps the most significant of all— is that in this ancient cave art there is nothing crude or incompetent, nothing "primitive" in the sense of ineptness or inability to achieve a desired artistic result. The Magdalenian was an accomplished artist, the more so when we consider the difficulty of drawing by scratching on rock or bone. In spite of this, his line is sure and bold, without working over, yet delicately sensitive at the same time. If there are certain unexplained peculiarities in this work, such as the superimposing of animals one over another, we must seek an explanation in the magic purposes which produced this art and which defined its apparent "limitations."

Surely, here is evidence that scientific *progress* and quality in art have no connection whatever. These ancient Paleolithic men, who had barely reached the stage of inventing the bow and arrow, who were the *first* known artists in the world, were also among the great artists of the ages. Their art evokes wonder and admiration today. Art came into the world full grown. Its creators were primitive people, but their art was not "primitive." It was not naïve. It was highly sophisticated.

21   Bronze Ancestors and Wooden Ghosts

Prehistoric art is by no means the only example of a sophisticated art produced by a so-called "primitive" people. Even more striking examples are provided by the relatively recent arts of the West African Negroes, the Polynesian islanders of the Pacific, and the American Indians. Of these, the art of the African Negroes has proved not only most stirring aesthetically, but also most important historically, especially in its influence on modern art.

About the year 1904 or 1905, some of the advance-guard modern artists of France, discontented with the art and the world of their time, and ever on the alert for new sources of inspiration, made an exciting discovery.

In a Paris curiosity shop they came upon some grotesquely carved wooden figures that looked unmistakably different from anything ever made by civilized man. The oddly carved figures were souvenirs brought back by the European conquerors of West Africa.

These figures, most of them less than two feet in height, also a number of equally exotic masks and small utensils, were just then finding their way into the London and Paris curiosity shops. Some of this plunder had been placed in the official ethnographic museums as specimens of the "industry" of the African "savages." But the greater part was being disposed of as curios, to be sold cheaply to anyone who cared for such oddities.

The possibility that these primitive sculptures might have real artistic value was undreamed of by the ethnographic museum curators. Even the first artists, who so eagerly pounced on their "finds" in the Paris shops, did not *fully* appreciate the artistic significance of the little statues. The "Fauve" discoverers of African art first collected it because it was exotic

and strange, but particularly because it was an art that was clearly *un-civilized*. It had symbolic value in the artists' battle with nineteenth century "civilization."

Not until a number of years later did clearer-eyed modern artists, led by Picasso, begin fully to appreciate the remarkable aesthetic qualities of the African sculptures and masks. Today, appreciation of African art has become general, and, at long last, these objects are gradually being moved from the ethnographic to the art museums, where they very properly belong.

There is little wonder the African statues and masks caught the eye of the artist collector. They are fascinating things. Oddly formed, with long bodies and short squat legs, with strange, haunting faces, they instantly attract attention. One senses in a glance a disturbingly profound difference between these primitive statuettes and the works of civilized man. There is something about them that instills a feeling of awe, and one is not surprised to learn that these are religious objects of one kind or another.

Longer acquaintance with the African sculptures—and with the elements of the primitive religion that fostered them—increases our appreciation of their haunting expressiveness. We seem to look into the African soul and sense its fear and superstition, its fatalism, and its brutally realistic attitude toward some of the harsher facts of a harsh life. We feel, uneasily, the throb of tom-toms and the sinister presence of dark jungle rites.

Michael E. Sadler writes: "Much of it indeed, like many of the masks from the Congo, becomes, as we concentrate our thoughts upon its form and meaning, even more horrible and terrible than when we first gave it a cursory glance. There are depths of cruelty in primitive religion. Spectres and bloodshed haunt much of West African sculpture. . . ."

Yet there is sympathy, and tenderness, and quaint humor in this carving.

Any attempt to find an "explanation" of this art in a study of its historical background, however, is likely to be unrewarding. The outlines of native African history are still very vague and cast little light on the creation of the Negro sculptures. Although the discovery of the famous "Benin Bronzes," produced in the sixteenth and seventeenth centuries, indicates cultural traditions dating far into the past, the best African art is more recent. Constructed of wood and other perishable materials, the most interesting objects cannot be more than two hundred years old. And yet again, they are not contemporary. The searing touch of European civilization has already completely destroyed native artistic traditions, and the fine African sculptures are no longer being produced. The richest period of this art, as we know it, probably lies between 1750 and 1875.

The little African statues are exactly what the missionaries thought them to be—idols and fetishes. But they exist in a great variety of types and were constructed for a great variety of purposes. Some, associated with ancestor worship, are actually stylized portraits. Others are fertility idols, and still others fetishes for conjuration, such as the nail-studded figures used for driving away illnesses.

The ritual masks represent an even wider variety of expression and purpose. Some are war masks, some hunting masks, some circumcision ritual masks, some masks to be worn at funeral and memorial ceremonies. Each tribe and each purpose had its own variation of type and materials. There are masks of wood, wicker, cloth, straw, parchment, ivory, and masks made of human skin. The masks had a particular purpose—to conceal personality. The wearer lost his own personality in the complete disguise of the mask and was "temporarily freed from the conventional restraints of common life." * Wearing a ghost mask, he believed himself to be a ghost in fact.

* Michael E. Sadler, *Arts of West Africa*.

Of these fetishes, it should be noted that their function is basically religious, or magic-religious, just as were the cave men's animals painted on the cave walls. It should also be noted that these sculptures are the products of a purely African and Negro artistic tradition; the effect of any outside influence is negligible.

It is not its exotic quality, nor its implications of mystery and terror, nor the circumstances of its creation, that give African Negro sculpture its enormous importance in the realm of art. It is its amazing *design*, brilliantly conceived in three dimensions.

If we close our eyes to the representational connotations of the Negro statues and study them only as examples of abstract design, we will quickly see how masterful is this design. The odd bumps and distortions which have little meaning as representation are discovered to be important elements in an over-all design conception. Studying the sculptures further, we begin to appreciate the Negro sculptor's remarkable sophistication as a designer, the almost unbelievable sensitivity of his touch. Subtle curves are executed with a delicacy and sureness seldom equaled in any art anywhere. Masses are related to one another with an intuitively perfect aesthetic sense. There is an economy of form, every part contributing importantly to a unified total effect. And finally, a tremendous surge of creative emotion flows through the entire work, giving it authority and life.

We have seen that the art of the Paleolithic Cro-Magnons was primarily an art of *two* dimensions, an art of contour presented on the flat background of a cave wall. The art of the West African Negro, in contrast, is almost totally *three*-dimensional—totally *sculptural*. It is sculpture conceived *entirely* in the round, not at all as the bas-relief so characteristic of archaic European art.

In his *Vision and Design*, Roger Fry writes:

> The sculptors seem to have no difficulty in getting away from the two-dimensional plane. The neck and the torso are conceived as cylinders, not as masses with a square section. The head is conceived as a pear-shaped mass. It is conceived as a single whole, not arrived at by approach from the mask, as with almost all primitive European art. The mask itself is conceived as a concave plane cut out of this otherwise perfectly unified mass.

Again, Mr. Fry casts light on what might seem to us to be oddity of proportion in Negro statues. He continues:

> Our emphasis has always been affected by our preferences for certain forms which appeared to us to mark the nobility of man. Thus we shrink from giving the head its full development, we like to lengthen the legs and generally force the form into a particular type. These preferences seem to be dictated not by a plastic bias, but by our reading of the physical symbols of certain inner qualities which we admire in our kind, such, for instance, as agility, a commanding pres-

ence, or a pensive brow. The Negro, it seems, either has no such preferences or his preferences happen to coincide more nearly with what his feeling for pure plastic design would dictate.

For instance, the length, thinness, and isolation of our limbs render them extremely refractory to fine plastic treatment, and the Negro scores heavily by his willingness to reduce the limbs to a succession of ovoid masses sometimes scarcely longer than they are broad. Generally speaking, one may say that his plastic sense leads him to give its utmost amplitude and relief to all the protuberant parts of the body, and to get thereby an extraordinarily emphatic and impressive sequence of planes. So far from clinging to two dimensions, as we tend to do, he actually underlines, as it were, the three-dimensionalness of his forms. It is in some such way, I suspect, that he manages to give to his forms their disconcerting vitality, the suggestion that they make of being not mere echoes of actual figures, but of possessing an inner life of their own.

As Mr. Fry and others have pointed out, the Negro sculptor shows an exquisite taste in the handling of his material, bestowing on it painstaking care to give it its marvelous texture and finish. Perhaps this is only a logical corollary to the obvious fact that material is a primary factor in the African sculptor's whole conception of his work. The cylindrical forms of the statues, for example, must have been strongly suggested by the tree trunks from which they were carved. Cowrie shells were found to be startlingly effective as "eyes," and so on.

Anyone who has actually *seen* some of these African statues (seeing them "in the round" gives a much better idea of their aesthetic subtlety than does a pictured reproduction) can have no doubts about the maturity and sophistication of this art. In its own special way, within its own areas of limitation, it is perhaps the most sophisticated art on earth—and one of the great arts of all time. Though produced by a so-called "primitive" people, it is in no way crude or childish or inept, a fact which we can readily perceive provided we clearly understand that the Negro sculptor has made no attempt to be accurately representational. The little statues are the embodiments of religious and aesthetic emotions, they are not representations of anything corporeal.

Many of the qualities that interest us in African Negro art are also to be found in the native Polynesian arts of the South Seas and in the several arts of the American Indians. Yet these arts are each quite different from that of Africa. Polynesian art is somewhat more decorative, more ornamental, but also less forceful in its emotional impact. The art of the nomadic Indians of North America is of the decorative type. On the other hand, the arts of the Mexican civilizations are notably architectural and display a peculiar affinity with the architectural sculpture of the Orient. But regardless of the locale or the time period of any of these "primitive" arts, one universal characteristic is always present—unceasing emphasis on *design*.

Why is this? In his *Art as Experience*, the philosopher John Dewey suggests an answer:

Order cannot but be admirable in a world constantly threatened with disorder—in a world where living creatures can go on living only by taking advantage of whatever order exists about them, incorporating it into themselves. In a world like ours, every living creature that attains sensibility welcomes order with a response of harmonious feeling whenever it finds a congruous order about it.

For only when an organism shares in the ordered relations of its environment does it secure the stability essential to living. And when the participation comes after a phase of disruption and conflict, it bears within itself the germs of a consummation akin to the aesthetic.

And:

All interactions that affect stability and order in the whirling flux of change are rhythms. There is ebb and flow, systole and diastole: ordered change. The latter moves within bounds. To overpass the limits that are set is destruction and death, out of which, however, new rhythms are built up.

Also:

The first characteristic of the environing world that makes possible the existence of artistic form is rhythm. There is rhythm in nature before poetry, painting, architecture, and music exist. . . .

The larger rhythms of nature are so bound up with the conditions of even elementary human subsistence, that they cannot have escaped the notice of man as soon as he became conscious of his occupations and the conditions that rendered them effective. Dawn and sunset, day and night, rain and sunshine, are in their alternation factors that directly concern human beings.

The circular course of the seasons affects almost every human interest. When man became agricultural, the rhythmic march of the seasons was of necessity identified with the destiny of the community. The cycle of irregular regularities and the shape and behavior of the moon seemed fraught with mysterious import for the welfare of man, beast, and crops, and inextricably bound up with the mystery of generation. With these larger rhythms were bound up those of the ever-recurring cycles of growth from seed to a maturity that reproduced the seed; the reproduction of animals, the relation of male and female, the never-ceasing round of births and deaths.

And finally:

Thus, sooner or later, the participation of man in nature's rhythms, a partnership much more intimate than is any observation of them for purposes of knowledge, induced him to impose rhythm on changes where they did not appear. The apportioned reed, the stretched string and taut skin rendered the measures of action conscious through song and dance. Experiences of war, of hunt, of sowing and reaping, of the death and resurrection of vegetation, of stars circling over watchful shepherds, of constant return of the inconstant moon, were undergone to be reproduced in pantomime and generated the sense of life as drama. The mysterious movements of serpent, elk, boar, fell into rhythms that brought the very essence of the lives of these animals to realization as they were enacted in dance, chiseled in stone, wrought in silver, or limned on the walls of caves. The formative arts that shaped things of use were wedded to the rhythms of voice and the self-contained movements of the body, and out of the union technical arts gained the quality of fine art. . . .

Now what else is design but the applying of order to the disorderly—the deriving of rhythm and form from the general chaos of the physical world! Inevitably, the great rhythms of nature—the ebb and flow of the tides, the alternation of night and day—led primitive man to rhythmic design in his art. His struggle to find an organized pattern in his life was paralleled by his struggle to reduce, in his art, the chaotic disarray of natural objects to simplified, orderly forms. He drew by designing. And in design he found a fundamental kinship with the great rhythmic forces of the universe.

Since its first appearance, African sculpture has served to inspire modern-thinking artists. In particular, it influenced the stream of modern art importantly at two different times.

First, about the year 1905 African art greatly excited the imaginations of the then most modern group of artists, the famous "Fauves." They were impressed both by its exotic nature and by its obvious freedom from the stamp of the hated Western "civilization." African art led them, along the lines of their own inclinations, toward the *primitivistic*.

Second, about four or five years later the impact of African sculpture on the ideas of the artist Picasso led to the development of Cubism. This influence was more fundamental, in a sense, than the earlier influence on the Fauves. Picasso's abstract design is more closely akin to the aesthetics of Negro sculpture than was the primitivism of the Fauves. Both influences, however, are historically significant.

It is the earlier influence that concerns us here. (The effect on Cubism will be discussed later.) The Fauves, in admiring the "primitive" Negro art, soon came to admire its distortions and oddities and were led to at least toy with the idea of introducing similar distortions in their own work. Their purpose was to recapture some of the *unspoiled, "childlike," anticivilized* character of primitive art.

160

"My five-year-old child can draw better than that!"

The intent behind this oft-repeated jibe at modern art is so transparent it hardly needs comment. Nevertheless, it is peculiarly interesting to us at this time because of the enormous misconceptions it implies—misconceptions not only of the aims of modern art, but also, more importantly, of the art of the five-year-old child. It clearly reveals that the parental adult looks down upon his child's rambling scribbles as nothing more than unskillful attempts at representation in the academic adult manner. Never once is there any suspicion that the child's artistic intentions might be something quite different from what the adults about him expect.

Yet such, precisely, is the case. It is now established beyond a doubt that the world of child art is entirely different from the world of adult art and is not to be judged by the alien standards of grown-up art. At the same time, the world of child art is aesthetically significant in its own right and has much to teach the more sophisticated artists of the adult realm. In many ways, the child is indeed the artistic father of the man; and in the peculiar processes of childish development we may see indicated a path that has often led, in the past, to the mature development of a great creative artist.

The child's approach to his art is intensely direct, honest, and fundamental to a degree that would be impossible of achievement by any adult. Because of this, child drawing reflects a freshness, a directness, and an inner sincerity that no adult work can quite duplicate, however superior adult work may be in other directions.

The basic developmental stages of child art are astonishingly alike among children of all social strata, among all races and among all the nations of the world, and apparently have been so throughout the ages. Here is the well-defined road trod by the great artists of both past and present. Out of the nebula of the childish scribble has emerged the universe of art.

We have the psychologists to thank for a great deal of our knowledge of child art. As far back as the end of the nineteenth century, psychological research workers began to collect and study children's drawings. Out of the mass of data gathered and analyzed since then has come a startling series of discoveries about the child's remarkable expression of himself in his art. The intent of the psychologists, of course, has been entirely scientific, but these scientists and educators have nevertheless also made an important contribution to the aesthetic appreciation of art.

Particularly interesting, from an aesthetic viewpoint, is the whole-heartedness with which the young child reveals his inner feelings—his emo-

Santa and the Pussy Cat, by Jimmy
T., aged 5.

A Lady in Her Garden with a Dog,
by Eileen, aged 5.

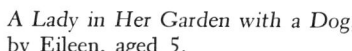

tions, his fears, his hopes, his imaginings, his thoughts—in his scribbly
drawings. The young child is a self-centered animal; he expresses *himself*
extensively in his childish art. As he grows older, he becomes more aware
of the presence of other people and other things about him; they appear
with growing emphasis in his art, which becomes less self-centered, more
self-critical, and more and more attentive to the ideas and opinions of
others.

As he grows older, the child's drawing "improves," but in a peculiar
manner. He goes through a sequence of *developmental stages* which,
with equal opportunities for drawing, tend to be approximately the same
for nearly all children of the same age and intelligence. Children start
drawing in the same way; do the same things as their development pro-
ceeds from phase to phase. As an artist, the child develops fastest if left
to himself. The imposition of adult "teaching" hinders him rather than
helps, and may completely stunt any further development.

This, basically, is because the child is not trying to be an "artist," is
not in the least concerned with "learning to draw," and never dreams of
trying to imitate nature (if given a model, he completely ignores it). *He*

162

Clown's Head, by John Browning, aged 12.

CHILDREN'S ART. The art of children and the art of adults belong to two different worlds. The child's drawings are a direct expression of his inner imaginative and emotional life and are not in the least concerned with imitation of nature. The child "draws what he knows, not what he sees." Because a child expresses his feelings in his pictures without inhibition, his natural sense of design quickly displays itself. The aesthetic qualities of such pictures were appreciated by the early modern artists. (Pictures reproduced from "Picture & Pattern Making by Children" by R. R. Tomlinson. Studio Publications.)

is merely trying to express himself, his feelings, and his ideas. His art is not really drawing at all, but a form of picture-writing, a means of communication. (It may also be considered a form of childish "magic"; the child-artist enjoys a sense of power in creating whatever he will on a piece of paper.)

Hence, the child consistently *"draws what he knows, not what he sees."* He emphasizes, even exaggerates, the essential, completely rejects the irrelevant. This is the key to child art, the explanation of much of its oddities, its stylized schematic approach to drawing (if a circle will express a "head," and that is all the child wishes to express at the moment, then a circle suffices), and of its progressive developmental stages (which represent not "improvement" in drawing, but actually a widening of interests and observations).

The age at which a child begins to draw depends to a considerable extent on when drawing materials are put in his or her hands. Babies as young as a year old (or perhaps even younger) will make haphazard marks if given a crayon and paper. The average beginning age, however, is slightly older. Florence L. Goodenough writes: *

> The baby of 18 months finds a pencil or crayon a fascinating object. Grasped in a chubby fist, it leaves visible results whenever it is moved over wall or paper. The baby looks at his accomplishments with amazement and delight.
>
> At first he has no interest beyond mere scribbling, but as the first edge of his joy in the movement and its immediate results begins to wear off, his attention is drawn more and more strongly to the lines he has drawn. . . .

The next step beyond the first chance lines is the scribble. Instead of just striking the paper haphazardly, the baby leaves the crayon on the paper and moves his hand about. Before long, the hand movement falls into an inevitable muscular expression, the hand swings back and forth in a natural rhythmic motion, and "wavy" or "rhythmic" scribble is produced. The child is delighted! From then on he scribbles with ever-increasing energy, often producing dense masses of the wonderful scribble.

The wavy scribble is the first conscious step of mankind along the road that leads to art. It occurs in all parts of the world and with children of all classes. It is as natural as learning to walk.

Later, the back-and-forth wavy scribble takes on variations, often becoming the woolly-looking "circular" scribble. If the two-year-old child is given paint and color, he applies it in blobby, scribbly masses, sometimes covering one color with another. In any case, the child becomes intensely absorbed in scribble-making and repeats the scribble or painted daubs again and again.

Psychologists (notably Rose H. Alschuler and La Berta Weiss Hattwick), studying these early efforts, decided that they were far from being the meaningless daubs they seemed to be to most adults. Close study discovered marked differences in the seemingly formless daubs, and that these special characteristics were remarkably revealing of the inner emotional life of the child. Use of *color* appeared particularly significant at the age of two to four.

In their *Painting and Personality*, Alschuler and Hattwick write:

> There is something fantastic about the notion that among young children the use of red connotes one emotional state, the use of yellow a different one, and the use of black means something else again. Although to an amazing extent this was found to be true, a bald statement of this kind smacks of charlatanism. A nondiscriminating use of the facts which we shall present would be just that.
>
> Yet systematic and objective investigation of the present field brought us to the conclusion that color, spontaneously used by young children of the age range studied, quite specifically seems to be a language of the feelings for which there tends to be, in our culture at

* "What Children's Drawings Tell Us," *Parents Magazine*, June, 1944.

least, a quite general, if not universal code. Once children begin to use colors realistically rather than symbolically, they take on different meanings or values than are found in the early years of abstract color usage.

More specifically:

As one observes children's paintings, one discovers that some children consistently choose warm colors, such as red, yellow, and orange, whereas others choose cooler colors, such as blue, black, green, and brown.

Those children who consistently favored warm colors tended, for the most part, to manifest the free emotional behavior, the warm affectionate relations, and the self-centered orientation natural for children of this age.

Those children who consistently favored cold colors tended as a group to stand out for their highly controlled, overadaptive behavior. They were likely to be critical, assertive, and/or undemonstrative toward others. . . .

Our observations suggest that individual nursery school children who consistently focused on cold colors tended to be restraining or repressing their inner feelings. Their paintings were likely to reflect their overt behavior and often gave no clue to their inner drives. . . .

Developmental data also support the view that emphasis on cold colors is not natural for the 2-to-4-year-old child who is adjusting happily. Once children have progressed naturally, as most of them do, from impulsive behavior to the level of conscious control and from mass technique to work with line and form, a preference for cold or cooler colors becomes natural, and such preference no longer reflects inadequate adjustment.

And so on, in fascinating detail.

The authors of *Painting and Personality* describe the pre-school child:

During the span of their lives between 18 months and 5 years children are in the process of making a striking transition both in their inner drives and in their overt behavior.

At 18 months children primarily do the things they *feel* like doing, regardless of what other people wish or think. They are likely to be continuously active, impulsive, and self-centered.

In contrast, the 4-or-5-year-old is beginning to do those things which other people approve and expect; he is attempting to control impulses in order to behave in socially acceptable ways.

While children are in the process of making the swing from impulsive toward reasoned responses and behavior, they are making a parallel shift from purely subjective self-centered interests to relatively objective concern for people and the world about them. These changes take place gradually throughout the nursery school years. During this period, as throughout life, dominance of interest shifts continuously from subjective to objective and back again.

The age of one to three is the age of unrestrained emotion, the age of transition from babyhood to childhood, the age of self, the age of the physical and of the mastery of the simple physical functions of life, the "age of manipulation." Its artistic expression is the *scribble*—wavy, circular, or variegated.

The following period, the age of three to six is the age of introduction to the outside world, the age of wonder and discovery, of entry into the land of imagination, of the beginning of mastery over self, of the first real awareness of others and the first social contacts, and the first momentous trip to school. Artistically, this age of discovery is characterized by the transition from the formless scribble to typical "child drawing" with its crude, but recognizable objects.

Form emerges from the scribble but gradually. The scribble at first becomes less haphazard, less prolific, and sooner or later the child gives part of the scribble a *meaning*. This tangle of lines becomes "mama" or "a flag" or a "man"—although actually there is as yet no attempt at representation; it is the same kind of scribble as before. This is the "naming" stage.

At this period, the child begins to develop some simple abstract forms, crudely of course: a rough simulation of a circle, a wobbly quadrilateral, crossing lines, and the like. Out of these develops the first attempt at a human figure—a rough circle representing a head, two shaky lines of varying length suggesting legs. Having thus discovered a formula for depicting a human being, the child repeats it many times, making the same picture-formula do for "papa," "mama," "baby" or anyone else. Only very gradually are improvements instituted, and these in the same schematized manner.

Perhaps the first addition is likely to be that of some enormous eyes, sometimes bigger than the head itself. There may be from one to a dozen or more of these eyes, the young child's conception of number being very hazy. Later the idea of "twoness" become established, and the eyes get smaller in size, but still consist of simple circles. What is particularly interesting about this is that this approach to drawing is practically universal; nearly all children, all over the world, depict their first human figures this same way.

Likewise, the ensuing developmental stages of drawing are remarkably similar (although the precise *ages* vary somewhat). Most children draw legs before arms, eyes before ears, hats before hair, and often buttons before torsos. The child draws what interests him, leaves out what doesn't, and buttons (also armholes in sleeves) are a matter of great importance to a three- or four-year-old. What the child finds exciting, he either repeats many times or exaggerates in size. (That's why a child who likes flowers— or buttons—draws *so many* of them.)

At all times, the drawing is schematic, a symbol, a handy form of picture-writing. The child draws a somewhat imperfect, but adequate, formalized symbol for a man. That is enough. He *never* tries to imitate the appearance of a man beyond his simple formula.

However, as the child artist grows older, his visual and imaginative horizon broadens and he feels a natural need to put more detail in the drawings that express his inner imaginings. Legs are not enough, hence arms and torsos develop and fingers sprout like grass at the ends of arms. Heads develop mouths, and eventually ears, but are seen full-face for many years. Much of this basic development occurs between the years of three and six.

What and why does the child draw—particularly if he is not *imitating* the appearance of the world about him? He draws what he is thinking about, what excites his emotions, and particularly what his imagination conjures up. He draws from within out. All child pictures "have a story," although frequently adults experience difficulty in finding out what it is. Sometimes the story is made up as the child draws and changes before the drawing is completed. It is because of its close tie with the inner imaginative life of a small child that the child's "art" often seems so remote to adults.

What adult would think, as one child did, of drawing a staircase from earth to heaven with a figure (God) carrying another (a dead man) upstairs to heaven?

What adult would think of expressing *Silence*—as did a child—by drawing a face without a mouth?

And then there was the little girl who thought the rain outside drab and depressing, so she improved on nature, drew a picture of the rain with each raindrop of a different bright color.

Finally (these instances could go on forever), there is the story told by Hilda Walley Oldham of the child of six who, in typical childlike "X-ray" fashion, "drew a cat full of mice; a mouse is shown 'going down its throat, so it is choking and bad breath is coming from its mouth because it has eaten too many mice!' "

This is the limitless world of childhood, not the cramped and ordered domain of adults!

The subject matter of child drawing tends to be much the same everywhere in the early years, although the effects of environment tend to become more and more important as the child grows older (country children draw more animals, city children draw more people).

Up to the age of ten, children prefer to draw the human figure (usually representing "mama," "papa," self, and other close acquaintances) in preference to any other subject. Universally, boys seem to like to draw ships, motor cars, airplanes, and "fierce men firing guns." Girls like flowers, houses, perambulators, and so forth, but especially houses. Flags are popular with all children, and at the age of six there is a particular fondness for vehicles.

As the school age approaches, many children delight in making imitation "writing" or in forming letters of the alphabet—sometimes accurately, but often upside down, backward, or otherwise incorrectly—of course, without understanding of the letters' meaning.

167   From the age of six on to eight or ten, *if the child is encouraged and is*

not interfered with by adult ideas about learning to draw, his proficiency in drawing should increase rapidly and naturally. This improvement will be along childlike lines, that is, it will continue to be imaginative, non-imitative, and will come from memory and knowledge instead of direct observation. Nevertheless, more will have been seen and remembered, and the childish figures will become more naturalistic and complete, the childish line firmer and more sophisticated.

Helga Eng, in her *Psychology of Children's Drawings*, writes:

> The study of the early drawing of children shows that a significant and regulated development is found in the apparently valueless and planless drawing of children. It appears on the one hand as a progress in ability to draw and in increasing mastery of line and form; on the other hand, progress in drawing is the expression of the gradual unfolding of the child's soul.
>
> For drawing is, like talking, a means of expression, crippled and undeveloped in the case of most grown-up people, but in the case of children, still alive and full of activity, however incomplete the products may appear to adult eyes.

If the child continues to draw in his school years and *if* his natural approach is not inhibited by adverse outside influences, he should make not only better and better drawings, but his natural senses of color and design should also find expression, enabling him to create ever more interesting and complex compositions. No subject will be too difficult for him, not even the roaring traffic of Times Square, or the bustle and color of a three-ring circus, or any other complicated scene. He can draw anything, because he is still drawing *what he knows*. Such a child, at the age of twelve or fourteen, is on his way to becoming an artist. He will teach himself, step by step, how to put objects in back of each other, how to give his figures action and life, and finally, in the years from fourteen to eighteen (or older) he will develop a true perception of form (oddly enough, only one thing needs to be *taught* him—*perspective!* *). He will, if he can continue to retain his childlike independence, imagination, and personal mastery over his work, not only absorb the dull and obvious requirements of "adult" art in due time, but proceed on to a richer and more exciting *creative* art of his own. *If*, an adult, he can retain the open eyes and individualized approach of the child, he will at least be treading the trail that leads to greatness in art and he should advance as far as his own capacities permit.

But in all this, there remains a great big *if*.

The big *IF* is this. Beginning at about the age of six and continuing until adolescence, the uninhibited child artist faces a number of developmental hazards—hazards so formidable that few children continue their natural artistic development beyond the age of ten or twelve, if they get that far.

The most destructive force acting to bring the child's natural artistic progress to an end is the constant pressure brought by adults—parents,

---

* Indicating, as many artists have maintained, that perspective is only an artificial convention and not nearly as much a "scientific law" as most laymen believe it to be.

teachers, and other older people—to "teach" the child adult art, that is, to induce him to copy or imitate nature. The effect of this effort is calamitous. As pointed out previously, the child has no intention of imitating nature, and the requirement that he do so at first confuses him and then, finally, bores him to the extent that he stops drawing altogether.

The child does not take criticism gracefully, and why should he? He sees no fault in his drawing, because it expresses exactly what he is thinking and feeling, perhaps better than he can express it in words. Criticism from an adult, who is thinking only of *drawing perfection* (which the child is *not*), is completely misunderstood and taken as a personal attack. The child, wounded, is discouraged from drawing further.

Even if adult pressure—well meant though it may be—does not obliterate the child's creative impulses immediately, it may inhibit the youngster's artistic expression to the point of mediocrity. It has been said that many a school child of ten is no longer able to draw what he could without effort at the age of six.

Fortunately, in some schools today, the child is encouraged to draw naturally in his own way; but these schools are still the exception rather than the rule. The result is seen in the decline of childish artistic expression in the school years.

Another important hazard to the development of the child artist is the perfectly natural competition of other interests. We have seen that the self-centered child of three gradually becomes more and more aware of the outside world as he approaches school age. In the grammar school years, from six to ten or twelve, the process continues, even accelerates. The child turns almost entirely away from self at times, becomes gregarious and increasingly desirous of winning the good opinion of others. Not only human beings, but interesting *things* about him increase in importance, and curiously, in the drawings of children of this age, human figures become smaller and smaller in relation to the surrounding scenes. Many a budding child artist drops by the wayside in this period because he is lured away by other (usually more social or otherwise more congenial) ways of expressing himself.

The age of ten (some authorities say twelve) seems to be the danger point, the low tide of most children's interest in art. If the child's interest, however, is kept alive through this difficult period by wise encouragement, he is quite likely to develop very rapidly in the following period of adolescence, a time when interest turns back again to *self*.

Throughout all this discussion, a vital question in connection with child art has remained to be answered. The question is, is it *art* at all? And if so, how "good" are children's drawings as works of art?

To the average adult, the child's scribblings—uncertain in line, out of proportion, lacking in conventional detail and the conventional mechanics of realistic representation—do not seem to be what the adult thinks of as "art" at all. But to many *artists*, children's drawings and paintings display aesthetic qualities not appreciated by the literal-minded layman. The child puts down what he has in mind with a directness, a freshness, and a boldness that is often the despair of many a mature professional. The child's work crackles with originality and imagination.

The child does not draw to imitate nature; neither does he draw for beauty, nor for any *conscious* aesthetic reason. Nevertheless, an unconscious aesthetic feeling underlies children's art; the child's natural sense of design plus his untrammeled freedom of expression often results in astonishing design patterns. Add to this the youngster's totally uninhibited use of color. (Until well along in years, the child applies color abstractly rather than naturally. That is, instead of making a tree brown and green, he may entirely disregard natural appearances and make it purple and red, or any other color that pleases his fancy.) As a result, child art abounds in aesthetic values.

Hence, the work af a sensitive child is undoubtedly *art*, in fact much more art than a dull but polished picture by an outwardly skillful, but inwardly uncreative, adult artist. Roger Fry, distinguished English art critic and one-time curator of paintings at the Metropolitan Museum of Art, wrote, "The fact is that almost all children's drawings have some merit."

In fact, he considered them to "have more aesthetic merit than all but the best art of the modern adult."

This is perhaps a highly enthusiastic statement, subject to quibble in some quarters, but it *can* be said that many of the *best* of child pictures are more deserving of a place on our walls and in our museums than many of the adult pictures now hanging there. On the other hand, the mature work of a really great adult artist will of course surpass in lasting interest the limited expression of a child. The difference is perhaps quantitative rather than qualitative. In fact, the work of a great creative artist will *include* a great deal of the child's originality and freshness of approach, and add to it the richness and power of a grown-up mind.

Attempts to find a close similarity between child art and the art of prehistoric or primitive peoples have largely failed. Child art—naïve, intensely individual, and "crude-appearing" in execution—is quite a different thing from the mature sophisticated arts of the Cro-Magnons or the West African Negroes. These arts are truly *primitive*, whereas child art is better described as *primitivistic* (although both terms are purely arbitrary).

At the dawn of the twentieth century, however, no one made any such distinction between primitive and primitivisitic. To the conservatives, African art, cave art, and child art *all* looked crude and inartistic. To the young revolutionaries in art, both primitive and primitivistic arts seemed to offer the same unspoiled, anticivilized qualities they were seeking.

These young artists were quick to appreciate the freshness, sincerity, and originality—the purity of vision—of children's drawings. Some of this they tried to incorporate in their own work, which itself became more and more primitivistic; and the influence of child art added itself to the influences of prehistoric and "savage" arts in turning the stream of modernism into new channels. The results of these primitivising influences are seen in the work of the Fauves, even more so in the paintings of the German Expressionists, and are also evident in the abstractions of the Cubists. In fact, to this day, a deep admiration for the primitive remains a basic tenet in the ideology of modern art.

170

23 Henri Rousseau and the Popular Masters

One other type of primitivistic art remains to be considered—the art of the *modern primitives* or *popular masters*.

This is the primitive-appearing, self-taught art of certain individuals who did not originally set out to be artists, but who took up painting in later life. These *modern primitives* were usually very simple people from humble walks of life, and their work is characterized by a peculiar naïveté of execution. Their unsophisticated and almost childlike painting is closely related to the anonymous folk art found in many countries of the world.

To academic-realistic eyes, the work of the modern primitives appears obviously faulty and "crude." Figures are often out of proportion, the so-called "laws" of perspective are flaunted, and the objects in a picture appear in strange relationships. In spite of the artists' meticulous attention to realistic detail, the pictures themselves give the impression of being disturbingly *un*realistic.

Hence, academic-realistic critics, interested only in the pictorial illusion of realistic appearance, have found little but "wrongness" in these naïve pictures. But more liberal minds have been attracted to the "child-adult" paintings and have discovered in them important aesthetic qualities, an undeniable vitality, a pleasing charm, and, above all, powerful and interesting patterns of *design*. A marked feeling for design characterizes every modern-primitive painting.

Not all modern-primitive painters are equal in artistic interest; some are more exciting than others; but all are interesting in some degree. Today, modern-primitive art is highly esteemed.

Because of a greater sensitivity, a finer color, a richer imagination, and a decorative poetry of design, the work of one modern-primitive painter stands out above all the others. This painter, Henri Rousseau, has won a well-earned place among the truly great in art. And because his paintings came into public view in the formative period just before the arrival of the twentieth century, Rousseau's modern primitivism greatly influenced the devlopment of modern art.

Rousseau was the first and the greatest of the popular masters. By coincidence, he happened to be a Frenchman. But France has had no monopoly on modern primitivism; there have been a considerable number of other interesting painters of this type in other countries, including our own. Since it is a characteristic of the modern primitive that he is peculiarly unaffected by current artistic traditions surrounding him, French modern-primitive artists have gained little comparative advantage from the supremacy of the French tradition in other forms of art, and American primitives, on the other hand, have not suffered from the relative

Rousseau: *A Game of Football*. Judged by academic-realistic stand ards, this picture could easily be criticized as being completely "o of drawing." But that is not the point of the picture at all. It is masterpiece of emotional design. Daniel Cotton Rich writes of "There is something festive and ballet-like in these four figures se against a luminous autumn landscape reminiscent of other ric surfaced views of the same time. Against the squared-off field, w rows of trees place at either side like columns, the players, striped jerseys, are depicted in jaunty movement, their poses rhy mically linked, one to another, the staccato of the hands repeated four distant trees. . . ."

weakness of American art traditions. Hence, it can be noted that, save in the individual case of Rousseau, the quality of American modern-primitive painting compares favorably with that of France or any other country.

Among the better known of American modern primitives are John Kane (1860-1934), Edward Hicks (1780-1849), Joseph Pickett (1848-1918), Patrick J. Sullivan (b. 1894), Lawrence Lebduska (b. 1894), and, more recently "discovered," Grandma Moses.

In France, in addition to Rousseau, the more important painters of this type include: Camille Bombois, André Bauchant, Dominique-Paul Peyronnet, Louis Vivin, and Séraphine Louis. The Swiss Adolph Dietrich has also attracted wide attention.

At first, after the initial shock of their appearance, modern-primitive pictures were taken somewhat as a matter of course by critics, both unfriendly and friendly. The unfriendly conservative critics treated these paintings as a huge joke, the inept daubings of those who hadn't learned how to draw. (How quick they were to apply that yardstick of "knowl-

edge of drawing"! How convenient a weapon it was to demolish anything the critic himself didn't understand!) On the other hand, the friendly critics offered nothing much better in the way of an explanation. The pictures were charming, yes. But they were made that way, the critics explained, because the artists were "naïfs," and that was that.

The "explanation" of modern-primitive paintings as being solely due to the naïveté of the artists is unsatisfactory. For one reason, because these artists—and particularly such a one as Rousseau—were far from being as naïve artistically as the critics made them out. In fact, we find the modern-primitive artist, when we try to analyze him, a rather complex and enigmatic creature.

Without question, the modern-primitive artists set out to be realistic painters. They called themselves realistic painters; they thought they *were* realistic painters. They painted carefully and tightly with immense attention to detail. They even copied photographs and postcards in lieu of models. Yet their painted photographs came out looking strangely unphotographic, and their intended realistic pictures contain grotesque violations of realistic appearance.

173

Was it then a matter of lack of "training," of amateurism, after all, as the academic critics maintained? One cannot continue to paint and not learn. All of the modern primitives spent many years painting. They were not, as inaccurate tradition has had it, merely "Sunday painters," but full-time professionals.

Henri Rouseeau spent many an hour in the Louvre (just as many other famous artists did) studying details that puzzled him. He copied leaves and plants at the Paris Botanical gardens and studied animals at the zoo. He made preliminary oil sketches of landscapes. He had the benefit of advice from outstanding artists. *It would not have been possible for an artist to continue to paint and study for as many years as Rousseau did and still remain an inept "amateur."* Yet, to the end of his days, Rousseau produced his primitive-appearing pictures. The reason cannot be ascribed to mere incapacity or lack of knowledge of his craft, but rather to something deeper in the make-up of the man himself.

His naïveté, again? As a *person*, he *was* simple and naïve. But there is too much in Rousseau's painting that is *not* naïve; that is, on the contrary, sophisticated and subtle. The design patterns in Rousseau's jungle pictures are remarkable in their complex, interwoven design organization. His painting technique—his use of color—is masterly. And if some of his "drawing" seems oddly ill-proportioned, there is also much of it that is delicately sensitive and indicative of close observation of nature.

No, there is some stubbornness—some compulsion—within the modern-primitive artist that prevents him from achieving the total realism he so often sets out to acquire.

If we study modern-primitive pictures carefully, we may note that the primitivisms and aberrations of drawing appear to be of one general type. We note a consistent impatience with *devices* used by academic artists to secure the *appearance* of reality. For example, *perspective* is almost ignored by the modern primitive. *Proportions* of parts of the body in figure drawing, action and foreshortening, are treated with childlike indifference. In fact, there is a great deal of the independent attitude of the child artists in the work of these grown-up primitives. Like the child, the modern primitive again and again will draw *what he knows* rather than *what he sees*; but on the other hand, unlike the child, the older man will combine this imaginative drawing with frequent meticulous copying of the details of nature. And where the child's picture is spontaneous and impromptu, that of the modern primitive is carefully planned and painstakingly executed.

It is interesting that the modern primitive utterly avoids special tricks relied on by academic-realistic artists to heighten the effect of reality. Such devices as studied light-and-shade juxtapositions and clever use of shadows are particularly avoided. Modern-primitive art is almost completely without shadow, without chiaroscuro.

Three hypotheses may be offered in explanation of the modern primitive's apparent "blind spot" in regard to drawing:

The *first* explanation is that the modern primitive is a man of such strong individuality that he cannot and will not paint any other way. One may tell him about his lack of shadows and such, but he still prefers to paint his own way. We have already noted the close analogy of the work of the adult modern primitive with that of the child artist. However, when the child artist comes of age and goes to art school, his child-like individuality is often beaten down and moulded into academic forms by the so-called "instruction" he receives. The older modern primitive escapes this "instruction." He not only continues his natural childlike individualism, but also, being a grown man, he is not afraid to pass judgment on it as a way of painting and boldly decide in favor of it. Having found it good, he stubbornly adheres to his decision in spite of ridicule and criticism. The things he draws "improperly" are simply things he isn't too much concerned about from a realistic standpoint.

The *second* explanation is that the design sense of the modern primitive is so strong that it automatically forces distortion in drawing. Whether or not this is the case, it is undeniable that the modern primitive loves to design and does so at every opportunity, with occasional resultant damage to realistic drawing.

The *third* explanation is that the modern primitive's very desire to be photographically realistic actually leads him away from the *appearance of reality*—the *illusion* of reality. Most of nature is too complex to be copied *exactly* by anyone except the photographer with his camera. The human artist does not seem to succeed when he tries to copy, *too* precisely, exactly what he sees. On the other hand, the skilled academic realist, by sacrificing some of the exact truth of what his eyes see, and by substituting the more generalized but tried-and-true tricks of his trade, can achieve a much more convincing *effect* of reality. The modern primitives are inwardly too honest to resort to these tricks, and, as a result, their attempted realism acquires its "primitive" look.

It can be said that what is missing in modern-primitive art is the fine collection of artistic tricks, devices, and illusions learned by the academicians in the art schools. In return for this lack, the modern primitive gains something else that the academicians miss—freshness, originality, pleasing design, and long-lasting interest.

Henri Rousseau was born in Laval in northwestern France, May 20, 1844. His father was a dealer in tinware, and the family was very poor.

At the age of eighteen young Rousseau is said to have gone to Mexico. He served in the ill-fated Emperor Maximilian's army as a flutist in the military band.* Some critics believe that the tropical Mexican forests and the primitive coloring of the Mexican marketplace were possible sources of inspiration for Rousseau's later jungle paintings. He returned from Mexico in 1866, and after an an interlude as a clerk, he was again in the army as a sergeant in the war of 1870.

Possibly as a reward for his military service, he was able to find government employment as a minor customs inspector, whence came his famous nickname, the *douanier*. About 1885, at the age of 40, he retired from this position on a very small pension and devoted himself to art. To eke

* The biographical facts of Rousseau's life are veiled in obscurity and it is not *proved* that he went to Mexico at all. The probability is, however, that he did.

out the meager pension, he taught music and drawing and sometimes played professionally as a musician (he "performed so adequately on the violin that he was hired for concerts in the Tuileries Gardens").* Throughout his life, however, he remained very poor.

Daniel Catton Rich writes of Rousseau's painting at this time:

Rousseau began with memories of anonymous portraits, flower pieces, little romantic landscapes—the whole retarded idiom of folk painting, which, especially since 1800, had been practiced all over Europe and the New World. Regardless of period and quality such works bear a family resemblance. Their forms are carefully adjusted to the surface of the painting and to the frame. The picture surface is developed geometrically, with an often inflexible rhythm of lines and spaces. The execution of details is minutely realistic. And because there usually lies at the bottom of such works the need to express a vital emotion, the result is full of expressive content. Figures with eyes gazing straight ahead are frozen in frontal pose. Perspective is centralized. Strong differences of proportion are stressed (tiny figures in a big landscape, an enormous figure against a dwarfed background) and severe contours surround areas of color, often without shadow or weight.

Rousseau found a place to exhibit his paintings in the new Salon of the Independents, which was open to all artists and had no juries or prizes. He made his debut here in the same year that Seurat exhibited his famous "Sunday Afternoon on the Island of La Grande Jatte." Rousseau continued to exhibit at the Independents year after year, trundling his often very large paintings to the exhibition in a borrowed wheelbarrow.

The oddity of his paintings immediately attracted a great deal of attention, most of it unfavorable. Then stories of his simplicity and naïveté began to go around, and he became the butt of innumerable practical jokes. He faced this ridicule and much uncomplimentary criticism in the press with surprisingly good grace and never allowed himself to be discouraged from exhibiting (as had Cézanne).

If Rousseau had many critics he also found many friends and defenders among the artists of Paris, artists as diverse in their views as the staunch academician Gérôme (who encouraged him to keep his "naïveté"), on the one hand, and Picasso and Braque on the other. He was also befriended by Degas, Odilon Redon, and Max Weber, and by the writers Guillaume Apollinaire, André Salmon, Alfred Jarry, Remy de Gourmont, Gustave Coquiot, and others.

Though very poor, Rousseau painted industriously until the end of his days. He died September 4, 1910, in the Necker hospital, Paris, at the age of sixty-six. Even the precise cause of his death is unknown, one writer ascribing it to a leg infection, another to a "chill." (His designation as an "alcoholic patient" was merely a ruse to get him, poor as he was, into the hospital at all. He does not seem to have been an alcoholic in

* Daniel Catton Rich, *Henri Rousseau.*

any sense.) As most of his friends happened to be out of the city at the time, only seven people attended his funeral.

Structurally, Rousseau's pictures fell in naturally with what might be called the developing "style" of modern art. They had the same leaning toward a near two-dimensional "flatness," the same growing emphasis on design for its own sake, that characterized the pictures of Cézanne, Gauguin, and Seurat.

It might be interesting to compare, briefly, Rousseau and Cézanne in this respect. We may recall Cézanne's agonizing struggle to combine his urge to design, which called for pictorial flatness, with an opposing desire to capture the solidity and roundness of objects, which called for pictorial depth. We have seen how Cézanne, after a bitter struggle and much mental turmoil, arrived finally at a passable compromise.

Rousseau, in his simplicity and naïveté, arrived at a similar compromise without any apparent struggle at all. Instinctively and immediately, he built his backgrounds in planes, that is, stage-set fashion, with objects in back of each other to delineate distance. Again, the modern primitive's inherent rejection of the academic artist's tricks and devices made it easy for Rousseau to subdue perspective, to avoid strongly modeled forms and disturbing chiaroscuro, and to achieve pictorial flatness. It came naturally —he could do nothing else. Furthermore, he was not in the least concerned, as was Cézanne, with preserving three-dimensional roundness and solidity.

Both Rousseau and Cézanne were designers, but because of the differences in their approaches, Cézanne's design was necessarily structural, architectural, and classical, whereas Rousseau's design was frankly decorative and poetical.

The design in Rousseau's pictures is easy to see (particularly if one turns the pictures upside down). Foliage and figures interweave in decorative, tapestry-like patterns. Sense of "pattern" (see Chapter 17) is particularly strong in Rousseau's painting. His delicate leaf shapes cross and meet each other in subtle rhythms. But what is most attractive about his art is the poetry that seems to infuse itself into every brush stroke, the feeling of mystery and drama, and the inspired imagination that is Rousseau's alone. He has been compared to the poet Blake, and his jungle pictures have been called pictorial equivalents of Blake's "Tiger."

Rousseau's painting increased in power and flexibility as he grew older. Although all types of his work are interesting, his masterpieces are probably to be found among his "dream" and jungle pictures.

Although Rousseau painted industriously until his death in 1910, and although modern-primitive art continues to flourish to this day, the *douanier* and his art may properly be considered as belonging to the nineteenth century. Seen in the light of the historical development of modern art, he may well be regarded as the last of the older group of founding masters.

After the turn of the twentieth century, a new and very different group of younger artists carry on the baton of modernism. Their work in-

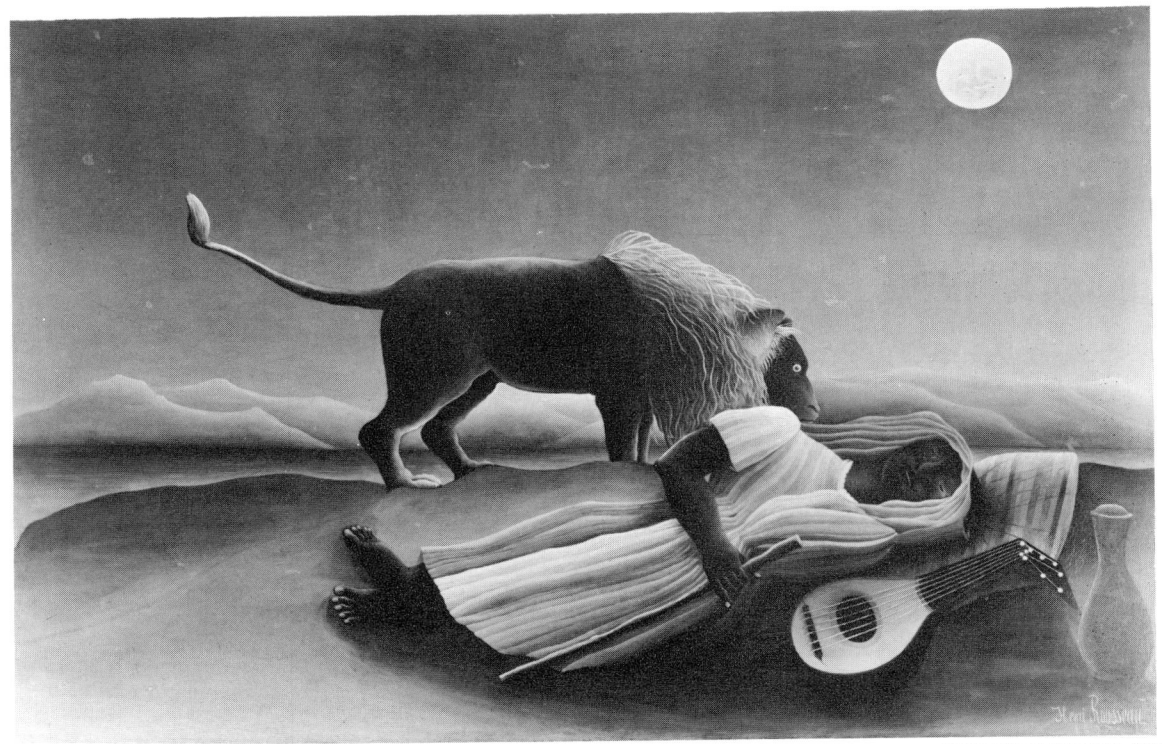

Rousseau: *The Dream* (right). Rousseau's art reaches its heights in his dream and jungle paintings. These pictures are notable for their interweaving lines and shapes, and for their rhythmic design patterns as well as their startling effects of color.

Rousseau: *The Sleeping Gypsy* (left). Strange, exotic, and dramatic in subject matter, this picture is also dramatic in drawing, design, and color. It is one of the artist's masterpieces.

corporated something of everything that went before—Cézanne's structure and pioneering approach, Van Gogh's emotion, Gauguin's color and pattern, Seurat's revolutionary boldness, and Renoir's freedom in drawing. Hardly less important was the new generation's respect for the *primitivism* suggested to them by the cave paintings of prehistoric man, the African native sculptures, the drawings of children, and the work of such modern primitives as Henri Rousseau. Primitivism has particular importance in its destructive effect on realistic drawing. It led more artists farther away from realism and brought closer the advent of Cubism and abstraction.

24   The Cage of Wild Beasts

> Matisse, once accused of drawing like a five-year-old child, replied: "That is what I am trying to do, I should like to recapture that freshness of vision which is characteristic of extreme youth, when all the world is new to it."
>
> —JAN GORDON, *Modern French Painters*.

In 1905, the sun rose on a new generation of painters. To these excited young men it was a bright new dawn, a fresh and beautiful morning, a happy springtime of art, once again. For them, 1905 was a year of liberation, of the breaking, at last, of the wearisome shackles of academic tradition that insisted so everlastingly on imitation of nature.

It was the year of the appearance of a second generation of modern artists, making their collective debut in a sensational public exhibition.

It was the year when modernism in art became a concerted group movement, instead of, as formerly, the expression of a few isolated individuals.

It was the year when revolution in art broke out openly; a revolution that has not ceased to this day.

Curiously, in the world outside of art, it was also the year when the cauldron of subterranean forces, seething and bubbling under the smug veneer of triumphant bourgeois civilization, suddenly boiled over. Socialism and liberalism became everywhere active, all over the world. In Russia there was an abortive revolution that failed to overthrow the government, but nevertheless forced reforms in the Czar's administration. In America, the era of trust busting and muckraking was in full swing, inspired by the "strenuous" leadership of President Theodore Roosevelt.

This liberal revolution in world affairs, however, lacked staying power and subsided quickly. It served only to relieve tension for a few years, until the arrival of the cataclysmic explosion of World War I. It served also to mark a turning point in the fortunes of the dominant nineteenth-century-type bourgeoisie, who, for the first time, found themselves clearly on the defensive. From then on, the supremacy of the old bourgeois masters—the merchant princes, the money lenders, the industrial barons, and the exploiters of men and resources—began slowly to disintegrate in a new and more complex machine age. As the twentieth century wore on, managerial control appeared to be replacing the old owner control, while a succession of wars and other political and economic upheavals seemed to threaten even more violent changes. But, throughout the first half of the century, there had been little or no diminution of the prevailing spirit of materialism.

Because of this, perhaps, the revolt in *art* did not subside after 1905, as did the socialist-liberal uprisings. Instead, the revolution in art developed rapidly in momentum and scope, reached a fever pitch in the second decade of the century, and has continued on for many years.

The years between 1900 and 1905 were years of growing excitement among the more progressive young artists working in Paris. The "old masters" of modernism (with the exception of Henri Rousseau) were no longer around. Seurat and Van Gogh had died some ten years before. Cézanne was to live until 1906, but he remained practically a hermit in distant Aix. Gauguin died in 1903 in even more distant Hiva-Oa. But although they were no longer present in person, the works of the pioneer moderns were very much in evidence and were creating a tremendous stir in Paris art circles. There was an important Seurat exhibition in 1900 and a Van Gogh show in 1901. Cézanne's pictures were shown regularly at Vollard's and in a special showing at the *Salon d'Automne* in 1904. Gauguin's pictures had been exhibited at the same Salon in 1903. Rousseau, of course, continued to exhibit every year at the *Indépendants*. The impact of these shows on the growing numbers of radical young artists was tremendous. Already, several groups of these artists, more or less united in their homage to the art of the older masters, had been formed.

One of these groups was to be pre-eminent—the group led by Henri Matisse, and including Georges Rouault, André Derain, Georges Braque, Raoul Dufy, Maurice Vlaminck, Albert Marquet, and Othon Friesz. This group surpassed the others in its greater originality and in the strength and character of its art. Its members began to draw together, one by one, in the years between 1900 and 1905. Matisse, somewhat older than most of the others, and more advanced in his ideas, became a natural leader.

In 1903, this group, in conjunction with other progressive artists, started a new group exhibition called the *Salon d'Automne*. "Conceived as a showing place for picked progressives and sincere radicals," writes Sheldon Cheney, "the *Salon d'Automne* was serving upon a ground between that of the overconservative official Salon and that of the no-jury and standardless *Indépendants* show." The exhibition of 1903, in a then-obscure gallery, was only a dress rehearsal for a greater show in 1905, in which an entire room was to be devoted to the radical Matisse group.

This *Salon d'Automne* exhibition of 1905 (which also included paintings by Cézanne, Manet, Toulouse-Lautrec, Henri Rousseau, and a tapestry by Odilon Redon) burst on the Paris art world with an explosive force exceeding even that of the Impressionist Exhibition of 1874. The critics

181

were outraged as they had not been outraged for years, and the publicity, pro and con, was enormous.

In the center of the hall where the paintings of Matisse and his radical friends were shown was a statue by the sculptor Marque—a small figure of a child, somewhat in the style of Donatello. The critic Louis Vaux-celles, seeing this, is said to have cried out, "Donatello among the wild beasts!"

"Wild beasts"—or *fauves*—became the name of the new group of artists. Their exhibition gallery came to be known as the *"Cage des fauves,* or the "Cage of the wild beasts."

The critics of the day roared their displeasure, and the Fauve artists were subjected to an amazing storm of bitter criticism and vilification. Today, after a lapse of nearly fifty years, when we look again at these paintings, we wonder what the shouting was all about. Having experienced Cubism, Dada-ism, and Surrealism, the work of the Fauves now appears to us very tame indeed. Indeed, today, for many people who have trouble appreciating modern art, the paintings of the Fauves are often the easiest of all to take because they seem the least disturbing.

But things looked very different in 1905. Sheldon Cheney, in his *Story of Modern Art*, writes:

> The exhibits seemed to the conservative critics to go further in irresponsibility and offensiveness than the pictures of Cézanne, Gauguin, and Seurat. Indeed, in those others there had been a quality of coloring harmonious and almost chaste, as compared to the flaming audacities of Vlaminck and Derain. The last vestiges of correct drawing seemed to have disappeared from the pictures of Matisse and Dufy, or to have been brutalized by Matisse and Rouault. The conservative critics were too blinded by the arbitrary coloring, and too enraged by the general flouting of the "principles of art," to mark these younger men as continuing the revolutionary work of the post-Impressionist masters. But the deluge had started. . . .

Even though it hardly appears to be noticeable in the pictures as seen today, there *was* a disturbing note of independence in these Fauve works that caught the eye of the antagonistic critics. There *was* a deliberateness, an unabashed intention, in the deformations of form and color instituted by the Fauves that was new, that was lacking or subdued, in the work of the older masters. The Fauves knew what they were doing in this respect —they *wanted* to do it—whereas the older pioneers were not always so sure. With them, the alteration of natural form and color was only incidental in the achieving of other aims.

This difference of intention resulted from the fact that the young and daring Fauves were carrying on from where the older masters had left off. The young men had looked at the pictures of Cézanne and Gauguin and Van Gogh and found them thrilling and inspiring. The pioneers had taken liberties with the depiction of realistic form. Very well, the young artists would start by taking even greater liberties and not think twice about it.

In fact, in this there was a joyous note of liberation—liberation from the stereotyped rules long imposed by academic tradition. As stated before, the artists were tired of looking at realistic pictures, tired of painting realistic pictures. They were seeking the lost *essence* of art that was no longer to be found in the lifeless academic-realistic pictures. This essence seemed to have been recaptured by Cézanne, Gauguin, and Van Gogh. They would follow Cézanne, Gauguin, and Van Gogh and let realism bury itself.

Again, the influence of *primitivism*, which strongly affected the Fauve group, strengthened the artists in their disrespect for academic-realistic painting. It was a Fauve who "discovered" African sculpture, and another Fauve who found child art worthy of emulation. Consciously or unconsciously, art was in revolt against the materialism of "traditional" nineteenth century civilization. Now art had taken the offensive; and if these so-called traditional rules stood in the way, down with traditionalism! Let us do something new, said the artists. Let us advance— let us discover—let us experiment! The deluge had started indeed.

The Fauve pictures do not exhibit this spirit of revolution being carried out to its fullest extent, but they do show a start. They do establish a philosophy of freedom for the artist. Within three years from the official inception of Fauvism, the *Cubists*, operating logically on this same philosophy, would begin to lead art into the uncharted fields of abstraction.

There is an important difference in spirit between the second generation of modern artists, the Fauves, and the first generation, Cézanne, Van Gogh, Gauguin, and Seurat. The first generation was largely self-taught —a generation of hardy pioneers who carved out a new art by the sheer force of their emotions. They were strong individuals, working alone, each solving his own problems in his own way. Each had a struggle of one kind or other to face, and each struggled alone.

The second generation was far less primitive and individual, far less deeply emotional, and far more sophisticated, far more intellectual, than the earlier generation. *Every important fauve artist was academically well trained, was a skilled academic-realistic artist before he turned to modernism.* This is particularly true of Rouault, Derain, and Matisse. For ten years, Matisse earned a living by making official copies of old masters for the Louvre, to be distributed to other museums.

Matisse: *Flowers and Ceramic*, 1911. 36 3/4 x 32 1/2 inches.

Picasso: *Still Life*, 1945. 39 x 26 inches.

PARKE-BERNET GALLERIES, INC.

The Fauves knew what they were about. Unlike the older artists, they acted as a group instead of as individuals. They were ideally fitted to develop, to polish, to guide, and to expand the somewhat undefined art handed down to them by their predecessors. The mission of the Fauves was to consolidate and give direction to the newly formed modern art, a mission they performed admirably. But their contribution as *artists* was somewhat less than that of the founders, and, with the possible exception of Matisse, there now seems to be no one of their number who comes up to the artistic stature of Cézanne, Van Gogh, Gauguin, or Seurat. Or of Picasso, who followed them.

The *intellectual* quality of their art, however useful to the modern movement at the time, may have been a source of weakness as far as individual artists are concerned, and Fauve art, while still interesting and important, does not quite attain the heights of greatness reached by some of the artists immediately preceding and following it. However, Fauve art makes up for its lack of dramatic greatness to some extent by being notably pleasant and comfortable—easy art to live with.

Although the Fauves were influenced by all of the four pioneer moderns, the greatest and most immediate influence undoubtedly came from Gauguin, followed in order by that of Van Gogh and Cézanne, with Seurat exerting a considerably lesser influence.

Some of the characteristics of typical Fauve art are (1) an extreme *simplification* both of means and of delineation of the subject, (2) the application of large, patterned areas of undifferentiated color, and (3) the use of pure and violent color, in startling combinations. All three of these stem from Gauguin. The Fauve lack of perspective and general flattening of the pictures might have been derived from any of the four earlier masters. The use of a broad, unfinished line, the roughness of execution and general apparent neglect of the "finish" of their painting, are all legacies of the several *primitive* influences with which the Fauves surrounded themselves.

The pre-eminence of Gauguin's influence in Fauve art is due, partly to his relative nearness to the Parisian art world, and partly to a possible affinity of spirit between him and the rather sophisticated young artists. The boldness of Van Gogh's color impressed them also. Cézanne's influence was exerted over a number of years both directly and indirectly through Gauguin.

Seurat's influence was lessened, partly because of the tight architecture of his design, which was opposed to the loose pattern-making of the Fauves, and partly because Fauvism was itself a reaction against both Impressionism and neo-Impressionism. If Seurat liked little dots, the Fauves, in contradistinction, preferred broad, flat areas of unbroken color.

Of the two main streams of modern art—the one headed by Van Gogh, favoring freedom and emotionalism, or *expressionism*; the other, sired by Cézanne, leaning to pictorial architecture and formal design—the Fauves may be best classified with the Expressionists. They are the French Expressionists.

Like all modern art, their art represents a seeking for *both* design and personal expressiveness. But while design is decidedly not absent (particularly in Matisse), it is characteristic of the Fauve movement as a whole that the emphasis was on personal expressiveness. The grand over-all key-note of Fauvism is liberation—liberation of the artist on a grand scale from the shackles of the past.

25   Matisse

> Expression, to my way of thinking, does not consist of the passion mirrored upon a human face or betrayed by a violent gesture. The whole arrangement of my picture is expressive. The place occupied by figures or objects, the empty spaces around them, the proportions— everything plays a part. Composition is the art of arranging in a decorative manner the various elements at the painter's disposal for the expression of his feelings. . . .
>
> —HENRI MATISSE.*

It is ironic that the lion among the "wild beasts" of art, Henri Matisse, should, in his domestic life, come to represent the very soul of bourgeois respectability. Throughout the years he has exhibited the manner, the appearance, and the personality of a cautious and proper college professor. "Tell the American people," he once said, "that I am a devoted husband and father—that I go to the theater, ride horseback, have a comfortable home, a fine garden that I love—just like any man." †

Matisse was born December 31, 1869, at Cateau-Cambrésis. Like Cézanne, he studied law before deciding to take up painting as a career. He entered the school of Beaux Arts, and among his masters there, odd as it may seem, were none other than Bouguereau and Gérôme, the out-standing exponents of academic-realistic art. Later, Matisse studied with Gustave Moreau, a more liberal teacher, whose occasionally unorthodox ideas may have aided in the subsequent development of Fauvism.

Matisse's first paintings were thoroughly academic, and, being unques-tionably talented, he soon developed such proficiency that he was commis-sioned to make official copies of old masters for the Louvre. He can boast, indeed, of having been able to sell some of his work to the most conserva-tive of all buyers, the French Government. But after a time, he tired of academic realism and—perhaps as a result of Moreau's influence, perhaps because of coming in contact with the work of the early moderns—he began to seek for more original ways of painting. At about this time the Fauve group began to form—Derain, Rouault, Matisse, and the others— and the whole group advanced step by step together in increasing revolt

---

* Robert Goldwater and Marco Treves, *Artists on Art*.
† *Time*, April 5, 1948.

against the prevailing academicism. It was not long before they were ready for the fateful 1905 exhibition.

In the drawings and paintings of Matisse (see pages 183, 190, 191), we may notice a certain roughness, a certain apparent carelessness or even "crudeness" of execution, that will be disappointing to those who prefer polished academic realism in pictures. In this willful roughness we can, of course, detect the influence of child art and of primitivism in general. Matisse admired children's art, but in this loose, rambling way of rendering there are other considerations than merely an attempt to imitate the drawings of a child. One consideration is Matisse's approach to drawing, an approach expounded by his own statement: ". . . Exactitude is not truth." The other consideration is Matisse's approach to design.

Every Matisse picture is a design pattern. It is a design pattern more than anything else. If we concede that this is the artist's paramount intention, and if we learn to seek out and discover the design patterns, we should have little difficulty in appreciating Matisse's art.

Matisse's design is of a special sort. It is a design of carefully placed patches and spots rather than of linear contours (this in spite of Matisse's skill as a pen-and-ink line artist, and also in spite of his *occasional* use of linear rhythms). It is a design of placement and of delicate *pattern* tensions (see Chapter 17) between colored areas of various "weights." And the patterns are over-all patterns covering the entire picture from edge to edge (perhaps a legacy from the "infinitely extending" patterns of Oriental art, which Matisse studied). No one part of the picture stands out importantly over any other part; the whole picture is the design, and the design is the picture. Matisse's rough, loose style facilitates the development of such a design pattern.

In a Matisse picture, even such an important element as a figure becomes only part of the design, and the accessories around the figure may often be of equal importance with or greater importance than the figure itself. This purely decorative handling of human figures was attempted by Cézanne, but his treatment is less adroit than Matisse's. Cézanne lacked the complete knowledge of the figure that is one of Matisse's outstanding characteristics.

The total effect of a Matisse picture is that of a blooming flower bed or an elaborate Oriental screen. It is always cheerful and gay. And these pictures, even though painted by one of the most sophisticated of artists, nevertheless retain much of the freshness and simplicity of a child's drawing.

Color is an integral part of Matisse's design; it is almost the *most important* element of his design. Without its color, a Matisse painting is incomplete (which is why his pictures often reproduce so disappointingly in black-and-white). With its color, the same picture sings.

Typical Matisse color consists of the brightest of vermilion reds, blues, greens, yellow, black, all balanced against each other and held in "place" by soft and delicate neutrals. It is the brightest of color—squeezed right out of the tube—yet always harmonious; each color is placed next to its adjoining color in perfect taste, the selection being made by an exquisite color sense.

187

Matisse's color is Gauguin's color carried out to its logical conclusions. It is *arbitrary* color, color for its own sake; abstract color, chosen with little regard for the realistic appearance of the objects painted. In its boldness and brilliance, it derives from Van Gogh as well as Gauguin. It is gay and happy; strong, yet everlastingly pleasing.

Of his own approach to color, Matisse wrote:

> I put down my colors without a preconceived plan . . . My choice of colors does not rest on any scientific theory; it is based on observation, on feeling, on the very nature of each experience.*

Roger Fry has noted an interesting fact about Matisse's painting—its "*equivoque* and ellipsis," he calls it—Matisse's solution of the old problem of *design* versus drawing that troubled Cézanne so much. Matisse's pictures have the "equivocal" quality of being seeable two ways. That is, one can look at the picture with an eye for drawing and see figure, objects, and background, all soundly drawn, though roughly rendered and with occasional distortions introduced for design purposes. Or again, one can forget subject matter entirely, and trace pattern and design from one end of the picture to the other.

Here is the old battle of the flat two-dimensionalism required by design versus the deep three-dimensionalism needed for drawing. Cézanne solved the problem of reconciling this conflict by a series of constructional compromises. Matisse, a far more facile draughtsman than Cézanne, was able to solve the problem somewhat more simply and cleverly.

First, as Fry points out, Matisse unhesitatingly abolished *chiaroscuro*—that is, strong light-and-dark shading or *modeling*—from his pictures. "For of all the aspects of the visible world," wrote Mr. Fry, "those that are included under the term of *chiaroscuro* are perhaps the most destructive of the picture surface." What little shading seemed necessary was done lightly, sketchily, and was incorporated into the design.

Then the item of drawing was accomplished in the *lines* of the picture (later to be filled in with more or less abstract color), with just enough alteration or distortion to incorporate the *drawing* element into the design elements of the painting. Matisse could do this with unusual ease because of his amazing skill in drawing and his immense knowledge of the human figure. He was able to give his figures and objects adequate three-dimensionalism, and yet almost completely suppress perspective, thereby keeping the picture flat for design purposes.

With his picture surface thus maintained, Matisse could design boldly and freely, relying on his natural sense of rhythm and pattern to achieve his design, and relying even more confidently on his skill in drawing to retain an effect of reality for those who asked for "truth."

All this was made possible by Matisse's rough, sketchy manner of painting; by his filling in of the areas between the outlines flatly, loosely, and incompletely. The observer's eye could readily respond to the *suggestion* of form offered by this style, or it could with equal ease forget form and

* Goldwater and Treves, *Artists on Art.*

concentrate on the picture's design pattern. On the other hand, had he painted otherwise, with strongly modeled forms, completely stated, this duality would have been impossible; the drawing would have been emphasized, but the design would have been irretrievably lost.

The subject matter of Matisse's painting has run to much the same thing year after year, the famous *odalisques*, nude or seminude female figures posed against a flat, pattern-making background. Matisse was deeply impressed by Mohammedan art early in his career. Inspired, perhaps, by the spirit of Delacroix, he made a painting trip to North Africa. He was familiar with both Persian manuscripts and Japanese prints. All of these influences are notably apparent in his paintings.

Matisse's paintings are famous for their happy color and decorative design patterns. But there is another branch of his art that sometimes appears even more exciting than his paintings—his pen-and-ink line drawings.

In these drawings, Matisse "lets himself go." They are obviously done very quickly, in a single daring line, without the slightest fear of making a mistake, without the slightest worry about precise correctness of proportion or exactness of detail. They are all feeling, emotion, and inspiration. In them, Matisse joyfully surrenders himself to the muse of art, and the result is magnificent!

To those who ask for "exactitude" in art over "truth," these drawings may seem crude and childlike. But to those who are willing to stop and look a while, these drawings seem to grow in realism and power. The loosely indicated forms seem to acquire a living reality that would not be possible if they were drawn in detail; the arms and legs and torsos, outlined in a single delicate pen line, appear to acquire an astonishing solidity of form; the line itself, that seemed to have been almost scribbled on the paper, is seen to be intensely sensitive, intensely understanding of the slightest subtleties of contour and direction. We begin to appreciate why Matisse has been called one of the greatest draughtsmen of recent times.

But draughtsmanship is not the only element of interest in these drawings. They, too, are marvelous examples of pattern design. In this, not only the lines, but the spaces between the lines, are of importance. Every mark is *just* the right distance from the next mark. Lines flow in lovely curves, and a decorative sense of rhythm pervades every part of the drawing. Matisse's drawings are livelier, more spontaneous and exciting, than his paintings—which is as should be, but which does not always happen with many artists.

Matisse's drawings contain the element of *comment* mentioned in the chapter on Renoir. His line not only describes the form he draws, but also includes the artist's feelings about the form, his artistic *comment* on it. Matisse's drawings also have the spontaneity desired by Gauguin; never once is there a hint of working over.

In his lively, decorative paintings and his lyrical drawings, Matisse added something to the treasure chest of art. In his bold experimentation —carried on, incidentally, throughout his life—he also furthered the development of the modern movement. He was the strongest individual, the greatest artist among the Fauves.

There are, however, some weaknesses, or near-weaknesses, in Matisse's art—failings which are also fairly typical of the other Fauves. For one thing, perhaps, a trifle too much intellectualism, and not quite enough depth of emotion. Matisse wrote:

> What I dream of is an art of balance, of purity and serenity devoid of troubling or depressing subject-matter in art, an art which might be for every mental worker, be he businessman or writer, like an appeasing influence, like a mental soother, something like a good armchair in which to rest from mental fatigue.

It is a perfect critique of his own art. It suggests its greatest greatness and its greatest weakness.

Most lacking in Matisse's pictures—when compared with certain others—is the element of *drama*. One misses the interplay of contrast and opposition, the strength that comes out of *struggle*. For this reason, Matisse's paintings often appear weak and flat when placed next to Picasso's, which rank far higher in visual drama. But this is no cause for discounting the

Matisse: *Drawing* (above). Drawn simply with a few lines, this picture nevertheless beautiful in design. Matisse: *Drawing* (right). In spite of t' free and loose drawing, we know exactly what this model looks li Though apparently inexact by academic standards, the line of this pictu is very sensitive and tells more about the model than a precisely realis drawing would. Note the feeling of "pattern" in the drawing; every line just the right distance from the next line, and the picture makes a pleas pattern of light and dark.

value of Matisse's art. There are many times when a "good armchair" is a most desirable thing to possess.

The other Fauves, though of interest to collectors of art, have little additional to offer us in a study of the basic principles of modern art. The collective case for the Fauves is most strongly presented by Matisse. Too great an intellectualism and a tendency to revert to academicism detracts from the importance of Derain. Dufy is charming and pleasant in his personal variety of artistic "shorthand," but seems to say the same thing year after year. Marquet (who nevertheless should be made better known in this country) leans backward toward early Impressionism, whereas Vlaminck, in spite of the gusto of his brush strokes, today appears to be almost an academic.

In recent years, Rouault has aroused considerable interest in America, but it is an interest that may not be so much due to a penetrating critical estimate of Rouault's art as to the possibility that Rouault's art is more understandable to many Americans than other examples of modern art. In other words, Rouault's pictures, in spite of their uncouth style, may be more academic and less modern than is generally admitted. For instance,

Rouault: *Figure*. As a boy Rouault worked in a shop for the repair of stained-glass windows. Later he adopted a style of coloring that reminds one of Gothic stained-glass windows. In spite of the apparent "crudity" of his work, Rouault has proved himself to be a skilled craftsman, and his rough, heavy manner is quite deliberate.

Derain: *Torso*. Derain's work can be characterized as frequently "hard and brittle." He is talented and clever rather than emotional in his approach to art.

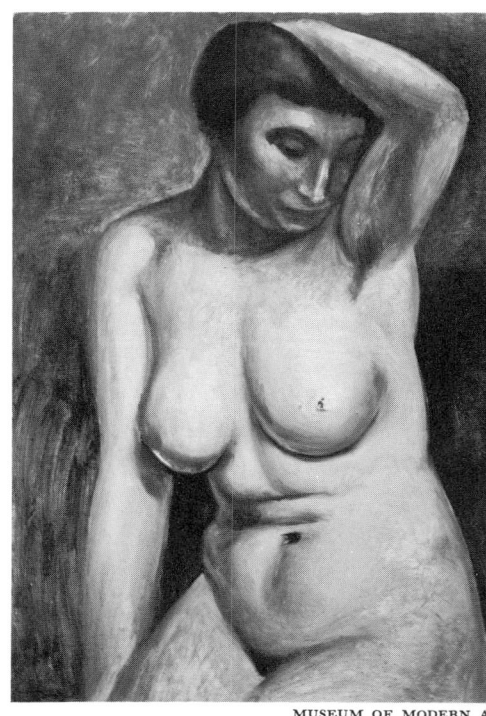

Dufy: *Window at Nice*. Dufy's gay water colors and gouaches have great charm. They have been much imitated by certain types of commercial artists, as also have, indeed, some of the mannerisms of Matisse. As in the case of the other *Fauves*, the works of Dufy are *not* primitive, in a real sense. They are the productions of a clever and accomplished artist.

they have a way of telling a story, which is a typical academic-realistic characteristic, and one readily understandable by the general public. Also, Rouault's paintings tend to be less concerned with design than most purely modern pictures. However, even though it *does* appeal to an audience part of which may not yet clearly understand the true aims of modern art, Rouault's art nevertheless thereby renders an important service to modernism by acting as a stepping stone to more formidable modern works.

In justice to Rouault, it must be pointed out that the limitations of his art are the limitations of Fauvism when not fully developed (as it is in Matisse). They may be the result of Fauve overemphasis on *personal expression* without similar emphasis on design, resulting, in the instance of such a skilled realistic draughtsman as Rouault, in some reversion to academic realism.

Rouault is a French Expressionist. He is also a caricaturist—or, to name it better, a visual *satirist*—of the line of Daumier, Forain, and Toulouse-Lautrec. There are literary connotations in his art which are alien to the true spirit of modernism. On the other hand, he is not without a modern decorative sense, and his roughhewn, apparently crude and careless painting technique conceals many beautiful color harmonies as well as much skillful drawing.

The apparent roughness of Rouault's style—and his personal background of great piety as a Roman Catholic—may mislead one into thinking of Rouault as a *primitive*, something like Rousseau or even Van Gogh. Nothing is more remote from the truth. Rouault is a skillful and sophisticated artist, and his apparent crudeness is deliberate and part of his art, as it was with all the Fauves.

Taken as a whole, the Fauve movement was a restatement of the ideas of the pioneer moderns. It emphasized the concept of the artist's right to paint as he pleased, regardless of subject matter, and proved by its work that such painting had artistic value. It contributed to and expanded the area of modernism, particularly in color and technique. And finally, it paved the way for the arrival, at last, of the full expression of modern art as we know it today. It was the prelude to the triumph of abstraction in art which first appeared under the name of *Cubism*.

26   Picasso

One day, late in October, 1900, a young Spaniard arrived in Paris from Barcelona. He had just attained his nineteenth birthday. Small, dark, and wiry, he looked very much a Latin, moreover, a notably good-looking one, with a fine head and alert, intelligent eyes that missed nothing whatever. He wore an artist's black slouch hat, tilted confidently at a saucy angle.

In a few years, this young Spaniard was destined to be acclaimed by many as the greatest artist of his time. He was to conquer the world of twentieth century art as spectacularly as Alexander the Great had conquered the world of the ancients. This boy would later lead the moderns in the most violent revolution art has known since the Cro-Magnons. But at the moment of this first trip to Paris—a cautious, two months' exploratory visit—his future conquests were as yet scarcely dreamed of, and he knew little, if anything, about modern art.

The young man's name was Pablo Ruiz Picasso. He was born October 25, 1881, at Malaga. When he was ten years old his parents brought him to Corunna, where he lived until he was about fifteen; then the family moved again, this time to Barcelona.

From an early age, the boy had displayed unusual skill as an artist. His natural talents were sharpened by the wise guidance of his father, himself an artist and teacher of art. When it came time to enter the Academy of Fine Arts, young Ruiz Picasso * was able, in a single day, to pass an examination considered so difficult that a whole month was usually allotted for its completion. At the age of fifteen, it could be said that Picasso was a completely trained academic-realistic artist. He had already painted some realistic pictures of Spanish beggars which, even today, startle us by their vigor and their competence of execution.

These highly realistic, rather tightly painted pictures can be considered as Milestone Number 1 in Picasso's long and changing career. Here is where he started. From this point, his art would pass through a long procession of phases, or "periods." These periods, these often apparently quite radical changes of style, represent not caprice or uncertainty; not a means of enhancing the prices of his pictures (as at least one rather cynical writer has suggested), but the natural, progressive stages of development of an extremely active and creative mind.

The five Barcelona years from 1896 to 1901—that is, from his fifteenth to his twentieth year—constitute Picasso's first period of development. While still at Corunna, the young artist had painted the aforementioned realistic pictures. At Barcelona, with its alert and lively cultural atmosphere, a series of new influences began to impinge on the youth's impressionable mind, with resultant changes in his style.

The stiff realism of the Corunna beggars was typical of accepted nineteenth century academic realism. The new influences that reacted on Picasso's style were more up to date, closer in spirit to the approaching twentieth century. What particularly caught Picasso's eye at this time were the paintings of artists whose work, though still realistic in spirit, had gone a bit beyond realism in style—Renoir, Toulouse-Lautrec, Steinlen, and the lively poster-maker, Chéret. Renoir's Impressionism intrigued Picasso for a while, and he painted a portrait of his sister in a soft, silvery Renoirish style. A little later, possibly as a result of his first contacts with Paris, he became fascinated by the satirical mannerisms of Henri de Toulouse-Lautrec. Sometimes he mixed Renoirish soft outlines with acid Lautrec-like satire.

These five years were a period of imitation and preparation, a type of

* Ruiz was his father's name, Picasso his mother's. He chose to use the latter as being more distinctive.

195

thing not too different from what one would expect from any talented young artist who had not yet really found himself. During this time Picasso sketched endlessly, sharpened the tools of his calling, increased his facility, and improved his techniques. But his development was mainly in the realm of technique; he had not yet begun to experiment with creative *ideas*.

Contact with Paris, and the arrival of full maturity, marked the beginning of a change. From his twentieth year (1901) on, Picasso's development shifted definitely from the field of technique to that of ideas. Technique, though he never ceased to experiment with it, was no longer a primary consideration. He had forged his tools—now he put them to work.

After making several more exploratory visits, Picasso settled more or less permanently in Paris in 1904. Unable to speak any French at first, he was for a long time completely unknown except to a few Spanish cronies. Gradually he became better known, but it was several years before he met such artists as Braque and Matisse.

Picasso's first Parisian period was the famous "Blue" period, lasting from 1901 to 1904. This was followed by a "Circus" period, a "Rose" period, a Primitive and a Negroid period, all rather closely related in spirit, yet noticeably different in the outward aspects of style.

In 1907-1909, working with Braque, Picasso created Cubism. Cubism itself developed through many stages—Analytic Cubism, Synthetic Cubism, Curvilinear Cubism, and so on. Each of these "periods" was marked by radical changes in Picasso's style.

Now this is remarkable. It has never happened before. There have been two or three changes in an artist's style (as in the case of Cézanne), or possibly even three or four, but never the long and continuous procession of changes that characterize Picasso's life work.

The explanation of this phenomenon will be found in an examination of Picasso himself. To those who have observed him superficially, he is likely to appear as an enigmatic and baffling personality, who does what he does from mysterious motives. Fortunately, however, there has now existed an opportunity to study Picasso at full length for a lifetime, to trace his development and examine his motives in detail. Looking back over the years, it seems to those who have taken the trouble to study him thoroughly that the essential integrity of his purpose is confirmed, his intensely individual character stands out clearly, and his immense stature looms up like a great mountain over the cultural horizon of our times.

Particularly to those artists who have worked in directions he has pioneered, it is beginning to be seen that this man is not only a talented artist but he is an intellectual giant. He is a true genius, a man whose innate abilities far exceed those of any other modern artist. To those able to appreciate his work fully, he is not only the greatest artist of his time but he is one of the monumental figures in the culture of the first half of the twentieth century, one of the creative interpreters of our civilization.

Considered just as an artist, taking only artistic qualities into account, he is remarkable. His sensitivity, his aesthetic emotion, his intensity of feeling are enormous; and instead of being inhibited by his powerful intellect (as indeed happened in the case of certain other intellectual artists of his time), that intellect combined with his other qualities in perfect proportion. As a result, Picasso's work is characterized by a tremendous *power* of expression.

It has been said that the greatness of an artist is often betrayed by the quantity of work he produces. In this respect, Picasso has been a veritable volcano, spewing forth drawings and paintings by the thousands. He has worked ceaselessly with a phenomenal energy from early boyhood to an amazing Titian-challenging old age.

Certain other typical Picasso characteristics are of particular interest to us, namely his originality, his imagination, and his creative restlessness. No other artist has been so consistently original; seldom, anywhere, has there been seen such an effervescent, apparently inexhaustible imagination. Picasso's originality is the more surprising in that he has drawn inspiration, almost as a matter of practice, from the arts and styles of other times. He has borrowed from innumerable sources, but (save in the early attempts of his boyhood apprenticeship) never has the borrowing been an imitation; it has always been transformed into something peculiarly original, something never seen before. In this there is a close analogy to Shakespeare, who also borrowed and transformed.

Picasso's creative restlessness is a typical characteristic. He cannot create once and then continue to go on doing the same thing. Repetition quickly bores him. Something within him demands that he create something new, something different. He may linger with a general *type* of creation for a while, but only to investigate its possibilities or to elaborate on a theme. Here is the reason for his succession of stylistic "periods." Having exhausted the creative possibilities of one set of ideas, he pushes on to another set. His eager mind, fueled by the flames of an inexhaustible imagination, drives forward like a mighty engine.

Several critics have already pointed to Picasso as the epitome of twentieth century civilization—as "the twentieth century man." In his restlessness of mind, his "tyrannous urge" * to create, his desire to tear down and rebuild—in his furious energy, his bewildering succession of changes of direction—he certainly typifies the spirit of our times.

He represents, too, the revolutionary bent of the modern movement in art, directed against certain specific aspects of that same twentieth century civilization. Alfred Barr, Jr., has written significantly: "In a world in which social pressures—democratic, collectivist, bourgeois—tend to restrict the freedom of the exceptional individual, Picasso's art assumes a significance far beyond its artistic importance." †

It is interesting to remember that, in the beginning, Picasso was not a *modern* artist. He was trained as an academic realist. Furthermore, his conversion to modern art was not sudden or spontaneous; he had his difficulties with modernism, too.

In the years between 1900 and 1905, when the modern movement in Paris was winning many new converts, when *Fauvism* was taking form, Picasso was relatively isolated. Handicapped temporarily by the language

* Harriet and Sidney Janis, *Picasso, The Recent Years.*
† Alfred H. Barr, Jr., *Picasso, Fifty Years of His Art.*

Picasso: (Blue Period) Mother and Child, 1901. T
strong design of this picture can be easily seen if
picture is turned upside down. Picasso works in lar
simple design areas in a manner reminiscent of G
guin. Picasso's pictures of this particular type are m
modern in spirit than many others that followed
some time.

barrier, it was a long time before he made real contact with the *avant
garde* artists who were carrying on the traditions of Cézanne, Gauguin,
Van Gogh, and Seurat. What Picasso had learned from the talkative intellectual hubbub of Barcelona came at second-hand and was full of misleading influences. Nevertheless, he clearly sensed that great things were
going on, that art was swinging in a new direction, and that he, too, must
find that direction.

The path taken by Picasso in finding his way to modernism was a long,
round-about detour; in fact, a detour that actually started in the wrong
direction. He was like a little boy who, arriving late for a parade, dashes
up a side street to overtake and meet the head of the procession.

Picasso's Blue Period, the Pink (or Rose) Period, and his Primitive-
influenced and early Negroid periods were all motivated by his somewhat
fumbling efforts to find his way to the core of modernism. The great
stumbling block in his advance was his early misdirected desire to base his
art on *literary* considerations, that is, to try to paint *story-telling* pictures.
Like many others, he did not at first appreciate that modern art is essen-

198

tially antiliterary, and that he was starting in the wrong direction. His strong sense of design, however, tended to correct his course, and in due time he found his way naturally and instinctively to the broad highway he was to follow for the rest of his life.

Nothing was lost by Picasso's taking this "detour." Indeed, the world has been enriched by a considerable number of very charming pictures that otherwise might not have been painted. In spite of their occasional almost mawkish sentimentality, these pictures have a strength that comes peculiarly from Picasso, and a lyricism of line, a visual poetry, that is not at all literary. Today, Picasso's Blue and Pink Period pictures are wisely prized by many collectors and museums.

Picasso made three trips to Paris before finally settling down there in a dilapidated studio-tenement in 1904. The first visit was for two months in 1900, the second was for the latter half of 1901, and the third, for three or four months in the winter of 1902-1903. During these trips, in addition to painting and sketching, he attempted to sell his pictures and also make arrangements for staying more permanently.

When not in Paris, he visited Madrid, but most of the remaining time he spent in Barcelona. From 1901 to 1904, Picasso painted more than two hundred pictures, about fifty of them in Paris, the rest in Barcelona. Although he had sold some pictures in Paris and had been given an exhibition by Vollard, his Parisian expeditions were not economically successful, and, after a taste of typical artist's poverty, he was forced to return to Barcelona, deeply discouraged, in 1903.

The pictures he painted during this period from 1901 to 1904 (from his twentieth to twenty-third birthdays) belong to what is now called his *Blue Period.* This is because so many of them (though not all) are painted entirely in shades and tones of blue. Why Picasso chose to paint in this blue near-monochrome has never been authoritatively explained (the many theories of critics on the subject are merely conjectures), but it is possible that he may have restricted himself to a single pervading color as an artistic tour-de-force, and he may have selected blue for no other reason than that he liked the color. Whether he intended it so or not, however, the blue is obviously appropriate to the melancholy mood that pervades the subject matter of these pictures.

These are pictures of unhappy people, sad people, hungry people. Lean beggars,* emaciated women with children, poverty-stricken youths, and wan prostitutes. A sentimental, frustrated symbolism of gloom seems to run through them all. Many years later, Jaime Sabartés, Picasso's friend and secretary, ascribed to the master the idea "that art emanates from sadness and pain." † It is more than probable, however, that the sadness in these paintings reflects Picasso's own discouragement at the time, his frustration, his youth, and his loneliness. In them one can sense a somewhat morbid, but understandable, note of self-pity.

These are story-telling pictures. Their emotional appeal is a literary one rather than a purely artistic one, and derives from the subject matter. In this respect, Picasso was still in the grip of his original academic-realistic thinking, a grip that he was not to break for some time. But in other directions he made great strides toward the modern point of view.

Some of the blue pictures exhibit a system of compositional design that is very reminiscent of Gauguin—and indeed may have been directly influenced by Gauguin's work. The rendering is drastically simplified and the pictures are painted in broad, flat areas of only slightly modified color, with little modeling. Backgrounds are simplified into a single curtainlike area. The outlines of the color areas, the wrinkles in clothing and draperies, and so on, are woven into a type of pattern design.

Most of these pattern pictures are strongly painted and are very lovely (see *Mother and Child,* page 199). Though Picasso distorted natural forms to force his design, this design was still essentially "compositional"— a design of *arrangement* rather than analysis—and a heritage from academic realism. It was not yet "analytical" or "structural," and hence, not yet fully modern in spirit. Youthful Picasso, the story-telling illustrator, compromised with Picasso the designer-to-be.

About 1905, the blue gloom began to lift from Picasso's pictures, per-

* Suggested, perhaps, by the elongated figures of El Greco.
† Jaime Sabartés . . . *Picasso, an Intimate Portrait.*

Rothko: *White Center.* 55 1/2 x 81 inches, oil on canvas.

Brooks: *Embo,* 1960. 48 x 44 inches, oil on canvas.

haps because he was in better circumstances. He was now firmly entrenched in Paris; he was beginning to meet other artists; and possibly he had by this time met the tall and beautiful model, Fernande Olivier, who was to be seen constantly with him for a number of years. He also met the American collectors Gertrude and Leo Stein, and Guillaume Apollinaire, the writer who would do much to make Picasso's art known to the world.

Whatever the cause, both the blue coloring and the heaviness of style began to disappear gradually from his painting, giving place to more cheerful *pinks* and *tans*, to somewhat better-fed figures, and to a lighter, more delicate and lyrical style which now achieved its effects, not so much by use of large areas of color, but by a poetical rhythm of outline. There is a sort of classic Grecian flavor to some of the facial types and poses of figures, which suggest today that Picasso had looked long at classic Greek examples in the museums. But this classicism was only skin deep—Picasso's dainty figures lacked the monumental calm of ancient Greek art—and nothing could be farther from the true classic spirit than the wistful sentiment that bathed all of his subjects at this time. Indeed, though the gloom had vanished, the sentiment had sweetened.

The subject matter of the paintings ran pretty much along one line, *saltimbanques,* or circus performers, harlequins, jugglers, acrobats, and the like, pictured not performing in the ring, but in a hypothetical family life before and after the performances. Even though there was an actual circus within easy reach of Picasso's studio, these pictures must not be thought of as an attempt on his part to make realistic records of the performers and their families. Instead, these figures are creatures of Picasso's imagination, vague symbols of aspects of life which must have appealed to him at the time. In fact, it is said that he painted them at night, without models, and that he slept during the day.

Picasso was still depending on *literary* effects to make his pictures interesting. But a new trend of thought is foreshadowed in some of the later circus pictures. The peculiarly literary symbols begin to slough off—that is, the trappings of clowns and acrobats begin to disappear, the harlequin loses his checks, and the figures become merely figures—nudes. A nude boy leads a horse without a bridle. Here is the first indication that Picasso's path has begun to turn; here is his first hint of abandonment of the literary in art, his first step toward abstraction.

Near the end of the 1905-1906 period, Picasso's color began to lean to a reddish terra cotta almost as persistently as it had formerly leaned to blue. As a result, these years are usually known as his Pink, or Rose Period.

Once Picasso's thinking began to turn in a different direction, it moved rapidly toward the position of the main stream of modern art. He did, however, keep aloof from *Fauvism,* although he probably met Matisse in 1905 or 1906,* and some of the other *Fauves* earlier.

* The exact dates of events during these days are matters of much controversy. The memory of Picasso himself is often contradicted by the memories of his best friends. Two particularly doubtful dates are (a) that of Picasso's first meeting with Matisse and (b) that of Picasso's first discovery of African sculpture.

PICASSO (PINK PERIOD)

La Toilette, 1906. Picasso's paintings of the Pink Period are characterized by a delicate, poetic quality of *line,* particularly in the outlines of the figures. They were warmer in color, happier in subject. Picasso himself was happier.

Boy Leading a Horse, 1905. This picture marks the beginning of Picasso's retreat from "literary" subject matter. His figures cease to be characters in a play or story— harlequins or circus performers—and now become simple nudes. In this picture the horse does not even have a bridle.

Iberian Influence. Self Portrait, 1906. Here Picasso has lost both the desire to paint a story-telling subject or to paint realistically. He has become a truly *modern* artist at last. The approach was suggested by primitive pre-Roman Iberian sculpture he saw in Spain.

PICASSO BECOMES A "MODERN" ARTIST.
PRELUDE TO CUBISM.

African Influence. The Dancer, 1907. This painting is influenced by African sculpture to the point of being imitative. Its design is more advanced than some of the Cubist pictures that immediately followed it, although the thinking that produced it is less creative and original on Picasso's part. Picasso learned much from these experimental studies.

Cézanne Influence. Bowls and Jug, 1907. Picasso discovered Cézanne at about this time. The influence of Cézanne plus the influence of primitive art led directly to the formulation of Cubism.

From the very beginning, there seems to have been a sort of professional rivalry between Matisse and Picasso, a rivalry that has continued throughout the years. A peculiar result of this rivalry was that, at this period and in the earlier stages of Cubism, Picasso and his friends deliberately painted in dull brownish and grayed colors and studiously avoided the bright colors favored by the rival *Fauves*. Picasso did not exhibit with the *Fauves*, nor with the *Indépendants*, whose mammoth 1906 "Salon" had 5,500 exhibits. He still sold his pictures at low prices to such dealers as would buy them.

Although Picasso carefully avoided affiliating himself with the *Fauve* painters, he was nevertheless too alert and too sensitive a person not to be affected by the new modern ideas that were bubbling up everywhere in a maelstrom of café-studio activity. In spite of himself, his thinking was swept into the main stream of modernism.

At the end of 1906, Picasso was twenty-five years old. It can be said that in that year he became a true modern for the first time. The literature and sentiment of his previous pictures vanished. The faces and poses of his figures no longer "told a story." Meanwhile, he developed an increased interest in form for its own sake. The soft, delicate, illustrative style

Picasso: *Les Demoiselles d'Avignon, 1907.* Sometim called the first Cubist picture. Actually, this la canvas is *pre*-Cubist. The three figures on the left deri from Picasso's "Iberian" style, whereas the two figu on the right indicate African influence. Apparent Picasso discovered African sculpture just at the ti he was painting this picture.

became more severe, more solid, more round. Shapes became "cruder," archaic-looking. But most significant of all, his faces took on a primitive, masklike form (see the two on page 203), which Picasso has testified was inspired by ancient pre-Roman Iberian sculpture.

In the spring of 1907 he painted the large and famous *Les Demoiselles d'Avignon*, often claimed to be the first Cubist picture, because it contains arbitrary planes and areas of color that break up natural form. The designation, however, although in some degree justified in details, is on the whole slightly premature; though it distorts faces and figures violently for purposes of design, the picture as a whole is still relatively naturalistic.

An interesting peculiarity of this picture (see below) is the fact that the three faces on the left are painted in Picasso's Iberian-influenced, masklike style, whereas the two faces on the right, painted later, resemble African masks. Obviously, Picasso had discovered African sculpture while the picture was being painted!

The impact of this discovery was tremendous, because Picasso, the first of all artists, really appreciated the design significance of African Negro art. Immediately, he produced some pictures more abstract, more advanced and nearer to Cubism than any yet painted—pictures that em-

bodied the well-learned lessons in design taught by the little Negro statuettes.

Almost coincidental with his discovery of African sculpture, Picasso made another all-important discovery—Cézanne. Cézanne had just died and, ironically, his paintings were then being brought before the Paris art world in a series of exhibitions. Again, Picasso saw Cézanne as no other artist had seen him before. The first fruits of this discovery were some pictures of bowls and jugs that suggest Cézanne's compositions and some near-abstract figures that suggest Cézanne's painting style. But there was also a touch of a restless something else that went beyond Cézanne, something wilder and more radical.

The next step was a culmination of all that went before—*Cubism*.

27   Cubism

The bombshell of Cubism exploded in 1908. The reverberations of this explosion have been felt around the world for more than half a century, and controversy over the baffling new kind of art introduced by the Cubists continues today with only slowly abating fury.

Picasso and Georges Braque, in rather close collaboration, are usually credited with the "discovery" of Cubism.

To the layman, unacquainted with the new trends taking form in the seething Parisian art world at the turn of the century, Cubism came as a distinct and sudden shock. It was like a slap in the face that came from nowhere. But to one who had observed the development of the modern movement from the beginning, the arrival of Cubism would have been seen as inevitable. Braque and Picasso arrived at Cubism almost simultaneously; if they had not "discovered" Cubism, one of the many other artists in the lively modern group would certainly have done so.

Cubism was the logical next step after *Fauvism*; the spirit of liberation instituted by *Fauvism* helped make Cubism possible. Primitivism, too, led to Cubism—particularly the Primitivism of the African sculptor-designers. And finally—and more fundamentally—the ideas of the early modern masters, Cézanne, Van Gogh, Gauguin, and Seurat, came to an inevitable conclusion in Cubism. If Picasso and Braque were the fathers of Cubism, Cézanne was its grandfather. In reality, Cubism did not arrive suddenly. It was the natural culmination of a long and gradual evolution.

What is Cubism?

Matisse is said to have coined the name—in ironic derision—when
 he saw an early Cubist picture by Braque, in which some farm buildings

had been simplified into abstract, cubelike forms. "Look at the little cubes," jeered Matisse, who liked graceful and flowing lines, and who instinctively recoiled from the sharp angles and straight edges of the new style.

Because of Matisse's remark, the new trend in art immediately acquired the label of *Cubism*. This term, however, is a misnomer because the picture seen by Matisse was one of the very few painted by Braque and Picasso at the very beginning of their Cubist experimentation—in which even approximately *cubic* forms occur. Save in these isolated early attempts, *cubes* as such are not to be found in Cubist pictures, and one will search long for them and in vain.

"Cubism is the art that started in 1908 and ended in 1910," writes one critic.

"No, indeed," writes another, "Cubism continued until 1914."

"1914? Cubism continued at least until 1933," comments a third critic.

There are numerous definitions of Cubism as an art bounded by certain dates. One quickly senses an arbitrary and unsatisfactory doctrinnaire quality about these definitions—plus more than a suspicion that the dates have been selected not so much for scholarly accuracy as to promote the merits or demerits of some certain artist or group of artists.

The fact is that important pictures are being produced today that are closely akin, in all essentials, to the first Cubist pictures painted in 1908. Once established, Cubism has not ceased to exist.

What is Cubism? Tentatively, we can find a simple and generally satisfactory answer. *Cubism is abstract art.*

Variations in style, or fine points of difference in the artists' philosophies, need not upset this simple definition. On the other hand, as we examine *all* abstract art produced in the modern period, we will find that such art falls into two basically different types, (1) abstract art *derived* from nature in some way, or (2) abstract art created independently of any particular natural model. Today, most critics seem inclined to associate abstract art *derived from nature* with the Cubist tradition, whereas they tend to think of the other type (usually geometric) as something else. As a matter of convenient usage, we might do well to adhere to the same distinction.

Hence, our definition could be improved to read: *Cubism is abstract art, derived or "abstracted" in some way from nature.*

The impact of Cubism on the world was heightened by the fact that it was a concerted outpouring of a remarkable group of able and productive artists. Picasso, one of the greatest artists of recent times, led the parade; but his confreres were scarcely a step behind him in artistic quality, and each had his own originality, his own personal contribution to make to the Cubist group effort.

207   Fauvism had been a group effort, too, but its artists lacked the

stature, the imagination, and the energetic drive of the members of the Cubist group. Indeed, the first members of the new group were those more able Fauves, such as Braque, who were dissatisfied with the leadership of Matisse, who felt that there was more to do, and who wanted to advance beyond the bounds of Fauvism.

Fauvism was the introduction to Cubism. Fauvism paved the way for great things—then stopped; Cubism *produced* the great things foreshadowed by Fauvism. The whole caliber of Cubism was more substantial, more effective, more militant than Fauvism. The Cubist artists were more imaginative, more creative; their emotions were stronger; their work was deeper in import.

With his tremendous imagination and boundless creativeness, Picasso usually led the advance of the radical young group. But not all the ideas that went into the formulating of Cubism were Picasso's, and many a time he found concepts to borrow from his fellow Cubists. For many years, Georges Braque matched picture for picture with the genius from Barcelona. Fernand Léger produced Cubist pictures in a style quite different from Picasso's and Braque's. Juan Gris, Louis Marcoussis, Jean Metzinger, Albert Gleizes, Francis Picabia, Marcel Duchamp, Duchamp-Villon, Robert Delaunay, and others each contributed works marked by strong individualities. In later years, Joan Miro taught all the Cubists, including Picasso, that curved lines could be quite as interestingly abstract as straight and angular ones.

While Cubism benefited from the advances made by Fauvism, and only too eagerly seized the baton of modernism from the somewhat tiring hands of the Fauves, Cubism also represented a strong reaction *against* Fauve ideas. Mention has already been made of Cubism's early rejection of the bright colors favored by Fauvism; its preference for austere angles and straight lines over the luxuriant curves of the Fauve masters. There were other types of reaction of even deeper import.

Fauvism drew its greatest inspiration from Gauguin, and to some extent, indirectly, from Van Gogh. Cubism, on the other hand, leaned strongly to Cézanne as a guide and found much to learn from Seurat, whom the Fauves had almost forgotten. This change of direction is highly significant. It meant not only that Cubism would be more austere in its approach than that of the rather gay Fauvism, but also that there would be a new emphasis on *design*, on pictorial structure and analysis, and that modern art's march toward *abstraction*, first set in motion by Cézanne, would be carried forward to a logical conclusion.

In the five years preceding World War I, the eager Cubist artists seemed to work in an atmosphere of electric excitement. Their enthusiasm was boundless as they pushed forward to explore the new worlds they had suddenly discovered. Their every brush stroke marked a new revelation. Yet, with all this enthusiasm, plus an immense productiveness in picture-making, a mature abstract art did not immediately emerge. It took Cubist abstraction nearly fifteen years to reach its full development.

208   The Cubist artists had to learn to be abstractionists step by step, and

their advance was undoubtedly delayed for years by the somewhat un-natural austerity to which they at first committed themselves, particularly by their insistent preference for harsh, angular forms and rigid straight lines—forms and lines that resisted rather than aided the creation of interesting designs. For this reason, not a few of the early Cubist paintings are today more interesting as historical documents than as important works of art. The Cubists tried to do everything the hard way; but often the way was a trifle *too* hard, and their art suffered. If, on looking at Cubist pictures, we remember that early Cubist abstraction was primitive and not yet fully developed—nor fully understood by the artists who were making it—we will find it easier to understand Cubism as a whole.

The first years of Cubism saw distorted but recognizably realistic images become more and more abstract, until nearly all trace of realism vanished from the pictures. To the layman, the pictures became, at this point, totally incomprehensible. (See pages 218 and 219.) He might well have asked at this time, what are the Cubist artists trying to do? What do they have in mind?

Some clues to this question are provided by checking back over the historical development of modern art. We have already seen that the Cubists were dissatisfied with realistic traditional painting; in fact, were up in arms in rebellion against it. Underlying this dissatisfaction was the Cubists' feeling that realistic-academic pictures were hackneyed and life-less, lacking in something artistically vital. On the other hand, when the Cubists looked at the pictures of Cézanne, they noted an intense vitality, an interestingness that was absent in the academic-realistic pictures. Similarly, years before, Cézanne himself had looked at the works of the great old masters and had found *them* more vital and interesting than academic-realistic painting.

Cézanne groped and struggled to reproduce the vitality of the old masters and to inject it into his own paintings. We have already seen that what he borrowed was the concept of *design*, enlivened by an artist's own *personal expressiveness*—his artistic *character*, or *personality*, as it were. Presumably Cézanne succeeded in his aim, because the vitality he sought was not only immediately noticed in his pictures by the Cubists, but also, over the years, by thousands and hundreds of thousands of other observers.

In the double series of influences, from Old Masters to Cézanne to Cubists, there was a crystallization, a strengthening of the idea of emphasis on design. The Fauves had already, successfully, made a point for personal expressiveness. The Cubists, influenced by both Cézanne and Seurat, and taught, too, by the fine design of African sculpture, did everything possible to make *design* the dominant factor in their paintings. Yet they were also wise enough to appreciate that this design they sought was itself a means to an end, namely, pictorial *vitality*; that design merely for its own sake was not enough, because hackneyed design could be quite as dull as academic realism. There had to be something creative, something expressive, about design to bring out its mysterious quality of lasting vitality.

209   The Cubists noticed that Cézanne had worked from nature and then

had distorted nature to create the interesting design pictures he envisioned. Of course, he didn't go very far (he didn't know he was "designing"), but the process was obvious. Furthermore, Seurat had done the same thing, with more abandon. The Cubists followed the same course as did Cézanne and Seurat, but unlike the older moderns, they knew that what they sought *was* design; they felt no compunction to be realistic at all; they were in an exploratory, rebellious mood, and hence pushed Cézanne's line of thought to its completely logical conclusion, *abstraction* —that is, art in which any resemblance of imagery to the original model is purely incidental and accidental; art in which vitality and interest of *design* is the only important consideration.

So much for the influence of the past. In the actual practice of making these *abstract* pictures, completely new factors of artistic importance came to light. Most important were the factors of *originality, imagination,* and *creativeness*. These, too, seemed to have a bearing on the eagerly sought quality of artistic vitality.

The Cubist artist not only distorted reality, he literally tore it to pieces and reassembled it in a new way to suit his fancy. An easy thing? Not unless one had the *imagination* to tear down and put together again interestingly, and the *originality* to do so in a manner different from his fellow painter. The whole process was *creative*—and from its mere quality of creativeness has come an additional new clue to artistic vitality. A picture rich in *creativeness*—like a picture rich in personal expressiveness and in design—also seems to exhibit the vitality that characterizes the great paintings of the old masters.

The new Cubist art, as it were, put a premium on creativeness, on imagination and originality. Because Picasso surpassed, and surpasses, all others in these three qualities, he has won the undisputed title of the greatest of the Cubists.

(A AND B) LINEAR CONTRAST. A straight line contrasts against a curve. The roundness of the curve seems to "bounce" against the straightness of the straight line. A dynamic aesthetic relationship is established between the lines. Parallel lines do not contrast, but merely lie passively side by side.

(C) CONTRAST AND SPACE. Contrasting lines organize the space *between* them. Three or more contrasting lines *tie* the included areas together.

(D) CONTRAST AND ABSTRACTION BUILDING. The "relating" or tying-together effect of contrasting lines and areas provides the aesthetic brick and mortar for the building of abstractions.

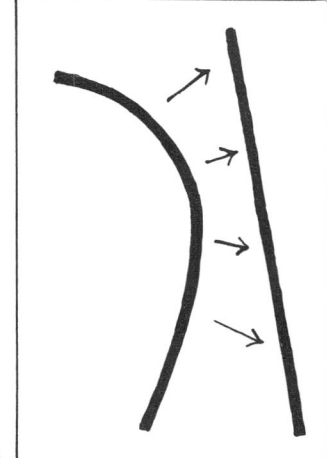

A

What is an abstraction? It is a design-picture; a picture that is also a design, and conversely, a design that is also a picture.

How does one make an abstraction? Today, after many years of abstraction-making, we can confidently say that the operation divides itself into two complementary parts: (1) the process of *abstracting*, or taking apart, and (2) the process of *re-designing*, or putting together. Most abstract artists are likely to do both at the same time.

The first process, that of abstracting, draws on the artist's imagination, originality, and courage. The second calls on his aesthetic sensibilities, his taste, his sense of design, his sense of drama, his ability to build and put together.

There are hundreds of ways of abstracting from nature. In general, however, the artist looks at the *forms* of nature and transforms them into other forms, according to his fancy. The eye and its pupil, for example, can be seen as two concentric circles. The abstracting artist might change these circles to two squares, or two ovals, or even two amorphous shapes, if he chose. He might make the eye very small and the nose larger than the rest of the head. He might change the position of the eyes and the mouth. He might reverse the curves of the body, change every line and every shape. But in making these arbitrary changes, we must remember, the artist is thinking solely in terms of shapes and forms. He thinks of the eye not as a corporeal eye, but only as a circular or oval *shape*, which he feels quite free to change into some other shape.

The artist's first intent is to break up the *forms* of nature, and convert them into other forms—more abstract forms—for the ultimate purpose of rebuilding them into a design-picture. A potent reason behind the determined breaking up of the natural appearance of nature is that the operation frees the artist from the tyranny that nature normally exerts over an artist when he attempts to design. One *can* design from the face of

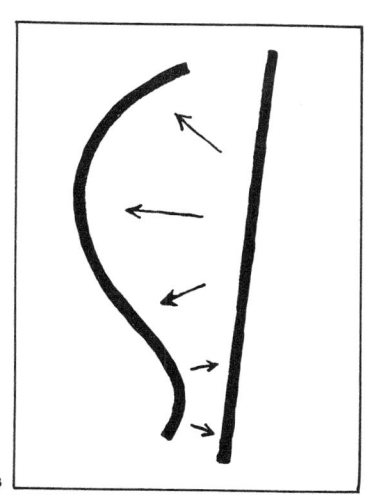

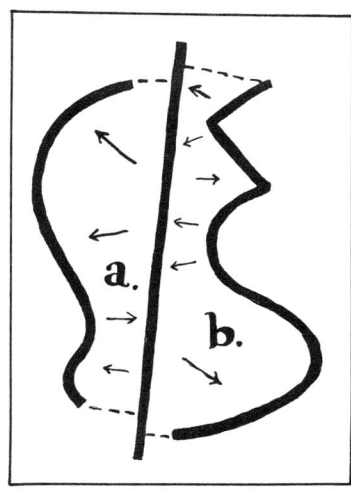

B

C

D

BLOCK CUBISM. The first step in Cubism was to convert the simplified forms of objects into *block* forms, forms that look as if cut out by a saw. Léger's *Seamstress* (1910) at *left* is an example of this style. A landscape by Braque of this type provoked Matisse to coin the name "Cubism."

FACET CUBISM. Picasso: *Head of a Woman, 1908-1909* (center). *Portrait of Braque, 1909* (right). Block Cubism obviously lacked possibilities for subtlety, and its usefulness was limited. Picasso and Braque moved quickly on to *Facet Cubism*, in which the crude block forms were refined into jewel-like facets. From left to right, the pictures lose solidity, become flatter and shallower in depth.

nature without too much altering its natural appearance, but designed face will look much like other designed faces that have been seen before. Somehow, lips, or a nose, suggest much the same sort of curved line to artist after artist. On the other hand, violent changes force the artist to draw on his own imagination, to create something new, to uncover ideas that were not exhausted by the Greeks or the Romans several thousand years ago.

In the abstracting process, the artist reveals himself—and particularly his power of imagination. The greater the imagination, the more color and interest the picture will have. At the same time, the secondary re-designing process is also important. The new shapes developed by the abstractor must be recombined in a picture that is not only a perfect design, but is also an interesting creative entity in its own right. It will reflect the artist's creative capacity, and the greater the capacity, the greater the picture.

How does the artist go about rebuilding his miscellany of shapes and forms into an organized picture? Ultimately and finally, his inherent sense of aesthetic fitness decides—he puts a form in a specific spot because he *feels* it belongs there. Also, over the years, artist-designers have developed a number of concepts which aid them in assembling their design pictures.

We have already considered two of these concepts. If we turn back to Chapter 17 (pages 117-133), we will find a discussion of the concept of "pattern." The artist maintains a feeling of pattern by maintaining each element of a design in exactly the right aesthetic relation to adjoining elements. In Chapter 13 (pages 79-91), the concept of "texture" was discussed. By varying areas of the picture with textural effects, the artist is able to give his design greater liveliness and interest.

212   There are a number of other such concepts, but it is not necessary to

discuss them all here. One concept of great usefulness in the construction of a design, however, should be mentioned—the concept of *contrast:* contrast not only in color and value (red vs. green, black vs. white) but also between *lines,* and between *areas* enclosed by lines. This linear contrast provides in an abstraction the element of aesthetic drama.

The gist of *linear contrast* is the idea that straight lines and curved lines (or angular lines), when placed side by side, *contrast* with each other. (Figure A, page 210.) That is, the roundness of the curve seems to "bounce" against the straightness of the straight line. (Two parallel lines, on the other hand, merely seem to lie passively side by side.)

The feeling of opposition—of "bounce"—between the curved and straight lines establishes an aesthetic relationship between the two kinds of lines. A mysterious dynamic interaction takes place, and artists say that the two lines *relate* to each other.

These contrasting lines also appear to organize the *space* between them. (Figure B, page 211.) This space ceases to be formless and tends to form a definite organized area. The two lines and the space in between them can be considered as a single unit.

Let us go on. Instead of *two* contrasting lines, think of *three* contrasting lines side by side (a straight line, a curve, another straight line, or two curves with a straight line between them). (Figure C, page 211.) The first two lines, and the area between them, constitute one unit, and the second two lines, another unit. But the middle line, being common to both units, tends to bind them together, like a line of cement between two courses of bricks. Now, not only do the lines relate to each other, but the two areas also relate to each other. The same thing can be done

213

with three areas, and so on, ad infinitum. Here are the construction materials of the design builder.

Contrast exists not only between straight lines and curves, but also between straight lines and angles. And contrast also exists between flat curves and more rounded curves. The effect of contrast is lost as lines approach the parallel. Shapes (areas) formed by contrasting lines seem to be *more active*, more interesting, than shapes formed by parallel lines.

Modern artists frequently make use of *contrast* in building their abstract pictures. In addition to linear contrast, they also use the effects of contrast of *value*—dark against light—to bind their pictures together; and contrast of *color*, of course, combined with textural variations.

Regardless of the means and devices (there are many) used by the artist in reassembling his pictures, his own aesthetic sense must finally determine where and how his lines and areas and colors go. His personality will make the picture, and conversely, the picture will reveal the artist's creative character. Hence, the real artistic value of an abstract picture will depend on the inherent creative capacities of the painter. Great pictures will be made by great picture-makers—trivial pictures, by men whose creative abilities are trivial.

28   Dissection in a Kaleidoscope

The first period of Cubist development—from 1908 to about 1912— is usually known as the period of *Analytical Cubism*. This is because the earlier phases of Cubism, quite naturally, should be most concerned with the basic problem of abstracting, and that emphasis at that time should be almost entirely on *analysis*. Later, after the preliminary lessons of analysis had been learned, emphasis would shift to the secondary stage of rebuilding or *synthesis*. This more mature secondary period—after 1912 —is today referred to as the period of *Synthetic Cubism*.

During the analytical period, the Cubist artists advanced from relative realism to almost complete abstraction in a series of consecutive steps. These can be enumerated as follows:

Step one. The simplification of realistic forms. The squat, heavy figures of Picasso's Iberian period are excellent examples of this preliminary stage of cubism.

What Braque and Picasso have done has been to *simplify* the large important *forms* of the human body, omitting minor details and fussy subtleties. To force the essential forms, they have made the figures round and squat, sculptural rather than descriptive. To emphasize their abstract-seeing point of view, they have made their drawing brutal rather than charming. If thought of realistically, as the true images of human beings, these nudes would be grotesque indeed. But the artists were not painting human beings at this moment, they were painting forms, and only forms.

Reduction of nature to a simplified form is almost invariably the first step in design-making. Hence, it was also the first step toward Cubism, toward abstraction.

Step two. To reduce the simplified figures to blocklike forms as if they had been cut out with a saw, as exemplified by Léger's *Seamstress* (page 212). This is called *Block Cubism* and is obviously an attempt at still further simplification. The early Cubist landscapes of Braque and Picasso, of the type that inspired the name "Cubism," are also examples of Block Cubism.

It is possible that these block forms may have been remotely suggested by the plaster cast "blocked" heads used in the training of academic artists. Many an art student has made charcoal copies of these simplified casts. They must, of course, have been familiar to the Cubist artists, all of whom had been exposed to academic training at one time or other.

Step three. The beginning of *Facet Cubism.* Inventive and imaginative artists like Braque and Picasso could hardly be satisfied very long working with crude wooden blocks. They quickly found ultrasimplified Block Cubism inadequate in painting such a complex form as the human face, so they promptly rejected the ideal of extreme simplicity for more complicated, but more flexible, methods. The blocklike forms were given more detail, more "cuts," until the forms became faceted as if cut by a jeweler (rather than a carpenter). (See *Picasso's Head of a Woman*, page 213.) Block Cubism became *Facet Cubism*, but in so doing, the early trend toward simplicity found itself turned into a trend toward *complication*—a trend that would continue for some time.

At first, the faceted paintings maintained a feeling of solidity. The basic integrity of the original image, even though sculptured in hard angular planes or facets, was retained in its essentials. A head still remained something of a head, even though it was no longer rendered realistically.

The facets were easy to make with oil and brush on canvas. It was easy to vary values, or the hard and soft effects of edges, the apparent angles of the facet-planes. They, therefore, were particularly adapted to the purposes of design. Soon the urge to design came in conflict with any disposition on the part of the artist to retain the integrity of the original image. Since these artists had very little of such disposition, it was not too surprising that the semblance of realism left should soon disintegrate.

Step four. The next stage of Facet Cubism marked just such a disintegration. As in Picasso's *Head of Braque* (page 213), the forms which vaguely suggested real things began to slip out of place. After this, the solidity of the image was soon lost and the picture became flatter. Foreground and background merged together in the picture plane (thereby completing a trend started by Cézanne).

Once the disintegrating process started, it proceeded rapidly, with the result that the faceted pictures became increasingly more abstract, more difficult to "recognize" for the realism-seeking eye. It was at this stage that casual observers were being more and more puzzled by Cubist art. The artists, however, were happier. They were learning to "abstract" from nature.

Step five. When the artists discovered what they were about, there was no holding them. All traces of reality disappeared in a welter of faceted planes. In fact, it seemed as if the artists had stopped painting nature entirely and were confining themselves to the painting of these angular facets—these "passages"—which indeed was just what they *were* doing. But they continued to derive inspiration, if not instruction, from the nature before them, and even in the most seemingly abstract Cubist paintings one can find, if he search intelligently, many an interesting vestige (if only that) of the original model.

How the Cubist artists of this period loved their planes, their angles, their "passages" and facets! They filled their pictures with them from edge to edge. Here was the culmination of Analytical Cubism—great canvases covered with hundreds of facets and angles and suggested planes (and painted, incidentally, in dull browns and grays and greens). The pictures were now utterly incomprehensible to the academic-realistically minded observer, but they were a delight to the artists who created them. For the artists had discovered a wonderful new process of taking apart the forms of nature—an interesting process that challenged the painter's brain and emotions and that gave him a sense of triumph whenever he carried it to a successful conclusion.

PROGRESS OF CUBISM. Gris: *Portrait of Picasso, 1* The breaking-up process has become more definite assured. The facets have become suggested plane "passages" and are interesting in themselves. The ar began to paint the planes and facets rather than figure. Three-dimensional depth flattens and disapp until the entire picture exists only at the picture face.

In their exuberance, at this point, it indeed seemed as if the Cubist painters had momentarily forgotten the second half of their design-making operation. The ultimate design—which is pretty much the point of an abstract picture—clearly seemed to suffer from the helter-skelter complexity of the planes and facets. Picasso and Braque, leading the Cubist parade and collaborating ever more closely, were quick to sense that they had gone too far in an unprofitable direction. About 1912 they began to reduce drastically the complexity of their pictures and to give more and more attention to over-all design. This turn-about marks the beginning of *Synthetic Cubism*.

If we look at Analytical Cubism as a whole, we note a characteristic appearance—pictures made up of intersecting and straight lines, angles, and incompleted planes, "passages," which fade into the background. There are few curves, and what curves there are are usually circles or segments of circles. But straight lines and angles dominate the compositions.

Angularity is not a necessary ingredient of abstraction. We have seen how Facet Cubism developed from Block Cubism. But there is no deep-seated aesthetic reason why simplification of natural form had to take a blocky or facet shape. It might as easily have been spherical or gracefully

THE CLIMAX OF
ANALYTICAL CUBISM

Cézanne: *Town of Gardanne*, 1885-1886.
Turn this picture upside down and compare it with *Ma Jolie*, below, and *L'Arlésienne*, right. Cézanne's brush strokes, his angular forms, his technique and mannerisms greatly influenced Cubist style.

Picasso: *Ma Jolie*, 1911-1912. Analytical Cubism becomes more and more complicated in structure—and grows more completely abstract. Only slight vestiges of the original model can be discovered in the picture.

Picasso: *L'Arlésienne, 1912.* A reverse trend to simplicity begins—there are fewer shapes; design is simpler and stronger. Mysterious planes which seem to cut through the figure have completely replaced early Cubist facets. As the artists put more emphasis on design and simplicity, Cubism moved over from its analytical to its synthetic phase.

Picasso: *Still Life, 1912-1913*

DEVELOPMENT OF COLLAGE IN SYNTHETIC CUBISM. Gris: *Fruit Dish, Glass and Newspaper, 1916.* Led by Braque, Cubist artists painted imitations of grained wood, newspaper headlines, and the like, in their paintings. Later they pasted bits of newspapers, labels, and so on, bodily on their canvases. This practice was called "collage." The collage led to the development of the "construction," in which the pasted up (or nailed up) materials become sculptural.

curved. Actually, the angularity of early Cubism—a little surprising from a design point of view—can be set down as a stylistic peculiarity of the Cubist period.

Two influences are probably responsible for the Cubist angular style: (1) the reaction against Matisse's gracefully curved *Fauvism*, which has already been mentioned, and (2), more important, the enormous influence of Cézanne on the Cubist artists at this time. Cézanne's pictures not only influenced the fundamental ideas of Cubist art, but his mannerisms, his way of putting paint on canvas, influenced Cubist style. It is from him that the facets and planes derive (see pages 218-219), and we find his chisel-like brush strokes repeated again and again in the paintings of Braque, Picasso, and the others of their group.

Is Analytical Cubism *art?* It is too early to tell. It will take years of critical estimate and re-estimate to evaluate the artistic value of the enormous number of paintings produced in the first quarter of the twentieth century. It is probable that many an early Cubist experiment will be lost in oblivion; that others will be regarded as of merely historical interest. But some of these pictures are already beginning to display a lasting charm that seems to grow over the years. Still others will be brought to light when critical attention, now focused on more recent painting, turns back again and re-examines this lively formative period of Cubism.

How can we view these complex and highly abstract pictures to best appreciate them? There are two ways. We can look at such a picture as if it were a fine Oriental rug and study its design, enjoy its aesthetic effect. Or, if we care to, we can also observe the picture as a sort of provocative puzzle. That is, knowing the painting to have been derived from nature, we can search for tell-tale indications of the original model; we can try to reconstruct the artist's mental processes as he proceeded to make his abstraction. It is surprising how much can be discovered, even in a very baffling abstraction, if one studies the picture for a while. This "detective" game adds interest to our appreciation of these pictures. It is, however, secondary in importance to the aesthetic enjoyment offered by the picture's artistic qualities—its design, its creative conception in shape and form.

29   Out of the Wastebasket up to Parnassus

During the period of Analytical Cubism, the artists looked often at the model for inspiration. In Synthetic Cubism they looked more at their canvas, and drew inspiration from their heads as often as not. The design shaping up before them became the important thing, and if the model's figure could not suggest the shapes and forms demanded by the design, so much the worse for the model. The artists could look elsewhere—and they did.

It would be only natural that an artist's eye, looking around thus, should be attracted by an unusual texture or shape somewhere in the room, and that this texture or shape should find its way into the picture. Furthermore, it was inevitable that such restless artists as Picasso and Braque should tire of painting picture after picture with Cézanne-inspired chisel-hatch brush strokes and would sooner or later seek something different in the way of textural effects. Hence, however curious the choice might seem, it was not too illogical that Braque, who happened to have learned an illusionist technique of simulating the grains of wood and marble from his house-painter father, should have introduced imitations of grained wood as textures in his abstractions.

The idea was adopted with enthusiasm by other artists. Between 1910 and 1912, many carefully painted imitations, not only of grained wood, but of letters from newspaper headlines or wine bottle labels, were introduced—but always abstractly, as part of the design of the pictures. Then the artists did something very logical and simple, but yet very daring from the standpoint of artistic tradition. Instead of meticulously painting imitations of newspaper lettering, the artists picked up the newspaper and pasted the part they wanted bodily on their pictures.

Soon these pasted-up additions became the most important part of the designs—the rest of the designs were painted in around them. All sorts of objects were pasted on; wastebaskets were emptied for odds and ends that might be useful in a design. This practice of pasting-up was called "collage" and became a popular device among the Cubist artists for several years. Furthermore, some of them carried the idea to its limits —they pasted more and more objects to the canvas until it became, no longer a picture, but actually a piece of sculpture called a *construction*. Other artists created actual textures by mixing sand, plaster, and fine gravel with their paints.

The effect of the use of *collage* on the artists themselves was that they continued to concentrate their attentions on the designs they were making and thus became less and less dependent on the model for direct inspiration. The Cubists did not completely abandon nature, they kept it before them; but their pictures became not portraits of nature, but rather improvisations on themes suggested by nature. Their designs became simpler, stronger, and more interesting purely as designs. Also some of the austerity that marked early Cubist work began to slough off, and gradually brighter and gayer colors reappeared. There were fewer angles and more curves, but the straight line still dominated.

It was about this time, just before the outbreak of World War I, that the greater artists commenced to really get the feel of creating abstractly. Thinking in terms of shapes and forms, they sensed the warm, expansive bulge of a curve, the cold contraction of a triangle, the drama of contrast, the interplay of shape against shape, the dominance of large areas, the rebellious chatter of small fragments. They used colors, unusual colors that would have frightened the academic realists half to death, in exciting new combinations solely for purposes of design. They made not merely

221

Picasso: *Three Musicians, 1921*. Often called the m
terpiece of Synthetic Cubism. It is certainly the m
interesting painting in Picasso's "poster" style.

designs, but real *design-pictures*—concertos in shapes and forms and colors
and textures comparable to the symphonies created by musical composers.
Into these picture-abstractions, the artists poured their full strength of
aesthetic emotion, of imagination, of originality and creative power.

The derivation of their designs from nature, however remote the connection may have seemed at times, gave their Cubist work a feeling of
authority that is absent in designs made otherwise. Indeed, the little tell-
tale indications of the abstracting process, the vestiges of reality hidden
in the paintings, added spice to an already interesting visual presentation.

It is on the basis of this complete *design-picture*, this over-all process
of creativeness, that Cubism could now submit its claim to be called *art*.
It offered a new art form, characterized by an obvious vitality. It combined the design and the personal expressiveness typical of the best of
traditional art with the intense, restless, highly inventive creativeness that
is characteristic of the twentieth century.

The cataclysm of World War I, though disturbing, did not halt the
continuing development of Cubist ideas or alter them in any important

ways. Nor did the rapid expansion of modern art in many *non*-Cubist

directions greatly affect Cubism itself. Occasionally, the Cubist artists borrowed an idea or two from other non-Cubist "isms," but they nevertheless maintained the essential integrity of their own Cubist purposes—of *abstraction derived from nature*. From time to time, postwar Cubism changed its outward appearance, but inwardly its basic abstracting process remained the same.

In 1914, Picasso's colors became warm and bright, his forms and textures sprightly and gay, in a style called *rococo* Cubism. He used little bright dabs of colors in a manner suggestive of, and possibly suggested by, the dots of Seurat; but his purpose, unlike Seurat's, was merely to create a new design texture.

From 1915 on into the 20's, Cubism underwent a somewhat more fundamental change in style. The facets, the "passages," tilted planes, and so on, all disappeared entirely. Instead, the designs were now expressed in flat, posterlike areas of color (a line of thought that doubtlessly evolved from the pasted-down areas of collage). Picasso's twin masterpieces in this postery style are his two versions of the famous *Three Musicians* of 1921 (see illustration above).

223

CURVILINEAR ABSTRACTION. Miro: *Person Thr*
ing a Stone at a Bird, 1926. No artist apprecia
the possibilities of curved forms in abstract
better than Miro.

CURVILINEAR CUBISM. Picasso: *Seated Woman,*
1926-1927. At long last, Cubism discovered the
curved line.

SURREALISM INFLUENCES CUBISM. Picasso: *Sea*
Bather, 1929 (left). The underlying philosop
of Surrealism was opposed to Cubism. Nevert
less, Surrealist and Cubist artists were often
surprisingly friendly terms, and the Cubists b
rowed what ideas they could from the youn
group. In this picture, the distant "horizon,"
relatively solid figure, and the vague hint
"menace" in the subject's appearance, all indic
the influence of Surrealism.

In the late 1920's occurred Cubism's most important stylistic change of all—the re-introduction of the curved line as a major design element. With the advent of *Curvilinear Cubism*, the nature-derived abstract art promulgated by Braque and Picasso nearly twenty years before at last attained its full maturity.

Credit for rehabilitation of the curving line belongs not to Picasso, the usual leader of the Cubists, but to a younger man, Joan Miro, whose work did not appear publicly until 1918. Miro, whose genius and originality challenges Picasso's, opened the eyes of all the Cubists as to the design possibilities of curved rather than angular forms.

Like Picasso a Spaniard arrived from Barcelona, Miro has often been classified as a Surrealist—was even included in the "official" Surrealist group in Paris. This is an artistic and stylistic anachronism. Miro is really an abstractionist—one who abstracts from nature—like the Cubists. His work has little or nothing in common with the ideas of the Surrealists.

In Miro's paintings, straight lines are used only as occasional and necessary foils to his exciting undulating curves. He frequently contrasts a sharply rounding curve against a flatter one and is a creator of interesting and unusual shapes delineated in sharply defined, but extremely sensitive, outlines. (See top illustration, facing page.)

In the late 1920's and early 1930's, Picasso and other Cubists adopted the curved line and incorporating it into their styles, something they perhaps should have done years before. (See *Seated Woman*, opposite.)

Another influence impinging on Cubism from the outside was that of *Surrealism*. Fundamentally, Surrealism is the antithesis of Cubism, but nevertheless, the Cubists were able to borrow something from the mannerisms of Surrealism without in the least subscribing to Surrealism's underlying philosophy. (See Picasso's *Seated Bather*, opposite.)

Much mention of Picasso has been made in this chapter on Cubism, for the simple reason that Picasso has so often been the leader in Cubist exploration of new ideas. But we must not think of Picasso as being the only Cubist, or even the *typical* Cubist. Other Cubists also are important as individual artists.

Picasso is a Spaniard. He paints as a Spaniard, because he so often thinks as a Spaniard. Georges Braque, an artist of nearly equal greatness, epitomizes the spirit of France in his beautiful and tasteful abstractions. The contribution of both men together is varied and enormous.

Fernand Léger, another Frenchman, arrived at a style quite different from Picasso's or Braque's—a more formal style reflecting, on the one hand, the influence of Seurat and, on the other, a liking for machinelike forms. Léger's predilection for cylindrical forms led to his work being facetiously labelled "tubism."

The Spaniard, Juan Gris, and the Pole, Louis Marcoussis, painted Cubist abstractions of great distinction, as did Albert Gleizes and Roger de la Fresnaye. Marcel Duchamp was an early member of the Cubist group and one of its more brilliant visual explorers, but his imagination frequently carried him beyond the limits of a purely Cubist style. He

Léger: *Breakfast, 1920* (above). Léger's painting is more formal, more architectural in quality, than the work of most Cubists. His forms suggest the influence of the machine in twentieth century life. Léger's pictures at this time have a monumental stability and were possibly influenced by Purism.

Boccioni: *Unique Forms of Continuity in Space, 1913.* This Cubist-Futurist sculpture combines abstraction of the figure with an expression of the Futurist ideal of dynamic motion. It is the masterpiece of Futurism.

Laurens: *Head, 1918.* The "construction" formalized into sculpture. The head is abstracted in Cubist style. Interesting new materials are added to these sculptures for textural effect.

anticipated *Futurism*, and in some stylistic respects, *Surrealism*. There were also numerous other artists, less well known, but who nevertheless made important contributions to Cubist art.*

The trend toward abstraction was not confined to the art of painting; it also found expression in painting's sister art of sculpture. Cubist painting found its natural counterpart in modern abstract sculpture (see Boccioni's *Unique Forms of Continuity in Space*, page 227), basically little different from painted abstraction, save that the sculptor works in three dimensions instead of two. Instead of the painted textures of the Cubists, the abstract sculptors developed new surfaces and new materials to carve.

There are numerous abstract sculptural works of individual importance, but on the whole, the role of abstract sculpture in modern art is historically secondary to the role of abstract painting. The essential growth and development of modern art took place in the realm of painting, as did the concept of abstraction. The application of these ideas to sculpture followed later.

The interest of modern artists in the progress of modern science has been mentioned earlier. Now that the abstracting process of the Cubists has been more fully discussed, we may better appreciate the remarkable analogy between the Cubist abstractionist and the twentieth century scientist in his laboratory. Just as the chemist analyzes his compounds and breaks them down into elements—into basic molecules, atoms, and electrons—so does the abstractionist artist break down the appearance of nature into essential shapes and forms. And also, just as the scientist finds ways to recombine his atoms and electrons to create new substances, so likewise does the artist recombine his abstracted shapes and forms into new design-pictures. Both artist and scientist are making use of an essential creative process—a process that is by no means confined to science or painting, but is seen wherever creation takes place.

It is in the exposition of this creative process that the spirit of modern art intertwines itself most closely with the spirit of the first half of the twentieth century. The Cubist artist is as much a twentieth century man as the scientific technician, and Cubist art is inevitably as much a part of twentieth century living as the automobile, the radio, or penicillin.

Cubism is not the only form taken by modern art in its explosive expansion since the beginning of the century. But, in spite of a lively competition from many other interesting ideas and approaches, Cubism still remains the *purest* example of modern art's way of thinking, the core of modern art's historical development. And today it is beginning to appear that, in its fully developed form, the Cubist style probably represents the highest pinnacle of modern art as *art*. Certainly, those modern artists generally conceded to be the greatest of all—Picasso, Braque, Miro, Léger —are the proponents of the Cubist line of thought.

The great Cubist artists have maintained their unceasing artistic production throughout the period between the two wars and up to the present. It has seemed that their work has continued to improve as time

* A listing of all the modern artists, or even of all the important ones, is not within the province of this book. This has been amply done elsewhere.

went on, and that their latest paintings appear to be the most interesting of all.

Over the years, after the early climax of Analytical Cubism, these artists have gradually but steadily retreated from too extreme abstraction to a type of picture in which there is more than a little indication of the original model. This trend is highly significant and revealing. It defines, by implication, both the limits and the essential purpose of Cubist art. It shows clearly, for example, that the Cubists have had no intention of abandoning nature as the raw material of their art. They have declined to "imitate" nature, but never have they banished nature. Never, in their abstractions, did they lose complete contact with nature.

As stated earlier, this tie to nature has given Cubist painting a feeling of *authority* that fades out of abstractions not so tied to nature. It has also tended to enrich the quality and increase the effectiveness of Cubist art. The subtle connotations of natural origins suggested by Cubist forms, the interesting evidence of the artist's creative processes (which become more apparent when paintings are not too completely abstract), the secret drama of the conflict between the artist's inner personality and the alien personality presented by the outward appearance of nature, plus a residual interest in the subject itself, all combine to pour a warm lifeblood into Cubist painting. This is *in addition* to the vitality and interest provided by the underlying *design* that is the integral basis of all Cubist art.

The Cubists created not merely designs but *design-pictures*. Their slow and gradual switch of emphasis, over more recent years, from the *design* element to the *picture* element of the combination not only indicates a rounding out of their artistic philosophy but also suggests a possible trend that may extend into the future.

30   Parade of the "Isms"

The explosion of Cubism was felt instantly around the artistic world. Artists in Germany, Holland, Italy, and Russia heard about it almost immediately. Eventually the news reached the Americas and Japan. The art colony in Paris, already in a turmoil, boiled up into an even madder frenzy.

Soon news came from Paris of a whole parade of artistic *isms* appearing one after another. Each new "ism" detonated into the limelight of world-wide publicity with bombshell effect, and each followed on the heels of the preceding "ism" with such bewildering rapidity that the puzzled average man could only throw up his hands and exclaim, "Will it never end!" To add to the confusion, the arrival of each new "ism" was often accompanied by a violent and bombastic *manifesto* denouncing

Picasso: *Guernica, 1937*. Picasso's later paintings display a sureness of taste and a skill in abstracting that set them above earlier works. *Guernica*, an enormous picture 25 feet in length and Picasso's most ambitious effort, was inspired by the bombing of Guernica in 1937. Though impressive, it is questionable whether or not the finished painting has been surpassed by Picasso's preliminary sketches, which are marvels of fluid and emotionally powerful design.

230

Duchamp: *Nude Descending a Staircase, 1912.* Although not painted by a member of the Futurist group, this picture is a good example of the basic ideas of Futurism, particularly of the idea of trying to suggest motion.

Balla: *Dog on Leash, 1912.* Futurist efforts to indicate motion are sometimes not unlike photographs that might have been taken with a stroboscopic camera.

231

all previous "isms" and claiming the pinnacle of artistic supremacy for itself.

In a short period after the founding of Cubism there came Futurism, Orphism, Purism, Synchromism, Vorticism, Suprematism, Rayonism, Non-Objectivism, Constructivism, Neo-Plasticism, Compressionism, Machinism, and Dadaism. Obviously, none of these names were very illuminating in the way of indicating what their particular brand of art was about. The artists, rather naïvely, liked the high-sounding names and enjoyed being mysterious; perhaps thought that being so might win their groups more publicity.

Actually, there is nothing at all mysterious about the "isms." They were all—up to Dadaism—variations of the new abstract art. Two of them, Futurism and Purism, were direct offshoots of Cubism. The rest were varieties of *non*-Cubist, non-nature-derived abstraction. Some of the "isms" were practically identical with certain others except for the artists' nationality: Italian *Futurism* and English *Vorticism*; French *Purism* and German *Compressionism*; French *Orphism* and expatriot-American *Synchromism*.

Noisiest of all the "ism" groups were the Futurists. The torrents of publicity that they managed to pour out into the world, the bombastic manifestos that heralded their exhibitions, were considerably more earth-shaking than their actual paintings.

The group was Italian. It included Umberto Boccioni, Giacomo Balla, Luigi Russolo, Gino Severini, Carlo Carrà, and the writer-politician Filippo Tommaso Marinetti, as well as an important American painter, Joseph Stella. The group's aims were resoundingly stated in the *First Futurist Manifesto*. Excerpts from this Manifesto, as summarized by R. H. Wilenski in his *Modern French Painters*, are as follows:

> A Racing Motor-Car, its frame adorned with great pipes, like snakes with explosive breath—a Roaring Motor-Car which seems to be running on shrapnel—is more beautiful than the Victory of Samothrace. . . .
>
> The Past is balsam for prisoners, invalids, and men on their death-beds who see the Future closed to them.
>
> We will none of it. We are young, strong, living—we are FUTURISTS.
>
> Museums are cemeteries—public dormitories. We will permit flowers once a year before *La Gioconda*—but no more daily walking in these gloomy mausoleums, no more libations of living sensibility into cemetery urns.
>
> We are out to glorify War—the only health-giver of the world—Militarism, Patriotism, the Destructive arm of the Anarchist, Ideas that kill, Contempt for Women . . .
>
> We are out to combat Moralism, Feminism, and all Opportunist and Utilitarian meanness. . . .

We extol aggressive movement, feverish insomnia, the double-quick step, the somersault, the box on the ear....

Poetry must be a violent onslaught. There is no masterpiece without aggressiveness....

We shall sing of great crowds in the excitement of Labor, Pleasure, or Rebellion; of the nocturnal vibration of arsenals and workshops beneath their electric moons; of greedy stations swallowing smoking snakes; of factories suspended from the clouds by strings of smoke; of adventurous liners scenting the horizon; of broad-chested locomotives galloping on rails—giant steel horses bridled with long tubes; of aeroplanes with screws whose sound is like the flapping of flags and the cheers of a roaring crowd.

It is from Italy that we launch this Manifesto of Destructive Incendiary Violence.

Italy has been too long the market place of the Second-hand Art Trade.

We must free our country from its canker of professors, archaeologists, cicerones, antiquaries and second-hand dealers.

On then, Good Incendiaries! Fire the libraries! . . . Turn the floods into museums! Let the famous pictures float! . . . We cast our Challenge to the Stars!

The expression of dynamism, energy, *movement* is the goal of Futurist art. The Futurists tried to indicate the movement of a dog's feet by a series of superimposed views such as might be taken by a stroboscopic camera (Balla's *Dog on a Leash;* see page 231). At other times an effect suggestive of magnetic lines of force was used to show power and motion.

Curiously enough, what is perhaps the most eloquent pictorial expression of Futurist ideas, the famous *Nude Descending a Staircase,* was painted not by a member of the Futurist group, but by a French Cubist, Marcel Duchamp. (See page 231.)

The real masterpiece of Futurism is Boccioni's sculpture, *Unique Forms of Continuity in Space*—a boldly striding figure made up of swirling forms which very effectively produce the feeling of motion so much sought by the Futurists (page 227).

In subject matter, the Futurists like to picture (abstractly, of course) the modern world of machinery—automobiles, locomotives, armored trains, and the like. They painted cabaret night-life scenes because they represented city life in its "brightest and most *kinetic*" form. But except for the attempt to delineate motion, Futurism was not essenially different from Cubism.

The impact of Futurism rocked the art world for a year or two, then the movement faded from the scene. Oddly, Futurist influence was felt more strongly in England than anywhere else. In Paris, Futurism lacked the artistic solidity necessary to get a secure foothold, and the Cubists' pre-eminence was not disturbed.

The *political* ideas expressed in the Futurist manifestos (derived from Anarchism) lived on later in the ideology of Mussolini's Fascism. It should be remembered, however, that Futurism preceded the establishment of Italian Fascism by a decade.

Futurism was a derivation of Cubism carried to one extreme. *Purism* was a form of Cubism carried to an almost diametrically opposite extreme. If Futurism stood for violent action, Purism leaned toward serene calm. If Futurism could not wait to plunge into the future, Purism looked wistfully at the past. Both Futurism and Purism revered the machine. But while Futurism idolized the roar of the speeding locomotive, Purism preferred the machine at rest, so that it could better contemplate the metallic severity of its straight-line forms.

Developed about 1918 by Amédée Ozenfant and the architect-artist Jeanneret (Le Corbusier), Purism was essentially a reform movement. Its founders, looking at the more recent works of Braque and Picasso (Rococo Cubism), decided that Cubism had become frivolously decorative and that it was time to return to the "classic" austerity of earlier days.

The Purists painted in geometrically simplified forms (see below), not too extremely abstracted, resembling a formal architectural design. Their design-pictures were pleasing but not very exciting. Intellectual theory, rather than emotion, dominated their art. A favorite conceit of the Purists was the trick called *equivocal space*, wherein a line which delineates one

PURISM. Le Corbusier: *Still Life*, 1920. This picture typical of the Purist style. Lines and forms are "designy," almost geometrical. Sometimes Purist pictures incorporated the concept of *equivocal space*, in which the outline of one object also happens to be the outline of another object.

shape is also the boundary of another shape. For instance, what appears to be the edge of a guitar also happens to be the outline of a milk pitcher or (at the same time) a water carafe. It is an amusing trick, but hardly very profound, nor can it be credited with any very serious artistic significance.

Purism, in spite of the lively writings of Monsieur Ozenfant, lacked staying power and, like Futurism, fell out of favor in a few years. Also like Futurism, its influence seemed greater in countries other than its own.

The names of two individual artists are sometimes linked with Cubism, although neither of them was in any sense a Cubist. Maurice Utrillo and his friend, Amadeo Modigliani, were both madcap Bohemians who led the wildest and weirdest of lives. They were also talented artists who produced pictures of great charm.

Utrillo was the son of Suzanne Valadon, trapeze performer, artist's model, and later herself an artist of note. The boy, brought up haphazardly in a Bohemian-gamin atmosphere, became in due time the Number 1 Bohemian of all Paris. He was an alcoholic of the wilder, madder type, and his pranks were soon internationally famous. Nevertheless, he produced a large number of paintings, notable not only for their pleasing quality but also for their essential sanity.

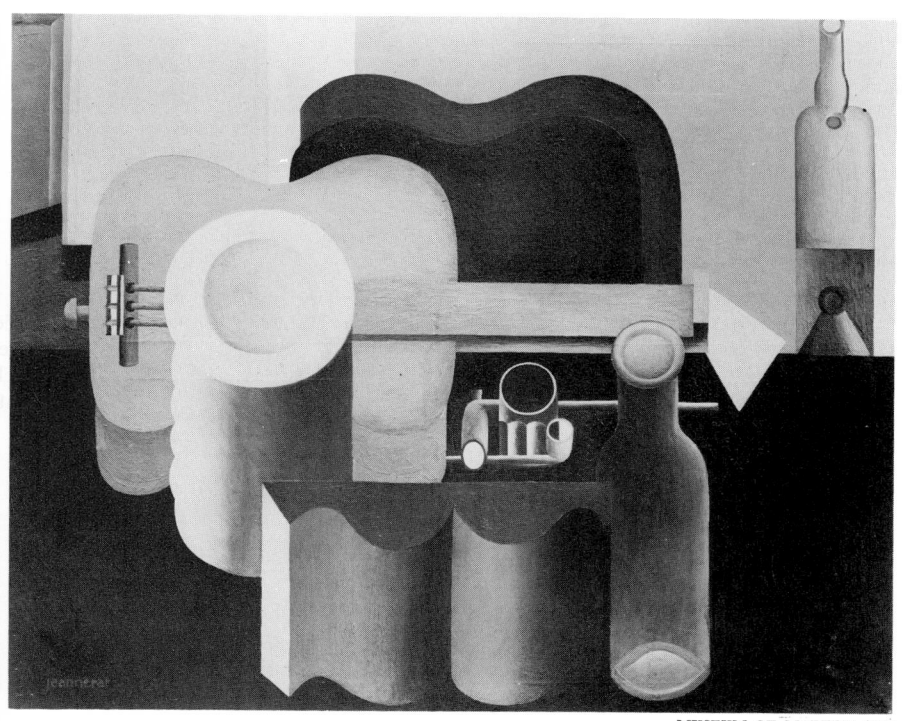

Modigliani: *Reclining Nude* (right). This picture
vides into three large design areas, two dark and
light in value. Modigliani's delicacy of line and de
beauty of area are shown here.

He painted buildings, city streets, the inns and houses of Montmartre.
Often he painted them from memory or from cheap postcards. But whatever he painted came to life. These pictures of winding streets and dram-
shops have a strange vitality that is peculiarly Utrillo's. He did not belong
to any particular school, the best description of his style being the paradoxical one of *sophisticated primitive*. He was a sophisticated artist who
painted almost realistically, yet there remained in his work a childlike
touch of the primitive that imbued everything he did with an artistic
vitality it would not have had otherwise. His painting was uneven—some
things are close to being commercial "pot-boilers,"—others are strong and
vital. But everything he painted has the quality of being appealingly
charming.

Utrillo is said to have finally conquered his alcoholic tendencies and
to have settled down to long years of more respectable living. Modigliani
was not so fortunate. *His* unbridled Bohemianism led to an early and
tragic death.

Utrillo: *Place du Tertre* (left). Utrillo's pictures have a quality of charm that comes in part from a touch of primitivism in his otherwise sophisticated work.

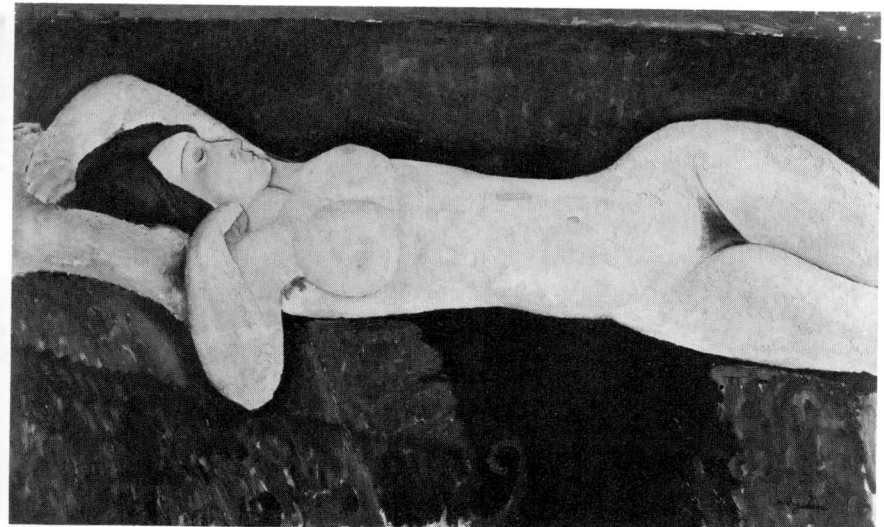

Of Jewish-Italian extraction, Modigliani came to Paris in 1906 and attempted to live as a Romantic aesthete—in the manner of Beardsley and Wilde. But his funds failed, his art did not pay, and he became a café character. He was very handsome, popular, and unusually attractive to women. But dissipation ruled—and ruined—his life. He died at the age of thirty-five of tuberculosis, brought on by alcoholism, starvation, and cold. After a fantastic funeral, attended by great multitudes of Parisians, Modigliani's mistress killed herself by throwing herself from a high window onto the pavement.

Modigliani's art is too personal and original to be classed with any one group. In broad stylistic approach, it is perhaps closest to Gauguin. That is, Modigliani's pictures are expressed in large, flat areas of color, areas decorative in outline. He paints very flatly with as little modeling as possible, and, what is more notable, composes with remarkable simplicity, confining his color areas to as few as possible. The simplicity and boldness of these large flat areas remind one of Japanese prints.

Modigliani was impressed both by African sculpture and by the early-Renaissance Primitive painters of his native Italy. Both of these influences are strongly reflected in the shapes of Modigliani's faces and heads and in the quality of his line.

But what distinguishes Modigliani's painting above all is his own creative touch—the sensitivity of his outline, the delicacy of his design, the grace which characterizes his shapes, and his perfect taste. The areas of color are beautiful in form, yet strong and interesting. It is this that makes him a great artist.

31   Rendezvous with Geometry

From Cézanne to Analytical Cubism, the major path of modern art's development has been a more or less straight road leading to abstraction. From the relatively realistic pictures of Cézanne to the planes and facets of the Analytical Cubists, the paintings of the modern artists had progressively, step by step, grown more abstract. But upon reaching a point of near—*but not quite complete*—abstraction, the Cubists stepped aside, as it were, and ceased their forward march in this direction.

It was inevitable, however, that the steady march to ever more complete abstraction should continue to its logical conclusion. If the Cubists were unwilling to go on, there were others only too eager to push forward. Such artists could well ask—if the Cubists could go as far as they had in tearing nature apart to make design-pictures, why shouldn't others go ahead and make design-pictures without any dependence at all on nature? After all, the movement toward abstraction had been a liberating revolt against the tyranny of naturalistic representation. Then why not take the final step—free the artist entirely and make *complete* abstractions, unfettered by any lingering ties to natural models?

An artistic expression of the answers to these questions was inescapable. From about 1912 on an abstract art arose in Europe in which all thought of derivation from nature was banished. The major development of this *complete* or *pure abstraction* took place, not in France, but in the northern Teutonic and Slavic countries—in Holland, Germany, and Russia. In contrast to the tight little Cubist cadre in Paris, *pure abstraction* was developed by widely separated groups, which nevertheless maintained a sympathetic contact with one another through personal acquaintanceship among the artists.

The name *non-objectivism* is sometimes given to this non-nature-derived art. It is a good name, but it has been claimed, somewhat narrowly, by two specific groups—one in Russia, and one, later, in America. To apply the name *non-objective* to all pure abstraction, though perfectly correct and descriptive, might perhaps cause some confusion. Hence, in this book, the term *pure abstraction* will be used.

If Cubism had its Picasso to lead and point the way, pure abstraction also had a great proponent—Wassily Kandinsky. Kandinsky was a Russian who had given up a law career at the age of thirty to devote his life to art. After studying at Munich, he traveled widely and, from shortly after the turn of the century on, kept in close contact with radical art movements in Holland, Belgium, Germany, and Russia, as well as Paris. Strongly influenced by the *Fauves* for a time, he found his way to abstraction quite independently of the Cubists. He did not free his art of nature derivations until about 1912, but once having abandoned nature as a source of inspiration, he never returned to it.

Unhampered by Cubist traditions, inhibitions, and prejudices, Kandinsky advanced rapidly to a mature system of design. There were no years of preoccupation with facets or planes to hold him back. Instead, Kandinsky proceeded directly from more and more abstract renditions of *Fauvism* to pure design, retaining, however, such useful characteristics of *Fauvism* as freedom of approach, Gauguin-inspired brilliance and gayety of color, and a flowing, rather than tight and architectural, conception of design.

Hence, in 1913, Kandinsky was able to paint such a masterpiece of loose, freely rendered *pure design* as his famous *Improvisation No. 30* (page 240). (Incidentally, the "cannons" in this picture were not nature-inspired, but are merely an accidental resemblance taken by pure design forms.) No picture quite like this had ever been painted before. Of this painting Kandinsky wrote:

> . . . This entire description is chiefly an analysis of the picture which I have painted rather subconsciously in a state of strong inner tension. So intensively do I feel the necessity of some of the forms, that I remember having given loud-voiced directions to myself, as for instance: "But the corners must be heavy!"

In the utter freedom of the artist's rendering, its personal and emotional expression, its disregard of any convention, this picture well deserves to be described as *expressionist*. The artist has put his personal emotions into paint with scarcely any restraint whatever. The picture is also, however, a design, although it might not seem so if viewed with a quick careless look.

If we study this painting at length (in color, of course, as here color is important) we will see that it does *not* consist of daubs of paint applied haphazardly without form or purpose. Instead, it will be seen that every brush stroke, every touch of color, is in exactly the right place, that each value and area relates aesthetically to nearby areas, and that all the various elements coalesce into an exciting, unified design-picture. It had to be a design because, of all artists, Kandinsky is inherently and completely a designer, and even in such a freely expressed, somewhat Fauve-influenced picture as this, his designer instinct dictated where every line and spot of color should be placed.

239 Kandinsky painted a number of these loose, freely expressed abstrac-

tions. But eventually his own nature made it necessary to change his style. The change was a violent one, from extreme looseness of approach to extreme tightness. In a sense it was a pity, because no one else has painted pure abstractions quite as intriguing and of the same type as *Improvisation No. 30* (below). On the other hand, the tighter forms of *Composition No. 1* (opposite) are more characteristic of Kandinsky's inner *designer* spirit.

As his art developed, Kandinsky became a master of the technique of design. He studied the aesthetic relations of points and lines and areas in minute detail. He analyzed color in its design implications. He could produce design almost as a form of calligraphy—he could literally write it down. It could be said that over the years—in contrast to the direction taken by the Cubists—Kandinsky's *design-pictures* became more and more *designs* and less and less *pictorial*.

Nevertheless, perhaps because of Kandinsky's aesthetic sensitivity and perhaps also because of his lively sense of movement and drama, his pictures display a vitality that is notably missing in the work of some of his followers and imitators. Kandinsky's work is especially interesting for its design, an intricate, active design of many delicately balanced elements. Kandinsky was an inventor, but unlike Picasso who invented from nature,

Kandinsky: *Improvisation No. 30, 1913.* Loose, free design. A pure abstraction, it is not based on nature. In spite of its apparent carelessness of execution, this picture is tightly knit as a design and is well composed aesthetically.

Kandinsky's invention was carried on entirely in the world of the purely aesthetic. Finally, there is a certain personal mysticism, a mysterious touch of the spirit, that keeps this master's painting well on the safe side of the fence that separates *art* from the purely mechanical.

Some thousands of years ago, Plato wrote: *

I will try to speak of the beauty of shapes, and I do not mean, as most people would think, the shapes of living figures, or their imitations in paintings, but I mean straight lines and curves and the shapes made from them, flat or solid, by the lathe, ruler, and square, if you see what I mean. These are not beautiful for any particular reason or purpose, as other things are, but are always by their very nature beautiful, and give pleasure of their own quite free from the itch of desire; and colors of this kind are beautiful, too, and give a similar pleasure.

* Alfred Barr, Jr., has on several occasions made effective use of this quotation in his illuminating texts on abstract art.

Kandinsky: *Composition No. 1, 1921.* Kandinsky's later, more typical "tight" style. Kandinsky was primarily a designer, and this picture typifies his complex, but well-integrated designs.

(Above) ORPHISM consisted of disks or planes of
lently bright rainbow colors. This *Disks of New*
(1912) by Kupka is a *pure* abstraction because it is
derived from nature as were the paintings of the C
ists.

Sooner or later, artists plunging into the world of pure abstract form
had to discover geometry, just as a traveler traveling from Denver to San
Francisco must sooner or later see mountains. Inevitably, if natural forms
are abjured, geometrical forms must be considered, and inexorably, the
path of pure abstraction in art led to a recontemplation of the geometrical.
Many of Kandinsky's shapes in his tighter style were geometrical; but other
artists had already discovered the beauties of geometry, and in this Kandinsky was a follower rather than a leader.

An early form of geometrical abstraction was the *Orphism* of Robert
Delaunay and Frank Kupka. These men painted disks and spirals of gay
prismatic colors or rainbow-colored "windows." Interest in these pictures
lies primarily in the bright rainbow colors, plus the simple but dynamic
design provided by the concentric circles of color. Similar pictures were
painted by a group who called themselves the *Synchromists*.

In Moscow, Michael Larionov invented *Rayonism*, a pure abstract style
based on radiating lines of light—splintery lines that are somehow reminiscent of the splintery folds of drapery in Byzantine and Russian Ikon
painting.

Both of these styles were primitive forms of geometrical abstraction
and too vague in their concepts of form to be of lasting importance.
Geometrical abstraction did not come into its own until it discovered the

242

SUPREMATISM: The Suprematists tried to reduce their abstract art to fundamental geometric forms. Their pictures, such as this one by Malevich, depend for interest on aesthetic perfection of detail, nicety of placement, arrangement, and balance.

square (and an occasional circle). This happened in Russia, where Kasimir Malevich tried to reduce art to its essential fundamentals by painting a few simple circles and squares on a rectangular background (see above). In this style, called *Suprematism*, the enjoyment given by the picture was to be entirely aesthetic—to be derived from the perfect aesthetic placement of the simple forms, the inherent beauty of the circles and squares themselves, and the aesthetic interest of the composition. The final pinnacle of the Suprematist movement, in fact, the ultimate in all geometical abstraction, came in 1918, when Malevich painted *White on White*—one white square painted within another larger square of a slightly different tone of white.

It was the utmost in simplicity. Curiously, this picture, far from being dull and obvious, is mysteriously interesting. The smaller, inner square, slightly tilted, is located within the outer square with delicate aesthetic feeling for placement and proportion, and the two nearly, but not quite, alike tones of white, one warm and the other cold, create an odd and intriguing color sensation that makes the picture seem to contain much more than a simple square.

This was as far as modern art could go in the direction of simple geometry. From here geometrical abstraction could only retrace its tracks, become more complicated, or adapt itself, as it did, to commercial uses.

243

Mondrian: *Pier and Ocean, 1914* (left). An early composition which was derived from a natural scene (a pier jutting out into water). Most of Mondrian's pictures are expressed in verticals and horizontals. Mondrian: *Composition, 1921* (right). A composition more typical of Mondrian's later work. Space in this picture is divided up according to a delicately balanced system of aesthetic checks and thrusts.

Gabo: *Monument for an Airport* (above). Pure abstraction in the field of sculpture. Work of this type was called *Constructivism*. Calder: *Mobile* (below). An interesting variation of Constructivism is Alexander Calder's fascinating *mobiles*, hanging metal forms that move in the wind.

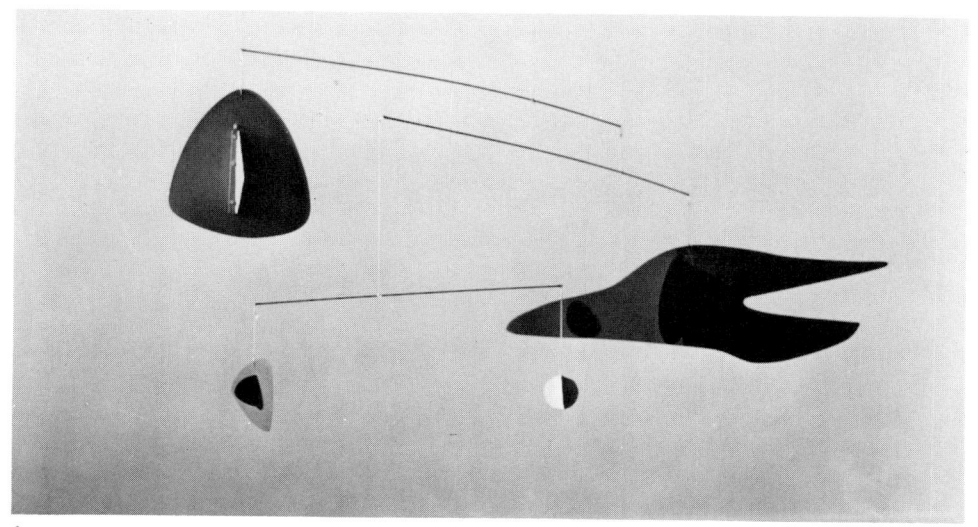

If geometric abstraction reached a "farthest north" of logic and simplicity in the square of Malevich, it reached other heights of subtlety and a near mysticism in the crossed lines and sliced-up spaces of Piet Mondrian. If anything, Mondrian's painting is even more an art of pure aesthetics than the simplified geometry of the Suprematists.

Mondrian, a native of Holland, had an academic art training, was impressed by Cubism, then developed an abstract style of his own. From a generously curving academic style he moved to a form of nature-derived abstraction based on slightly curving lines. This gave way to an abstract but still nature-derived style, consisting only of vertical and horizontal lines (as *Pier and Ocean*, page 244). Later, Mondrian painted only of horizontals and verticals, meeting or crossing at right angles. He wrote:

> I found that the right angle is the only constant relationship, and that, through the proportions of dimension, its constant expression can be given movement, that is, made living.

His mature style (called *Neo-Plasticism*) consisted of black lines (of occasionally varying width) crossing a white background, cutting it into rectangles of varying sizes and proportions. Occasionally, a rectangle would be "filled" with gray or a primary color. Here was the simplest *means* of expression possible. Obviously, the essence of Mondrian's art was to be found in the perfect aesthetic relationship between the various included rectangles (including the lines themselves when they had thickness). It gained interest from the delicate aesthetic tensions and balances arising from the thrusts and weights of the rectangular divisions of space, from the advancing and receding effects of the occasional colors, and from the rhythms of alternating contrasting areas.

It has been said of Mondrian that his "fundamental aim was to transcend the particular to express the universal. He was the great uncompromising classicist of the early twentieth century."

That is true of the means used by Mondrian to develop his pictures. The converse applies to the appreciation of his art on the part of the public. Of all modern artists, Mondrian's pictures are the hardest to understand, not only on the part of the pictorially ignorant, but also of the relatively sophisticated. The pictures do *not* have—nor ever will have—universal appeal to the average observer. They are for a select few. To this select group, however, the subtleties of Mondrian's design, his severe classicism and untainted aestheticism, will have a strong and lasting appeal.

All pure abstraction—all geometric abstraction, particularly—is an art of aesthetic nicety, of precise and pleasing proportions, and interesting, but purely aesthetic, relationships between the elements of design. It is a truly abstract art, and is to be enjoyed as such. It is no more than this, nor any less.

As in the case of Cubism, pure abstraction had its counterpart in sculpture, notably in the work of Naum Gabo (see page 245) and Antoine Pevsner. Even more importantly, pure abstraction had an enormous influence on modern architecture, modern furniture, and the design of innumerable domestic articles. The face of our modern living has been changed by the work of commercial designers carrying out ideas first promulgated by the pure abstractionists of Holland, Germany, and Russia. Especially influential in the development of these ideas into practical channels was the famous German *Bauhaus*, a remarkable school which was as much a creative workshop and a forum for ideas as a place for instruction.

32   The Soul—and the Pixies

In tracing the development of modern art, we have thus far followed only the largest trunk of the tree that grew out of the four roots of Cézanne, Seurat, Gauguin, and Van Gogh. We have explored that particular stream of artistic ideas that had its source in Cézanne and Seurat, which inspired the Cubists, and which came, finally, to a logical conclusion in the geometrical abstraction of Mondrian and the Suprematists. Following this one line of approach, we have seen the roughly stated design of Cézanne become more and more emphatic, more formal, and more abstract, until an ultimate point of no farther possible advance was reached in the simple geometric square of Malevich.

The Cézanne-Seurat inspired, design-dominant trend of development does not, however, constitute the whole of modern art. There is another trunk of the tree, another stream of growth of rival importance, which had its source in Van Gogh and Gauguin. The work of the artists who were guided by the inspiration of Van Gogh led in quite a different direction from that of those who followed the trail to abstraction.

We have seen how Van Gogh's art leaned toward disorder of presentation and informality of statement, to violent personalized emotion, and to mysticism. Van Gogh's ideas, transmuted and made more palatable by the catalytic agent of Gauguin (who was also nearer to the younger artists' set in Paris), had much to do with forming the style of the *Fauves*. The *Fauves*, however—inhibited perhaps by their classical French sense of "taste" and by their intellectual sophistication as artists—did not develop Van Gogh's turbulent *expressionism* to its full possibilities.

That remained to be done, with unrestrained enthusiasm and Teutonic thoroughness, by the artists of Germany. In Germany, *Expressionismus* became not only a dominant trend in art and a way of making pictures, it even came to be a philosophy of life. The German artists plumbed the possibilities of personal expression in painting to its utmost limits, to the point of incoherence and incomprehensibility.

German Expressionism took shape under a number of influences, which were generally different from those characteristic of French art. First and foremost was the ancient, deep-seated, underlying spirit of German art—a spirit traceable to the Middle Ages and somehow irremovably entwined in the Teutonic character. The German was a Romantic. He was relatively uninterested in form and style as ends in themselves, and he could never quite grasp the Mediterranean Classical point of view. On the other hand, he was deeply moved by introspective emotional values, by "feeling," by brooding soul-searching, and by mysticism. In naming their earliest Expressionist group "The Bridge" (*Die Brücke*), the German artists asserted they were "seeking for the bridge which leads from the visible to the invisible." They sought to paint the soul.

It should follow without surprise that German art has seldom been a *pure* art. Not only aesthetic emotions, but also moral, social, and philosophical considerations have been included in its scope. If Van Gogh confused art and life, so did his Expressionist followers; so also have Northern artists done since time immemorial. A favorite and typical undertone in German psychology, the sense of catastrophe, recurs again and again in German Expressionist art.

The basic impurity of German art has had several effects on the nature of Expressionist painting in the early twentieth century. For one thing, the output of the Expressionist group has been notably uneven in artistic quality. Some (but not all, of course) of the paintings have been difficult to understand and appreciate—by anybody. It is all very well for an artist to express his soul, but what the world can comprehend—what art "pays off on," as it were—is what goes down on the canvas. If what is on the canvas contains symbols or other expression of ideas and feelings locked in the artist's mind, and if no key is provided, the painting becomes merely an irritating puzzle. Unless there are other redeeming qualities, such paintings must soon be cast aside and forgotten. Perhaps a feeling of more or less well-justified irritation moved the German critic Trog to remark: "What cannot be defined is considered Expressionism."

Another reflection of the general impurity of German art, as art, is its persistent *literary* quality, an important consideration from the modern point of view. Moral, social, and philosophic motivations are literary in spirit, as opposed to the purely *artistic*, which has to do with form, design, color, and other aesthetic factors. A strong literary intent runs through German Expressionist art; and it is not surprising that Expressionist work occasionally leans to caricature, which is highly literary, and sometimes to fantasy, which is also literary in essence.

Since the literary in art is constantly opposed by the philosophy of modern art as a whole, it may be questioned why these pictures are included under the name "modern." Indeed, if these paintings were executed more realistically, they might well have been considered as belonging to traditional academic-realistic art. But they are not realistic pictures; they are saved for modernism by the Expressionists' implacable and intense hatred of realism in painting. Because of this fierce denial of realism, other modern and purely *artistic* qualities become possible in the pictures, in spite of the artists' occasional literary intentions. In other words, a compromise is effected between antimodern literary considerations and the antiliterary artistic and aesthetic requirements of a true modern picture.

That this compromise was accomplished successfully by the better Expressionist artists is historically significant. The trend in French, Cézanne-inspired modern art ran consistently (at least until quite recently) against literary manifestations. The reinjection of literary themes into otherwise modern pictures by the German Expressionists was the first step in a reverse trend—a trend that would later culminate in the almost completely literary productions of the Surrealists.

What is startling about German modern art is that while it readily condoned literary intent on the part of the artist, it was at the same time so violently opposed to *realism* of execution. All modern artists eschew representational realism, but the Germans went beyond all others in the vehemence with which they distorted it or struck it from their paintings. The explanation of this is to be found in the artistic and cultural atmosphere that rather peculiarly surrounded the German artist in the early years of this century.

First, there was the Teutonic teaching of academic-realistic art. The rules of academic realism were clamped down harder on art students' necks by the thoroughgoing German teachers than would be possible anywhere else on earth. As a result, when artistic revolt came, it reacted more violently, more bitterly, against academic shackles in Germany than elsewhere.

Second, at the time when Expressionism came into being, Germany's industrial expansion was accelerating. Prussian militarism was rampant. The German citizen found himself more and more subject to the discipline of a bureaucracy dedicated to imperial control. In the words of Horace Kallen, "the boundaries of personal freedom were contracting." Expressionism was itself a form of revolt of the individual against repression. It struck back at the symbol of authority implied by traditional academic-realistic teaching.

Otherwise, German Expressionism grew from sources common to modern art in France, and generally paralleled the development of *Fauvism*. Like *Fauvism*, German Expressionism sprang from Van Gogh—with an assist from Gauguin. The Norwegian, Edvard Munch, first of the Expressionists, had been influenced directly by Gauguin.

Like the *Fauves*, the Expressionists delighted in the use of bright colors, but while the effect of *Fauve* color was gay but tasteful, Expressionist color was violent and often lacking in taste. In fact, Expressionism as a whole was far more violent, more brutal, and more emotional than *Fauvism*.

As German Expressionism established itself more firmly, it reacted somewhat against French influences. Part of this reaction was due, no doubt, to German nationalist pride; but it was also due to the more fundamental Teutonic reaction against the classical formalism of Cubism.

Expressionism was enormously influenced by primitive and primitivistic art. African masks and statuettes, prehistoric art, primitive folk art, the art of the insane, and the art of children were studied with zest, and the artists tried to incorporate these primitive strains into their own paintings. Generally, children's art seems to have had the greatest direct influence;

whereas African Negro art with its emphasis on subtle design was the least understood.

The Expressionists frequently painted pictures of masks, but they were not masks that looked like the creations of African or Polynesian savages. They were northern masks, such as actors' masks or Hallowe'en masks. Often the Expressionists painted masks that looked like faces and faces that looked like masks.

The characteristics of Expressionist style are deliberate roughness and crudeness of painting, broad slashing lines, slap-dash impasto effects, violent color, and distortion of nature reveled in for the sake of greater emotional expression. The artist painted from within, literally throwing himself at the canvas. Strength was sought, rather than grace.

Design, when it occurred, seemed to come as something of a happy accident, although the better Expressionist painters were not lacking in natural design sense. On the whole, the formal elements of design were too frequently neglected. The artists painted to express their feelings, their emotions, their souls. That was the main idea.

Most profound of the German Expressionists and the most typical and eloquent exponent of the Expressionist style at its best is Emil Nolde. His work is rough, savage, powerful, mysterious, tragic, and deeply emotional. His brush stroke is broad and heavily laden with pigment. But behind the purposely crude technique, there is the touch of a great artist, and a sad, sensitive poetry underlies the heavy, somber forms. An innate sense of design, felt rather than arrived at formally, organizes his pictures better than most other Expressionists, and lifts his art to a higher level.

More completely than the others, Nolde carries on the spirit of Vincent Van Gogh. He has much of the excitement and inner vitality so

Kokoschka: *Portrait of Dr. Tietze and His Wife, 190*
The rough Expressionist style of Oskar Kokoschka do
not conceal his penetrating draughtsmanship (nor h
pleasing, Gauguin-influenced color). His pictures a
well organized, but the organization is essentially cor
positional rather than strongly designed, somewh
similar to the *Fauve* pictures.

characteristic of the earlier master. Nolde's subject matter is sometimes religious, sometimes satirical. Sometimes it borders on fantasy and the supernatural. Like several others of his contemporaries, Nolde seems to have an obsession for painting strange, grimacing masks.

Another Expressionist of great reputation is the Austrian, Oskar Kokoschka. Kokoschka is less "primitive" than Nolde and less deeply poetical. Kokoschka's brushwork is heavy and pigment-laden in the usual Expressionist manner, but what is less typical is the Austrian artist's masterly draughtsmanship and his beautiful color. He is a remarkable painter of faces. Kokoschka has been compared to Van Gogh, but the resemblance is superficial. Kokoschka in drawing is nearer to Rembrandt than to Van Gogh; in color he is nearer to Gauguin.

Nolde and Kokoschka are the outstanding exponents of the Expressionist style in its purest sense. There were other artists of importance connected with the Expressionist group in one way or other, who, however, have made a name for themselves for other things than their Expressionism as such. Kandinsky, for example, for his abstraction. Georg Grosz for his caricature and satire. Klee for his fantasy and design.

And there was Franz Marc, who fell before Verdun in 1916, who combined sentiment, Expressionist ideas, and a form of Cubist abstraction in charming pictures of animals. Though overlaid with almost sugary sentiment, Marc's design is active and dynamic. There is life and movement in his abstract forms. A wind blows through his work.

In Paris, Chaim Soutine, a Russian Jew who had no connection whatever with the German Expressionist groups, has painted pictures more expressionist in spirit than those of the Expressionists themselves. Soutine's painting combines a Rembrandtlike richness of surface with good

design and sharply felt emotion—and extreme distortion. His rather hot and raw colors are sometimes harshly clanging, however, and detract from the pleasure given by his pictures otherwise.

Fantasy, as a subject matter for art, has interested painters for thousands of years. The names of Hieronymus Bosch and William Blake come quickly to mind when we think of the art of the unearthly and unreal, and there have been scores of others in the past who have preferred to paint from the untrammeled imagination rather than from matter-of-fact nature as normally seen.

Early in the course of the modern movement, one such painter appeared in the person of Odilon Redon, a contemporary of Cézanne. Redon, a gentle and wraithlike personality, was fascinated by the weird and unreal, and frequently painted mysterious dream fantasies, some of which seem to be direct precursors of modern Surrealism. His pictures, though interesting in subject matter (and often delightful in color), are somewhat weak in design organization, and hence are of rather incidental importance in a study of modern art.

It was inevitable, sooner or later, that fantasy would appeal strongly to more than one modern artist. We have already seen, in Chapter 27, how the Cubists found imagination and originality important to their art as artistic factors that seemed to increase pictorial vitality. The Cubists, however, did not base their work wholly on imagination, but rather started from the factual basis of nature and then *applied* imagination to their abstracting process.

Fantasy is a natural expression of imagination. In addition, fantasy has a special usefulness to the imaginative artist who wishes to design. The fixed forms of nature are sometimes balky; they do not always easily conform to the needs of the designer. The world of fantasy, on the other hand, is under complete control of the designer's imagination. If he needs a certain form or shape, he can create it at will, or he can borrow from nature whatever image suits his fancy and meets the needs of his design.

The German Expressionists approached close to fantasy on a number of occasions. In their examinations of their souls, they seldom crossed over the borderline of the unreal and the fantastic, perhaps because they took themselves too seriously. But at last, from their group, an artist *did* come forth who did *not* take himself too seriously nor the world around him too factually. Highly imaginative, and a great designer at the same time, he understood how fantasy could be put to work to help him construct his pictures. His name was Paul Klee.

Paul Klee was born December 18, 1879, near Berne, Switzerland. His father was a Bavarian, his mother, Southern French. His education, however, was primarily Germanic. After some debate as to whether he should be a musician or an artist, young Klee went to Munich at the age of nineteen to study painting.

He at first intended to be a caricaturist; but there was too little acid and too much poetry in his make-up for such a career. His early attempts at satire were too decorative, too fraught with happily soaring imagination and gentle, whimsical humor to be really satirical; they belonged rather to a slightly grotesque fairyland or to some other strange realm of fantasy.

Klee's first works were etchings and black-and-white pen drawings. Traveling about Europe, he came in contact with French modern art, learning about color from the Fauves and about abstraction and design from the Cubists. He belonged to a group of artists called the Blue Riders, or the Blue Knights (*Der Blaue Reiter*), who did much to establish Expressionism firmly in Germany. After World War I, he taught at the famous Bauhaus. Most of Klee's life was spent in Germany. The triumph of Hitlerism, however, forced him to go into "exile" in Switzerland, where he died in 1940.

Though Klee's drawings and paintings were often madly fantastic, there was nothing at all eccentric about his life, which was calm, serious, and studious. He was a gentle, sensitive man, noted for his common sense and mild, pleasant sense of humor.

Klee's art defies description or classification. It cannot quite be pinned down. It is as inventive and varied as the art of Picasso, but unlike Picasso's, Klee's art does not fall into successive styles or periods. Rather, it has always seemed to be going all ways at once, at all times. Nor does Klee's work seem to show any progressive development; it was born practically full grown.

However, a few things *can* be said. Most Klee pictures are essentially abstract (regardless of any literary connotations invoked by his provocative titles), and there is no Klee picture whatever that is not brilliantly, exquisitely designed. Klee was as thorough a designer as Kandinsky, and far warmer, richer, and more colorful in general feeling. His inventiveness has been compared constantly with Picasso's, and he also rivals Picasso in the vivid personality which animates his work.

Klee's "thin, incalculably spry line" * is intensely sensitive, and he is a master, in design, of linear movement and activity. The direction in which a Klee line points, the velocity with which it whirls around a curve or loop, or the timbre of its statement on the paper, are all very important.

Also important is the textural treatment of the background in which the line exists. Klee was a great technician and worked in a wide variety of media, all of which he handled with remarkable skill. He combined water color and ink, oil and gouache, and used all sorts of texturally interesting surfaces to work on. He was an accomplished water-colorist and a great and subtle colorist in all media.

Many influences can be traced in Klee's work. The influence of child art is perhaps most impressive, because better than any other artist Klee has succeeded in capturing both the mannerisms and the spirit of the child artist. He has seemed to have been able to make himself *see* as the child sees; to partake of the child's wonder and delight in his discovery of a most fascinating world about him; to sympathetically comprehend the child's child-world problems and emotions. Yet—without loss—Klee has also retained the better judgment and more sophisticated picture-organization of

253   * James Thrall Soby, *Paintings, Drawings, and Prints by Paul Klee.*

Klee: *In the Grass* (above); *Twittering Machine* (right). Klee successfully combined fantasy and gentle humor with abstract design. His pictures have "literary" connotations (as indicated by their titles), but the touch of the literary does not impair their purely "artistic" qualities.

maturity. His pictures, along this line, look more like actual children's painting than those of most other artists, but they are also obviously productions of a great and fully developed artistic ability.

The influence of Cubism can be seen in certain Klee pictures. In others one can detect the influence of African masks, which Klee, like Picasso and unlike most German artists, quite thoroughly understood. Klee did not copy the appearance of African masks in his work. He had no need to borrow from their exotic connotations (as the *Fauves* tried to do); he had his own overflowing personal store of imaginative fancy to draw from at will. But he did find in the Negro art *design* ideas which he effectively translated into his own peculiar artistic idiom.

Klee studied the strange pictures of the insane—pathetic and disturbing pictures, but often beautiful in design and other artistic qualities. He was also interested in the subconscious mind and in "automatic drawing," wherein the hand goes where it will. From these sources, too, came ideas which influenced his art.

Klee looked at nature and often saw things that other artists missed, usually small intimate things, like a bit of colored cloth, a feather, or a sea shell. In these he found infinite possibilities for design. To him the arrow seemed an interesting symbol, and he used it many times in his compositions.

The greatest source of Klee's artistry, however, was his own inexhaustible imagination, enriched by a quaint, whimsical sense of humor. The fairies and the pixies lived happily in his paint box and gayly bewitched his palette and brushes. In his art he could go anywhere, do anything. He could see into the predatory mind of a cat about to pounce on a bird, meet strange creatures in a grassy field at midnight, visit villages among the stars, or mourn at the death of flowers. But always his fantasy was closely linked with the design shapes, the directional lines, the subtle colors and studied textures of his pictures. The combination was Klee's great accomplishment.

It is interesting to note that Klee's fantasy was not motivated by "escape." Rather it is a fantasy of joy, of discovery, of the thrill of creation. Where there is an occasional touch of the somber, it is relieved by sympathy, beauty, and wistful, elfin humor.

Klee nearly always worked on a small scale, which sometimes gives his work a deceptive effect of slightness. A favorite size of his pictures was 18 by 12 inches, or smaller. But they are pictures of high quality, and great art does not necessarily need a great canvas. The intimacy of these pictures is part of their charm, and the humility of Klee's approach has given his art an immense profoundness, regardless of the apparent smallness and simplicity of his subject matter.

The titles given to pictures in modern art have a special interest in the light they sometimes shed on the artist's purposes. In *academic-realistic* art, the role of the title is usually quite simple—the picture *illustrates* the title. For example, if the title is "Nymph at Fountain," the painting is a picture of a nymph at a fountain; if the title is "Henrietta," the picture is probably a portrait of Henrietta, and so on.

In modern art, this does not hold. Modern art denies that its intent is descriptive, or that it is trying to reproduce an image *of* something. It claims, instead, that the subject matter is unimportant, that it is the picture itself and the manner in which it is painted (or designed) that really counts. Hence, theoretically, a truly modern picture needs no title at all —the picture should be enjoyed for itself as is.

So much for theory. There are practical considerations, however, that make titles a necessity, such as the need for identifying pictures in print for cataloguing at exhibitions. Consequently, modern artists have been forced to give their pictures titles whether they wanted to or not. The types of the titles given under these conditions often reveal the artist's essential purpose in picture making.

For example, Picasso's titles always identify the subject of his abstractions, even though that subject may be practically unrecognizable in the picture. Among Picasso's titles are:

> Girl with a Mandolin
> Portrait of Kahnweiler
> Guitar, 1912
> Three Musicians
> Seated Woman

The titles are very simple, but adequate to name the subject. In Cubist, *derived* abstraction it is interesting to know the subject from which the artist's design had its derivation. Therefore, the simple descriptive title has a usefulness in relation to the artist's purpose.

When we turn to Kandinsky, we find such titles as:

> Improvisation No. 30
> Composition No. 1
> Yellow Surrounding
> Scherzo
> Great Fugue

Kandinsky's *pure abstractions* obviously have no subjects, and so there are no subjects in the titles. Instead, there are *Improvisations, Compositions, Fugues*, and so on. The titles cannot describe the pictures, but they do hint at the *type* of picture painted. The type of title used by the *geometric* abstractionists also indicates the type of approach:

> Suprematist Composition
> Composition in Gray
> Composition in White and Blue
> Painting, 1932
> Painting, 1936

Here the simplicity and severity of the geometrical abstractionists' pictures is paralleled by the severity of the titles.

If we look ahead to the *Dadaists* (to be discussed in the next chapter), we find an entirely different type of title:

> Mask for Insulting Esthetes
> Very Rare Picture Upon the Earth
> Why Not Sneeze?
> Amorous Procession
> The Little Tear Gland That Says Tic-tac

These titles are much more interesting from a literary point of view, but the reader should be warned that they do not in the least describe the Dadaist pictures. Irreverent, facetious, they *do* reflect the bitter, disillusioned Dadaist attitude toward art and life. In *Surrealism* (also to be discussed in a later chapter), the literary elements in both pictures and titles are emphasized even more:

> The Engima of the Hour
> The Disquieting Muses
> A Chemist Lifting with Extreme Precaution the Cuticle of a
>   Grand Piano
> The Persistence of Memory
> Mama, Papa Is Wounded!
> Two Pieces of Bread Expressing the Sentiment of Love
> 2 Children Are Menaced by a Nightingale

These Surrealist titles are not only literary, but literary in a peculiar way. Retaining some elements of Dada facetiousness, they nevertheless introduce elements of strangeness, shock, incongruity, and disquietude. Also, for the first time, they begin to be descriptive of the subjects of the pictures. All this is reflective of the ideas of the artists interpreting Surrealism.

This discussion of titles may appear to be in the nature of a digression, but it has point in that the titles of Paul Klee's pictures have considerable significance, not only in revealing the nature of his own art, but also as indications of developing trends in modern art as a whole. Klee himself insisted that the titling of his pictures was important.

Some of Klee's titles were simply descriptive, but a great many were definitely literary and had a literary connection with his pictures. They were not facetious, like Dadaist titles, but were sometimes humorous. For example:

> A Girl Possessed
> Little World
> Around the Fish
> The Little Man Is Off on His Own

Apparatus for the Magnetic Treatment of Plants
The Mocker Mocked
Mount of the Sacred Cat
Dance You Monster to My Sweet Song
She Moos, We Play
Child Consecrated to Suffering
One Who Understands

There is an important point of difference between these titles and the titles of academic-realistic pictures. In academic realism, the pictures illustrate the titles; in Klee's work the titles illustrate the pictures, which is something different entirely. In other words, Klee's pictures came first, the titles later. The picture is the text, the title the embellishment. Klee selected his titles carefully, he said, because "such and such a person may see in one of my pictures something which I myself do not see at all." *
His titles were intended to help the observer see the literary connotations of his pictures in the same way he himself saw them.

The titles of the Cubists, the pure abstractionists, and the geometric abstractionist were mere labels to identify the pictures (also, in the case of the Cubists, the type of subject matter). The fact that Klee's titles are far more than labels, and that they inject unquestionably literary considerations into the enjoyment of his pictures, constitutes something of a milestone in the continuing history of modern art. They signify a beginning of a new trend *away* from pure abstraction—a trend that might lead back not only to the literary in painting, but possibly also to realism.

In Klee's case, however, the abstract artistic qualities of his pictures were not in the least disturbed by the slight literary connotations Klee read into them. Probably, in some instances, he did not begin to decide what the literary "meaning" of his pictures would be until some time after he had painted them.

Critics have more than once compared Klee to Picasso. For Klee it can be said that not only does his art vie with Picasso's in quality and interest, but he also challenges the Cubist master in the latter's own specialties—imagination, originality, and creativeness. Indeed, Klee's is perhaps the only artistic reputation that has been steadily climbing in relation to Picasso's. On the other hand, it seems unlikely that Klee's modest and intimate art, however gemlike in quality, will ever quite supplant in pre-eminence the excitement, the drama, and the sheer power of Picasso.

Nevertheless, whatever Klee's rank among the foremost names in modern art, he is a great artist. With his kindliness, his gentle humor, his fantasy and imagination, his magic-touched offerings of color and beauty, he has made a contribution not only to modern art but to modern civilization—for which we may be grateful.

If Klee stands for abstraction "tainted" by mild literary leanings, Marc Chagall's brand of fantasy can be described as gayly mad literature slightly

* Herbert Read, *Klee*.

touched by abstract design. Klee saw things smaller than they were. Chagall saw them larger than life—giant figures striding across the village rooftops or flying helter-skelter through the air. Klee's art is whimsical, Chagall's intensely sentimental; Klee's, precisely designed, Chagall's, loosely and sweepingly poetical.

In spite of its imaginative sources, Klee's design is akin in spirit to that of the Cubists. Chagall's art embraces the lyrical qualities of a Gauguin, the sweeping grace of a Matisse, the primitive manner and loose, free brushwork of the Expressionists. Klee is a musician—Chagall, a poet.

Marc Chagall was born July 7, 1889, in the city of Vitebsk, Russia. His father worked in a herring depot. The family was Jewish and devoutly religious. They belonged to an ancient sect called Chassidim, whose attitude toward life bore a relation in the Jewish religion vaguely parallel to the spirit of St. Francis in Roman Catholicism.

When only a boy, young Chagall decided to be an artist, and his family aided him in his desire as best they could. He received desultory art schooling at Vitebsk, St. Petersburg, and Bakst. At the age of nineteen or twenty he painted his "first illogical painting." His approach to painting was somewhat Expressionist in style with poetical Russian overtones.

Visiting Paris, Chagall's native and primitive Expressionism was deeply influenced by Cubism, which taught him the importance of design. For a while, Chagall's art was perhaps overinfluenced by Cubism; it stiffened the natural fluidity of his painting and cramped his imagination in its rigid angles and planes. But eventually he outgrew this, and it is said that he became less interested in breaking up forms, and more interested in breaking up memories. Nevertheless, he retained the essentials of what he had learned. He did not lose his sense of design, but expressed it intuitively and emotionally rather than formally.

In 1914, Chagall returned to Russia and in 1915 married his sweetheart Bella. In that year he painted the first of a long series of paintings of lovers, each of which celebrated an anniversary of his marriage with Bella. These are "love pictures," deeply sentimental and usually beautifully poetical. They were also often wildly fantastic. Sometimes the lovers fly through the air; sometimes they embrace in a gigantic bowl of flowers or appear in utterly impossible but tender and loving poses.

For years, Chagall has painted, in gorgeous colors and flowing compositions, his moving sentimental fantasies. Anything can happen in a Chagall picture. It is part of his art that the unreal comes to seem real.

Chagall's handling of people and animals is fairly realistic, though drawn in an intentionally primitive style. His fantasy is entirely literary in substance—much more so than that of Klee. Chagall needs no hinting titles to point out what his pictures are about; it is all clearly stated in the paintings themselves. There may be a secret symbolism in the pictures, but if so, no one cares, because the pictures are so beautiful in their mysterious poetry, so fascinating in their gayly jumbled subjects, that meanings are not needed.

A large part of Chagall's poetry is literary, involving his subject matter. But another part of his poetry is purely visual, modern, and artistic. It derives from his glorious color harmonies, and from an innate sense of

Chagall: *Double Portrait* (left); *The Lovers in the Flowers* (below). Chagall's fantasy is more literary, more poetical, less organized in design than the fantasy of Klee. On the other hand, in Chagall's better pictures, a natural sense of rhythm, placement, and color creates an intuitive poetical design which more than makes up for the lack of any rigid, formal organization. Klee made things seem smaller than life; Chagall made them appear larger.

flowing design that makes his paintings true art. For this reason Chagall stands among the greater modern artists.

On the other hand, Chagall's relative realism of drawing and his literary subject matter are symptomatic of those growing trends in modern art which have been moving away from abstraction and nearer to realism.

33 Dada

One thing about modern art as a whole that particularly confuses the layman is the apparent disorder of its aims, the seeming incongruity of its many different and sometimes conflicting types of approach. If one goes to a general exhibition of modern paintings, he may see a severe geometrical abstraction of the Mondrian type hung side by side with a painty Expressionist picture that is not in the least abstract. A third picture might be an example of Surrealism, or even a pointillist effort in the manner of Seurat. And so on. The confused layman my well ask, "What are they all driving at?"

The answer, of course, is that modern art is not all of one piece; it didn't happen all at one time. It is a succession of different ideas and approaches developed by different artists at different times. Nevertheless, confusion still exists because these individual and group efforts did not start and end in a neat chronological order. They constantly overlap. The *Fauves* did not stop painting when the Cubists arrived on the scene, nor the Cubists when the Expressionists appeared. Instead, each group kept right on turning out pictures, until, as in a Dixieland jazz band, everybody seemed to be doing everything at once.

In an effort to restore some semblance of historical order to this jumble of styles, one is not helped much by adherence to precise dates of first appearance. In the first place, there are few if any such dates that any sizable group of critics or artists could agree upon as the precise and true beginnings. Changes in artistic style are almost always gradual and indefinite. Then again, a first appearance of a particular style might precede by many years the period when the style was most influential on the artistic scene. This is pointedly the case with the type of paintings associated with the name *Dadaism*. A few such paintings appeared on the artistic stage almost on the heels of early Cubism, yet Dadaism, as such, did not attain its full stature and import until nearly a decade later.

Our only choice (as attempted in this book) is to follow general trends of thought in a broad way—to trace influences and ideas in approximate chronological order without too close adherence to precise datings of individual pictures. By thus observing the flow of ideas roughly and in the large, we find ourselves almost surprisingly successful in discovering a readily understandable over-all pattern for the development of modern art.

We have seen, for example, how modern art's powerful trend toward abstraction had its beginnings in the design qualities of Cézanne's pictures and arose to dominance in the Cubist period. We have also observed an important counter trend—a reaction *against* abstraction—beginning to appear more and more insistently as modern art progresses. The turning point—when the antiabstract reaction steps to the front of the stage—is signalized by the arrival of *Dada*.

Dada represented a violent emotional reaction to the frustrations and destruction of values caused by the cataclysm of the First World War. But also, in a larger sense, Dada marked an artistic stylistic transition from one type of art to another—a transition that would probably have occurred even if there had not been a war. It linked abstraction-loving, design-conscious modern art with a new, antiabstract, antimodern, literature-influenced kind of art called Surrealism.

Dada has been described, with justice, as the first stage of Surrealism. Dada's ideas flowed naturally into the ideas of Surrealism, and most of Dada's champions later became the official Surrealists. On the other hand, with equal justice, Dada can be described as a lingering stage of abstract modern art. During this curious transition period, both trends—the old and the new—seem to overlap.

As a movement, Dada started officially in February, 1916, and continued until 1921, when the movement, as such, disintegrated. Pictures in a more or less Dadaist style were painted both before and after this five-year period of group activity.

An immense bitterness underlies and motivates every expression of Dada. As the chaos of World War I increased, as its senseless blood bath swallowed the lives of talented writers and artists, as its frightful destruction callously shattered the irreplaceable monuments of European civilization, many sensitive persons were moved to disgust and despair. Helpless, disillusioned, frustrated, these unhappy spirits became enraged at the hollow mockery implied by the pretentious facade of "modern Civilization," and they found themselves drawn together in nihilistic revolt against all the cultural pretenses of that civilization—its literature, its art, its morals, and its manners.

Immediately after the war, the disillusionment continued. The pompous oratory of statesmen booming out in a ceaseless cacophony while the cause of true peace was being strangled, the scandals of an unbelievably reactionary capitalism reinstated to influence on a wave of war-weariness and inflation, and the resurgence of a greedy materialism on every hand, only added fuel to the fiery hatred of those who had already set themselves against the status quo.

The Dadaists took the lead in actual, active revolt against established culture during the war and early postwar years. The bitterness of their disillusionment, the intensity of their frustration, does much to explain the bizarre violence of some of their actions. They sought to fight destruction with destruction; futility with a greater futility; senselessness with a more extreme irrationality.

The gathering place of the men who were to found Dada was Zurich, in neutral Switzerland. Zurich, at the time, was full of refugees from

Central Europe—German pacifists, Rumanians, Hungarians, even Russian revolutionaries. Lenin waited there while preparing to make his historic trip to Russia.

Meanwhile, other future Dadaists, had gathered in New York, where Marcel Duchamp and Francis Picabia had gone at the beginning of the war. These artists later joined the Zurich group.

In 1916, the German poet, Hugo Ball, opened a literary café in Zurich, which he called the *Cabaret Voltaire*. This café became the headquarters of a number of voluntary and involuntary exiles, including the young Rumanian poet, Tristan Tzara; Hans Arp, an Alsatian artist; Richard Huelsenbeck, a German poet; and Dr. Val Serner of the University of Geneva. This group soon found a common cause in its hatred of world conditions, and prepared to take action to express that hatred.

On February 8, 1916, the group gave itself a name. During a tumultuous gathering at the Café Terrasse, Tristan Tzara, who had become the leader, plunged a paper cutter at random into the pages of a *Dictionnaire Larousse*. By a remarkable coincidence, on opening the book, he found the paper cutter pointing to the silly word "Dada" which, in French, is an infantile expression approximately meaning "horse" or "hobby horse."

Writing of the event, Hans Arp said: "I affirm that Tristan Tzara discovered the word Dada on the 8th of February, 1916 at 6 o'clock in the evening. I was there with my twelve children when Tzara pronounced for the first time this word, which aroused legitimate enthusiasm in all of us. This took place at the Terrace Café in Zurich, and I had a roll of bread up my left nostril. I am persuaded that only imbeciles and Spanish professors can be interested in dates. What interests us is the dada spirit, and we were all dada before Dada began. . . ." *

The Dada group did not confine itself to writing poems and painting pictures. By means of concerts, exhibitions, soirées, mass meetings—which often ended in riots—and other public performances, the Dadaists attempted mightily to fling their destructive doctrines in the face of an astonished world.

In June, 1916, they published a review called *Cabaret Voltaire*, which was followed by the opening of a Dada art gallery. On July 14, 1916, Tzara read his first Dada manifesto, ridiculing art, science, philosophy, and psychology. In 1919, at the end of the war, the expanding Dada movement transferred its center of operations from Zurich to Paris. Smaller Dada groups were formed in Cologne, Berlin, Hanover, and other cities.

Dada demonstrations grew progressively more and more insane and more riotous. At one, five people dressed in stovepipes performed a dance called *Noir Cacadou*, and a poet, instead of reading his poems as advertised, walked across the platform and laid a bunch of flowers at the feet of a dummy figure. At another exhibition, in Cologne in 1920, the gallery was entered through a public lavatory. Once inside, visitors were provided with hatchets with which, if they wished, they could attack the objects and paintings exhibited. In one part of the hall, a young girl dressed for her first communion recited obscene poems.

* David Gascoyne, *A Short Survey of Surrealism*.

Sometimes two or more poets would recite poems at the same time, to the accompaniment of the ringing of electric bells or of loud music. Or the artist Picabia would draw pictures on a blackboard, only to have them rubbed off as fast as he drew them. Bewildered members of the audience were chosen chairmen. In 1917, Marcel Duchamp sent to the New York Exhibition of the *Indépendants* a porcelain bathroom fixture which he entitled *Fountain* and signed *R. Mutt*. The exhibit was rejected by the jury, from which he promptly resigned.

The audience at the public demonstrations of Dada soon caught the spirit of the performances, and their jeers and shouting rapidly created a state of pandemonium which seldom ended until the arrival of the police. At one of the later performances, a Dadaist manifesto—which turned out to be merely an excuse to fling insults and abuse at the audience—was greeted by a shower of tomatoes and pieces of raw meat. The delighted Dadaists hurled the missiles back at the audience, and again the usual riot ensued.

In spite of the avowed intent to discredit all art and literature—even reason itself, in spite of the horseplay and nonsense, there lurked, behind the bitterness of Dada, real wit and humor. The Dadaist *anti-poet*, in spite of himself, wrote interesting poems, and the Dada *anti-artists* painted pictures of historical importance. And while it is possibly true that Dada produced no artistic masterpiece, Dadaist ideas and innovations neverthe-less influenced many other artists for years to come.

The poetry of Dada is disjointed in form and derisively satirical in spirit, but its mumbo-jumbo contains frequent gems of poetic imagery. This is evidenced in a typical Dada poem by Tristan Tzara:

> in your inside there are smoking lamps
> the swamp of blue honey
> cat crouched in the gold of a flemish inn
> boom boom
> lots of sand yellow bicyclist
> chateauneuf des papes
> manhattan there are tubs of excrement before you
> mbaze mbaze bazebaze mleganga garoo
> you turn round rapidly inside me
> kangaroos in the boat's entrails . . . *

Dada poetry leads directly into the more assured, more subtle and free-flowing poetry of Surrealism. Tzara himself eventually became a Sur-realist, and the leaders-to-be of Surrealism—Breton, Eluard, Aragon, and Soupault—first belonged to the Dada group in Paris.

Dada art likewise led into Surrealism, but its path was not quite so direct, and it developed several contributions of its own before merging into the main body of Surrealist endeavor. Indeed, the Dadaist artists were confused and uncertain about their own motives when Dada began. They still had an enormous respect for Picasso and Cubist abstraction, and even though their art developed in a direction opposed to Cubism, the Dadaists

265   * Gascoyne.

never ceased to include *design* as a requisite element in their pictures. Early Dada exhibitions included both Cubist and Futurist paintings, as well as the work of Klee, Kandinsky, Arp, Ernst, Chirico, and Modigliani.

Gradually, however, as the Dada movement acquired more solidarity, new Dada artistic ideas appeared, frequently prompted by Marcel Duchamp who, in spite of his refusal to enter any organized activity, nevertheless exerted as much leadership over the Dada artists as Tristan Tzara did over the poets. Duchamp saw clearly that Cubism belonged to its masters, Picasso and Braque, and that the path of younger artists must point in some other direction. With the other Dadaists he searched about, rather fumblingly at first, to find that new direction.

The first manifestation of an independent Dada approach was a new interest in the *machine* and other mechanical objects as important elements in modern life. Typical pictures embodying this interest are Duchamp's *The Bachelors*, Picabia's *Very Rare Picture Upon the Earth* (see page 268), and Ernst's *The Little Tear Gland That Says Tic-tac* (page 268).

All of these genuine Dada pictures contain as much design as any Cubist abstraction, yet they also include literary connotations of a type avoided by the Cubists. The Dada machines would never run, but somehow they look as if they *almost* might—a *suggestion* of possible mechanical operation is there. The odd, somewhat facetious titles reflect not only the derisive Dadaist attitude toward "serious" art but also serve to warn the beholder that here are pictures dedicated to the imagination—pictures that are not merely pedestrian imitations or dissections of "life."

A second manifestation of the Dada spirit is found in the Dadaist's *revolt pictures*, none of them of any real value as works of art, but immensely valuable as warning signals of an important change of mind on the part of the artists. They are faint thunder peals announcing the approach of a new counterrevolution in art.

A typical example is the little calendar picture—a banal "chromo"—representing a woodland glen, on which Duchamp painted two tiny bulblike bottles, one red and one green, hanging from the limb of a tree. He entitled the picture *Pharmacie*. More famous, but similar in spirit, is the incident of Duchamp's painting a moustache on a reproduction of the Mona Lisa and entitled the result *LHOOQ*.

Behind these actions lies a particular subdivision of Dada revolt—revolt based on irritation at the false "aestheticism" of the twentieth century world. The Dadists were disgusted by the vast amount of supposedly explanatory writings—the now-familiar artistic "double talk"—that appeared on the heels of Cubism. They were also disgusted by the pretentions of that part of the public who eagerly worshipped art as Art, without discrimination—the people who at long last had discovered Cézanne merely because it was now fashionable to do so.

In reply to these pretenders, Picabia wrote:

> I have a horror of the painting
> of Cézanne
> it bores me stiff,

and a year later, he put a toy monkey in a frame and labeled it "Portrait of Cézanne."

A turning point, indeed!

Carrying the revolt against aestheticism still further, Duchamp invented the *"Ready-made"* to replace the precious *objet d'art*. The *Ready-made* was any commonplace object of ordinary life, manufactured by machine and found in any department store.

He loudly praised the beauty of these objects, claiming that they had an accidental quality which raised them far above the labored work of sculptors and artists. Soon he proclaimed his preference for them over the greatest masterpieces of art.

Duchamp's purpose, of course, was bitterly satirical, obviously directed at the overprecious cult of untouchable "Art," but it also included overtones of sincere purpose. Inferentially, he called attention to the possible beauty of so-called non-artistic materials—wood, glass, metals, and so on. Also, he anticipated future Surrealist ideas in suggesting the possibility of artistic interest in the sudden chance appearance of an otherwise familiar and commonplace object.

The final achievement of Dadaism was the development of a new type of collage. It is in this development that Dadaism and Surrealism begin to merge together.

Collages were invented by the Cubists when they pasted bits of newspapers and other objects on their paintings and incorporated them into the abstractions they were painting. In doing so, the Cubists regarded the pasted-on objects as bits of *texture*, to be woven abstractly into the pictures' design. (See page 219.) They rather carefully avoided permitting the pasted-up material to carry into the picture any important *literary* connotations of its own. In other words, they were not interested in the words printed on the piece of newspaper; what was wanted was the over-all gray textural effect of the black lines of type on the white paper.

The Dadaist approach to collage was different. They pasted up their bits of paper with due regard for design, but they thought also about what was pictured on the paper. They preferred to use photographs, and pasted up not only bits of texture, but also a face, a building, an animal, or a machine. These they delighted to put together in strange combinations: a woman's head fastened to an inanimate object, disembodied legs or arms flying through the air, Josephine Baker and a statue of a medieval saint in weird juxtapositions. The pictures had literary, "subject matter" significance, as well as abstract design (see Hoch's *Collage*, page 268).

This introduction of the literary into what was formerly a device used only by abstractionists indicates the strength of the new trend developing in art—a trend noticed in the paintings of the German Expressionists, Klee and Chagall, and soon to culminate in the almost totally literary, storytelling pictures of the Surrealists. Indeed, the Dadaist collages constitute the first stage of Surrealism, not only because of the literary connotations, but also because the collages brought together recognizable images in strange and unusual combinations.

Picabia: *Very Rare Picture Upon the Earth*, 1915 (above right).

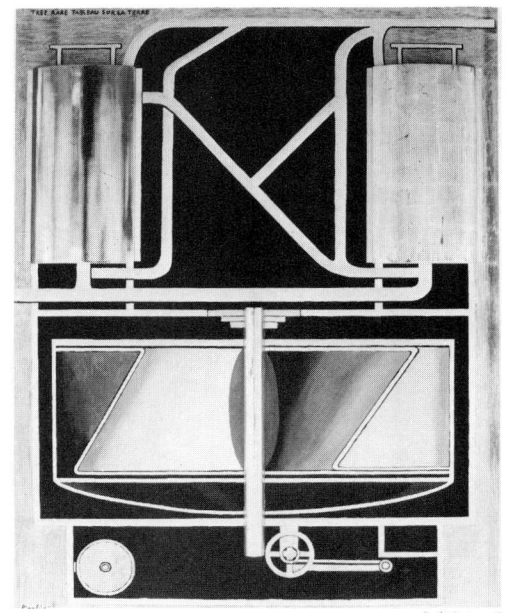

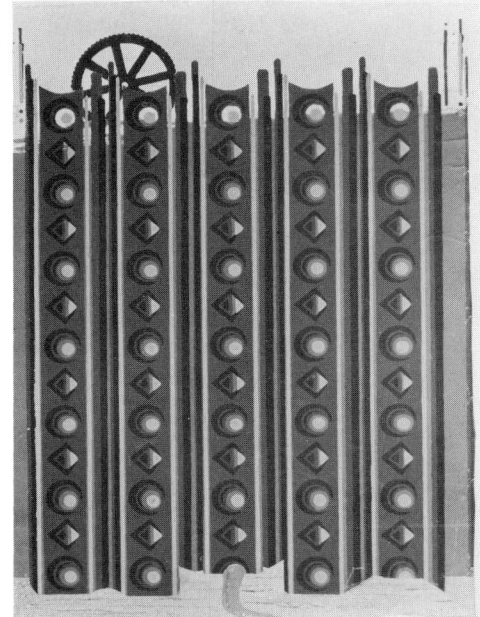

Ernst: *The Little Tear Gland That Says Tic-tac*, 1920 (above). The Dadaists had an unabashed admiration for the modern machine and delighted in painting machinelike forms that look as if they might *almost* work. The work of the Dadaists is more *literary*, less *abstract* than the paintings of the Cubists.

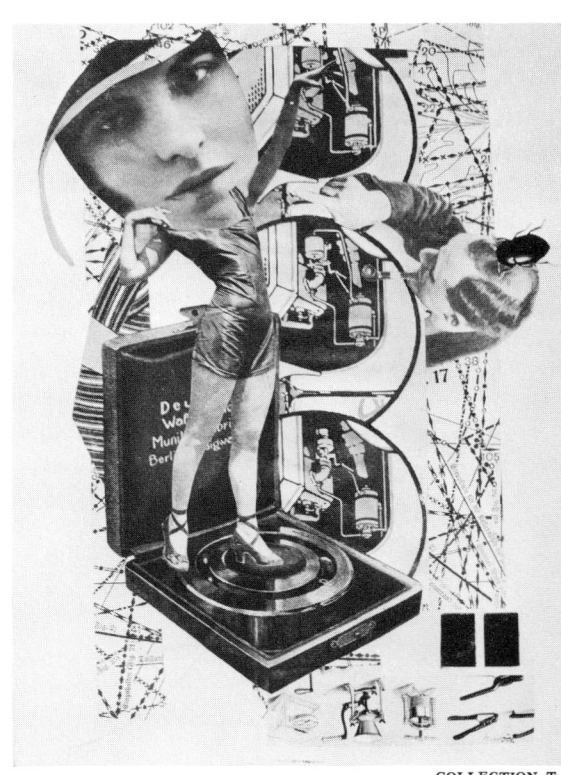

Hoch: *Collage*, 1920 (right). Startling effects were sought by Dada collage makers. Their use of collage was more "literary" than the collages made by the Cubists, who pasted up materials only as *textures* in an abstract design. Dadaist collages were a preliminary stage of Surrealism.

Later, the Surrealists would make collages of their own, exploiting the astonishing effects made possible by the paper-cutting and pasting process. There would be a traveler on a train with the head of a lion, a sphinx with a blinking eye, and so on. But there remains an essential difference between purely Surrealist collage and the earlier collages made by the Dadaist group: the Dadaist consistently maintained an underpinning of design in their "montages," whereas the Surrealists overlooked design entirely in their effort to obtain an astonishing literary effect.

Dada, as a movement, collapsed in 1921. Internal dissension split the group. Behind this dissension was the emergence of a new Surrealist group who felt that purely negative and destructive Dada had had its day, and that it was now time to move on to something constructive.

Seen in another light, Dada, as one writer describes it, "died of cheerfulness." The world was changing. Throughout Europe a new optimism was dispelling the wartime feeling of despair. A new romanticism was arising. Dada found itself out of date, with no longer sufficient justification for its snarling bitterness.

But before it faded into the past, along with other fantastic memories of a strange, unhappy period, Dada left an indelible mark. The new Surrealism that was to take the center of the artistic stage for the next decade was built on the foundations of Dada; nor did Surrealism ever quite entirely rid itself of many important ideas first established by the Dadaists.

34   Surrealism

Insofar as new ideas, new discoveries, are concerned, the original creative impulse of modern art comes to an end with Surrealism. Since the full development of Surrealism, there has been a great deal of modern painting, but no new *major ideas*. Surrealism is the last of the "isms."

In spite of some weak links tying it superficially to modernism, Surrealism is actually a complete negation of practically all that modern art stands for. It marks the completion of a cycle: modern art started as a revolt against academic realism; Surrealism attempts to lead modern art back again to a thinly disguised form of that same academic realism.

Surrealism has one thing in common with the main body of modern art—it continues to rebel against the prevailing materialism that appears to be increasingly characteristic of twentieth century culture. On the other hand, Surrealism is the antithesis of true modern art in at least two vitally important respects. First, in Surrealism, the influence of literary, story-telling subject matter is completely paramount. Second, as a result, realistic representation becomes more desirable; design fades in importance.

Desiderio: *Legend of St. Augustine.* The details of tl[
mysterious picture reveal a strange life. "It is populate[
not by beings of flesh and blood, but the solemn a[
passionless citizens of another dimension." This pictu[
is very close to Surrealism in its spirit and in the d[
turbing effect of psychological tension it imparts [
the beholder.

The motivation of Surrealism is extremely complex. Some of its roots extend as far back as the Middle Ages, others are quite recent. Its spirit is definitely Romantic and has an affinity with various manifestations of Romanticism in the past. Indeed, Surrealism seems to be a crossroads of a considerable number of converging influences and ideas. Among the trends and influences leading to Surrealism can be listed:

1. An ancient tradition of fantastic and Romantic art, dating back to Bosch, Piranesi, and Desiderio.
2. The direct influence of the French Surrealist *poets*, whose poetry, in turn, derived from the revolutionary Romantic literature of France in the nineteenth century.
3. The influence of an individual Romantic artist, Giorgio de Chirico.
4. The more recent manifestations of fantastic and imaginative art in general; the work of Klee and Chagall, as well as Chirico, leading to *Neo-Romanticism.*
5. Dada.
6. The writings of Sigmund Freud.
7. Stylistic reaction against Cubism; against the classical and abstract in modern art.

The general complexity of Surrealism is heightened by the fact that Surrealism is not only an *artistic* movement, but also a *literary* movement. Indeed, the literary aspects of Surrealism will probably prove the more important in history, since they have already overshadowed and dominated Surrealism's purely artistic expression on numerous occasions.

Looking back over the history of art, it is not hard to find fantastic paintings that anticipate the odd, disturbing pictures of Surrealism. The work of Hieronymus Bosch (c. 1450-1516) is a classic example. Not only do his nightmarish creations—witches, devils, and sorcerors—precede in spirit the work of Dali, Tanguy, and Ernst, but his *style* also shows similarities to the technical painting methods of modern Surrealism.

The Italian painter Giuseppe Arcimboldo (c. 1530-1593) delighted in painting heads made up of flowers, fruits, and animals. Nearly four hundred years before Dali, he created double images—faces concealed in landscapes. At about this time, or perhaps a little later, other artists drew figures made up of cabinets and chests of drawers, also anticipating certain Dali pictures.

A sense of psychological disturbance and frustration permeates the half-mad prison scenes of Giovanni Piranesi (1720-1778)—pictures of vast, almost living staircases that spiral up to nowhere.

But probably most Surrealist of all was the mysterious seventeenth century painter Monsú Desiderio. Describing Desiderio's *Legend of St. Augustine*, William Gaunt writes: *

It is a wild and mad picture, ruinous in essence.

Against a dead and black sky is silhouetted a nightmarish port which seems to have grown from rather than settled into decay; there is a fungus-like flourishing in the column that is encrusted with statuary as if it will rise still higher as the process goes on. The fall of masonry on a building in the foreground is held strangely in mid-air

271   * W. Gaunt, *Bandits in a Landscape.*

as if it were a shifting of position only, imbued with a strange and unnatural life. The sculptures, which are in profusion, seem almost like corpses that have rotted on their pedestals and sink in a marble putrefaction.

A hooded figure walks upon the beach, where there is a tiny naked child, towards a derelict ship whose anchor is visible in the silt of the channel. In the background the solitude is the more frightening because of certain evidences that it is populated, not by beings of flesh and blood, but the solemn and passionless citizens of another dimension.

The possible influence of these ancient pictures on the modern Surrealists is hard to determine. Certainly, the moderns did not have to delve into the past for a source of inspiration, although a few of them may, at times, have found occasion to borrow a bit of technique here and there. Rather, the link between the old and the new is primarily a psychological one—the artists of both times, facing similar frustrations in a hapless world, produced a surprisingly similar type of art.

Referring again to modern Surrealism, it must be recalled that the Surrealist poets preceded the Surrealist artists. The leader of the Surrealist group in Paris has been André Breton, a poet; and the poets have dominated the movement from the beginning. This domination has done much to give Surrealist art its characteristic form.

Surrealist poetry is not a sudden development of recent times. Rather, it is the most recent blossom of a rebel-Romanticist literary tradition that goes far back into the nineteenth century. Although Surrealist propagandists claim as their forerunners such writers as J. J. Rousseau, the Marquis de Sade, Coleridge, Edgar Allan Poe, Baudelaire, Alfred Jarry, Lewis Carroll, and J. K. Huysmans (as in his A *Rebours*), modern Surrealist literature derives more directly from two mid-nineteenth century poets, *Arthur Rimbaud* and Isidore Ducasse, the so-called *Comte de Lautréamont*. Both of these men revolted against the stupidity, the conventions, and the morality of self-satisfied nineteenth century bourgeois civilization.

Rimbaud, in particular, centered his attack on the forms of poetry. Tired of the everlasting poetical clichés of his time, he tried to replace them with startling innovations, which in turn made possible a new and fresher imagery. For example: *

From *After the Deluge:*

As soon as the idea of the Deluge was abated,
A hare stopped in the clover and swaying flower-bells, and said a prayer to the rainbow, through the spider's web.
Oh! the precious stones that were hiding,—and the flowers that had already looked around.

* Rimbaud, *Illuminations*. (Translated by Louise Varese.)

In the dirty main street, stalls were set up and boats were hauled toward the sea, high-tiered as in old prints. . . .

In the big house with window panes still dripping, children in mourning looked at the marvellous pictures.

From *Scenes:*

Boulevards of raised platforms . . .

In the corridors of black gauze, following the promenaders with their lanterns and their leaves,

Bird actors swoop down onto a masonry pontoon swayed by a covered archipelago of spectators' boats.

From *Barbarian:*

The banner of raw meat against the silk of seas and arctic flowers; (they do not exist).

By constructing his images of paradoxical and apparently illogical combinations of words, Rimbaud created a richer and more exciting imagery, an imagery that might not entirely satisfy the carping requirements of the reason, but one that would certainly appeal to the imagination.

Other startling images were created by the Comte de Lautréamont in his gigantic epic of Satanism, the amazing *Maldoror.* Among the more famous are two which perfectly embody the spirit of the Surrealism to come:

I let fall one by one, like ivory balls onto a silver platter, my sublime lies.

As beautiful . . . as the chance meeting upon a dissecting table of a sewing machine with an umbrella!

More of this strangely combined imagery and much of the spirit of literary Surrealism are contained in this description by David Gascoyne of the poetry of Charles Cros:

I only know that I shall never forget Paul Eluard read, in his inimitable voice, the poem of Cros' that tells of a tall white wall with a ladder against it, a herring lying on the ground, and one who came with a heavy hammer, a long piece of string and a nail; who mounted the ladder and nailed the string to the top of the wall, tying the herring to the other end; and then climbed down and went far, far away, leaving the herring slowly swaying there ever after. . . .

The type of poetry pioneered by Rimbaud and Lautréamont, developed
273   further by Cros, and still later by such Dadaists as Tristan Tzara, had its

final culmination in the modern Surrealist poetry of Breton, Eluard, and others of their group. From Breton's *Young Cherry Trees Secured Against Hares:*

> If a dishevelled woman follows you, pay no attention.
> It's the blue, you need fear nothing of the blue.
> There'll be a tall blond vase in a tree.
> The spire of the village of melted colors
> Will be your landmark. Take it easy,
> Remember. The dark geyser that hurls fern-tips towards the sky
> Greets you.

> ... The letter sealed in three corners with a fish ...
> A brazier was already yielding
> In her bosom to a lovely romance of cloaks
> And daggers.

> He is coming and that is the wolf with teeth of glass
> The one who eats the time in small round boxes ...

It can well be said that this poetry does not make *sense*, but it does evoke beauty and excites the imagination. One cannot follow the thought of a Surrealist poem with humdrum, daily-life logic, but one's delighted imagination can leap from image to image without the slightest impediment. Given the wings of imagination, a logical connection between words is unnecessary. Surrealist poetry is to be enjoyed, not dissected.

In another sense Surrealism transcends the bonds of ordinary logic. As will be discussed later, the outward irrationality of Surrealist poetry has an intentional similarity to the irrationality of dreams, which, nevertheless, can have an intense reality for the dreamer.

It is on the combination of illogicals—"the chance meeting"—that Surrealist literature is based. The same idea carries over into Surrealist art.

For fifteen years before the Surrealist group was formed officially in 1924, a lone artist had been painting pictures highly Surrealist in quality. He belonged to no school (save that of *pittura metafisica*, which he more or less founded himself), and his Surrealist point of view seems to have been developed quite individually, a natural result of his own Romantic and introspective nature.

When this artist, Giorgio di Chirico, arrived in Paris in 1911, he had already embarked on his nostalgic, dreamlike style of painting. Significantly, he had entitled a self-portrait, painted in 1908, "*What shall I love unless it be the Enigma?*" From 1910-1911 on into the twenties, he painted a long series of "enigma" pictures, pictures with such titles as *The Enigma of the Oracle, The Enigma of an Autumn Evening, Nostalgia of the Infinite, The Enigma of the Hour.*

In all of these pictures, there is a strange, dreamlike mood, a sense of foreboding, an "illusion of romantic isolation and silence, of a still and

Chirico: *The Disquieting Muses* (above); *Melancholy and Mystery of a Street* (right). Long before Surrealism had started officially, Giorgio de Chirico had set the Surrealist mood with his pictures that are both nostalgic and ominous. Chirico's paintings of this period are strongly *designed*, in contrast to the picture of later Surrealism.

remote nostalgia." * Perspective was exaggerated, led to infinity by repeated archways of buildings or by the abrupt scaling down of figures in the background. Colors were toned down, moody and Romantic, bathed in a strange half-light. Here was a dead world, peopled by invisible ghosts.

Adding to the feeling of the ominous, there was unbelievable action in the pictures. Long, dark shadows went the wrong way. "A ghostly locomotive (repeated again and again in these pictures) passes in the foreground or against the horizon and leaves the silence inviolate; a child rolls her hoop towards the forbidding shadow of an unseen statue." Solemn, threatening towers climb to disquieting heights. Everywhere there is an oppressive silence, a feeling of secret psychological tension.

The mood of these pictures—particularly in its enigmatic, subtly disturbing qualities—is intensely Surrealist, even though these paintings were created a decade before official Surrealism was proclaimed. The symbol-like devices—the arcades, the towers, the clocks, the mysterious locomotive—are also Surrealist in essence. In fact, there is only one quality of Chirico's painting at this time that was not Surrealist—a strong sense of *design*. This design Chirico derived from his contacts with the Cubists, and its effects, over the years, has been to strengthen, rather than weaken his work. Indeed, because of its design, Chirico's early work continues to grow in critical estimation and may well outlive the more realistic paintings of some of the Surrealists who followed him.

Chirico's painting enormously influenced Dadaists, Neo-Romanticists, and Surrealists. His extreme perspective, his "nostalgia of the infinite," his weird, dreamlike moods, became hallmarks of all Surrealist painting. Curiously, his painting was rescued from obscurity by the loud praise and propaganda of the Surrealists, and then later, when his style changed, was consigned again to a near-obscurity by the abusive attacks of those same Surrealists. During this latter period of disagreement, feelings boiled up to heights, and it is said that when Chirico "saw a Surrealist coming toward him, he made the sign of the cross, and hastened to the other side of the street." †

The official Surrealists, in a characteristically arbitrary manner, drew the line between Chirico's "good" and "bad" styles at the year 1917. Actually, however, Chirico painted many pictures, of both high quality and unquestionably Surrealist mood, long after that date. On the other hand, there *does* seem to have been a gradual diminution, over the years, of his original creative spirit, with his later work passing finally from the commercial to the near-academic. But long before this occurred, Chirico had provided a firm foundation on which, first Neo-Romanticism, and then pure Surrealism could build.

From the influence of Chirico, and from the fantasy of Klee and Chagall, grew another type of early Surrealism—the type of art known as Neo-Romanticism. The new painting, which appeared about 1926, was literary, anecdotal, and highly *sentimental* in spirit. Its protagonists were

* Soby. † Ibid.

Christian Berard, Pavel Tchelitchew, Eugene Berman, Kristians Tonny, and Leonide (older brother of Eugene Berman); and they painted as a group until 1930.

The first Neo-Romantic pictures were dark and gloomy as a reaction against the over-clear statements of abstract art. The hero of the Neo-Romantics was the Picasso of the almost forgotten Blue period, and the Neo-Romantics imitated the sad sentiment, the emaciated figures, and the somber blue color of that period. These painters sought, not design or structure, but *poetical intensity*.

Their paintings were characterized by a mood of languid sadness, of futility and melancholy. Figures were often painted asleep, or sitting idly in a darkened room, as if overcome by an overwhelming weariness. There is much in Neo-Romantic work that goes back to similar Romantic painting in the past; Berman, for example, is obviously much indebted to Guardi's depiction of the ruins of Venice.

One characteristic of Neo-Romantic art that found its way into later Surrealism was the development of distant horizons (going even beyond Chirico) and of long, accentuated perspectives leading either into vast distances or, perversely, pointing all emphasis toward relatively miniature objects in the paintings (creating an element of surprise that such objects should be there at all). The quality of highly developed Romantic mood is perhaps Neo-Romanticism's greatest contribution to the formation of Surrealist art.

As a movement, Neo-Romanticism collapsed within five years of its inception, but its artists continued to develop as individuals. Tchelitchew has progressed to a more extreme, "shocker" type of Surrealism. Berard has become closely associated with commercial art. Berman's art, reversing the usual trend of Surrealism, has shown an increased interest both in design and in rich color, which has had the effect of strengthening his painting and increasing his stature as an artist. It may be that Berman, by thus accomplishing an apparently successful compromise between the interesting literary connotations of fantastic Surrealist art and the sounder design and pictorial construction of the earlier moderns, has made himself one of the most modern of the moderns, and also, perhaps, one of those artists who may have a possible great influence on the art of the future.

The direct line of Surrealist thought, if we think in terms of the official Surrealist group in Paris, stems straight from Dada, and more specifically from the Dadaist collage and Dadaist poetry. This official group, dominated by André Breton and the poets, was a tight little Parisian coterie who undertook to direct all Surrealist thought. It became established with the publication of the *First Surrealist Manifesto* of 1924, and continued its activities until the arrival of the Nazi troops in World War II. Throughout the group's existence, literary Surrealism maintained at least a spiritual ascendancy over artistic Surrealism; indeed, it has frequently seemed as if the major function of the "official" Surrealist artists was simply to translate the ideas of the poets into another medium.

277 The first period of official Surrealism has been termed the "period of

the sleeping-fits," during which the Surrealists sought, by means of séances, hypnotism, automatic writing, and other devices, to liberate a flow of words from the subconscious mind. André Breton, then much influenced by Freudian ideas, wrote (as quoted by Gascoyne):

> I resolved to obtain from myself . . . a monologue poured out as rapidly as possible, over which the subject's critical faculty has no control—the subject himself throwing reticence to the winds—and which as much as possible represents *spoken thought*.
>
> It seemed and still seems to me that the speed of thought is no greater than that of words, and hence does not exceed the flow of either tongue or pen. It was in such circumstances that . . . I began to cover sheets of paper with writing, feeling a praiseworthy contempt for whatever the literary result might be . . .

The actual result was a disjointed flow of words, not unlike the poetry of the Dadaists, in which an occasional striking poetical image appeared from time to time to be gathered up triumphantly by the Surrealist experimenters. This *automatism* in writing was duplicated artistically by such artists as Masson (page 280), who created pictures by allowing their pencils to wander idly over the paper as if guided by the subconscious mind alone.

Encouraged by many such experiments, Breton defined Surrealism: *

> SURREALISM, *n.* Pure psychic automatism, by which it is intended to express, verbally, in writing, or by other means, the real process of thought. Thought's dictation, in the absence of all control exercised by the reason and outside all aesthetic or moral preoccupations.

> ENCYCL. *Philos.* Surrealism rests in the belief in the superior reality of certain forms of association neglected heretofore; in the omnipotence of the dream and in the disinterested play of thought. It tends definitely to do away with all other psychic mechanisms and to substitute itself for them in the solution of the principal problems of life.

Automatic writing and drawing were not the only means employed by the Surrealists to create the strange, illogical imagery—the "revelation of the marvellous"—that they sought in fact. Another means was the "collage poem," a poem composed from random newspaper cuttings or words drawn from a hat. These literary collages were analogous to the artistic collages made by the Dadaist artists, who combined many incongruous objects in their collage pictures.

Still another device was the "Exquisite Corpse," which, likewise, had both literary and artistic variations. In the literary version, a number of people sat at a table and passed around a piece of paper. Each one, with-

278   * Gascoyne.

out noting what the others had written, wrote a word—the first an adjective, the second a noun, the third a verb, the fourth an adjective, the fifth a noun, and so on. In this way such Surrealist sentences were produced as: "The winged vapor seduces the locked bird," "The Senegal oyster shall eat the tri-colored bread." The name of the device, "Exquisite Corpse," is said to have come from such a sentence.

Pictures were made in the same way. One person drew part of a picture, folded the paper, and passed it on to the next person, and so on. A peculiar oddity of Surrealist thought is revealed by the fact that literary men, as well as artists, took part in the making of pictorial "exquisite corpses," which were sometimes later exhibited. The group effort was not only intended to break down any individual "preconceived logic" of execution, but it also provided a democratic plane wherein both writers and artists could work together. The Surrealists, following a line of thought derived from the "ready-made" philosophy of the Dadaists, believed that achievement of the "the marvellous" should be within reach of everybody. That there may have been some fallacy in this reasoning is indicated by the fact that, years later, some of these "corpses" exhibit a banality which is directly traceable to the artistic limitations of the literary Surrealists.

The anti-individualistic trend of Surrealist thought was also responsible for group or collaborative poems, which were made by the collaboration of three or more poets working on the same poem at the same time. The results of this procedure, however, were said to have turned out surprisingly good.

Just as emphasis on automatism marked the early period of Surrealist literature, so the *collage* was characteristic of early Surrealist art. The first collages were much like those of the Dadaists, but soon the Dadaist respect for design gave way to the sole purpose of creating astonishing pictorial combinations. Max Ernst became a master of this scissors-and-paste picture making.

The first period of artistic Surrealism—that of automatic or accidental pictures—was followed by a second period of dream pictures. It was in these dream pictures that all of the influences impinging on Surrealism came together—the Romantic mood; the illogical combination; the search for the shocking, the astonishing, and the marvelous; Freudian influence and sexual symbolism; and realistic, anti-Cubist representation.

The desire to shock and surprise became a frequent characteristic of these pictures. The motivation was partly a reflection of the old Dadaist rebellion against the world, and partly a deliberate Surrealist attempt to deprive the beholder, by shock, of preconceived standards, to break down apathy, and thus open the mind to new impressions. Together with the attempt to shock and surprise, went the characteristic Surrealist desire to awaken in the beholder a childlike delight in "the revelation of the marvellous."

The influence of the writings of Dr. Sigmund Freud on all of the Surrealists has been enormous. André Breton, who had studied to be a
neurologist, was familiar with Freud's ideas and enthusiastically attempted

AUTOMATISM. Masson: *Furious Suns*, 1925 (above). In the automatic drawings made by the early Surrealists, the hand was allowed to wander aimlessly over the picture, as if guided by the subconscious. Surrealists believed that the subconscious mind had a greater reality than the conscious, controlled type of thinking which had resulted in much stupidity.

Exquisite Corpse made by Knutson, Hugo, Breton, and Tzara. The *Exquisite Corpse* was a combination drawing made by a group of people. The banality of forms found in some is due to the frequent collaboration of nonartists.

Ernst: *2 Children Are Threatened by a Nightingale, 1924.* An early Dada-Surrealist picture. Essentially Dadaist is the constructed gate. The picture becomes more Surrealist in its suggestion of mystery and menace.

to include them in his Surrealist theory. It was Freudian psychology that gave a borrowed validity to the Surrealist idea that the subconscious mind provided a truer reality (super-reality, or sur-reality) than that revealed by the conscious mind, which indulged in stupid, traditional reasoning (as evidenced by the War, and so forth). Furthermore, the importance of the dream in Freud's writings suggested to the Surrealists the dream as a subject field for their painting and writings. This, in turn, inspired the interest in sexual symbolism and the frank approach to the erotic, which occurs so frequently in later Surrealist painting.

Salvador Dali, greatest technician of all the Surrealist painters, carried this Freud-inspired type of thinking further than all others. To other Freud-Surrealist concepts, he added one of his own, which he called his *paranoiac method of criticism*. By *paranoia*, Dali is said not to have been thinking of "persecution mania," the usual general significance of the word, but rather of the idea of *obsession*, particularly an obsession that makes unreal things seem real.

The seeing of imaginary faces in a landscape by the obsessed one has been made a favorite theme in many pictures by Dali. Dali paints some buildings, figures, or foliage in a landscape—however, at the same time, it can be seen, rather obviously, that the objects also form the shape of a head or face. Sometimes there are many such faces in the same picture. These multiple images have been aptly described as "visual puns," and they occur so frequently in Dali's paintings as to seem to constitute, in themselves, a most insistent obsession on the part of Dali himself.

Dali, a Catalan Spaniard born in 1904, had his first Surrealist exhibition in 1929. Though a late-comer to the Surrealist group, he soon surpassed the others, not only in the completeness and complexity of his Surrealism, but also in stature as an artist. He brought to his work a precise realism of execution—the detailed realism of miniature painting. His technical virtuosity in paint is amazing, as is his remarkable draughtsmanship, best evidenced in his drawings. He is also a brilliant and colorful writer, and has collaborated in the production of Surrealist movies. Much of Dali's philosophy is contained in his statement: "For one thing is certain: I hate simplicity in all its forms."

Two other artists of importance in the realm of Surrealist dream painting are Yves Tanguy and Rene Magritte. Tanguy paints tightly in a technique somewhat similar to Dali's, but his semiabstract shapes are touched with a good-natured fantasy that is quite different from Dali's paranoiac obsessions. Tanguy's figures stand out strongly in an atmosphere that melts away into invisibly infinite distances.

Magritte, perhaps the most consistent of all the Surrealists, paints a more dynamic type of picture, one in which elements of sudden surprise and appearance of the "bewildering object" and the "accidental encounter" are generally present. His astonishing effects are provocative and titillating in their effect on the imagination.

The paintings of Max Ernst and Kurt Seligmann are also of interest, but they tend more to the fantastic than to the purely Surrealist. The forms of Seligmann, like those of Tanguy, are quite abstract in conception, and thus display a kinship with the non-Surrealist modern art of design.

An interesting late development of Surrealist expression was the invention of the *Surrealist object*. A classic example is Oppenheim's famous *fur-lined teacup*—an actual teacup and spoon, carefully lined with fur. Other such objects were a bronze glove and a statue of an attractive female nude torso studded with projecting razor blades.

Quite succinctly, these objects symbolize the basic Surrealist concept of illogical, contrasting juxtaposition. Nothing could be more illogical—yet imagination-provoking and Surrealist—than a fur-lined teacup, a wall "papered" with feathers, watches that droop and bend, or a soft, smooth female form from which menacing razor blades project.

Seen entirely from the viewpoint of purely artistic considerations, the strength of the Surrealist reaction against Cubist, abstraction-conscious modern art quickly becomes evident. In earlier modern art, design is structural, all-important. In Surrealism, it is merely compositional and incidental, if present at all.

In Cézanne-inspired modern art, there is a constant flattening of depth, an increasing identification of all parts of the picture with the picture surface itself. Surrealism restores depth with its infinite horizons; gives its objects and figures a solid roundness of a type avoided by the earlier moderns.

Modern art moved away from academic realism; Surrealism re-embraces it "to make its sur-reality more effective and convincing." Later, Surrealism becomes tight, detailed, and intensely realistic in its manner of painting, if not in subject matter. Even its distortions are covered, as it were, by a skin of realism.

Most of the attributes of the Surrealist style are not such as might prevent it from having durable qualities. Its one Achilles' heel, however, is its more recent insistence on realism of execution—an unfortunate attribute of late Surrealism that has already, in a few years, done much to vitiate lasting interest in Surrealist work generally, and which, eventually, must minimize the permanent artistic importance of much Surrealist painting, regardless of all its other interesting facets.

The story of Surrealism has a strange epilogue. During the troubled years between the two world wars—particularly the latter years when the whole world seemed gripped in a spiritual paralysis of fear and futility before the rise of militant fascism—Surrealism flourished. The height of its popularity almost seemed to coincide with Munich.

Obviously, Surrealism offered a "crazy" form of escape from an apparently "crazy" world. Also, Surrealism inherited from Dada a deeply ingrained pacifism which was in sympathetic tune with a widely current popular mood before the inevitable outburst of hostilities.

When at last, finally, Hitler's tanks and airplanes did roar into action, Surrealism became one of the first casualties. Almost magically, its pictures seemed to disappear from galleries and exhibitions; as far as the general public was concerned, its voice seemed to be stilled.

283

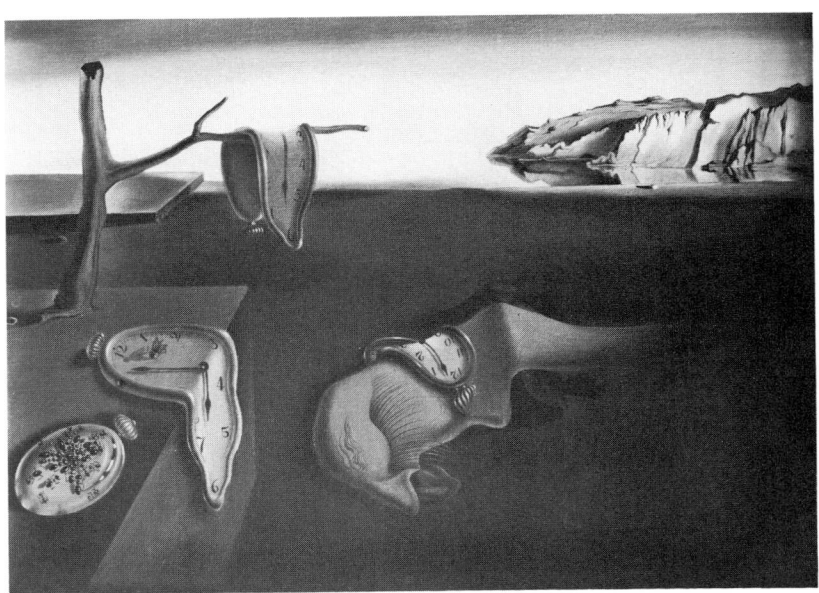

Dali: *The Persistence of Memory, 1931* (above). Like the other Surrealists, Salvador Dali was immensely influenced by the writings of Freud. The finest technician of all the Surrealists, his dream paintings are executed in the detailed style of a skilled miniature painter.

Magritte: *Mental Calculus, 1931*. Magritte's pictures are usually characterized by an element of startling surprise. In a sense, though less notable as a technician, he is more typically a Surrealist than Dali.

Tanguy: *Mama, Papa Is Wounded!, 1927.*
Tanguy succeeds in painting abstract forms
in an entirely Surrealist manner. His style
of painting, precise, detailed, carefully
brushed, is somewhat similar to Dali's.

THE SURREALIST OBJECT. Oppenheim: *Fur-lined Teacup, etc.,* 1936.
The *Surrealist object* replaces the
Cubist's *construction.* These Surrealist objects were conceived symbolically and are intended to convey an
emotional reaction such as might
be given by a Surrealist painting or
poem.

And almost as suddenly, *abstract art*—the art of Picasso and Braque (and a host of imitators)—regained first place in the public estimation. Somehow, abstract art's more stubborn, vigorous spirit of revolt seemed more appropriate to the clash of arms than Surrealism's slinking refuge in a land of fitful dreams.

35   Götterdämmerung

Throughout the entire period of the Surrealist ascendancy—the 1920's and 30's—the Cubists and abstractionists continued painting with undiminished vigor. During World War II, public interest in modern art grew by leaps and bounds. At the time France was liberated and Picasso was found unharmed in Paris, public enthusiasm for Cubist abstract art reached a peak, and Picasso's own reputation soared to heights it had never reached before.

There was no longer any question about it—Picasso was firmly enthroned as an "old master," and the other leading moderns—Braque, Matisse, Miro, Léger—sat as demigods around him. Mondrian, Kandinsky, and Klee—who had died during the war period—had also become deified as artists. Those of these "old masters" who were still alive continued to paint vigorously throughout the 1940's.

However, while the general public seemed to take a greater interest in modern art, it also became apparent that something disturbing was happening internally to the modern movement itself. One noted an odd situation: the now-enthroned "old masters" of the movement were running alone; no new revolutionary groups, no new "isms," were appearing on the scene—there had been none of importance since the Surrealists in the thirties.

In the 1940–1950 decade, it looked as if the grand creative impulse that had boiled and bubbled for seventy years was finally completing its cycle. It looked as if modern art's mighty revolution was over at last.

It wasn't—quite. But part of it, the European part, had indeed come to a resting place. The continuity of the *international modern art movement centering in Paris*—the procession of pioneering artists and ideas from Cézanne on—had been broken. It was a Götterdämmerung—a twilight of the gods!

Possibly, this story might well have ended here, at the time when the original impulse of modern art, in its original character, seemed to have burned itself out. Art does not die, however, as long as there are artists who keep on painting—and thousands of artists did go on painting, and in the modern idiom.

Modernism continued, of necessity—but the tone and character of its development changed in important respects; instead of a straight-line passing of the baton from man to man in the narrow art world of Paris, it became a broadening diffusion of inspiration among many, many artists. Its widening circles of influence leaped across oceans and continents, spread out over the world. As its original revolution was repeated in country after country, in slightly blurred facsimile, it seemed also to acquire new sources of vigor. Eventually—though altered in character—a militant modern art again began marching forward, but its headquarters was no longer in Paris.

The difference between the earlier period and the after–1945 period had been evolutionary, rather than revolutionary. The second period "continued" modern art—but in a new spirit, in the new ways of a new generation. Its changing face reflected the gradual change in our culture over a period of years.

A favorite concept of modern art is its idea of *exploration* of the space contained in the picture area; its persistent experimentation in the many ways of dividing up that space. In this exploration, the "masters" of the primary period were like the great continent-discoverers—Columbus, Cabot, etc.

But while the continent-discoverers—both geographical and artistic—opened up vast areas, they also, naturally, left much for other, later explorers to map more thoroughly. In art, the deeper exploration of areas merely touched on or indicated by the original masters became the special task of the newer artists.

Another aspect of the newer art—perhaps not deeply significant, but nevertheless indicative of a change in the artistic atmosphere—was the inevitable reappearance of a new academicism. Once again, some artists were looking too hard at the handiwork of other artists.

At exhibitions, one saw more and more repetition of ideas. In the schools, hordes of students "studied" abstraction. Most frightening of all, the art critics and dealers talked glibly of a "world-wide international *style* in modern art"—a contradiction of terms. Modern art cannot be a "style." By definition, it is a revolt against style. The spirit of modern art prevents any "style" from staying in force very long before someone starts to change it.

Perhaps the most startling fact involved in the development from the first to the second period of modernism was the decline of France as the world's center of art. After World War II, art in France did not rebound with the usual Gallic vitality. French art remained strangely weak. In France's neighboring European countries, the forward pace of modernism also seemed to slow down. Only in West Germany were there signs of a fresh, vigorous spirit in a revived modern art—which had developed from the old moody expressionism to a strong, bright-colored, and extreme abstraction.

By the late 50's, the real forefront of the postwar modern movement was not to be found in Europe at all. For the expanding circles of the modernist explosion had spread to sections of the world that, in the 1880's

287

and 1890's, had never heard of Cézanne and Van Gogh. The "international" modern movement had become "intercontinental." Its greatest vitality of expression appeared in Japan, Mexico, Canada, and—most of all—the United States. New York replaced Paris as the pioneer city of contemporary art.

In Japan and Mexico, the impact of modern art served primarily to reignite the fires of ancient native artistic cultures. These fires had been almost smothered by the imposition of too much European culture of the nineteenth-century academic variety. Modern art, with its emphasis on expression, on design, and on freedom of approach, brought to the old native arts a new prestige and dignity.

For in all the world there are three naturally artistic countries—Persia (Iran), Japan, and Mexico. Even the simplest common people of these lands seem to be blessed with unusual artistic taste and talent. They see things beautifully. In Japan, thanks to modern art, the Japanese are now returning to the guidance of their own beautiful prints and paintings—the same inspiration that, years before, contributed so much to the beginnings of modern art itself. And in their ancient and graceful calligraphy, the Japanese can see models for the more recent "calligraphy" of ultra-modern Abstract Expressionism.

In Mexico, the pre-Cortez art of the Mayans, Toltecs, and Aztecs is today gradually being fused with the traditions of modernism. The simple but infinitely sincere and sensitive art of the Indian people sprouts everywhere over the countryside, usually in little objects made of cheap materials, but exquisitely artistic. Underneath, like a slumbering volcano, there is a stubbornly independent native culture; a culture that resists, on the one hand, immense and growing pressures from the institutions of the United States—and, on the other hand, the more traditional blandishments of Spanish and European civilization.

In the work of Rivera, Orozco, Siqueiros, Tamayo, and others, Mexico's art circles were early identified with the modern movement—perhaps because modern art was revolutionary, and the Mexicans like to think of themselves as a revolutionary country. But this was an art of leftism and propaganda, an art with more interest in realism than the more formal, purely artistic aesthetics of genuine modernism. The influence of these artists of great reputation indeed tended to slow up the advance of a more profound modernism in Mexican art. There are signs, however, that this influence is waning. Meanwhile, the natural art of the people flourishes, and the powerful design of the Aztec is studied with increasing respect.

In Canada, quite recently, a school of ultramodern abstraction developed from dual streams of influence—one from the United States, the other from the most advanced art circles in France. The work of these Canadian artists has been fresh and vigorous, but generally followed in the path of the more advanced American painters—the mid-century's international leaders.

Most amazing of all the developments in recent art history was the removal of the world center of artistic inspiration from Paris to New York —a Cinderella story of a chimney-corner American art, backward and laggard for years, suddenly casting off its rags.

288

The United States was not only a Johnny-come-lately in the realm of modern art, but it was also the scene of the longest and bitterest struggle between the forces of artistic reaction and modernism. In fact, it took our culture nearly fifty years to accept fully some of the more fundamental tenets of modern art. Let us go back a half century or more . . .

36   America—Flying Shingles in an Armory

In 1900, the situation in America's art world was like that of France in 1880. It seemed as if the clock had been held back for twenty years on the west side of the Atlantic. American academicism, led by New York's National Academy of Design—and supported by somewhat jealous sister academies in other cities—completely dominated the art of the country. There was no other kind of art but academic. The American brand of academicism at times even approached the *hauteur* and arrogance of the great Academy of France.

The American academies, of course, were imitations of their European prototype. But the Yankee versions had served a special useful purpose during the nineteenth century—a difficult century for all American artists, a period when most other robust American citizens were involving themselves in the exciting and more profitable occupation of making a buck out of the Industrial Revolution. Among a practical people, art had never been highly regarded. When everybody was very busy trying to get rich, or trying even more desperately to keep from getting poor, the artist was certainly an odd number. Consequently he found himself in need of a friend and helper. The academies, in their fashion, fulfilled that function.

The academy became a spiritual rallying point and, at the same time, a caretaker for American art. The academy supplied needed prestige to the artist. Also it helped him sell his pictures. Because the academy had a reputation for being stern, authoritative, straight-laced, academic approval of a painting assured a businessman purchaser that he was getting a good buy—and no nonsense.

Hence, as earlier in Paris, the exhibition juries of the academies became the taste-makers and the sales-makers of American art. Through their selections, they dictated what subjects were permissible for pictures, and in what way they should be painted—even down to considerations of brushwork. Naturally, an art produced under such conditions must eventually become sterile, imitative, and lacking in inspiration. But the late nineteenth century demanded only "beautiful" subjects, accurately painted, and, if possible, presented in a mood of charm and sentiment.

A point of special importance to be noted is this great power, this symbolic authority, of the academic system in America. Because, later, when revolt in art came, a certain part of its attack would be directed specifically against academicism as such.

289

A second significant fact about American art in 1900 was that, though its subject matter was limited to the conventionally beautiful, its *manner* of painting was almost photographically realistic. Americans had always painted realistic pictures and never dreamed there could be any other kind.

At the same time, American painting had always been characterized by a tendency to want to "tell a story" in its pictures—even if it were only in the form of a little allusion or an anecdote. In other words, this art had a *literary* motivation. It was attempting to depict an incident or bit of life, not in words, but pictorially.

Americans came by these dual tendencies—to paint with literary intent and to paint realistically—quite naturally and honorably. In the nineteenth century, the United States was a country dominated by Anglo-Saxon literary traditions. A realistic and literary bent is characteristic of English art. The American colonists had brought their English art traditions with them (at a time when English art was at its greatest strength).

A corollary of the Englishman's ingrained love for the literary and realistic was his relative lack of interest in formal design, in the nonliterary. He described an abstractly designed object, such as an oriental rug, as "merely decorative"—in other words, something ordinary and unimportant.

Both Englishman and American had a deep-seated artistic inheritance diametrically opposed to the philosophy of modern art. Hence, it is not surprising that the progress of modern art in America (and in England, too) was slow and difficult, with many a last-ditch battle on the part of the traditionalists, and with much backsliding on the part of those who had gone forward without complete conviction.

It is curious that interest in formal design, while outlawed from traditional English easel painting, has been allowed in the past to develop effectively in the minor arts, such as furniture-making, and the chaste decoration of neoclassic architecture. The English seemed quite capable of design, and good design. But they didn't regard it as being important enough for easel painting. Could it be that this peculiar Anglo-Saxon twist of thought explains why the English and Americans have turned to abstract *sculpture* with facility, assurance, and success—while their progress in painting has been halting and retrograde?

In America, some of the power of the Anglo-Saxon tradition was, at long last, sapped by continued immigration from the continent. Alien traditions were beginning to flow rather easily into our own. And, at the same time, peculiarly English habits of thinking were losing their hold; the old Anglo-Saxon tradition was diluted, giving way to a new and culturally more fruitful consmopolitanism.

A third consideration casting light on the coming of modernism to America is the surprising gap between the art scene in 1900 America and the more progressive art in Paris. Particularly notable was America's almost total ignorance of what had been going on in nonacademic European art. At a time when Cézanne, Van Gogh, Seurat, and Gauguin had come and gone, when the wild Fauves and wilder Cubists were about to burst noisily upon the European scene, Americans were still arguing about the Barbizon school, discovering the brushwork of Franz Hals, and being annoyed by such watered-down samples of Impressionism as had come to their notice.

Because of the odd time gap between French and American art, it is only natural that the arrival of modern art should strike unprepared American sensibilities with bombshell force. Furthermore, because so much revolutionary art history had been lost to Americans, it is also not surprising that, after the first shock, they would misunderstand the strange new art and be confused by it. Unfortunately, the confusion would linger on—for nearly fifty years.

Indeed, *confusion* as to what art was "modern," confusion as to which artists were "modern," confusion as to what direction modern art should take was the characteristic curse of American art in the first half of the twentieth century. The confusion delayed America's progress in the production of truly modern art.

As John I. H. Baur has so instructively pointed out, when the art revolution did come to America, it came in the form of not one, but *two* revolutions—pointed in opposite directions. One was the previously mentioned revolt against the academy, which, however, was directed *only* against the academy and its restriction, rather than being a revolt against the literary-realistic approach.

On the other hand, the second revolution, which was the true modern art revolution of France and Europe, was against realism per se. It was in favor of the artist's *expression* in paint of his aesthetic emotions—in a way totally different from anything previously known in American art.

But this vitally significant difference between the two revolutions was not understood in 1900, nor in 1913, nor for many years afterward. The resulting confusion underlies the tortured history of even relatively recent American art, particularly in the 1930's.

In the limelight around 1900 were academicians, the neoclassicists, the accomplished craftsmen, and the slick brushworkers. The best of these —John Singer Sargent and William M. Chase—had passed their peak, and were being supplanted by more anemic painters. The academy, though supreme in authority, was tired. Its art was rapidly and obviously becoming more dull, more weak, and more imitative.

In contrast, outside the realm of art, the social, industrial, and political disturbances that had so much to do with the birth of modern art in Europe were also operating in America—including a similar cultural reaction against the evils of the Industrial Revolution. The world-wide unrest of the years 1900 to 1905 was felt by American artists as well as by Europeans—and was directly reflected in the first concerted revolt by American artists against academicism.

This was the revolt of "the Eight." The Eight were a group of artists centered in Philadelphia and led by Robert Henri. Included in the group were John Sloan, William Glackens, Everett Shinn, Ernest Lawson, George Luks, Maurice Prendergast, and Arthur B. Davies.

Robert Henri is today known to practically all American artists as the author of the art-wise book of maxims on painting called *The Art Spirit*. Nearly every artist owns or has read this book. For while there exist some doubts as to Henri's greatness as an artist, he is widely famous as a great teacher. He was an inspirer. He could teach others less gifted than himself to paint better than himself. He was also a great fighter and crusader—as Milton W. Brown calls him, "the great white knight of American art."

Sloan, Glackens, Shinn, and Luks—the active core of the group—originally were artistic journalists, illustrators for newspapers, first in Philadelphia and later, after 1895, in New York. It was Henri, with whom they studied, who imbued them "with a sense of destiny"; induced them to paint more seriously. It was also Henri, back from Germany with a trunkful of ideas about painting techniques, who probably led them to paint in a much more fluid and looser style than was considered proper by the academies.

But it was not Henri alone who inspired their revolutionary choice of subject matter. This part of the revolution was in the very air around them. President Theodore Roosevelt voiced it loudly when he took a big stick to the trusts and to the "malefactors of great wealth." The young writers from Chicago and the West—Theodore Dreiser, Maxwell Anderson, Carl Sandburg, Edgar Lee Masters—with their down-to-earth literary realism, later put it in words on paper. The Eight caught the idea—and would put it in paint on canvas.

With a new spirit of social consciousness, they would (and did) paint *the people*—ordinary people as they looked and lived, in factories, in slums, in cheap theaters and saloons, and in the market place—regardless of whether they were "ugly" or "beautiful." They would paint real life—humanity. And let the academy stick to its stereotyped genre pictures and silly neoclassicism, its nymphs in nightgowns. In standing for truth and reality as against artificially defined "beauty," the new school brutally flouted the favorite tenet of academic thinking. As the young artists went to work with gusto, painting and exhibiting pictures embodying their new doctrine, the academy roared its disapproval and dubbed the upstart group the "Black Gang" and the "Ash Can School."

The eight did its most colorful painting in the early years of the twentieth century. In 1908, these artists put on a now-famous group exhibition in the Macbeth Galleries in New York—a bold gesture, further throwing the glove of challenge in the face of the academy.

It is true that the Eight was not a tight homogeneous group in all respects. Not all of its members painted or thought the same way, not all were equally socially conscious. Its artists were not the first to paint poor people. Nor did the group include *all* the important American artists who painted contemporary human beings with the same gusto and spirit, and in the same free, loose manner as they did. George Bellows, for example, who was also strongly influenced by Henri, did work that closely paralleled theirs, but was not a member of the group.

The real significance of the Eight was that it was a group, and that as a group it had power to create publicity, to call public attention to its aims, and to get its challenge to the academy in the public prints. As a group

Henri: *Laughing Child*. Henri's own art was not very radical. His rough, sketchy brushwork was borrowed from Franz Hals. But Henri's inspired teaching did much to stir up revolutionary ideas among his students.

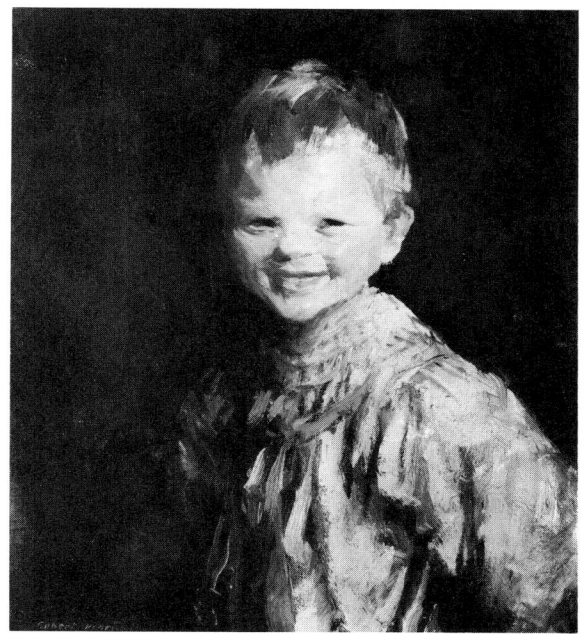

Sloan: *Sixth Avenue Elevated at Third Street*. Instead of striving for idealized "beauty," an early group of American radicals—"the Eight"—painted ordinary people in everyday scenes. Because of their choice of commonplace subjects, these artists became known as the Ash Can School.

it could appeal to other artists and extend the influence of its ideas. Indeed, it could take a hand in fashioning art history—and it did.

The Eight were the first to take the field in revolt against the citadel of the academy—the first fighters in a continuing art revolution that was to go on for many years to come. For that reason, they were considered by many people, including themselves and other artists, as the first American moderns. This was the beginning of a misconception that would cloud understanding of what was going on in American art for the next forty years.

Actually, the Eight were *not* moderns. Their paintings were lively, fresh, colorful, charming, loosely painted—but they were still essentially *realistic*, still literary in intent. They were descriptions of life, but the life came from the depicted subject matter, not more than incidentally from the manner of painting. They definitely were not "modern" as defined by modern artists in Paris—Cézanne, Matisse, Picasso.

As we look back, the paintings of the Eight seem today to be far from shocking. Instead, they are charming, often joyous, a pleasure to look at. In depicting the teeming life of a rich and colorful period in American social history, the artists were eminently successful in putting their enthusiasm on canvas. They added something worthwhile to America's historical collection of art.

It was very much of its time and it was very American. Its artists, generally, were stay-at-homes. The only foreign influence that had any effect on this effort was the somewhat stale one imported by Henri, when he promoted the free brushwork of Franz Hals and, perhaps, some of the vision of Manet. In this provincialism, the Eight were of course much nearer to the American academy than they were to the moderns of Europe.

The assault of the Eight had smirched the academy's proud banners. And soon, the academy would face a far more formidable and destructive blow. This blow would gather its strength from across the ocean.

After all, it was not possible for America to remain in artistic isolation forever. In the early years of the twentieth century, unprecedented numbers of young art students flocked to Paris to complete their academic art education. In Paris, most of them saw nothing but academic art. Nevertheless, there were at least a corporal's guard of others who quickly became aware of the modern revolution then approaching a climax of excitement abroad.

One by one, in a thin, trickling stream, these young Americans brought back word of the strange new art. It was almost like an "underground railroad." At the Paris end were people like the art-collecting Steins—Leo and Gertrude—who helped many Americans come in contact with the leaders of modern art and with modern paintings. At the other end, in New York, another center came into being—the studio of Alfred Stieglitz in an attic at 291 Fifth Avenue. Stieglitz, an advanced and expert photographer, already in conflict with conservatism in his own art, found it easy to befriend radical—that is, modern—painters. He turned his Fifth Avenue studio into a gallery to exhibit radical work of all kinds, with a predilection for that which came from France. The studio-gallery soon became known as "291."

The general public and the uncurious official art world heard little or nothing of "291." But the news did get around to a smattering of young artists interested in new directions and ideas. The circle of influence of "291" was small, but within that circle its achievement was substantial and qualitatively of high order.

In 1908, for the first time in America, Stieglitz exhibited fifty-eight Rodin drawings. Later in the year, he presented drawings by Matisse. Within the next few years, he exhibited works by Cézanne, Manet, Renoir, Toulouse-Laùtrec, and Picasso. Stieglitz also showed the advanced art of his young American friends—John Marin, Max Weber, Alfred Maurer, Edward Steichen, Abraham Walkowitz, and others.

As a gallery with formal exhibitions, "291" was able to gain publicity, if only in the form of unfavorable reviews. Through this publicity, through the exhibitions themselves, and through artists' word of mouth, a larger and larger nucleus of American artists learned that something very exciting was going on in the European art world. Because this growing awareness and interest existed, the 1913 Armory Show became possible.

In 1908, another small gallery was opened in Greenwich Village, a friendly gallery that was tolerant of "advanced" thinking in art. It became noted for giving wall space to progressive young artists who could not get a showing elsewhere. This was the Whitney Studio Gallery on West 8th Street, made possible by Gertrude Vanderbilt Whitney and her friend, Juliana Force. Over the years, it has grown into the Whitney Museum of American Art. In its first years, however, its influence was slight, being confined to its role of friend of the artist.

Another early "friend of the artist" was John Cotton Dana, director of the Newark Museum. In 1910, Dana put on a modern exhibition at the New Jersey museum. One of the exhibitors was John Marin. But it would be a long time before other museums would dream of showing anything modern (although the Brooklyn Museum early became interested in primitive art and was the first to exhibit African Negro sculpture—as *art*).

In its impact, in the way it came into being, in the colorful events that surrounded its showing, and in its aftermath, the Armory Show of 1913 is one of the most fantastic exhibitions in all art history. It has certainly been the most influential and important exhibition in American art.

It was conceived, about 1911, by those progressive painters who felt that the time had come for a large exhibition of all the advanced or revolutionary work then being done. It included the Eight, but by this time there were also many others eager to tweak the nose of the academy, and they were welcome to join in the fun. To add interest, someone suggested including a few of the more radical things from abroad.

But basically the idea was to popularize the new American art and build sales for it. An organization was formed, known as The Association of American Painters and Sculptors. It was headed by J. Alden Weir, Gutzon Borglum, Elmer MacRae, and Walt Kuhn. However, difficulties were encountered in arranging and financing, and the project was almost abandoned.

Then Walt Kuhn induced Arthur B. Davies, who was known to have influential contacts with wealthy patrons, to take over. Davies, gentle painter of romantic dream-world pictures, proved to have unsuspected abilities as a determined leader and as an executive. Helped by the energetic Kuhn, he soon had things moving. Davies' influence with the wealthy patrons turned out to be very genuine and substantial, and with their assistance, he signed up the Sixty-Ninth Regiment Armory at 26th Street and Lexington Avenue for the exhibition.

George Bellows was put in charge of hanging the show and planned a series of eighteen rooms formed from burlap partitions. Walt Kuhn was rushed to Europe to see what he could find in the way of examples of revolutionary foreign art. The grand stroke of genius was the collecting of the foreign works, originally intended as a stunt to add color to the show. Davies, more cosmopolitan and better informed than some of his colleagues, and well aware of the nature and importance of what was going on overseas, decided to make the foreign moderns the central core of the exhibition. To this end, he joined Kuhn and his committee in Paris—where they even succeeded in enlisting the aid of the famous art dealer Ambroise Vollard.

Together they assembled an amazing cross section of nearly everything that was going on in European modern art, as well as examples of earlier art that seemed to lead in a modern direction. Included were works of Cézanne, Van Gogh, Gauguin, Renoir, Redon, Matisse and the Fauves, Kandinsky, Picasso, Braque, Léger, Ingres, Delacroix, Daumier, Corot, Monet, Duchamp, Picabia, Brancusi, Lehmbruck, Maillol, Munch, Kirchner, and Monticelli. It was planned to locate these importations in the central portion of the floor.

Difficulties arose. One was a prohibitive tariff against the foreign imports, but John Quinn (an influential member of the party in power) was able to get the tariff repealed against works of art less than twenty years old. Then nature intervened. The ship bringing the foreign art was caught in a gigantic Atlantic gale, and arrival was delayed two weeks. When the ship landed, the works had to be rushed to the Armory, just in time to make the opening of the show.

And, of course, there was dissension. In an outspoken letter to the press, on the eve of the opening, Gutzon Borglum resigned as vice president. Nevertheless, others pitched in with increased energy, and a score of volunteers worked twenty-four hours without rest to get the show on.

And it did go on—February 17, 1913—with band music and speeches. The press came, gasped, and called for photographers and cartoonists. The next day, the show had moved to the front pages of New York's newspapers, stirring up a turbulent roar of publicity, ridicule, discussion, and angry criticism. Conservative critic Royal Cortissoz was utterly outraged; younger critic Henry McBride, in one of his first assignments for the *Sun*, had the insight to be enthusiastic.

But for ten days the public stayed away. Then, when the insistent publicity told the world that this Armory Show was really different, a sensation, the public picked up and arrived—in armies. And when they did, they made the show a complete success.

So many came that the price of admission had to be raised. In three weeks, more than one hundred thousand people saw the show at the Armory. Later, the exhibition was taken to Chicago (where an investigation of immoral nudity was baffled by the Cubist technique), and then to Boston. By the end of the tour, the show had been seen by two hundred and fifty thousand people.

To a sensation-seeking press and public, the great hit was the foreign section, whose mad-looking paintings might just as well have suddenly plummeted in from Mars. Next to these, the American efforts looked safe and conservative. The greatest furor of all—and for a long time to come—was aroused by Marcel Duchamp's *Nude Descending a Staircase* (page 231). Possibly it was because this picture seemed more incomprehensible than the others. Or it may have been because the title seemed so grotesquely incompatible with what was pictured, a welter of abstract Cubist-Futurist planes. Some critics renamed it "explosion in a shingle factory."

Generally, the public regarded the show with amusement and enjoyed it as a freakish novelty. The academic side of the art world, critics and artists, were furiously angry. Editors moralized. The revolutionary artists were happy, and when the show closed just before St. Patrick's Day, there was a champagne supper in the Armory, and a jubilant parade and snake dance. The festivities lasted all night.

What had been accomplished? First of all, modern art—the genuine modern movement of Europe—had arrived in America in complete, full-grown form. Though it would be a long time before it became naturalized, and though its growth would be painfully slow and difficult, it was here to stay. Second, the academy had been dealt a lusty blow, which crumbled its prestige and ended its right to speak for all American artists.

The Armory Show made tremendous news, and stirred up controversy that lasted for four or five years—until greater news came, the entry of America into the World War.

As a promotional device, the show was a great success. Within a year, there were half a dozen new galleries in New York devoted to what the critics called "faddist" painting. And new collectors appeared, who would specialize in the new painting. There was a wry twist to this promotional success, however. The lion's share of the benefit went to the foreign artists of France and Italy and Germany. The Americans, whose pictures now seemed much less revolutionary, attracted correspondingly less attention.

This added hurt and heat to the dissension that had boiled up among the artists who had put on the show, and the show organization was disbanded. Davies was attacked as an "internationalist." With all the heat of the discussion, however, there was little light. Everyone was aware of the direct economic competition of foreign painting; few seemed to sense that there was a deeper division between two very different kinds of art, and that one was in a different world, far more advanced than the other. Even at the birth of modern art in America, confusion was rampant.

The Armory Show, successful as it had been in every other respect, failed in one aspect of lasting importance. It was unable to provide an adequate explanation of the new modern art it had introduced. Modern art was here but, like an unfamiliar foreign language, nobody could understand it.

America's first adventurers in modern art, themselves often lacking clear information as to its motives, history, and philosophy, were ill-equipped to cope with a world that loudly demanded an explanation but would not stay around for an answer. The resultant lack of understanding underlies the painfully slow progress of modernism in the years immediately after the Armory Show, even though that show had been so unusually successful in presenting and publicizing the new art.

37   Old Realism in Modern Dress

Since 1913, the history of modern art in this country falls naturally into four periods—each strongly influenced by the social, political, and economic climate of American life at the time. The first period, from 1913 to 1919, was heavily colored by the impact of the Armory Show, the influence of foreign abstraction in the form of Cubism and Futurism, and by an apparent temporary eclipse of the American realists.

The second period, that of the 1920's, saw a complete reversal—the collapse of early abstraction and a revival of the native urge for realism, modified somewhat by Expressionist techniques.

The third period, from 1930 to 1945, was a period of transition and reawakening. Its first years were molded by the depression; the realist tradition was continued, with a new social-consciousness twist. The latter years were characterized by a new advance of modern abstraction, mixed with some of the Surrealism which had arrived from abroad. With the war years, there was a public vogue for Picasso, although many artists were reacting against the tyranny of Picasso's stylistic devices.

The fourth period marked a final triumph of the modern movement in America—in the form of an extreme, uncompromising, and advanced abstraction. Along with this internal conquest came more and more evidence of the surprising fact that world leadership in the modern movement had moved from Paris to America.

Throughout the four periods, a continuing struggle went on between forces tending to pull American art back to realism in the one direction, and forward into abstraction in the other. This has been the grand drama of American art in the first half of the twentieth century. The greater part of the struggle took place on middle ground—for ultraconservative academic realism had been soundly defeated at the beginning of the era, and the ultraradical abstraction did not arrive until the end of it.

The first period, 1913–1919, was clearly an aftermath of the Armory Show—chiefly characterized by the attempt of Americans to assimilate the new Expressionism, Cubism, and Futurism. Those artists who had made the trip to Paris had an advantage here, and were the first to work in the new style. Notable in the group were some who had already exhibited at Stieglitz's "291."

Conversely, the Ash Can school of painting seemed to fade into the background in this post–Armory Show period. One reason was that the painters were themselves being confused by the new ideas from abroad. They did not realize how great was the rift between their Ash Can realism and the new modern formalism, and, having a natural inclination to be sympathetic rather than antagonistic to new conceptions, they tried to find compromises, not too successfully. Another rather simple explanation for the decline of the Ash Can painting was that the colorful Ash Can world was disappearing. It came to an end in 1914, swallowed up by the war, and by the rapid-fire series of colossal social changes brought into being by the war.

As a matter of fact, the other, temporarily more successful group, the American abstractionists of this 1913–1919 period, would only have these five or six years to state *their* case before the changing world would write "finis" for them, too. As long as the controversial reverberations of the Armory Show echoed and re-echoed in the public prints, as long as the word "Cubism" still denoted novelty and news, the Cubist artists could hold the public's attention. Finally, when America entered the war in 1917 in a singing, cheering atmosphere of tense excitement, the Armory Show and its art were forgotten completely, and Cubism ceased to have any news value at all. When the Phillistine and extrovert twenties moved in, America's first Cubist period of modernism was very dead indeed.

During the 1913–1919 period, Cubism and its lively variant, Futurism, held the center of the stage. Expressionism, perhaps because it was a little less startling and newsworthy, took second billing at first. Then Expressionism (both the Matisse and the more conservative Derain variety) began to grow in popularity, as increasing numbers of American artists found themselves more at home with this free emotion than with the severity of Cubist formalism.

And at this point, another element of confusion entered to bedevil the future—a triple confusion of abstraction, Expressionism, and realism. Though both modern abstraction and modern Expressionism have much in common, there are significant differences. A typical Expressionist, as personified by Matisse, does not usually have to move far from the appearance of reality to achieve his ends. His pictures are usually seen as distorted reality—distorted to express his aesthetic feelings about form and arrangement. The abstractionist, on the other hand, is more thoroughgoing. He rather completely destroys the appearance of reality, before reassembling its broken segments into a new, *reorganized* picture.

299   The pioneer American moderns, whose concepts of all modern art

Benton: *Homestead* (right). After experimenting with abstraction in Paris, Benton abjured modernism and came back to paint the American scene in an essentially realistic manner. Nevertheless, strong elements of modern design and Expressionism remain evident in his work.

Weber: *Adoration of the Moon* (left). Max Weber was one of the first of the young Americans who helped "import" modern art from Paris. Though Weber has painted in many modern styles—his forte has always been Expressionism.

Marin: *Maine Islands* (left). Another pioneer American modern, John Marin's painting has a superficial Cubist look, but his fine watercolors are not very abstract —and are really more Expressionist than Cubist in their inspiration.

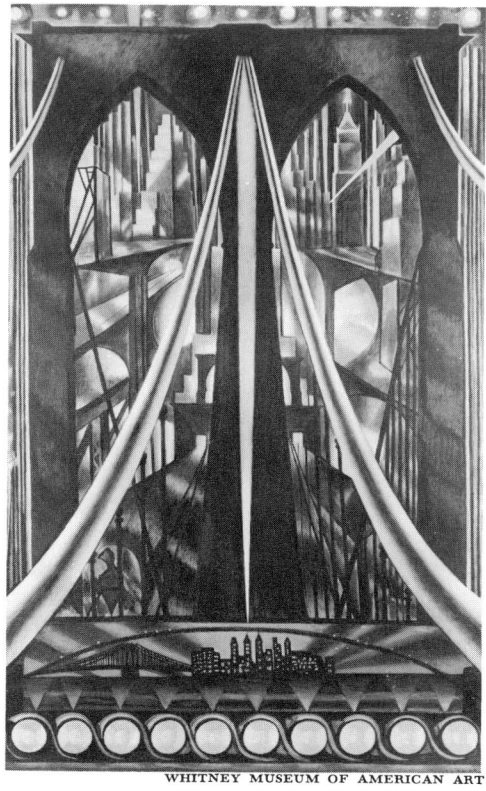

Stella: *Brooklyn Bridge* (right). Stella took part in the original Futurist movement in Europe, and his Futurist style is able and authoritative.

were necessarily second-hand, imitative, and blurred, very frequently mingled the loose, tolerant thinking of the Expressionist with the formal-mindedness of the abstractionist. And, in the other direction, they also confused Expressionism with loosely painted realism. Underlying these recurring confusions was the American artist's timidity in going to extremes, his desire for a comfortable compromise.

Many of the first Americans who called themselves "Cubists" were not temperamentally abstractionists at all—they were, deeply and spiritually, natural Expressionists. This was particularly true of Max Weber and Abraham Walkowitz, as well as of John Marin and Marsden Hartley; and there was a strong strain of Expressionism in Thomas Benton. Max Weber, a well-informed, sophisticated artist with a chameleonlike ability to paint well in many styles, was one of the first Americans to paint in the Cubist manner with an authentic Cubist "look"—but his pictures, though interesting in their individuality, somehow lack the true Cubist crispness and sparkle. Later, when Weber turned wholeheartedly to pure Expressionism, his painting seems to rise much higher in effectiveness, completeness, and emotional power.

In John Marin, Cubism, Expressionism, and a good measure of realistic representation were all combined in a charming and peculiarly personal style. Many of Marin's paintings give a superficial impression of being abstract, but for Marin abstraction was only a handy device for carrying out his basically Expressionist purposes. At the same time, one catches more than fragmentary glimpses of realism—bits of Maine coast line, hills, pines, rock—executed by a master of the difficult water-color medium. These nostalgic touches are intentionally realistic. Nevertheless, it is Marin's Expressionism that dominates his painting.

In the early days of American modernism, Thomas Benton, at the urging of his friend Stanton MacDonald-Wright, tried his hand at abstraction in Paris and later in New York. But Benton, who had a strong urge for literary realism, could not convince himself that modern abstraction—"jumping cubes" and "cockeyed tables"—was for him. He turned deliberately to realism, to paint "the world of America."

Nevertheless, modernism left an indelible stamp on Benton's style (possibly in spite of himself), in a nervous Expressionist manner of drawing and constantly recurring abstractionist tricks of design. Result—another unique and individual style, containing many finely designed details, but sprawling and disorganized in overall design; meticulous story-telling realism combined with mad distortions; a style occasionally sensitive and delicate in form and color, but more often heavy-handed, loud, brutal, and blatant; sometimes exciting to look at, but just as often dull and boring. An individual! But certainly not a Cubist. And though there is modernism in his work, and though he has been many times labeled "modern," Benton most properly belongs with the realists in American art.

The first attempts of Americans in Cubism seem quite frequently to miss the lively spirit of French Cubism. This was partly because Americans painted Cubism as a *fait accompli*, as a set style that had arrived at a static point—whereas to Frenchmen, Cubism had been a dynamic path of progress, a series of exciting experiments, not stopping, but constantly moving forward to new revelations. The Cubist of Paris was as much intrigued by the process of abstraction as he was by its sometimes unpredicted end results.

However, there was one American who was not a follower but an original participant in a European modern movement—and one American who was unquestionably and uncompromisingly an abstractionist—Joseph Stella, a true Futurist and an important one. Stella had taken part in the Futurist movement in Italy and brought back to America an authoritative and accomplished Futurist style. His paintings are among the masterpieces of Futurist painting, and in several cases are equal to or superior to similar works by the European leaders of the movement.

There were others, such as John Covert, with his Cubist collages, who were true abstractionists. But, by and large, most of the American Cubist examples of these years are not truly Cubist in spirit. After all, though our artists were often eager students of Cubism, they had little opportunity to know much of its historical background or where its Parisian leaders were going with it. And, unfortunately, before they could learn more, hard times intervened and put an end to their efforts.

The period ended, as if chopped off. Even before the troops came back from France, the public had lost interest in Cubist abstraction—for good. The fashionable fad had run its course, and the Armory Show had been forgotten. The war had blotted it out. And the Cubist artists suddenly found themselves without a market. They couldn't sell a picture. Neither could they teach, for whoever heard of teaching Cubism in an art school? The artists were faced with a prospect of long-lasting poverty —poverty much harder to take in New York than in Paris.

As a result, most of the advanced modern artists gave up painting entirely and went into other businesses, or went back to more conservative painting. Those who had Expressionist leanings moved in that direction, because Expressionism, being somewhat more realistic and hence more understandable, suffered less from public neglect than abstractionism.

When the returning doughboys marched triumphantly up Fifth Avenue, which artist celebrated the flag-flying gayety of that avenue for posterity to see? Childe Hassam—popular American Impressionist! There was something symbolic in this. For once again, at the beginning of the 1920's, America was turning the clock back. The old urge for story-telling subjects, the old demand for recognizable realism insisted on being placated. A return to *realism*, partially if not totally, would be the keynote of America's art for the next ten years. And—to maintain the prevailing fog of confusion—the realism would be labelled, in blissful ignorance, "modern."

This period of reaction in art only re-echoed the spirit of reaction in everything else—reaction against the war, principally. But also reaction against Wilsonian idealism, reaction against prewar Puritan morality, reaction against prohibition, reaction against anything that might inter-

Marsh: *Twenty Cent Movie*. The "14th Street School," of which Marsh was a prominent member, seemed to revive the old Ash Can tradition. This art was basically realistic, only slightly touched by modernism.

Hopper: *New York Movie*. Though contemporary, Hopper's painting is realistic, not at all modern. His subjects are story-telling to a marked degree.

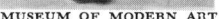

Burchfield: *Pippin House, East Liverpool, Ohio.* Burchfield painted realistic subjects bathed in a subdued romantic atmosphere. He carried some of these subjects into semiabstract fantasy.

od: *Landscape Near Chi-* This "regional" painting is typical of America's art of 920's and early 1930's. It ins modern elements of de- and Expressionist feeling, is picture remains realistic rit. Details of subject mat- re more important than would be in a truly modern fere with a return to "normalcy." In these years, Europe had its bitter Dada movement, but Dada had little real meaning in America. Prosperity—and the rising stock market—were more important. It was only natural that art should slip back to an earlier, more comfortable, more understandable way of painting.

But not all the way back. In art's previous advance, a few bridges had been irrevocably burned—a few permanent footholds had been established. The academy could not take over—even though one would see near-academic work carelessly classed as "modern." For, in spite of the irresistible trend toward realism, modernism held one fortress and would not be dislodged—the fortress of *Expressionism*. The Expressionist touch would be on everything done in this decade that was not outright academic. Expressionist distortion grafted onto story-telling realism chiefly characterizes American art in the 1920's.

This art was called "modern" by everybody, but essentially it was not modern at all. It was, in truth, the old realism slightly concealed by a thin veneer of modern mannerisms and cautious distortions—a pseudo-modern art, an odd hybrid which was peculiar to America.

An astonishing large number of artists made wide reputations for themselves at this time—possibly because of the generous publicity afforded by various magazines, which frequently reproduced the artists' paintings in full color. There were numerous schools, and old-timers of the Ash Can School remained, such as Sloan, Bellows, Glackens, Luks, Kuhn. There were Expressionists like Weber and Hartley, and hybrid individuals like Marin and Benton. For a while there was a very popular near-academic school, that prided itself on its lushness of style and its high "paint quality"—and which appealed to the public with its sentimental or voluptuous subject matter.

There was a 14th Street school that came very close to reviving the old Ash Can tradition. Kenneth Hayes Miller, Reginald Marsh, and the Soyers also had a hand in portraying the teeming world of Union Square.

Another compromise school peculiar to the twenties was the so-called *Immaculates*. The compromise this time, however, was between realism and *abstraction*, rather than between realism and Expressionism. The Immaculates—best represented by Charles Sheeler—painted very simplified pictures of buildings, and machines, designing the large simple shapes and their shadows into something that had the look of a Cubist abstraction. But it still remained a realistic picture—sometimes a very realistic picture. This form of art, with its mechanical and industrial connotations, its flimflam pretense of modern style, and its meticulous representation of reality (later Immaculate pictures deliberately imitate photographs), was very popular for a long time.

Two artists—Edward Hopper and Charles Burchfield—loom up so individually that they hardly seem to be part of the period at all, but rather to link up with such unclassifiables of the past as Albert Ryder and Winslow Homer. Hopper and Burchfield are not modern, though the directness and strength of their painting suggests they might have learned from the moderns; nor can they be classified properly with the Expressionist-realists of their day. Their reputation has climbed steadily over the years.

Hopper and Burchfield have been called "romantic realists." Their styles are quite different, but both favor romantic subjects. Burchfield, in a sure, subdued-tone water-color technique, painted the dreary Victorian houses of old Buffalo—either literally or frighteningly bewitched into mad, semiabstract fantasy. Hopper used oil in a simplified but haunting style, focusing on silent visual dramas of city life. Nevertheless, both painters have something in common: both have developed the literary, story-telling aspects of their art to a most unusual degree—so much so, that their work almost becomes a special type of art. Each picture becomes practically a novel in paint. Hopper and Burchfield are perhaps the most persuasive exponents of this type of art yet seen.

At the end of the twenties and going on into the thirties, "regional" painters—painters of the midwestern "American Scene"—became more and more in evidence. A typical regional painter is Aaron Bohrod, who also combines realism of subject with an Expressionist manner.

The twenties belonged to the realists. Nevertheless, near the end of the decade, abstraction-minded modern art began slowly to revive in new forms quite different from the old, primitive Cubism. Despite bleak economic prospects, new men were trying to get started, critics and art journals slowly became less hostile, and gradually a more accurate understanding of modern art began to seep in from Europe. More and more artists began to move over to an intelligent acceptance of modernism.

Then, at the end of 1929, came the momentous stock market crash—to be followed by the great depression. This affected American art strongly for the next five years. However, also at the end of 1929, another event occurred that would affect American art more deeply and much longer than the depression. In November of that year, three wealthy ladies started the Museum of Modern Art in New York.

38   The Tide Ebbs, the Tide Flows

The first years of the 1930's continued to belong to the Expressionist-realists, the latter years to the abstractionists.

In the early years, the regional painters—especially Benton, Curry, and Grant Wood, rose to great heights of popular esteem, with the astounding best-seller success of Thomas Craven's book, *Men of Art*, in which these artists were portrayed as titans equal to the greatest of the old masters. This book, enticingly written by a skilled and colorful writer, convinced many laymen that native greatness in art was here, but the professional art world was less enthusiastic. Later, with the return of a resurgent modernism, the reputations of Benton and the others declined almost as unreasonably as they had been previously built up by the extravagant puffery of Craven. Again the same confusing error was repeated: these artists had been touted as representing the essence of modernism, which, of course, they did not at all.

The effect of the great economic depression of the early 1930's was to strengthen the trend of Expressionist-realist art, but with a new twist. Art became "socially conscious," but in a far more wholehearted way than in the old Ash Can days. Artists, for a long time forgotten men themselves, seemed to have a special affinity for the victims of the depression, and a special hatred for those villainous individuals who were supposed to have brought on all the misery. A group of these artists came out fighting—with angry, bitter pictures that were more like political cartoons than wall paintings. Many artists had moved far to the left in political philosophy. After the nation recovered from the depths of the depression, art's socially conscious subject matter rather quickly lost its appeal to almost everybody except the die-hard leftists.

Viewed technically, this painting was really not very different from the Expressionist-realist art from which it grew. The only difference was the change of subject matter, with a little cartoonery and caricature thrown in. Today, only one artist of this school remains memorable—Ben Shahn. Shahn's art transcended his propaganda, and his pictures retain a haunting interest that has nothing to do with yesterday's political implications.

Shahn: *Handball*. The socially conscious painting of the depression-haunted 1930's combined a small amount of modern Expressionism with considerable realism. Shahn's art is valued for its interesting personal touch.

Up to the middle of the thirties, at least, the pseudomodern art of Expressionist-realism continued to be confused with true modernism, but the era of confusion was approaching an end. Soon, at long last, America would learn what Cubist painting was all about. Information was on the way—and the greatest single force in bringing it about was the new museum founded in New York by Lillie Bliss, Mrs. John D. Rockefeller, Jr., and Mrs. Cornelius Sullivan—the Museum of Modern Art. It is said that the death of Arthur B. Davies, the man most instrumental in introducing modern art to America in 1913, inspired these ladies to go ahead and make the long-talked-of museum a fact.

Collector and business executive A. Conger Goodyear was installed as president, and Alfred H. Barr, Jr., a young Princetonian then teaching art at Wellesley, was made professional director. From the beginning, the Museum of Modern Art knew where it was going. Significantly, its first exhibition in November, 1929, in the Heckscher Building, was devoted to paintings by Cézanne, Van Gogh, Seurat, and Gauguin.

Well-supported financially, fed from numerous wealthy collections, and managed with almost awesome skill, the new museum grew rapidly. Word of it spread among the artists and public eager to know more about modern art, and almost from the beginning its exhibitions drew full houses. In 1932, it moved from its rooms in the Heckscher Building to a brownstone building on 53rd Street. In 1939, ten years after its founding, the Museum of Modern Art moved into its present modern building on 54th Street—and that building has since been considerably enlarged.

MUSEUM OF MODERN ART

Among its many functions, the Museum's greatest service has been its educational function. It taught everybody—artists, critics, editors, collectors, teachers, students, and the public—exactly what modern art was, how it developed, and who started it. It did this in a series of novel and effective exhibitions reinforced by informative captions and catalogs.

Despite criticism, this museum has concentrated, with a stubborn single-mindedness, on the presentation of the modern movement founded by Cézanne. In selecting the early blue-chip masterpieces of modernism, the museum has displayed an almost clairvoyant taste—a taste that enhanced its reputation and imbued its decisions with great authority in later years. Its scholarly research has influenced almost everything written about modern art in any depth.

By supplying hungry-eyed artists in the early days with the visual information they needed, the Museum of Modern Art to a tremendous degree helped to form America's modern art of today. And through its constant activity, it has gone far in accomplishing what must have been an objective of its original founders—the popularizing of modern art with the general public.

Criticism of the museum has centered around its so-called "foreign-mindedness"—its apparent disinterest in American art as such, and its lack of extensive aid to American artists in general. In answer to this, the museum can point to the word "modern" in its name; and it can also point out that another museum already exists—the Whitney—whose declared function is to do just the things the Modern museum is criticized for not doing.

But the return of abstraction in the 1930's can by no means be ascribed merely to the museum's activities. With an influx of ideas—and artists—constantly arriving from abroad, a return of abstraction was inevitable. The beginnings were slow. It was like the turn of the tide in a seaside inlet, imperceptible at first, then growing to an impressive flood.

New artists appeared on the scene. One was Stuart Davis with his gay postery style. Another, Arshile Gorky, whose personalized disintegration of Miro-esque shapes would lead to a new art movement in later years. There was Arthur G. Dove, a somewhat nonconformist old-timer of Cubist days, whose loosely curved forms were now becoming more up-to-date. There was Morris Kantor, a man whose personal sweetness of character finds its way into his pictures, notably in his famous "Farewell to Union Square." Unlike many other American artists, Kantor, a true modern, turned away from near-realism and moved eagerly into poetic abstraction. And there was young Byron Browne, struggling with the strong Picasso influence he would eventually throw off.

Near the midpoint of the decade, Surrealism enjoyed its great days in America. For a time, Julien Levy's 57th Street gallery—which specialized in top Surrealist artists—became the number-one gallery of the nation. Salvador Dali had several wonderful shows there—and there were also exhibitions by Chirico, Tanguy, Ernst, Lenore Fini, and other Surrealists.

In 1936 the Museum of Modern Art put on a spectacular, comprehensive show of "Fantastic Art, Dada, and Surrealism"—which, among other things, fascinated the American public with its tantalizing *Fur-Lined Teacup* (page 285). And there was a continuing Surrealist show at Peggy Guggenheim's out-of-this-world barrel-shaped gallery, where the pictures literally jumped out at you from the curved wall. Dali's *Dream of Venus* was exhibited at the World's Fair. And, as a grand finale in 1942 (for War had been declared, and the movement was fast fading), there was an International Surrealist Exhibition in the gilt-encrusted Whitelaw Reid Mansion—which had to be viewed through a mile of string, hung cobweb-fashion around the exhibits by Marcel Duchamp. Incidentally, the ubiquitous *mobiles* of Alexander Calder, though not particularly Surrealist in themselves, were among the notable hits of the show.

To all outward appearances, Surrealism was a great success. On every American artist's tongue were the names of Dali, Magritte, Tanguy, Masson, Ernst, Seligmann, Paul Delvaux, Man Ray, and Tchelitchew. The public loved Surrealism and even bought Surrealist pictures.

Nevertheless, Surrealism displayed a strange fragility and lack of staying power. The public instantly dropped Surrealism's fun, fright, and fancy when war came. In its place was substituted a new public interest in abstraction, an interest that may have been stimulated by the figure of Picasso as a symbol of resistance against the Nazis.

Again, with all its publicity and penetration among both artists and public, *pure* Surrealism did not create a school in American art. One can think of a few pure Surrealist artists—Federico Castellon, Peter Bloom, Joseph Cornell, Lorser Feitelson—but not many others. This failure of Surrealism to take root in America might be because its inner spirit is somewhat alien to American culture. It has sinister implications and depths of meaning—menace and fear and secret drama—that are understandable to Europeans, but do not successfully cross the ocean.

On the other hand, while pure Surrealism failed as a movement, the impact of Surrealism and Surrealist techniques on other forms of art was enormous. It influenced both the realistic and the abstract wings of American art, the abstract more decisively.

On the realist and semirealist side one can see strong Surrealist shadings in the rather grim art of Henry Koerner, Louis Guglielmi, Alton Pickens, Ivan Albright, and Philip Evergood. It is also present in the happier semiabstractions of Ernest Fiene, Julian Levi, and Yasuo Kuniyoshi—and in the strong realism of Walter Murch and Andrew Wyeth. Surrealism also encouraged a reappearance of the art of sheer fantasy, in the paintings of Darrel Austin, Loren MacIver, and Morris Graves—continuing a tradition dating far back in American art, including the early twentieth-century mysticism of Arthur B. Davies and Louis Eilshemius.

Of more interest to modern art, and more significant historically, was the influence of Surrealism on the new abstract art movement beginning to take form in the middle nineteen thirties. The realistic and literary aspects of Surrealism were of little interest to the abstractionists—but the methods, the mannerisms, and the widened visual territory of Surrealism were of vast importance. For Surrealism, liberated the abstract imagina-

311

tion—made possible a whole world of new shapes, new combinations, and new ways of thinking visually. It also brought liberation from the overwhelming and oppressive influence of Picasso.

When an artist made a nature-derived abstraction—in the manner developed by Picasso and the Cubists—he found himself almost automatically constructing his abstraction from the bits of nature before his eyes. If he were doing a head, for example, he might develop shapes from the curve of an eye, or the angle of a nose shadow—or he might throw in something he has noted nearby in the room. He could disguise these shapes or elaborate on them or improvise on them or recombine them, but nevertheless their presence as nature would have a limiting effect on the scope of the picture-making.

The enterprising artist, trying to create something new, tried many methods and concepts of abstractions, but, all too often, later found that Picasso had been there before him. For this was Picasso's invention, and a vital part of his genius has been his special mastery of the process of abstraction, his inexhaustible ability to take nature apart and put it together again in an endless variety of ways.

One of the great problems facing the sincere abstractionist of the 1930's was to throw off this yoke of Picasso's creative dominance. Of course, there were at the time many less conscientious artists—immature students sometimes, or sheer imitators—who attempted to appropriate as much of Picasso's style, including his favorite tricks and characteristic shapes, as possible. These imitative artists were labeled *Picassoids* by the critics.

Surrealism upset the tyranny of nature, firstly,—by changing nature. Instead of just drawing from a head, an artist could work from a head with a tree growing out of the top of it. Or a torso could have two heads, or three. A telephone could melt, and so on. Anything was possible, and the unbridled imagination could set the limits to what the artist could work from. Shapes now became fluid, flexible, and unrestrained by the logic of nature. Picasso insisted on working from nature in his studio— but the younger artist could now escape from Picasso's studio by flying out the window into never-never land.

Surrealism made possible many new systems of design and vastly widened the visual world of abstraction. It became a great rule-breaker. It favored looser paint techniques, amorphous and curvilinear forms, and freedom of mental approach. It told the artist, "Now you can do anything you want. *Anything!* There is no law against it." It was not surprising that automatism began to creep into the new Surrealist-influenced abstraction.

The amalgamation of Surrealism with abstraction took place gradually and naturally, and in different degree with different artists. Meanwhile, a great awakening of the true modern spirit was going on among artists everywhere, and many new ones were turning their hands to abstraction for the first time.

From 1935 to 1945, abstraction gathered strength, rather more rapidly among little groups of artists than among the galleries. One such group arose at Buk Ulreich's sketch class on East 40th Street, and should be better known. The class was conducted on a very informal basis by Buk, a capable modern muralist who painted with great purity and grace of design, and his wife Nura, also an accomplished modern artist and illustrator. Buk and Nura's sketch class became a Mecca for young modern artists eager to work in modern directions. Most advanced were Harry McGinnis and Howard Hardy. McGinnis, whose extreme and exciting abstractions, only lightly touched by a mad Surrealist inspiration, antedated by a decade or more many of the ideas now only beginning to appear publicly, is apparently one of the lost pioneers of American modern art.

These years saw much exploration, much slow education, and much review of European modernism. Older forms of abstraction, such as geometric abstraction, were reprobed by various artists, including George L. K. Morris, Irene Rice Pereira, Balcomb Greene, and Lyonel Feininger. Georgia O'Keeffe painted flower and animal forms, combining realism and abstraction in a manner vaguely reminiscent of the Immaculates.

The Solomon Guggenheim Museum of Non-Objective Art, founded in 1939, made an invaluable contribution to the developing American art by exhibiting its large and fine collection of the paintings and drawings of Kandinsky. This presentation of Kandinsky was not lost on the American artists seeking an escape from Picassoism. For here was a non-nature-derived abstractionist art that had obvious possibilities for further development. Kandinsky's loose, Expressionist-approached, free-form abstractions of the "cannon" style (see page 240) rang out like a bell, and seemed to say: "This is the direction to follow."

It *was* followed. The favored abstract art of today, as a result, is the art of Kandinsky, rather than that of Picasso. Unlike Picasso, the continent-discoverer Kandinsky, after making his basic discovery, left large subareas unexplored. The intense exploration of these areas, however, would not come until after the Second World War.

The third period (1930–1945) of post–Armory Show American art came to an end with the Second World War. At the end of the period, modernism seemed to have slowed up as if waiting for some new development. There existed for a time an atmosphere of frustration, a feeling of fear that American art had shot its bolt without quite arriving, and that perhaps it never would arrive. Then, suddenly, something *did* happen . . .

39   Break-Through

About 1950, the typical art fan would probably have learned about the new avant-garde art, not by seeing an exhibition—but by reading about it in print. Continued and militant publicity were highly instrumental in focusing the public's attention on the extreme abstract artists

313

who were called at first the avant-garde—and later the Abstract Expressionists.

The artists were not exactly newcomers. Most of them had been around a long time, and had been seen in individual exhibitions, but without attracting special attention. When, however, they found ways to promote themselves as a group, the whole art world sat up and took notice.

At the time, there seemed to be a vacuum in modern art leadership, both in America and in Europe—and an extreme type of art, such as that presented by the avant-garde, was a natural type to fill such a vacuum. Furthermore—and this is the happy miracle—the artists had the ability to assume leadership. They were, the best of them, competent, daring, imaginative, and talented.

The avant-garde triumph made possible a sudden rise in the international prestige of American modern art. And internally, America's modern art movement was at last purged of its half-century-old cloud of confusion—and was set firmly on a track, facing forward.

As artists, the avant-garde did not act with any great unity or coherence as a group. There was no group credo, no war cry, no Futurist Manifesto. Each artist painted in a different style; in fact, if anything, a rather proud and jealous individualism characterized the group. Though these people came to be known as Abstract Expressionists, they did not hesitate, if the spirit moved them, to paint in other ways—such as nature-derived abstraction. One of their early pioneers, Arshile Gorky, died in 1948—the same year Willem de Kooning put on a first one-man show. It was the spoken and written word, rather than concurring paint brushes, that really created the concept of "group" and linked these artists together.

However, if one throws on his critic's robe and steps back a little for a broader-gauge look, he can observe certain group similarities. First, *complete modernism*. No shilly-shallying with realism in any form or degree. Also, a passionate eagerness to be *extreme*, as extreme as man can go in art. And, generally, these artists were concerned with *non*-nature-derived abstraction—with complete abstraction.

These are the similarities. But there is also an obvious area of difference in the types of art produced by members of the group. The group's art splits into two directions: the spirited, highly Expressionist, actively emotional direction favored by de Kooning, Jackson Pollock, and Franz Kline, called *Action Painting*—and the more static *pure abstraction* direction, exemplified by William Baziotes, Clyfford Still, James Brooks, and Mark Rothko.

From the standpoint of the historian and critic, this divergence has interesting implications. Action Painting continues the straight-line forward movement of the modernism of the past. It is the wing that seems to have the greatest international appeal and impact. On the other hand, the *pure abstractionists* represent a *widening* of the movement, a trend to variety and diversity—which may well be the inevitable trend of the future, and which also seems to be a natural characteristic of American art.

314   In the Action Painting approach to Abstract Expressionism, the

artist's aesthetic emotion and paint supply the entire substance of his picture. What he feels goes on the canvas, whether it be in the form of a blob, a line, or just a spatter of the brush. As he works, sometimes calmly, but often in an increasingly high degree of excitement and concentration—a picture takes place. It might be good, bad, or indifferent. If, over a period of time, a considerable number of sensitive-eyed people can look at the canvas and find it interesting—if they can sense some of the emotion that went into the picture-making—it is a good picture.

These artists are being totally self-expressive, and producing, for the first time, *total* Expressionism. At the same time they are totally abstract. Hence, the very valid name—*Abstract Expressionism*.

In thus combining Abstraction and Expressionism, today's modern artist at last joins together the two great streams of modern art—the one that started with Cézanne, and the one that started with Van Gogh. Abstract Expressionism also continues the exploration of a great continent of art—discovered years before by Kandinsky in his "cannon" type paintings, but never investigated to its full possibilities.

In naming the postwar avant-garde artists more or less chronologically, it is customary to start with the name of the Armenian-born Arshile Gorky. In Gorky, many streams of modern art came together—the acceptance and rejection of Picasso, a deep veneration for the vision of Miro (though Gorky exploded Miro's tight forms), the liberating influence of Surrealism, and automatism.

Gorky, a sensitive, interesting, and sophisticated artist, may be seen as a steppingstone linking the older abstract art of the Cubist and the Surrealism-influenced abstractionists with the newer art of today. Until his death in 1948, he acted as a dean and mentor of the younger avant-garde artists.

To the general public, the first of the Abstract Expressionist artists to become well known was the late Jackson Pollock. Pollock was an automatist if there ever was one. His flying brush slashed around the canvas, guided only by his restless spirit. Then he discovered a new way to paint —put his canvas on the floor, and walked wildly around it, literally hurling paint at the canvas. The result often looked more like a section of paint-spattered linoleum than what most people would call a picture. But there was really something there. If one takes a good long look at a Pollock picture and sits with it a while one notes that the painting gradually loses its violence, and that instead of disturbing, it becomes calming, soothing, and pleasing. For Pollock was gripped by an overpowering (and often rather orderly) sense of design. The drippings fall and spatter, but they make lines that flow gracefully back into the picture. Loose ends are sewed up. Pollock's control of the dripping paint was greater than lazy eyes suspect. And thanks to Pollock's sense of design, one finds ultimately in his pictures, not violence, but peace. One could make a similar observation about Vincent van Gogh.

In Pollock, and with the other Abstract Expressionists, a favorite American painting device, the *accidental* effect, comes into frequent use. For a hundred years, water-colorists have exploited the accidental paint effects they couldn't avoid, such as unevenly drying pools of color, to add

Pollock: *The She-Wolf.* True modernism returned to American art in *abstract expressionism*—the combination of intense Expressionist feeling with complete abstraction. This "early" painting demonstrates Pollock's strong sense of design.

Pollock: *Full Fathom Five*. Pollock's later pictures became very complex, with innumerable swirling lines and paint droppings. There are many "accidentals" and the total effect is that of an over-all texture. However, the artist skillfully controlled his seemingly haphazard technique, and his strong design-sense becomes more and more evident the longer one studies these paintings.

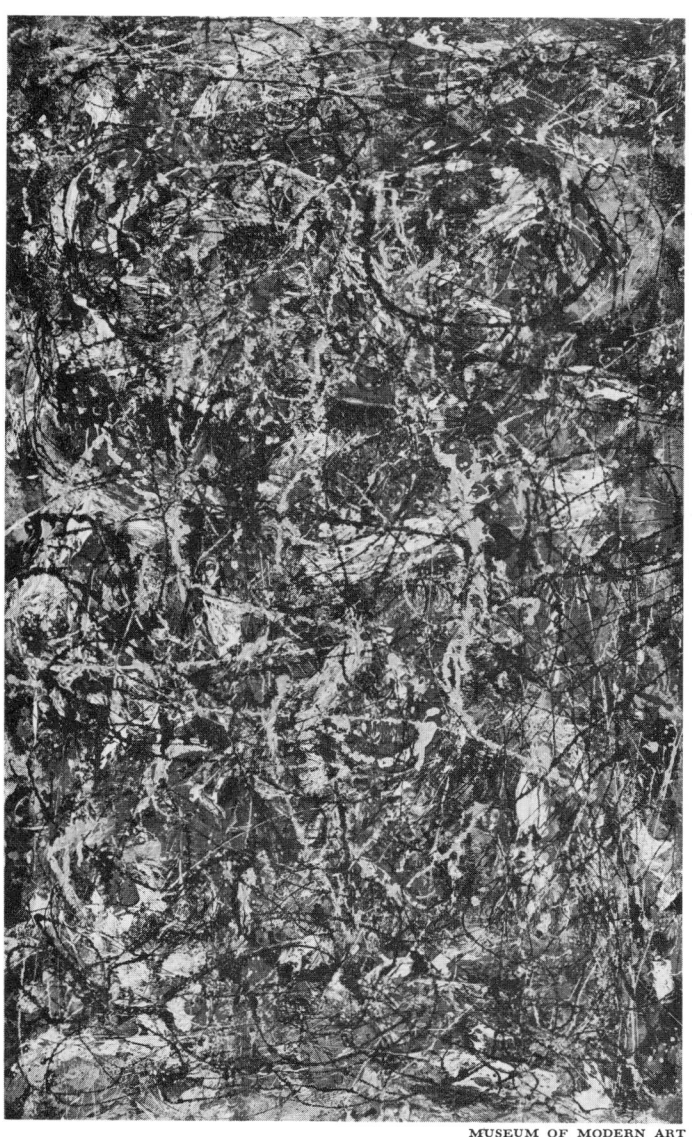

interest and variety to their pictures. Though not quite so easy to achieve—it comes under the head of "tricks of the trade"—similar effects have been essayed in oil. Pollock's spatterings and drippings belong in this accidentalist tradition.

Similarly, textural effects become more important. Indeed, in Pollock's more complex later paintings, the multitudinous lines and drippings have the effect of turning the entire picture into a texture—though it might be questioned whether this is advantageous, and whether the earlier, simpler pictures are not more powerful and more interesting.

Though it, too, contains violent brushing, the art of Willem de Kooning differs greatly in spirit from that of Pollock. De Kooning's abstraction is less lyrical, more powerful. What stands out in de Kooning's painting is *strength* and stability. The forms are strong, the structure is strong. The painting is direct—and strongly felt. De Kooning is the Cézanne of the Abstract Expressionists.

Comparison of the handiwork of de Kooning and Pollock is fascinating—perhaps because, though there are outward, superficial similarities, they are in essence so different. Time may find de Kooning's struggled-with painting more substantial and profound than the fierce, free-emotion expressions of Pollock. Struggle adds lasting value in art. Again, the classical quality of de Kooning's Abstract Expressionism may be found more pure than that of Pollock. On the other hand, the lyricism and design of Pollock may be more admired.

A third artist, related to the other two in spirit, and characterized by simple forms of great strength—is Franz Kline, who paints in black and white, in a style called "calligraphy." The earlier calligraphers painted lines of what looked like lines of lettering in an unknown language—designed into a picture. Kandinsky had pioneered in this form. Kline's approach, however, differed from the others—instead of many letters, he made a single letter, blown up to huge proportions, the subject of his picture. His vigorous brush stroke, but even more, the sheer gigantic mass of black form (or the "negative" white form), give his pictures overwhelming power. His approach (unlike the other calligraphers, who are pure abstractionists) is brutally Expressionist. Kline's importance is growing—and it would seem as if some of the other Abstract Expressionists are beginning to follow his leadership.

The calligraphers Bradley Walker Tomlin, Mark Tobey, and Adolph Gottlieb were among the first of the avant-garde group to be known to the gallery-going public. Tomlin was perhaps the purest and most typical calligrapher, and his investigation of this special type of art was deeper than the others. Tobey's calligraphy became less formal, and became eventually so complex that it was almost a form of texture painting. Gottlieb dealt in little symbols and pictographs that might have been taken from an American Indian sign language. For the Museum of Modern Art Exhibition shown in eight European countries in 1958 and 1959, Gottlieb blew up some of these symbols to enormous size. Indeed, huge pictures—eight or ten feet on a side—seem to have become a favorite practice of this group.

The Abstract Expressionists generally, and the lively Action Painter

De Kooning: *Woman 1*. In this painting, the abstraction is derived from a material subject, as are the abstractions of Picasso. De Kooning's later pictures are completely abstract—but display the same vigorous brushing and powerful forms shown here.

wing in particular, have provided the iron point of America's spearhead operation in the international art world. Europe had nothing to compare with these powerful pictures. But also important was the other sub-division of Abstract Expressionism, the *pure abstractionists*. In this second group, Expressionism is subdued to little more than a mannerism of painting. The emphasis is on the "abstract."

To a group of three artists—William Baziotes, Clyfford Still, and James Brooks—goes credit for creating an abstract art in which the word "abstract" means exactly what the dictionary defines it to mean. Total "abstractness" is the essential characteristic of this painting; there is nothing else mixed in (as there is in such styles as Cubism and Futurism). The paintings are conceived abstractly, painted abstractly, and are intended to be seen abstractly.

If de Kooning is the Cézanne of the avant-garde, William Baziotes might well be called its Gauguin—because of his pleasing, harmonious color and decorative design. Baziotes ranges far in search for interesting abstract shapes which nearly always seem to surprise. Also surprising is Clyfford Still's original handling of near-amorphous shapes and areas. And, although not as startling, the free-shape abstractions of James Brooks have a lively vitality and a brusque freshness of color.

Woven into the new American "non-figurative" (non-nature-derived) abstraction are reminiscences of the old Suprematism and the severe and simplified aestheticism of Mondrian. This can be detected in another group, including notably Robert Motherwell and Mark Rothko.

Motherwell's *manner* of painting, with its loose, free brushing, is similar to the Action Painters—but the structure of his pictures and his stable forms (including the frequent egg-shape form that has become almost a trade mark) are far more abstract than Expressionist in spirit. His painting seems to be imbued with an aestheticism very much akin to that of Mondrian, although the outward appearance of the pictures is quite different.

Mark Rothko's paintings often look like Mondrians in soft focus. The shapes are rectangular, but the edges are blurred, which turns out to be startling, but not at all silly—for deprived of Mondrian's hard edges, the masses of color are now felt clearly *as masses*. Mondrian's hard, contrasting straight lines, we suddenly realize, were more than fences around a color-mass area—they were battle lines of opposing tensions, of contrasting colors facing each other at bayonet point. Their belligerancy drew our attention away from the weights and values of the masses themselves. Rothko's blurred edges correct this. Furthermore, Rothko's warm, resonant, subtle, and varied color, with its frequent suggestion of light, adds a whole new dimension of excitement to the cold and bleak Mondrian aesthetics.

As the Abstract Expressionists and extreme abstractionists grew in importance, the rest of the modern sector of the art world seemed to rally around them, and their pictures became the central feature of many exhibitions. Then, in 1955, an event occurred of tremendous importance in the history of American art. In that year, the Museum of Modern Art put on a show, "The New Decade—22 European Painters and Sculptors."

The show presumably represented the best of contemporary European art, selected with the critical acumen and consistency characteristic of this museum. Simultaneously, the Whitney Museum exhibited a twin show, "The New Decade—35 American Painters and Sculptors." The Whitney show was less consistent, even including an incongruous selection of oddly chosen realists. Here was a clear-cut showdown, right in the center arena.

As one walked from the back door of the Modern museum into the back door of the Whitney, one could not fail to be surprised and impressed. There was no question about the American superiority. The American exhibit, in spite of its occasional incongruous examples, looked strong, lively, progressive. In comparison, the European examples seemed relatively weak, languid, uncertain of direction. The Abstract Expressionist pictures, the core of the American show, seemed far in advance of anything seen in the other museum. Nothing like this had ever happened before. Nothing like this could have happened before.

The painters of France, and of Holland, Belgium, and the other European countries had begun imitating the painters of America. In American art circles an almost unbelievable new phrase had become current—"the School of New York." The replacement for "the School of Paris"! Some time in the late 1950's—by painting more substantial, more vital, and more advanced pictures—America moved to the forefront of the modern movement.

How long it will stay there cannot be predicted. At the time of writing these words, the prospect looks good for quite awhile. Of course, Paris will struggle to regain its eminence. It has touted a new "ism," *Tachism* (from patches of paint), named from the stylistic mannerisms of certain French painters. But thus far, Tachism has been too thin and pale to challenge seriously the American upsurge.

In April 1959, there was another exhibition of considerable significance —the mammoth "Art U.S.A.—59." It filled an entire floor of the New York Coliseum—probably the largest and certainly the most overwhelming presentation of art since the World's Fair Exhibition, twenty years earlier. The lion's share of the show was devoted to extreme abstraction, with the Abstract Expressionists in the place of honor. A secondary section was devoted to the semiabstractionists, and somewhat less space to the realists. Nearly every American artist of note was represented (there were a few notable exceptions, due, perhaps, to the peculiar manner in which the artists were selected)—and the exhibition served as a remarkable and reasonably accurate cross-section of contemporary art. Also included were a number of very exciting pieces of sculpture.

The whole exhibition breathed power and vitality and diversity. The total impact was tremendous. One thought of a long-chained Titan suddenly breaking his bonds.

If nothing else, this exhibition indicated a widespread awakening and revitalization of the *whole* of American art—and showed that the small group who had led the advance were not alone in a wilderness. Today they are surrounded by many other top-rank artists, such as the poetic abstractionist, Byron Browne, whose now skilled and experienced abstraction is especially distinguished by its lyrical, poetic quality—a rich visual poetry that assures his paintings will continue to satisfy the eye for a long time to come.

Along with American painting, American sculpture also stands at the top in world modern art. Less plagued by an urge for realism than painting, American sculpture has been more consistently modern than its sister art—but not nearly as well publicized. From early modern-art pioneer William Zorach on, American sculptors have moved slowly but steadily forward. For a period of time, their almost too great respect for material—their fetish for closely following the original shape of the block they worked on—seemed to slow their pace. The newer sculptors, however, have broken away from this attitude, and seem to be working much more freely.

One hesitates to mention just a few names of American sculptors— there are so many who are so talented and productive. Alexander Calder's *mobiles* have achieved world fame. Jose de Rivera, with his *Brussels Construction*, has gone far beyond the European Brancusi. And there are many others who have opened up new worlds of form—Peter Grippe, Isamu Noguchi, Richard Lippold, Chaim Gross, Ibram Lassaw, Louise Nevelson, Theodore J. Roszak, Leo Amino, Herbert Ferber, David Hare, Seymour Lipton—and others. Today, the strength of American sculpture parallels that of American painting. What a pity that stiff-necked official conservatism allows so little of this fine sculpture to be seen by the American people in public places.

The arrival of American art at the forefront of the world's modern movement has been one great achievement of today's radical abstract artists in this country.

Another great achievement has been the clearing of the air of American modernism—the banishing of the fog of confusion that has lingered since the Armory Show. By their very existence as the dominant example of present-day modern art, the extreme abstractionists have torn the veil of pretense from *pseudomodern* painting. No longer can essential realism, masking itself under a thin veneer of Expressionist distortion, claim to be "modern art." Now, realism can be only one thing—realism. Semi-abstraction will be called semiabstraction. And so on.

This does not mean that there will be no more realistic pictures painted in the world. In this country, certainly, we can be sure that realistic pictures will continue to be painted; artists like to depict. And similarly, it is unlikely that artists will stop making abstractions; they like to design, to create, to express what they feel. It also seems unlikely that semiabstractions and nature-derived abstractions will disappear—because artists enjoy abstracting from nature.

But with today's clearer view of modern art, all of those approaches are seen as merely different ways of making a painting—in fact, there is no reason why the same artist should not try his hand at any or all of them as he chooses. In thus clearing the air, the extreme abstractionists have actually brought liberation to other, more conservative forms of art.

Modern art, in America and in the world, has now come to a traffic circle, with roads leading out in every direction. One feels that the original surge of modern art initiated by Cézanne has now completed a cycle, and that we have already started to proceed on to a new period of art. That is to say, today's artists are painting forward from the art of today; they are no longer referring back to Cézanne, or Matisse or Picasso, as a source of inspiration.

Now, more than ever, it is hazardous to guess in what direction art will be moving in the future. Though art will move in all directions, one particularly hesitates to predict which of the roads leading out from the traffic circle will be tomorrow's main highway. Indeed, with present-day abstraction carried out to what seems an almost ultimate extreme, it is not impossible that the favored road may be the one bearing the startling sign: "Counterrevolution!"

Rumblings of the counterrevolution, that is, a return to some form or degree of realistic representation, have been heard for some time. The rumblings appear to be growing louder. There have been artist manifestos. Young modern artists—not conservative old academics—have begun to question the nature of modern art itself. The untutored public, of course, would be delighted by a return to realism.

At this moment of writing, however, the realistic counterrevolution has not developed into any very definite movement in any specific direction. Whether some new form of realism will grow importantly remains to be seen. Nor can one say for sure that modern art's long-persisting advance into abstraction has come to a final conclusion, to a last dead end, in thin, austere Abstract Expressionism. Perhaps the abstractionists can turn up something new, although doing so seems increasingly difficult.

Another suggestion of a future direction comes from the long history of art, with its pendulum swings of action and reaction. The history of art teaches that classical and anticlassical periods of art have a tendency to alternate. Modern art, with its emphasis on flatness of pictorial depth, its tightly knit design structure, its abstractness, and the relative calmness and stability of its forms is essentially *classic*. A possible new art, then, might probably veer away from the classic spirit and bear a relation to modern art not too different from the relation of baroque art to the art of the Renaissance. In particular, it would not be at all surprising if modern art's most consistent characteristic—its "flatness," its identification of the picture with the picture surface—should be completely abandoned in favor of an art of greater depth, richness, and roundness.

Beyond this, even in the realm of speculation, one dare not go. The shape of the art to come will be molded finally by the civilization in which it exists. The artist is only a pencil in the hand of his time.

323

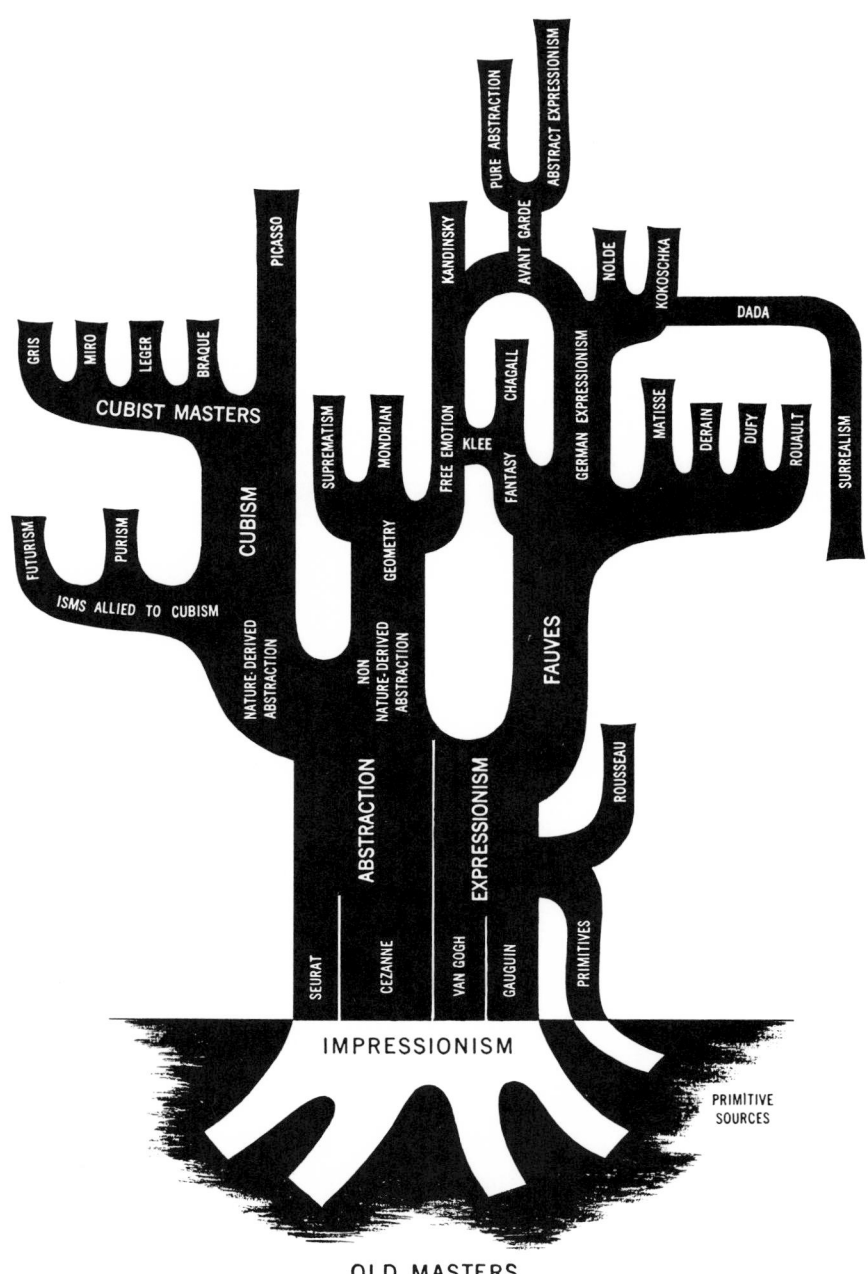

Growth Diagram of Modern Art

Bibliography

MODERN ART—GENERAL

Barr, Alfred H. *First Loan Exhibition—Gauguin, Cézanne, Seurat, Van Gogh* (Museum of Modern Art, New York, 1929).

———. *Masters of Modern Art* (The Museum of Modern Art, New York, 1954).

———. *Painting in Paris* (Museum of Modern Art, New York, 1930).

———. *Art in Our Time* (Museum of Modern Art, New York, 1939).

———. *Painting and Sculpture in the Museum of Modern Art* (Museum of Modern Art, New York, 1942).

———. *What Is Modern Painting?* (Museum of Modern Art, New York, 1943).

Basler, Adolphe; and Kunstler, Charles. *The Post-Impressionists* (William Farquhar Payson, New York, 1931).

———. *The Modernists* (William Farquhar Payson, New York, 1931).

Baur, John I. H. *Revolution and Tradition in Modern American Art* (Harvard University Press, Cambridge, 1951).

Bell, Clive. *Art* (Chatto and Windus, London, 1921).

———. *Since Cézanne* (Chatto and Windus, London, 1922).

Belmont, J. J. *The Modern Dilemma in Art* (Harbinger House, New York, 1944).

Benton, Thomas Hart. *An Artist in America* (University of Kansas City Press, New York, 1951).

Bourgeois, Stephan. *The Adolph Lewisohn Collection of Modern French Paintings and Sculptures* (E. Weyhe, New York, 1928).

Bulliet, C. J. *Apples and Madonnas* (Covici-Friede, New York, 1930).

———. *The Significant Moderns* (Covici-Friede, New York, 1936).

Cahill, Holger. *American Folk Art* (Museum of Modern Art, New York, 1933).

———. *Aztec, Incan and Mayan Art* (Museum of Modern Art, New York, 1933).

———. *New Horizons in American Art* (Museum of Modern Art, New York, 1936).

Catalogs:

The Lee Ault Collection of Modern Paintings (Valentine Gallery, New York, 1944).

Painting in France, 1939-1946 (Whitney Museum, New York, 1947).

(See also Barr, Cahill, Dale, Halpert, Miller, Rich, Soby, Wheeler.)

Charlot, Jean. *Art from the Mayans to Disney* (Sheed & Ward, New York, 1939).

Cheney, Sheldon. *A Primer of Modern Art* (Liveright Publishing Co., New York, 1933).

———. *Expressionism in Art* (Liveright Publishing Co., New York, 1934).

———. *The Story of Modern Art* (Viking Press, New York, 1941).

———. *A World History of Art* (Viking Press, New York, 1945), chapters 26-28.

Craven, Thomas. *Modern Art* (Simon & Schuster, New York, 1934).

Dale, Maud. *Twentieth Century French Paintings from the Chester Dale Collection* (Art Institute of Chicago, 1943).

Davidson, Morris. *Painting for Pleasure* (Hale, Cushman & Flint, Boston, 1938).

———. *An Approach to Modern Painting* (Coward-McCann, Inc., New York, 1948).

Dewey, John. *Art as Experience* (Minton, Balch & Co., New York, 1934).

Dreier, Katherine S.; Sweeney, James J.; and Gabo, Naum. *Three Lectures on Modern Art* (Philosophical Library, New York, 1949).

Earp, T. W. *The Modern Movement in Painting* (Studio, Ltd., London, 1935).

Faure, Elie. *History of Art—Modern Art* (Garden City Publishing Co., Garden City, New York, 1936), pages 325-508.

Flexner, James Thomas. *A Short History of American Painting* (Houghton Mifflin Company, Boston, 1950), chapters 6-8.

Frost, Rosamund. *Contemporary Art* (Crown Publishers, New York, 1942)

Fry, Roger. *Vision and Design* (Brentanos, New York, n.d.).
——. *Transformations* (Chatto and Windus, London, 1926).
Gallatin, A. E. *Of Art* (Wittenborn and Co., New York, 1945).
Gardner, Helen. *Art Through the Ages* (Harcourt, Brace & Co., New York, 1936), chapters 23, 24, 28-30.
Goldwater, Robert J. *Primitivism in Modern Painting* (Harper & Brothers, New York, 1938).
Goldwater, Robert J.; and Treves, Marco. *Artists on Art* (Pantheon Books, New York, 1945).
Goodyear, A. Conger. *The Museum of Modern Art. The First Ten Years* (Museum of Modern Art, New York, 1943).
Gordon, Jan. *Modern French Painters* (John Lane, London, 1936).
Graham, John D. *System and Dialectics of Art* (Delphic Studios, New York, 1937).
Grosser, Maurice. *Painting in Public* (Alfred A. Knopf, New York, 1948).
——. *The Painter's Eye* (Rinehart & Company, New York, 1951).
Guggenheim, Peggy. *Art of This Century* (Art Aid Corp., New York, 1942).
Halpert, Edith Gregor. *"Nature Vivre"* by William M. Harnett (Catalog: The Downtown Gallery, New York, 1939).
Henri, Robert. *The Art Spirit* (J. B. Lippincott Company, Philadelphia, 1939).
Hind, Charles Lewis. *The Post Impressionists* (Methuen & Co., Ltd., London, 1911).
Holme, Bryan. *Master Drawings* (American Studio Books, New York, 1943), plates 92-129.
Kepes, Gyorgy. *Language of Vision* (Paul Theobald, Chicago, 1944).
Kirstein, Lincoln. *The Latin-American Collection of the Museum of Modern Art* (Museum of Modern Art, New York, 1943).
Kuh, Katherine. *Art Has Many Faces* (Harper & Brothers, New York, 1951).
Langui, Emile. *Fifty Years of Modern Art* (Frederick A. Praeger, New York, 1959).
Larkin, Oliver W. *Art and Life in America* (Rinehart & Company, New York, 1949), books 5-6.
Laver, James. *French Painting and the Nineteenth Century* (B. T. Batsford, Ltd., London, 1937).
Lee, Kathryn Dean; and Burchwood, Katherine Tyler. *Art Then and Now* (Appleton-Century-Crofts, Inc., New York, 1949), chapters 22-23.
Leepa, Allen. *The Challenge of Modern Art* (Beechhurst Press, New York, 1949).

Lemaitre, Georges. *From Cubism to Surrealism in French Literature* (Harvard University Press, 1941).
Lewisohn, Sam A. *Painters and Personality* (Harper & Brothers, New York, 1937).
Louchheim, Aline B. *5000 Years of Art* (Howell, Soskin, New York, 1946), pages 145-197.
Marriott, Charles. *Modern Movements in Painting* (Charles Scribner's Sons, New York, n.d.).
Mather, Frank Jewett. *Modern Painting* (Garden City Publishing Co., H. Holt & Co., New York, 1927).
McCausland, Elizabeth. *Work for Artists* (American Artists Group, New York, 1947).
Meier-Graefe, Julius. *The Development of Modern Art* (G. P. Putnam's Sons, New York, 1908), 2 vols.
Miller, Dorothy C. *Modern Masters* (Museum of Modern Art, New York, 1940).
——. *The Sculpture of John B. Flannagan* (Museum of Modern Art, New York, 1942).
Miller, Dorothy C.; and Barr, Alfred H. *American Realists and Magic Realists* (Museum of Modern Art, New York, 1943).
Moholy-Nagy, L. *Vision in Motion* (Paul Theobald, Chicago, 1947).
Museum of Modern Art. *John Marin* (Museum of Modern Art, New York, 1936).
——. *20 Centuries of Mexican Art* (Museum of Modern Art, New York, 1940).
Myers, Bernard S. *Modern Art in the Making* (McGraw-Hill Book Company, Inc., New York, 1950).
Newmeyer, Sarah. *Enjoying Modern Art* (Mentor Books, New York, 1957).
Nicolaides, Kimon. *The Natural Way to Draw* (Houghton Mifflin Company, Boston, 1941).
Orpen, Sir William. *The Outline of Art* (G. P. Putnam's Sons, New York, 1938), chapters 22-25.
Ozenfant, Amédée. *Foundations of Modern Art* (Brewer, Warren & Putnam, New York, 1931).
Pach, Walter. *The Masters of Modern Art* (B. W. Huebsch, Inc., New York, 1924).
——. *Queer Thing, Painting* (Harper & Brothers, New York, 1938).
Pearson, Ralph M. *How to See Modern Pictures* (Dial Press, New York, 1925).
Ramsden, E. H. *An Introduction to Modern Art* (Oxford University Press, London, 1940).
Rathbun, Mary C.; and Hayes, Bartlett H. *Layman's Guide to Modern Art* (Oxford University Press, New York, 1949).

Raynal, Maurice. *Modern French Painters* (Tudor Publishing Co., New York, 1934).

——. *History of Modern Painting* (Skira, Incorporated, Publisher; New York, 1949).

Read, Herbert. *Art Now* (Harcourt, Brace & Co., New York and London, 1933).

——. *Contemporary British Art* (Penguin Books, Baltimore, 1951).

——. *The Philosophy of Modern Art* (Faber & Faber, London, 1952).

Reinach, S. *Apollo* (Charles Scribner's Sons, New York, 1935), pages 337-353.

Rich, Daniel Catton. *Abstract and Surrealist American Art* (Art Institute of Chicago, 1947).

Ritchie, Andrew C. *Charles Demuth* (Museum of Modern Art, New York, 1950).

——. *Sculpture of the Twentieth Century* (Museum of Modern Art, New York, 1952).

Robb, David M.; and Garrison, J. J. *Art in the Western World* (Harper & Brothers, New York, 1942), chapters 13, 14, 22, 30-32, 35.

Rodman, Selden. *Portrait of the Artist as an American: Ben Shahn* (Harper & Brothers, New York, 1951).

Ruckstuhl, F. W. *Great Works of Art* (Garden City Publishing Co., Garden City, New York, 1925).

Rutter, Frank. *Evolution in Modern Art* (George G. Harrap & Co., London, 1926).

——. *Modern Masterpieces* (George Newnes, Ltd., London, n.d.).

Sicre, José Gomez; and Riddle, Harold T. *Cuban Painting of Today* (Maria Luisa Gómez Mena, Havana, 1944).

Sloan, John. *Gist of Art* (American Artists Group, New York, 1939).

Smith, S. C. Kaines. *An Outline of Modern Painting* (William Morrow & Co., New York, 1931).

Soby, James Thrall. *Art in Progress* (Museum of Modern Art, New York, 1944).

——. *Ben Shahn* (bulletin, Museum of Modern Art, New York, 1947).

—— and Barr, Alfred H. *Twentieth Century Italian Art* (Museum of Modern Art, New York, 1949).

—— and Miller, Dorothy C. *Romantic Painting in America* (Museum of Modern Art, New York, 1943).

Stites, Raymond S. *The Arts and Man* (McGraw-Hill Book Co., New York, 1940), chapters 18-19.

Sweeney, James Johnson. *Plastic Redirections in 20th Century Painting* (University of Chicago Press, 1934).

Toor, Frances; and Merida, Carlos. *Modern Mexican Artists* (Frances Toor Studios, Mexico City, 1937).

Venturi, Lionello. *Painting and Painters* (Charles Scribner's Sons, New York, 1945).

Watkins, C. Law. *The Language of Design* (Phillips Memorial Gallery, Washington, D. C., 1946).

Wheeler, Monroe. *Modern Painters and Sculptors as Illustrators* (Museum of Modern Art, New York, 1938).

——. *Twentieth Century Portraits* (Museum of Modern Art, New York, 1942).

——. *Modern Drawings* (Museum of Modern Art, New York, 1944).

Wilenski, R. H. *The Modern Movement in Art* (Faber & Faber, London, 1935).

——. *French Painting* (Hale, Cushman & Flint, Boston, 1936).

——. *Modern French Painters* (Faber & Faber, London, 1946).

Wölfflin, Heinrich. *Principles of Art History* (G. Bell & Sons, Ltd., London, 1932).

Wright, Frank Lloyd. *The Future of Architecture* (Horizon Press, New York, 1953).

Wright, Willard Huntington. *Modern Painting* (Dodd, Mead and Co., New York, 1922).

IMPRESSIONISM

Barnes, Albert C.; and De Mazia, Violette. *The Art of Renoir* (Minton, Balch & Co., New York, 1935).

Bertram, Anthony. *Edouard Manet* (Studio Publications, New York, 1935).

Blanche, J. E. *Manet* (Dodd, Mead & Co,. N. Y., 1925).

Dewhurst, W. *Impressionist Painting* (George Newnes, London, 1904).

Duret, Theodore. *Manet* (Crown Publishers, New York, 1937).

——. *Renoir* (Crown Publishers, New York, 1937).

Frost, Rosamund. *Pierre Auguste Renoir* (Hyperion Press, Inc., New York, 1944).

Fuller, William H. *Claude Monet and His Paintings* (catalog, Lotus Club, New York, 1899).

Gwynn, Stephen. *Claude Monet and His Garden* (Macmillan, New York, 1935).

Jean, René. *Ten Water-colours, Sanguines, and Pastels by Auguste Renoir* (Georg & Cie, Paris, 1921).

Jewell, Edwin Alden; and Crane, Aimee. *French Impressionists* (Hyperion Press, Inc., New York, 1944).

Mauclair, Camille. *Claude Monet* (John Lane, London, n.d.).

McKinney, Roland J. *The Development of Impressionism* (catalog, Los Angeles Museum, 1940).

Raynal, Maurice. *The Nineteenth Century: New Sources of Emotion* (Skira, Incorporated, Publisher; New York, 1951).

Rewald, John. *Camille Pissarro, Letters to His Son Lucien* (Pantheon Books, New York, 1943).

——. *The History of Impressionism* (Museum of Modern Art, New York, 1946).

Uhde, Wilhelm. *The Impressionists* (The Phaidon Press, Vienna, 1937).

Vollard, Ambroise. *Renoir, an Intimate Record* (Alfred A. Knopf, New York, 1934).

CÉZANNE

Barnes, Albert C.; and DeMazia, Violette. *The Art of Cézanne* (Harcourt, Brace & Co., New York, 1939).

Bertram, Anthony. *Paul Cézanne* (Studio Publications, New York, 1935).

Catalogs:

Renoir, Cézanne and Their Contemporaries (Alex, Reid & Lefevre, Ltd., London, 1934).

Corot to Cézanne (Alex, Reid & Lefevre, Ltd., London, 1936).

Cézanne and the Impressionists (Bignou Galleries, New York, 1935).

Memorial Exhibition—The Collection of Miss Lizzie P. Bliss (Museum of Modern Art, New York, 1931).

Loan Exhibition of Paintings by Cézanne (Paul M. Rosenberg & Co., New York, 1942).

Cézanne . . . Gauguin (Toledo Museum of Art, Toledo, 1936).

Loan Exhibition—Paintings by Paul Cézanne (Wildenstein Galleries, Paul Rosenberg, New York, 1928).

(See also Museum of Modern Art, First Loan Exhibition.)

Cogniat, Raymond. *Cézanne* (French Library of Fine Arts, New York, 1939).

Faure, Elie. *Cézanne* (Association of American Painters and Sculptors, New York, 1913).

Fry, Roger. *Cézanne—A Study of His Development* (Hogarth Press, London, 1932).

Jewell, Edward Alden. *Cézanne* (Hyperion Press, Inc., New York, 1944).

Klingsor, Tristan L. *Cézanne* (Dodd, Mead & Co., New York, 1924).

Loran, Erle. *Cézanne's Composition* (University of California Press, Berkeley and Los Angeles, 1944).

Mack, Gerstle. *Paul Cézanne* (Alfred A. Knopf, New York, 1942).

Meier-Grafe, Julius. *Cézanne* (Ernest Benn, Ltd., London, 1927).

Museum of Modern Art. *First Loan Exhibition—Cézanne, Gauguin, Seurat, Van Gogh* (Museum of Modern Art, New York, 1929).

Novotny, Fritz. *Paul Cézanne* (The Phaidon Press, Vienna, 1937).

Rewald, John. *Paul Cézanne, Letters* (Bruno Cassirer, London, 1941).

Sutro, Esther. *Nicolas Poussin* (The Medici Society, Boston, 1923).

Taubes, Frederic. *You Don't Know What You Like* (Dodd, Mead & Co., New York, 1942), pages 164-169.

Venturi, Lionello. *Cézanne—Son Art—Son Oeuvre* (Catalog of Cézanne's paintings and sketches, 1600 illustrations) (Paul Rosenberg, Paris, 1936), in French.

——. *Paul Cézanne Water Colours* (Bruno Cassirer, Oxford, 1943).

Vollard, Ambroise. *Paul Cézanne—His Life and Art* (Crown Publishers, New York, 1937).

VAN GOGH

Barr, Alfred H. *Vincent Van Gogh* (Museum of Modern Art, New York, 1935).

Bertram, Anthony. *Vincent Van Gogh* (The Studio, London, 1930).

Brooks, Charles Mattoon. *Vincent Van Gogh—A Bibliography* (Museum of Modern Art, New York, 1942).

Burra, Peter. *Van Gogh* (Duckworth, London, 1934).

Catalogs:

Paintings by Vincent Van Gogh (Netherlands Information Bureau, New York, 1943).

Vincent Van Gogh Exhibition (Montross Gallery, New York, 1920).

Masterpieces by Van Gogh (Paul Rosenberg & Co., New York, 1942).

Loan Exhibition in Aid of American and Dutch War Relief (Wildenstein, New York, 1943).

(See also Barr, Rich.)

De La Faille, J. B. *Vincent Van Gogh* (Hyperion Press, Paris, 1939).

Earp, Thomas W. *Vincent Van Gogh* (T. Nelson & Sons, London, n.d.).

Elgar, Frank. *Van Gogh* (Fernand Hazan, Paris, 1949), text in French.

Faille, see De la Faille.

Fierens, Paul. *Van Gogh* (Braun & Cie, Paris, 1949).

Goldscheider, L.; and Uhde, W. *Vincent Van Gogh* (Phaidon Press, Oxford University Press, London, 1945).

Lord, Douglas. *Vincent Van Gogh—Letters to Emile Bernard* (Museum of Modern Art, New York, 1938).

Ludovici, A. M. *The Letters of a Post-Impressionist* (Constable & Co., London, 1912).
Magazine articles:
  Van Gogh issue (*L'Amour de L'Art* Paris, April, 1937.
  Henry Thannhauser. Van Gogh and John Russell (*Burlington Magazine*, London, September, 1938).
  "Vincent Van Gogh" (*PM* magazine, New York, April, 1936).
  Mary Fantin Roberts. "Vincent Van Gogh: The Supreme Colorist" (*Touchstone*; New York, September, 1920).
Meier-Graefe, Julius. *Vincent Van Gogh* (Harcourt, Brace & Co., New York, 1933).
Muensterberger, W. *Vincent Van Gogh, Drawings, Pastels, Studies* (F. G. Kroonder, Bussum, Holland, 1949).
Pach, Walter. *Vincent Van Gogh* (Artbook Museum, New York, 1936).
—— and Van Messel, Rela. *Letters to an Artist—From Vincent Van Gogh to Anton Ridder Van Rappard, 1881-1885* (Constable & Co., Ltd., London, 1936).
Piérard, Louis. *The Tragic Life of Vincent Van Gogh* (John Castle, London, 1925).
Rich, Daniel Catton; and Rousseau, Theodore. *Van Gogh—Paintings and Drawings* (Metropolitan Museum of Art, New York, 1949).
Stone, Irving. *Lust for Life* (Grosset & Dunlap, New York, 1937).
——. *Dear Theo—The Autobiography of Vincent Van Gogh* (Houghton Mifflin Co., Boston, 1937).
Van Gogh, Elizabeth Du Quesne. *Personal Recollections of Vincent Van Gogh* (Houghton Mifflin Co., Boston, 1913).
Van Gogh-Bonger, J. *The Letters of Vincent Van Gogh to His Brother 1872-1886* (Constable & Co., London, 1927) 2 vols.
——. *Further Letters of Vincent Van Gogh to His Brother 1886-1889* (Constable & Co., London, 1929).

GAUGUIN

Barr, Alfred H. *First Loan Exhibition—Cézanne, Gauguin, Seurat, Van Gogh* (Museum of Modern Art, New York, 1929).
Bertram, Anthony. *Paul Gauguin* (The Studio, London, 1930).
Brooks, Van Wyck. *Paul Gauguin's Intimate Journals* (Crown Publishers, New York, 1936).

Burnett, Robert. *The Life of Paul Gauguin* (Oxford University Press, New York, 1937).
Catalogs:
  Baltimore Museum of Art, Baltimore, May-June, 1936.
  Cézanne-Gauguin Exhibition (Toledo Museum of Art, Toledo, 1936).
  Paul Gauguin Loan Exhibition (Wildenstein Galleries, New York, 1946). (See also Barr.)
Fletcher, John Gould. *Paul Gauguin, His Life and Art* (Nicholas L. Brown, New York, 1921).
Gauguin, Paul. *Noa Noa* (Nicholas L. Brown, New York, 1920).
——. *Noa Noa* (Lear Publishers, New York, 1947).
Gauguin, Pola. *My Father Paul Gauguin* (Alfred Knopf, New York, 1937).
Malingue, Maurice. *Paul Gauguin, Letters to His Wife and Friends* (World Publishing Co., Cleveland, 1949).
Pielkovo, Ruth. *The Letters of Paul Gauguin to Georges Daniel de Monfried* (Dodd, Mead & Co., New York, 1922).
Rewald, John. *Gauguin* (Hyperion Press, Paris, 1938).
——. *Gauguin—Letters to Ambroise Vollard and André Fontainas* (Grabhorn Press, San Francisco, 1943).
Rey, Robert. *Gauguin* (Dodd, Mead & Co., New York, 1924).
Rousseau, Theodore, Jr. *Gauguin* (The Art Institute of Chicago and the Metropolitan Museum of Art, New York, 1959).

SEURAT

Barr, Alfred H. *First Loan Exhibition—Cézanne, Gauguin, Seurat, Van Gogh* (Museum of Modern Art, New York, 1929).
Catalogs:
  Joseph Brummer Galleries, New York, December 1944.
Evans, Myfanwy. *The Painters' Object* (Gerald Howe, London, 1937), Article by Hélion, Jean: *Poussin, Seurat and the Double Rhythm.*
Magazine articles:
  Fry, Roger. "Seurat's La Parade" (*Burlington Magazine*, London, December 1929).
  Goldwater, Robert J. "Some Aspects of the Development of Seurat's Style" (*The Art Bulletin*, New York, June, 1941).
  Hélion, Jean. "Seurat as a Predecessor" (*Burlington Magazine*, London, July, 1936).
Pach, Walter. *Georges Seurat* (Duffield & Co., New York, 1923).

Rewald, John. *Georges Seurat* (Wittenborn & Co., New York, 1943).

Rich, Daniel Catton. *Seurat and the Evolution of the Grande Jatte* (University of Chicago Press, 1935).

PRIMITIVE

Breasted, James Henry. *Ancient Times* (Ginn & Co., Boston, 1935), pages 3-48.

Burkitt, M. C. *Our Early Ancestors* (Cambridge University Press, Cambridge, 1929).

Cahill, Holger. *Masters of Popular Painting* (Museum of Modern Art, New York, 1938).

Catalog:
   Exhibition of Rare African Sculptures (Valentine Gallery, New York), 1930).

Christensen, Erwin O. *Popular Art in the United States* (Penguin Books, Baltimore, 1948).

Dewey, John. *Art as Experience* (Minton, Balch & Co., New York, 1934).

Douglas, Frederic H.; and D'Harnoncourt, René. *Indian Art of the United States* (Museum of Modern Art, New York, 1941).

Fox-Pitt-Rivers, A. H. L. *Antique Works of Art from Benin* (privately printed, London, 1900).

Frobenius, Leo; and Fox, Douglas C. *Prehistoric Rock Pictures in Europe and Africa* (Museum of Modern Art, New York, 1937).

Goldwater, Robert J. *Primitivism in Modern Painting* (Harper & Brothers, New York, 1938).

Guillaume, Paul; and Munro, Thomas. *Primitive Negro Sculpture* (Harcourt, Brace & Co., New York, 1928).

Hedger, George A.; and others. *An Introduction to Western Civilization* (Doubleday, Doran & Co., Inc., New York, 1933), pages 11-47, 117-129.

Linton, Ralph; Wingert, Paul S.; and D'Harnoncourt, Rene. *Arts of the South Seas* (Museum of Modern Art, New York, 1946).

Lipman, Jean; and Winchester, Alice. *Primitive Painters in America* (Dodd Mead & Company, New York, 1950).

Magazine articles:
   Anti, Carlo. "The Sculpture of the African Negroes" (*Art in America*, New York, 1923).
   Von Sydow, Eckard. "African Sculpture" (*Africa*, London, 1928).

Moses, Grandma. *My Life's History* (Harper & Brothers, New York, 1952).

Osborn, Henry Fairfield. *Men of the Old Stone Age* (Charles Scribner's Sons, New York, 1936).

Raphael, Max. *Prehistoric Cave Paintings* (Pantheon Books, New York and Washington, 1945).

Rich, Daniel Catton. *Henri Rousseau* (Museum of Modern Art, New York, 1942).

Sadler, Michael E. *Arts of West Africa* (Oxford University Press, London, 1935).

Smith, Sydney Ure. *Art of Australia* (Museum of Modern Art, New York, 1941).

Sweeney, James Johnson. *African Negro Art* (Museum of Modern Art, New York, 1935).

Underwood, Leon. *Figures in Wood of West Africa* (John Tiranti, Ltd., London, 1947).

Wells, H. G. *The Outline of History* (Garden City Publishing Co., New York, 1930), pages 1-105.

Wingert, Paul S. *Art of the South Pacific* (Columbia University Press, New York, 1946).

CHILD ART

Alschuler, Rose H.; and Hattwick, La Berta Weiss. *Painting and Personality* (University of Chicago Press, Chicago, 1947), 2 vols.

d'Amico, Victor. *Creative Teaching in Art* (International Textbook Co., Scranton, 1942).

Bannon, Laura. *Mind Your Child's Art: a Guide for Parents and Teachers* (Pellegrini & Cudahy, New York, 1953).

Beck, Walter. *Self Development in Drawing* (G. P. Putnam's Sons, New York, 1941).

Bland, Jane Cooper. *Art of the Young Child* (Museum of Modern Art, New York, 1957).

Cane, Florence. *The Artist in Each of Us* (Pantheon Books, New York, 1951).

Cash, Margaret C. *Creative Art for Use in the Elementary Schools* (Denver Public Schools, 1949).

Eng, Helga. *The Psychology of Children's Drawings* (Harcourt, Brace & Co., New York, 1931).

Goodenough, Florence L. *Measurement of Intelligence by Drawings* (World Book Co., Chicago, 1926).

Johnstone, William. *Child Art to Man Art* (Macmillan, London, 1941).

Magazine and Newspaper Articles:
   "Children's Art" (*Ford Times*, Dearborn, September, 1947).

"Research Shows That Children's Daubs Are Pictures of Emotions" (*Life* Magazine, New York, June 8, 1942).

Bach, Julian. "Your Child's Pictures Can Talk" (*Collier's*, New York, October 25, 1947).

Fry, Rogers. "Children's Drawings" (*Burlington Magazine*, London, June, 1917).

———. "Children's Drawings" (*Burlington Magazine*, London, January 1924).

Goodenough, Florence L. "What Children's Drawings Tell Us" (*Parent's Magazine*, New York, June, 1944).

Lindstrom, Miriam. *Children's Art* (University of California Press, Berkeley and Los Angeles, 1958).

Lowenfeld, Viktor. *Your Child and His Art: a Guide for Parents* (Macmillan, New York, 1954).

Mackenzie, Catherine. "They Paint As They Feel" (*New York Times Magazine*, New York, October 7, 1945).

Mendelowitz, Daniel M. *Children Are Artists* (Stanford University Press, 1953).

Newton, Eric. "Child Art—Art or Myth?" (*New York Times Magazine*, New York, August, 1947).

Spoerl, Dorothy Tilden. "Encourage the Artist in Your Child" (*Parent's Magazine*, New York, August, 1947).

Oldham, Hilda Walley. *Child Expression in Color and Form* (John Lane, London, 1940).

Perrine, Van Dearing. *Let the Child Draw* (Frederick A. Stokes Co., New York, 1936).

Pictures by Young Americans (Oxford University Press, New York, 1946).

Tomlinson, R. R. *Picture and Pattern Making by Children* (Studio Publications, New York, 1934).

Viola, Wilhelm. *Child Art and Franz Cizek* (Austrian Junior Red Cross, Vienna, 1936).

MATISSE AND THE FAUVES

Barnes, Albert C.; and De Mazia, Violette. *The Art of Henri-Matisse* (Charles Scribner's Sons, New York, 1933).

Barr, Alfred H., Jr. *Matisse, His Art and His Public* (Museum of Modern Art, New York, 1951).

Bertram, Anthony. *Henri Matisse* (Studio Publications, London, 1943).

Cahiers d'Art. *Dessins de Henri-Matisse* (Cahiers d'Art, Paris, n.d.).

Cassou, Jean. *Paintings and Drawings of Matisse* (Braun & Cie., Paris, 1939).

Catalogs:

Henri Matisse (Philadelphia Museum of Art, 1948).

Henri Matisse (Museum of Modern Art, New York, 1952).

Fry, Roger. *Henri-Matisse* (E. Weyhe, New York, 1935).

Hendy, Philip. *Matthew Smith* (Penguin Books, Harmonsworth, England, 1944).

McBride, Henry. *Modern Art—Matisse* (Alfred A. Knopf, New York, 1930).

Rewald, John. *Les Fauves* (Museum of Modern Art, New York, 1952).

Romm, Alexander. *Henri-Matisse* (Isogiz, Moscow, 1937).

Soby, James Thrall. *Georges Rouault* (Museum of Modern Art, New York, 1945).

PICASSO, CUBISM, ABSTRACTION

Apollinaire, Guillaume. *The Cubist Painters—Aesthetic Meditations* (Wittenborn & Co., New York, 1944).

Armitage, Merle. *2 Statements by Picasso* (Merle Armitage, New York, 1936).

Barr, Alfred H. *Cubism and Abstract Art* (Museum of Modern Art, New York, 1936).

———. *Picasso, Forty Years of His Art* (Museum of Modern Art, New York, 1939).

———. *Picasso, Fifty Years of His Art* (Museum of Modern Art, New York, 1946).

Basler, Adolphe. *Modigliani* (G. Crés & Cie, Paris, 1931), text in French.

Bertram, Anthony. *Picasso* (Studio Publications, London, 1943).

Betjeman, John. *John Piper* (Penguin Books, Harmondsworth, England, 1944).

Cahiers, d'Art. *Guernica* (Cahiers d'Art, Paris, Nos. 4-5, 1937), text in French.

———. *Picasso—Le Greco* (Cahiers d'Art, Paris, Nos. 3-10, 1938), text in French.

Cassou, Jean: *Picasso* (Braun & Cie., Paris, 1937).

Catalogs:

Thirty Years of Picasso (Alex, Reid & Lefevre, London, 1931).

Picasso (Durand-Ruel Galleries, New York, 1948).

Picasso Before 1907 (Knoedler Galleries, New York, 1947).

Picasso 1947 (Samuel M. Kootz Gallery, New York, 1948).

Picasso "Blue" and "Rose" Periods 1901-1906 (Jacques Seligmann & Co., New York, 1936).

1910-1912, The Climactic Years in Cubism (Jacques Seligmann & Co., New York, n.d.).

Abstractions of Picasso (Valentine Gallery, New York, 1931).

Exhibition of Paintings by Picasso and Matisse (Victoria and Albert Museum, London, 1945).

Pablo Picasso (Wadsworth Atheneum, Hartford, 1934).

Clough, Rosa Trillo. Looking Back at Futurism (Cocce Press, New York, 1942).

Coughlan, Robert. The Wine of Genius, a Life of Maurice Utrillo (Harper & Brothers, New York, 1951).

Couturier, M. A.; and others. Fernand Léger (Les Éditions de L'Arbre, Montreal, 1945), text in French.

Dale, Maud. Modern Art—Picasso (Alfred A. Knopf, New York, 1930).

Danz, Louis. Personal Revolution and Picasso (Longmans, Green & Co., New York, 1941).

Desnos, Robert. Picasso, Peintures 1939-1946 (Les Éditions du Chêne, Paris, 1946), text in French.

D'Ors, Eugenio. Pablo Picasso (E. Weyhe, New York, 1930).

Eddy, Arthur Jerome. Cubists and Post-Impressionism (A. C. McClurg & Co., Chicago, 1914).

Eluard, Paul. Pablo Picasso (Philosophical Library, New York, 1947).

——. Voir (Editions des Trois Collines, Geneva-Paris, 1948), text in French.

Fumet, Stanislas. Braque (Collection des Maîtres) (Braun & Cie., Paris, n.d.).

——. Braque (Colours of Masters) (Braun & Cie., Paris, 1946).

Gallatin, A. E. Georges Braque (Wittenborn & Co., New York, 1943).

Gleizes, Albert; and Metzinger, Jean. Cubism (T. Fisher Unwin, London, 1913).

Grigson, Geoffrey. Henry Moore (Penguin Books, Harmondsworth, England, 1944).

Hess, Thomas B. Abstract Painting (The Viking Press, New York, 1951).

Hope, Henry R. Georges Braque (Museum of Modern Art, New York, 1949).

Janis, Harriet and Sidney. Picasso—The Recent Years—1939-1946 (Doubleday & Co., New York, 1946).

Kahnweiler, Daniel-Henry. Juan Gris, His Life and Work (Curt Valentin, New York, 1947).

Kandinsky, Wassily. Concerning the Spiritual in Art (Wittenborn, Scultz, Inc., New York, 1947).

——. Point and Line to Plane (Solomon R. Guggenheim Foundation, New York, 1947).

Larrea, Juan. Guernica: Pablo Picasso (Curt Valentin, New York, 1947).

Mack, Gerstle. Toulouse-Lautrec (Alfred A. Knopf, New York, 1942).

Mackenzie, Helen F. Pablo Picasso (University of Chicago Press, 1940).

Melville, Robert. Picasso: Master of the Phantom (Oxford University Press, London, 1939).

Miller, Dorothy C. 15 Americans (Museum of Modern Art, New York, 1952).

Mondrian, Piet. Plastic Art and Pure Plastic Art (Wittenborn & Co., New York, 1945).

Museum of Modern Art. Bulletin, Picasso (Museum of Modern Art, New York, January, 1945).

Picasso—Forty-nine Lithographs (Lear Publishers, New York, 1947).

Putnam, Samuel. The Glistening Bridge—Leopold Survage and the Spatial Problem in Painting (Covici-Friede, New York, 1929).

Read, Herbert. Paul Nash (Penguin Books, Harmondsworth, England, 1944).

Rebay, Hilla. Art of Tomorrow (Solomon R. Guggenheim Foundation, New York, 1939).

Regler, Gustav. Wolfgang Paalen (Nierendorf Editions, New York, 1946).

Ritchie, Andrew C. Abstract Painting and Sculpture in America (Museum of Modern Art, New York, 1951).

Sabartés, Jaime. Paintings and Drawings of Picasso (Braun & Cie., Paris, 1946).

——. Picasso, an Intimate Portrait (Prentice-Hall, Inc., New York, 1948).

Sackville-West, Edward. Graham Sutherland (Penguin Books, Harmondsworth, England, 1943).

Soby, James Thrall. Modigliani (Museum of Modern Art, New York, 1952).

Stein, Gertrude. The Autobiography of Alice B. Toklas (Harcourt, Brace & Co., New York, 1933).

——. Picasso (Charles Scribner's Sons, New York, 1946).

Sweeney, James Johnson. "Picasso and Iberian Sculpture" (The Art Bulletin, New York, September, 1941).

——. Joan Miro (Museum of Modern Art, New York, 1941).

——. Henry Moore (Museum of Modern Art, New York, 1946).

Tériade, E. Fernand Léger (Cahiers d'Art, Paris, 1928), text in French.

Tzara, Tristan. Picasso et les Chemins de la Connaissance (Albert Skira, Geneva, 1948), text in French.

Valentin, Curt. *Pablo Picasso Lithographs 1945-1947* (Curt Valentin, New York, n.d.).

Verve. *Couleur de Picasso* (*Verve*, Paris, 1948), text in French.

Zervos, Christian. *Pablo Picasso, Vol. 1 (1895-1906)* (*Cahiers d'Art*, Paris, 1932).

——. *Pablo Picasso, Vol. 2, Part 1, (1906-1912) Cahiers d'Art*, Paris, 1942).

——. *Pablo Picasso, Vol. 2, Part 2, (1912-1917)* ·(*Cahiers d'Art*, Paris, 1942).

——. *Pablo Picasso, Vol. 3* (Cahiers d'Art, Paris, 1950).

——. *Pablo Picasso, Vol. 4* (Cahiers d'Art, Paris, 1950).

——. *Pablo Picasso, Vol. 5* (Cahiers d'Art, Paris, 1952).

GERMAN EXPRESSIONISM

Barr, Alfred H. *German Painting and Sculpture* (Museum of Modern Art, New York, 1931).

Bayer, H.; and Gropius, W. and I. *Bauhaus* (Museum of Modern Art, New York, 1938).

Catalogs:
Max Beckmann (City Art Museum of St. Louis, 1948).
Five Expressionists (Oberlin Allen Memorial Art Museum, Oberlin, 1946).

Cheney, Sheldon. *A Primer of Modern Art* (Liveright Publishing Co., New York, 1933), pages 191-216.

——. *Expressionism in Art* (Liveright Publishing Co., New York, 1934).

Colin, Paul. *James Ensor* (*Junge Kunst*, Berlin, 1931), text in German.

Cogniat, Raymond. *Soutine* (*Éditions du Chêne*, Paris, 1945), text in French.

Deknatel, Frederick B. *Edvard Munch* (Museum of Modern Art, New York, 1950).

Faure, Elie. *Soutine* (G. Crés & Cie., Paris, 1929), text in French.

Goldwater, Robert J. *Primitivism in Modern Painting* (Harper & Brothers, New York, 1938).

Hodin, J. P. *Edvard Munch* (Stockholm, 1948), text in Swedish.

Hoffmann, Edith. *Kokoschka, Life and Work* (Faber & Faber, London, 1947).

Kallen, Horace M. *Art and Freedom* (Duell, Sloan & Pearce, New York, 1942), section on German Expressionism, vol. 2.

Landau, Rom. "Modern Movements in German Art" (*The Arts*, New York, July, 1928).

Payró, Julio E. *James Ensor* (Buenos Aires, 1943), text in Spanish.

Plaut, James S. *Oskar Kokoschka* (Chanticleer Press, Inc., New York, 1949).

Roethel, Hans Konrad. *Modern German Painting* (Reynal & Company, New York, 1957).

Sauerlandt, Max. *Emil Nolde* (Munich, 1931), text in German.

FANTASTIC AND IMAGINATIVE ART

Adler, Jankel. "Memories of Paul Klee" (*Horizon*, London, October, 1942).

Ayrton, Michael. *Chagall* (Faber & Faber, London, 1948).

Barr, Alfred H.; Feininger, J. and L.; and Sweeney, J. J. *Paul Klee* (Museum of Modern Art, New York, 1945).

Catalog:
Paul Klee (Buchholz Gallery, New York, 1948).

Cooper, Douglas. *Paul Klee* (Penguin Books, London, 1949).

Grohmann, Will. *Paul Klee* (*Cahiers d'Art*, Paris, 1929).

Klee, Paul. *Pedagogical Sketch Book* (Nierendorf Gallery, New York, 1944).

Mellerio, André. *Odilon Redon* (Paris, 1923), text in French.

Museum of Modern Art. *Tenth Loan Exhibition—Lautrec-Redon* (Museum of Modern Art, New York, 1931).

Nierendorf, Karl. *Paul Klee, Paintings, Watercolors, 1913-1939* (Oxford University Press, New York, 1941).

Read, Herbert. *Paul Klee on Modern Art* (Faber & Faber, London, 1949).

——. *Klee* (Pitman Publishing Corporation, New York and London, 1949).

Schmidt, Georg. *Paul Klee* (Wittenborn, New York, 1946).

Soby, James Thrall. *Paintings, Drawings and Prints by Paul Klee* (Museum of Modern Art, New York, 1949).

Sweeney, James Johnson. *Marc Chagall* (Museum of Modern Art, New York, 1946).

Tannenbaum, Libby. *James Ensor* (Museum of Modern Art, New York, 1951).

Venturi, Lionello. *Marc Chagall* (Pierre Matisse Editions, New York, 1945).

Wheeler, Monroe. *Soutine* (Museum of Modern Art, New York, 1950).

DADA, SURREALISM

Balakian, Anna. *Literary Origin of Surrealism* (King's Crown Press, New York, 1947).

Barr, Alfred H. *Fantastic Art, Dada, Surrealism* (Museum of Modern Art, New York, 1936).

Breton, André. *What Is Surrealism?* (Faber & Faber, London, 1936).

——. *Young Cherry Trees Secured Against Hares* (View Editions, New York, 1946)

——. *Yves Tanguy* (Pierre Matisse Editions, New York, 1946).

Brill, A. A. *The Basic Writings of Sigmund Freud* (Modern Library, New York, 1938).

Catalogs:

Dali, Dali, Dali (Bignou Gallery, New York, 1938).

Dali News (November 25, 1947 New York).

First Papers of Surrealism (Coordinating Council of French Relief Societies, New York, November, 1942).

Magritte (Hugo Gallery, New York, 1948).

Eugene Berman (Institute of Modern Art, Boston, 1941).

Dali, Salvador. *Conquest of the Irrational* (Julien Levy, New York, 1935).

——. *The Secret Life of Salvador Dali* (The Dial Press, New York, 1942).

Gascoyne, David. *A Short Survey of Surrealism* (Cobden-Sanderson, London, 1936).

Gaunt, W. *Bandits in a Landscape* (The Studio, London, 1937).

Huysmans, Joris Karl. *Against the Grain (A Rebours)* (Hartsdale House, New York, 1931).

Josephson, Hannah; and Cowley, Malcolm. *Aragon—Poet of the French Resistance* (Duell, Sloan & Pearce, New York., 1945).

Lautréamont, Comte de. *Maldoror* (New Directions, New York, 1943).

Lemaitre, Georges. *From Cubism to Surrealism in French Literature* (Harvard University Press, Cambridge, 1945).

Levy, Julien. *Surrealism* (The Black Sun Press, New York, 1936).

Mackworth, Cecily. *A Mirror for French Poetry, 1840-1940* (George Routledge & Sons, London, 1947).

Motherwell, Robert. *The Dada Painters and Poets* (Wittenborn, Schultz, Inc., New York, 1951).

Raymond, Marcel. *From Baudelaire to Surrealism* (Wittenborn, Schultz, Inc., New York, 1949).

Rimbaud, Arthur. *A Season in Hell* (New Directions, New York, 1945).

——. *Prose Poems from the Illuminations* (New Directions, New York, 1946).

Soby, James Thrall. *After Picasso* (Dodd Mead & Co., New York, 1935).

——. *Salvador Dali* (Museum of Modern Art, New York, 1941).

——. *The Early Chirico* (Dodd, Mead & Co., New York, 1941).

——. *Tchelitchew* (Museum of Modern Art, New York, 1942).

AMERICAN

Barr, Alfred H. *The New Decade—35 American Painters and Sculptors* (Whitney Museum of American Art, New York, 1955).

Blesh, Rudi. *Modern Art U.S.A.* (Alfred A. Knopf, New York, 1956).

Boswell, Peyton, Jr. *George Bellows* (Crown Publishers, New York, 1942).

Brown, Milton W. *American Painting from the Armory Show to the Depression* (Princeton University Press, Princeton, 1955).

Cahill, Holger, and Barr, Alfred H., Jr. *Art in America in Modern Times* (Reynal & Hitchcock, New York, 1934).

Catalogs:

Art: USA: 58 (Madison Square Garden, Art Expositions, Inc., New York, 1958).

Art: USA: 59 (Coliseum, American Art Expositions, Inc., New York, 1959).

Pioneers of Modern Art in America (Whitney Museum of American Art, New York, 1946).

The American Vision (Wildenstein—American Federation of Arts, New York, 1957).

The Museum and its Friends (Whitney Museum of American Art, New York, 1959).

Zorach, Retrospective Exhibition (Art Students League, New York, 1950).

Craven, Thomas. *Thomas Hart Benton* (Associated American Artists, New York, 1939).

Du Bois, Guy Pène. *Artists Say the Silliest Things* (American Artists Group, New York, 1940).

Eliot, Alexander. *Three Hundred Years of American Painting* (Time Incorporated, New York, 1957).

Fox, Milton S., Editor. *Art Since 1945* (Harry N. Abrams, Inc., New York, 1958).

Hess, Thomas B. *Abstract Painting* (The Viking Press, New York, 1951).

Hunter, Sam. *Jackson Pollock* (bulletin, The Museum of Modern Art, New York, 1957).

Irvine, Rosalind. *Bradley Walker Tomlin* (The Whitney Museum of American Art, New York, 1957).

Kootz, Samuel M. *New Frontiers in American Painting* (Hastings House, New York, 1943).

——. *15 Americans* (Museum of Modern Art, New York, 1952).

——. *12 Americans* (Museum of Modern Art, New York, 1956).

—— and Barr, Alfred H. *American Realists and Magic Realists* (Museum of Modern Art, New York, 1943).

——. *The New American Painting* (Museum of Modern Art, New York, 1959).

Pagano, Grace. *Encyclopaedia Britannica Collection of Contemporary American Painting* (Encyclopaedia Britannica, Inc., Chicago, 1945).

Ritchie, Andrew·C. *Abstract Painting and Sculpture in America* (Museum of Modern Art, New York, 1951).

——. The New Decade—*22 European Painters and Sculptors* (Museum of Modern Art, New York, 1955).

Saarinen, Aline B. *The Proud Possessors* (Random House, New York, 1958).

Seuphor, Michael. *Dictionary of Abstract Painting* (Tudor Publishing Company, New York, 1957).

——. *Recent Sculpture U.S.A.* (bulletin, Museum of Modern Art, New York, 1959).

—— and Miller, Dorothy C. *Romantic Painting in America* (Museum of Modern Art, New York, 1943).

Whitney Museum of American Art. *The Whitney Museum and its Collection* (Whitney Museum of American Art, New York, 1958).

Index

341

343

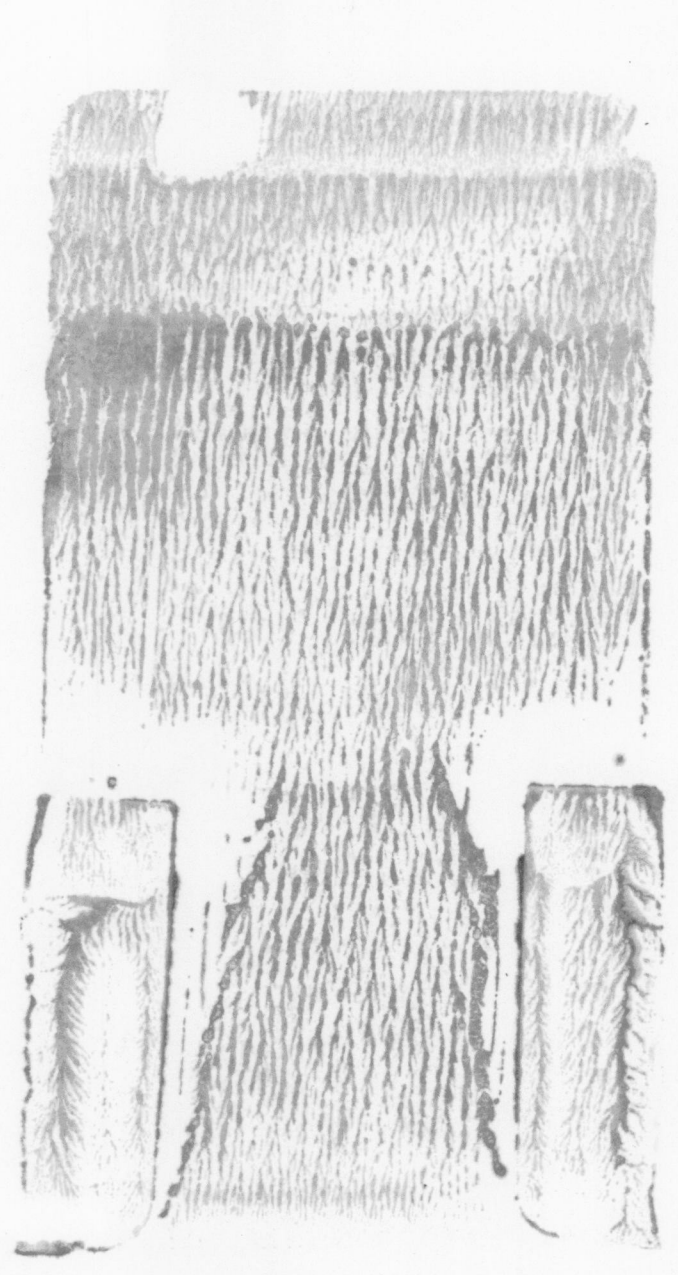